RAILROADIANA
THE
OFFICIAL PRICE GUIDE

RAILROADIANA THE OFFICIAL PRICE GUIDE

For the year 2000 and beyond

Bill & Sue Knous

RRM PUBLISHING

RRM PUBLISHING

A DIVISION OF RAILROAD MEMORIES

1903 S. NIAGARA ST.

DENVER, COLORADO 80224

303-759-1290

FIRST EDITION

PRINTED IN THE UNITED STATES

ISBN 0-9674373-0-X

This book is dedicated to all of the wonderful people we have meant along the way. The dedicated and seasoned collectors who were the temporary caretakers for a while of these great relics who have taken the last ride from the depot. We hope that the items they left behind are being as enjoyed and treasured as they were in the hands of these wonderful people. Many names will be familiar to those of us who have been around. Some will be strangers but all of us have had one thing in common a love of the trains and their relics that live on today because of collectors like you and me. We thank each and everyone one of them for saving these items so we could enjoy them. It is our job now as temporary caretakers to cherish and preserve the items for future collectors. In their memory we dedicate this book.

NYLE BARLOW

BILL FLOOD

CHUCK HESLER

MARTY NEROS

CHRIS PEASE

ERNIE PEYTON

DOUG RAMSEY SR

VIC RAWSTRON

RAY SCHMORANCE

HORACIO VALDEZ

And many more wonderful folks who have completed their journeys!

RAILROAD ABBREVIATION KEY

A & S .... ALTON & SOUTHERN RR
AERR .... ARIZONA EASTERN
A&LM ..... ARKANSAS & LOUISIANA MIDLAND
A&BB .... AKRON & BARBERTON BELT
AC&Y ...... AKRON CANTON & YOUNGSTOWN
AGSRR .... ALABAMA GREAT SOUTHERN
A RR .... ALASKA RR
A&NRR .... ATCHISON & NEBRASKA RR
AT&SF .... ATCHISON TOPEKA & SANTA FE
A&LG .... ATLANTA & LA GRANGE
A&PRR .... ATLANTIC & PACIFIC
ACL .... ATLANTIC COAST LINE
A&WP .... ATLANTIC & WEST POINT
B&O .... BALTIMORE & OHIO RR
B&OSW BALTIMORE & OHIO SOUTHWESTERN
BAR .... BANGOR & AROOSTOOK RR
B&LE .... BESSEMER & LAKE ERIE
B&A .... BOSTON & ALBANY
B&L .... BOSTON & LOWELL
B&M .... BOSTON & MAINE
BR&P .... BUFFALO ROCHESTER & PITTSBURGH
B&MR RR .. BURLINGTON & MISSOURI RIVER RR
BCR&M .... BURLINGTON CEDAR RAPIDS & MINNESOTA
BCR&N .... BURLINGTON CEDAR RAPIDS & NORTHERN RR
BN .... BURLINGTON NORTHERN RR
BR .... BURLINGTON ROUTE
BA&P .... BUTTE ANACONDA & PACIFIC
CYR&PRY .. CANANEA YAQUI RIVER & PACIFIC RY
CNR .... CANADIAN NATIONAL RR
CPR .... CANADIAN PACIFIC RY
CCRY .... CARBON COUNTY RY
CPRR .... CENTRAL PACIFIC RR
CRR OF GA ..... CENTRAL RAILROAD OF GEORGIA
CRR OF IO .... CENTRAL RAILROAD OF IOWA
CRR OF NJ CENTRAL RAILROAD OF NEW JERSEY
CVRY .... CENTRAL VERMONT RY
C&O .... CHESAPEAKE & OHIO RR
C&A .... CHICAGO & ALTON RR

C&EI .... CHICAGO & EASTERN ILLINOIS RR
C&IM .... CHICGO & ILLINOIS MIDLAND
C&NW .... CHICAGO & NORTHWESTERN RR
C&WI .... CHICAGO & WESTERN INDIANA
CB&KC .... CHICAGO BURLINGTON & KANSAS CITY
CB&Q .... CHICAGO BURLINGTON & QUINCY
CGW .... CHICAGO GREAT WESTERN
CH&D .... CHICAGO HAMILTON & DAYTON
CI&LCHICAGO INDIANAPOLIS & LOUISVILLE
CI&W ...... CHICAGO INDIANA & WESTERN RY
CK&N ...... CHICAGO KANSAS & NEBRASKA RY
CM&PS CHICAGO MILWAUKEE & PUGET SOUND
CM&STP ... CHICAGO MILWAUKEE & ST. PAUL
CMSTP&P .... CHICAGO MILWAUKEE ST. PAUL & PACIFIC
CP&STL .... CHICAGO PEORIA & ST. LOUIS
CRI&P ..... CHICAGO ROCK ISLAND & PACIFIC
CSF&CRRCHICAGO SANTA FE & CALIFORNIA
CSTP&KC CHICAGO ST PAUL & KANSAS CITY
CSTPM&O .... CHICAGO ST PAUL MINNEAPOLIS & OMAHA
CSS&SB .... CHICAGO SOUTH SHORE & SOUTH BEND
C&DM .... CHILICOTHE & DES MOINES
CO&G ... CHOCKTAW OKLAHOMA & GULF RR
CNO&TPRY .... CINCINNATI NEW ORLEANS & TEXAS PACIFIC
C&NE RY .... CISCO & NORTHEASTERN RY
CCC&STL ... CLEVELAND CINCINNATI, CHICAGO & ST. LOUIS
C&OW .... CLINTON & OKLAHOMA WESTERN
C&S .... COLORADO & SOUTHERN RR
C&SE .... COLORADO & SOUTHEASTERN
C&W .... COLORADO & WYOMING
CM .... COLORADO MIDLAND RY
CS&CCD . COLORADO SPRINGS & CRIPPLE CREEK DISTRICT
C&G .... COLUMBIA & GREENVILLE
CdRR .... CONCORD RR
CRRR .... CONNECTICUT RIVER RR
CC&CS .... CRIPPLE CREEK & COLORADO SPRINGS
C&MRR .... CONCORD & MONTREAL RR
DL&WDELAWARE LACKAWANNA & WESTERN
DMURY .... DEMOINES UNION RY
D&RGRR .... DENVER & RIO GRANDE RR
D&RGWRR .... DENVER & RIO GRANDE WESTERN RR
D&SL .... DENVER & SALT LAKE
DL&G .... DENVER LEADVILLE & GUNNISON
DNW&P ... DENVER NORTHWESTERN & PACIFIC
DSP&PRR ... DENVER SOUTH PARK & PACIFIC RR
DT&G .... DENVER TEXAS & GULF
DTRR .... DETROIT TERMINAL RR
DT&I .... DETROIT TOLEDO & IRONTON
D&TSL ...... DETROIT & TOLEDO SHORE LINE
DBC&W .... DETROIT BAY CITY & WESTERN
D&IR .... DULUTH & IRON RANGE
D&MRR .... DULUTH & MANITOBA RR
DM&IR ..... DULUTH MISSABE & IRON RANGE
DM&N .... DULUTH MISSABE & NORTHERN
DW&P .... DULUTH WINNIPEG & PACIFIC
EP&NE .... EL PASO & NORTHEASTERN
EP&SW .... EL PASO & SOUTHWESTERN
EJ&E .... ELGIN JOLIET & EASTERN
ERR .... ERIE RR
EL .... ERIE LACKAWANNA EP&NE
E&MC .... EVERETT & MONTE CRISTO
FRR .... FITCHBURG RR
F&PM .... FLINT&PERE MARQUETTE
F&KRR .... FRANKFORT & KOKOMO
FE&MV .... FREMONT ELKHORN & MISSOUR VALLEY
FEC .... FLORIDA EAST COAST
FL&CCRR ... FLORENCE & CRIPPLE CREEK RR
FTDDM&S .... FT DODGE DES MOINES & SOUTHERN
FTS&W .... FT SMITH & WESTERN
FTW&DC .... FT WORTH & DENVER CITY
FWSYCO .... FT WORTH STOCK YARD CO
FRISCO .... ST LOUIS & SAN FRANCISCO
GR&I .... GRAND RAPIDS & INDIANA
GTR .... GRAND TRUNK RY
GTW .... GRAND TRUNK WESTERN
GNRY .... GREAT NORTHERN RY
GWRY .... GREAT WESTERN
GB&W .... GREEN BAY & WESTERN
GC&SF .... GULF COLORADO & SANTA FE
GM&O .... GULF MOBILE & OHIO
H&STJRR .... HANNIBAL & ST. JOSEPH
HBL .... HARBOR BELT LINE
HVRY .... HOCKING VALLEY RY
H&TC .... HOUSTON & TEXAS CENTRAL
HB&T .... HOUSTON BELT & TERMINAL
HE&WTRY .... HOUSTON EAST & WEST TEXAS
ICRR .... ILLINOIS CENTRAL RR

ICG .... ILLINOIS CENTRAL GULF
ITRR .... ILLINOIS TERMINAL
IHB .... INDIANA HARBOR BELT
II&I RY .... INDIANA ILLINOIS & IOWA RY
I&STLRR .... INDIANAPOLIS & ST. LOUIS
I&GN ..... INTERNATIONAL & GREAT NORTHERN
IACRY .... IOWA CENTRAL RY
INRY .... IOWA NORTHERN RY
JSE .... JACKSONVILLE SOUTHEASTERN
JCL .... JERSEY CENTRAL LINES
K&IT .... KANSAS & INDIANA TERMINAL
KCSF&G .... KANSAS CITY FT SCOTT & GULF
KCSF&MKANSAS CITY FT SCOTT & MEMPHIS
KCKV&W .... KANSAS CITY KAW VALLEY & WESTERN
KCM&O ..... KANSAS CITY MEXICO & ORIENT
KCNW .... KANSAS CITY NORTHWESTERN
KCP&GRR .... KANSAS CITY PITTSBURGH & GULF
KCS .... KANSAS CITY SOUTHERN
KCT .... KANSAS CITY TERMINAL
KO&G .... KANSAS OKLAHOMA & GULF
KP .... KANSAS PACIFIC
LE&W .... LAKE ERIE & WESTERN
LS&MS .. LAKE SHORE & MICHIGAN SOUTHERN
L&A ....LOUISIANA & ARKANSAS
LS&I .... LAKE SUPERIOR & ISHPEMING
LIRR .... LONG ISLAND RR
LA&SL .... LOS ANGELES & SALT LAKE
LA&T .... LOUISIANA ARKANSAS & TEXAS
L&N .... LOUISVILLE & NASHVILLE
MC&CLRR .... MASON CITY & CLEAR LAKE RR
MCRR .... MICHIGAN CENTRAL RR
MTRY .... MIDLAND TERMINAL RY
MVRY .... MIDLAND VALLEY
M&STP .... MILWAUKEE & ST PAUL RY
MNRY .... MILWAUKEE NORTHERN RY
M&STL .... MINNEAPOLIS & ST. LOUIS
MN&S .... MINNEAPOLIS NORTHFIELD & SOUTHERN
MSTP&SSM .... MINNEAPOLIS ST PAUL & SAULT STE MARIE
MD&W ..... MINNESOTA DAKOTA & WESTERN
MTRY CO ....MINNESOTA TRANSFER RY CO.
MK&T .... MISSOURI KANSAS & TEXAS
MPRR .... MISSOURI PACIFIC RR
MOPAC .... MISSOURI PACIFIC RR
M&ORR .... MOBILE & OHIO RR
MRR .... MONONGAHELA RR
NC&STL .... NASHVILLE CHATTANOOGA & ST. LOUIS
NY&LB ....NEW YORK & LONG BRANCH
NY&NE .... NEW YORK &NEW ENGLAND
NYC .... NEW YORK CENTRAL
NYCS .... NEW YORK CENTRAL SYSTEM
NYC&STL .... NEW YORK CHICAGO & ST. LOUIS
NYLE&W ... NEW YORK LAKE ERIE & WESTERN
NYNH&H .... NEW YORK NEW HAVEN & HARTFORD
NYO&W ....NEW YORK ONTARIO & WESTERN
NYS&W .... NEW YORK SUSQUEHANNA & WESTERN
NKP .... NICKEL PLATE
N&W .... NORFOLK & WESTERN
NSRR .... NORTH SHORE RR
NAR .... NORTHERN ALBERTA RY
NPRR .... NORTHERN PACIFIC RR
OHRR .... OHIO RIVER RR
ONRY .... OKMULGEE NORTHERN RY
OCRR .... OLD COLONY RR
OR&N .... OREGON RAILWAY & NAVIGATION
OSL .... OREGON SHORT LINE
OWRR&N CO . OREGON WASHINGTON RAILROAD & NAVIGATION CO.
OCCRR .... OZARK & CHEROKEE CENTRAL
OSRY .... OZARK SOUTHERN
PERY .... PACIFIC ELECTRIC RY
PGE .... PACIFIC GREAT EASTERN
PVCRRCO ... PAJARO VALLEY CONSOLIDATED RR
PRR .... PENNSYLVANIA RR
PENNA CO .... PENNSYLVANIA RR
PRSL .... PENNSYLVANIA READING SEASHORE LINE
PC .... PENNSYLVANIA CENTRAL
P&PU .... PEORIA & PEKIN UNION
PD&E .... PEORIA DECATUR & EVANSVILLE
PMRR .... PERE MARQUETTE RR
P&R .... PHILADELPHIA & READING
P&LE .... PITTSBURGH & LAKE ERIE
P&WV .... PITTSBURGH & WEST VIRGINIA
PC&STL .... PITTSBURGH CINCINNATI & ST. LOUIS
PCC&STL .. PITTSBURGH CINCINNATI CHICAGO & ST LOUIS
P&S .... PORTLAND & SEATTLE RY
QA&P .... QUANAH ACME & PACIFIC
QO&KC .... QUINCY OMAHA & KANSAS CITY

RCO .... READING COMPANY
RDGCO .... READING COMPANY
RF&P .... RICHMOND FREDERICKSBURG & POTOMAC
RGS .... RIO GRANDE SOUTHERN
RRI & STL .... ROCKFORD ROCK ISLAND & ST. LOUIS
RW&O .... ROME WATERSTOWN & OGDENSBURG
RS&P .... ROSCOE SNYDER & PACIFIC
RRR .... RUTLAND RR
RUT RR.. RUTLAND RR
R&BRR ....RUTLAND & BURLINGTON RR
SNRRCO .... SACRAMENTO NORTHERN RR CO
STJ&GI ....ST JOSEPH & GRAND ISLAND
STJ&DC................. ST JOSEPH & DENVER CITY
STL&H ....ST LOUIS & HANNIBAL
STLIM&S .... ST LOUIS IRON MOUNTAIN & SOUTHERN
STLKC&C .... ST LOUIS KANSAS CITY & COLORADO
STL&SF................ ST LOUIS & SAN FRANCISCO
STL&SE ....ST LOUIS & SOUTHEASTERN
STL&SW .... ST LOUIS & SOUTHWESTERN
STLRM&P ..... ST LOUIS ROCKY MOUNTAIN & PACIFIC
SSW ....ST LOUIS SOUTHWESTERN
STLB&M.. ST LOUIS BROWNSVILLE & MEXCO
STPUSYCO...... ST PAUL UNION STOCK YARDS
SL&O .... SALT LAKE & OGDEN
SLR ....SALT LAKE ROUTE
SA&AP .... SAN ANTONIO & ARANSAS PASS
SD&A .... SAN DIEGO & ARIZONA
SD&AE........SAN DIEGO & ARIZONA EASTERN
SFN&C..... SAN FRANCISCO NAPA CALISTOGA
SPLA&SL......... SAN PEDRO LOS ANGELES & SALT LAKE
SR&RLRR .... SANDY RIVER & RANGELY LAKES
SFP&P .... SANTA FE PRESCOTT & PHOENIX
SF ROUTE ....SANTA FE ROUTE
SAL ....SEABOARD AIR LINE
SCL .... SEABOARD COAST LINE
SPC .... SOUTH PACIFIC COAST
SSRY .... SOUTH SHORE RY
SO RY .... SOUTHERN RY
SRR .... SOUTHERN RR
SOURY .... SOUTHERN RY
SP .... SOUTHERN PACIFIC
SPCO .... SOUTHERN PACIFIC COMPANY
SP LINES .... SOUTHERN PACIFIC LINES

SURR .... SOUTHERN UTAH RR
SP&S .... SPOKANE PORTLAND & SEATTLE
TERY .... TACOMA EASTERN RY
TENN RY .... TENNESEE RY
TCRY .... TENNESEE CENTRAL
TMRR .... TENNESEE MIDLAND
TRRA .... TERMINAL RAILROAD ASSOCIATION OF ST. LOUIS
TMRR .... TEXAS MIDLAND
T&PRR .... TEXAS & PACIFIC
TO&E.............. TEXAS OKLAHOMA & EASTERN
T&NO .... TEXAS & NEW ORLEANS
TSE .... TEXAS SOUTHEASTERN
TSRR .... TIDEWATER SOUTHERN
T&OC .... TOLEDO & OHIO CENTRAL
TA&W .... TOLEDO ANGOLA & WESTERN
TP&W............. TOLEDO PEORIA & WESTERN
TSL&KC .. TOLEDO ST. LOUIS & KANSAS CITY
TSTL&W .... TOLEDO ST. LOUIS & WESTERN
TW&W .... TOLEDO WABASH & WESTERN
T&G .... TONOPAH & GOLDFIELD
TH&B .... TORONTO HAMILTON & BUFFALO
TH&D .... TORONTO HAMILTON & DAYTON
T&BV .... TRINITY & BRAZOS VALLEY
UP .... UNION PACIFIC
UPD&G ...... UNION PACIFIC DENVER & GULF
UPMP&CUNION PACIFIC MOTIVE POWER & CAR
VRR .... VIRGINIAN RR
VGN .... VIRGINIAN RR
V&T .... VIRGINIA & TRUCKEE
WRR .... WABASH RR
WAB .... WABASH RR
WSTL&P .... WABASH ST LOUIS & PACIFIC
WBT&SRY WACO BEAUMONT TRINITY & SABINE
W&OV .... WARREN & OUACHITA VALLEY
WP .... WESTERN PACIFIC
WVRR .... WESTERN VERMONT RR
W&LE .... WHEELING & LAKE ERIE
WM .... WESTERN MARYLAND
WP&YR .... WHITE PASS & YUKON
WC.. WISCONSIN CENTRAL
WIS&MICH ...... WISCONSIN & MICHIGAN RR
Y&MV .... YAZOO & MISSISSIPPI VALLEY
Y&N .... YOUNGSTOWN& NORTHERN
Y&S ....YOUNGSTOWN & SOUTHERN

CONTENTS

	FOREWORD	*xiii*
	ACKNOWLEDGEMENTS	*xv*
	INTRODUCTION	*xvi*
1	*ADVERTISING*	*1*
2	*ASHTRAYS*	*12*
3	*BAGGAGE TAGS*	*17*
4	*BOOKS*	*22*
5	*BREAST BADGES*	*26*
6	*BROTHERHOOD*	*35*
7	*BUILDERS PLATES*	*39*
8	*BUTTONS & PINS*	*45*
9	*CAP BADGES*	*50*
10	*CAPS & UNIFORMS*	*70*
11	*DEPOT & RAIL YARDS*	*74*
12	*DINING CAR CHINA*	*85*
13	*DINING CAR GLASSWARE*	*121*
14	*DINING CAR LINENS*	*128*
15	*DINING CAR MENUS*	*131*
16	*DINING CAR SILVER*	*136*
17	*EXPRESS*	*156*
18	*KEYS*	*165*
19	*LANTERNS SHORT GLOBE*	*193*
20	*LANTERNS TALL GLOBE*	*208*
21	*LANTERNS PRESENTATION*	*241*
22	*LIGHTS -SWITCH, CLASS, MARKER & MISCELLANEOUS*	*246*
23	*LOCKS BRASS SWITCH*	*252*
24	*LOCKS SPECIAL PURPOSE*	*265*
25	*LOCKS STEEL*	*274*
26	*PASSES*	*279*
27	*PHOTOS PRINTS & POSTERS*	*289*
28	*PLAYING CARDS*	*295*
29	*TIMETABLES*	*302*
30	*TOOLS & TINWARE*	*314*
31	*TRAIN COLLECTIBLES*	*319*
32	*TRAVEL BROCHURES*	*331*
33	*MISCELLANEOUS*	*340*
34	*REPRODUCTIONS*	*343*

FORWARD

A wise and valuable guide to the treasured artifacts and historic relics of bygone days of our American railroads has at last come into being. The striking volume now in the hands of the reader - comprehensive, authoritative, a well-illustrated new dictionary and price guide -- will find a ready and happy welcome.

No longer must we despair over the great gulf of ignorance, the little interest, the lack of recognition among otherwise renowed authorities, in the fields of antiques, to this wonderful field so fascinating to us all.

The new presentation here is the product of more than a decade of diligent attention and devoted study by Bill & Sue Knous to the diverse fields of railroad memorabilia. Their lengthy sequence of quality, attractive and reputable mail-order auction catalogues over the past thirteen years provides the knowledgeable basis for this effort.

Now at last, we are presented with this new guide, comprehensive in its coverage, authoratative in its classifications and varieties, appropriate in its copius photographic illustrations, and with great integrity and intelligence as a guide to the rarity, desirability, and monetary values of countless numbers of items.

Jackson Thode,

Author & Railroad Historian

Denver, Colorado

December, 1999

ACKNOWLEDGEMENTS

The task of writing any book can and is mounumental and would usually not be complete without the help of many qualified and generous people. This book of course was a large effort but made possible because of several people. We would like to take a moment to thank each and everyone of those wonderful friends and colleagues that helped make this project possible.

Beth & Bill Sagstetter who without their constant inspiration and support this would never have happened. Co-authors of "*Mining Camps Speak*" they offered much of their time and technical support to help us along the way. We are very grateful and highly recommend their book to anyone who enjoys the history of mining and railroads as well.

We consulted with many colleagues along the way who not only assisted in proof reading selected chapters, but also reviewed the suggested prices and we do appreciate and value their opinions. Chuck Albi with the Colorado Railroad Museum, Bill Cunningham, Rob Holt, Jim Johnson, Ron Kaminski, John McCaslin, Bill Pelozzi, Lee Reed, Bud Richie, Neil Shankweiler, Steve Spalding, Jack Thode, Sid White, Rick Wright & Dick Zinn. We thank those of you as well for loaning photographs and items we needed to complete the project. Your support and help were greatly appreciated.

Many years ago when Bill & I first started dealing in railroad artifacts a couple originally from Covina, California by the name of Bob & Lou Jones came into our store one day in Georgetown, Colorado. We want to thank them for trusting us and giving us the opportunity to handle their collection of railroadiana. Our first catalogs featured many items from their collection. They really launched us from a part time hobby to a full time business and we are very grateful.

Finally, we have to thank our children, Amanda, Billy & Andrea for putting up with us and continually hearing the words, *"When the Book Is Done!"* You three have always made us very proud and guess what, *"THE BOOK IS DONE!!!!"*

INTRODUCTION

There is something magical about a train. The sound of a whistle, the sight of a railroad light invoke wonderful memories in people still today. Many of us are too young to have experienced the height of train travel. The bustling Union Stations where the traveling public prepared for their journeys. A brochure readily available would show the many scenes a passenger might see along their trip. The timetable would give them a rigid schedule to plan their journey. Once on board they would experience a memorable and exciting event. Flanked by the best of everything the railroad passenger enjoyed the finest foods served on beautiful china placed on irish linens and accompanied by exquisite silver setting pieces. Meals were chosen from thoughtfully created menus. After enjoying a meal on board a passenger might retire to the lounge car where they would be again surrounded by smoking stands, ashtrays, lamps & advertising posters. In their sleeper cars they would find, linens, pullman items and of course soaps & advertising giveaways to take home as a complimentary gift. Upon arrival at their destination they would be greeted at the door of the coach by a fully uniformed conductor who would graciously offer a step stool to disembark the train. The depot would be fully appointed with various signs, clocks, ticket cabinets, ticket dater machines, wax sealers, photos and a host of other items that collectors hoard and cherish today. From the rail yards where the lanterns, locks, keys, lights, and other items were found the railroads were host to what has become today a very valuable and rewarding collecting hobby.

This book is based on 13 years of auction experience dealing strictly in railroadiana. Bill & Sue Knous the owners and proprietors of Railroad Memories have brokered literally thousands of different pieces of railroadiana through mail bid auction and private retail sales. They have spent the past two years compiling and tabulating the information found here. The prices shown are based on what they have seen versus what the general public is offered. When a piece sells at auction the price is often times based on two bidders who truly want the item. Willing to pay whatever it takes, the final price is many times more than what the general collecting community might want to pay. The prices found here are based on the average of the majority of the bidders. We feel in this way we are supplying the collecting community with a more realistic price than the finalized bidder frenzied price. We have also conferred with colleagues who are specialists in their own collecting fields such as just collecting lanterns, locks, keys, china or silver to include their imput in regard to the pricing. In this way we feel this book offers a wide variety of expertise and knowledge to compliment its contents. We feel you will find this book to be helpful not only in the values that are offered but more importantly in the amount of information that the reader will find. With over 900 photographs to lead the way this book will be the preferred guide for the new millenium.

The railroadiana hobby has come a long way. There are two collecting organizations that we highly recommend whether you are a collector, dealer or just plain curious. Both offer a wide variety of information for the collector as well as giving you the opportunity to become acquainted with other collectors. Your subscription fees insure you quarterly magazines that feature collections, articles about different railroad collectibles, reproductions, shows around the country and all the information you were looking for. This is the best way to find and learn about the hobby. The information provided below will get you started and will provide you with the cost and where to send your yearly subscription fees. This money is well spent and you will find the best way to begin your collecting adventure. We highly recommend joining both organizations as they each supply invaluable information to collectors.

RAILROADIANA COLLECTORS ASSOCIATION, INC.

yearly subscription fee of $20.00

send to:

RCAI

c/o Bob Chase, Secretary

550 Veronica Place

Escondido, California 92027

KEY LOCK & LANTERN INC.

yearly subscription fee $22.00

send to:

Marie Brainard, Vice President-Membership

35 Nordhoff Place

Englewood, New Jersey 07631

READERS: THE SUGGESTED VALUES PRESENTED IN THIS PUBLICATION ARE INTENDED FOR A REFERENCE GUIDE ONLY. MARKET CONDITIONS VARY GREATLY BY REGION AND COLLECTOR. VALUE IS ALWAYS SUBJECTIVE. THIS PUBLICATION IS NOT INTENDED TO DICTATE, WARRANT OR GUARANTEE THE SUGGESTED VALUE OF THE ARTICLES DESCRIBED. AUTHORS ASSUME NO RESPONSIBILITY, STATED OR IMPLIED, FOR ACQUISITIONS, SALES, OR TRANSACTIONS CONDUCTED RELYING UPON THIS GUIDE.

Cover designed by Ken White of ULTIMAX, INC., Wheatridge, Colorado

Printed by UNITED GRAPHICS, INC., Mattoon, Illinois

CHAPTER 1

ADVERTISING

As with any business, the railroads were in fierce competition with one another to lure the traveling passenger. Constantly touting their own horns the individual companies came up with their own logo which was put on everything from swizzle sticks to rain caps and given away daily to the traveling public. Many of these items have become quite collectible and scarce making their discoveries a true treasure for the lucky recipient. Many items were also sold to the traveling public. These items are often more valuable due to the limited number that were made available. Unlike the giveaway items where thousands were at one time distributed, the items that were sold as memento's were more likely treasured and taken care of. The railroads also gave away thousands of items to shippers as a thank you for using their road for the transportation of their freight. These items are included in this section as well. Remember that with all collectibles condition is very important. Items must be in excellent to mint condition showing little wear or use to command the suggested prices shown here.

REMEMBER: PRICES SHOWN ARE SUGGESTED VALUES ONLY. VALUES VARY FROM REGION TO REGION. THIS IS MEANT ONLY AS A GUIDE. (◆) **Denotes value over $1000.00**

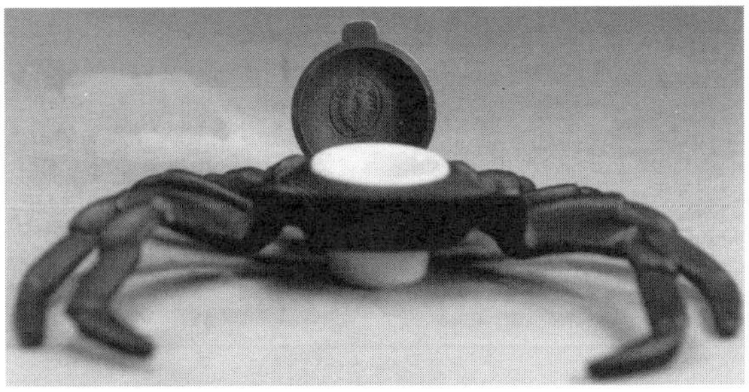

ADAMS & WESTLAKE- *inkwell* brass advertising piece. Crab design with porcelain insert for ink. **400-500**

ATLANTIC & EAST CAROLINA RY- *pearlized mechanical pencil* with calendar on one end **15-25**

ACL- *clipboard* wooden with metal clip cast "ACL". Measures 6"x 8" **20-30**

AMTRAK *celluloid buttons* with various designs. Advertising giveaway **1-2**

B&O- *letter opener* , red plastic with B&O capitol logo on top edge................................. **3-5**

B&O- *vinyl tote bag*, blue & white. Shows B&O in circle over engines and reads, "Student Tour" **20-25**

B&O- *tape measure* leather bound with embossed "B&ORR" on side **20-25**

B&O RR- *paperweight*, oval cast iron measures 3 ¾" diameter with B&ORR cast in center **60-70**

B&O- *bottle opener*, chrome plated in shape of letters. **15-20**

B&M- *paperweight*, clear glass measures 4 x 2 ½" with "Bellows Falls", VT" railroad bridge picture **15-20**

BN- *belt buckle* brass with high relief engine & BN logo **10-15**

BN- *tape measure* 10 foot size has green & white BN logo on cover **5-10**

BR- *license plate reflector*. Measures 4" diameter and shows BR logo in center, "EVERYWHERE" on top & "WEST" on the bottom **60-70**

BR- *smoked glass tray* measures 9"x7" with "Chuck Wagon, Denver Zephry" shows various cattle brands **45-55**

BR- *red glass tray* measures 9"x 7" with BR box logo and shows various cattle brands **65-75**

BR- *wall map* measure 34"x46" circa 1950's. Shows BR logos in each corner, given to shippers **50-60**

BURLINGTON ROUTE- *stainless steel match case* cover for boxed matches shows Zephrus on the front **25-35**

BURLINGTON ROUTE- *desk ornament* shows model of BR Vista Dome car. Measures 2" x 7 ½" with felt base. Base reads, "*The First Vista Dome Car 1945*" BR box logos on both sides. Must be complete with all four logos in tact **100-125**

BCR&N- *brass cast paperweight* measures 2 ¾" diameter reads, "Albert Lea Route, The Burlington Cedar Rapids & Northern Ry" on one side, reverse lists all the stations on the line **200-250**

CALIFORNIA ZEPHYR- *stainless steel tray* 2" diameter with Zephrus logo in center. Marked on bottom, "Solid Chrome Nickel Stainless Steel, The CH Hanson Co. Chicago." Giveaway for the first stainless steel car **25-35**

C&ORY- *paperweight.* showing Lima-Hamilton Allegheny type locomotive pewter engine mounted on high relief base. **150-175**

C&ORY- *plastic coasters* with Chessie logo in center. "Box reads, "Safety Our Watch Word". 6 yellow coasters in black plastic holder **10-15**

C&EI RR- *advertising plaque.* Aluminum cast piece shows "C&EI" cast on side of boxcar over "Ship by Rail". Measures 8" x 3" **90-100**

C&NW- *cigar box.* Wooden box shows C&NW logo on lid. **25-35**

C&NW- *metal advertising wall thermometer.* Reads, "Think Safety" on top **10-15**

CGW- *paperweight* double sided measures approximately 3" diameter with Mapel Leaf Route Herald on celluloid covering both sides. Metal rim 3/8" thick. Circa 1890's. **300-350**

CM&STPRY- *Grizzly Bear* bronze desk ornament mounted on base. Base reads "Chicago, Milwaukee & St. Paul Ry" to Puget Sound Electrified". Reverse reads, "Gallatin Gateway to Yellowstone Park" Felt bottom **100-125**

CM&STPRY- *desk ornament* Bi Polar Electric Engine. Opposite side of base reads, "To Puget Sound Electrified" 100-125

CMSTP&P- *pearlized mechanical pencil* advertising the "Route of the Hiawatha". 15-25

CSS&SBRR- *mechanical pencil.* Black pencil with white letters. MFg. Autopoint. 10-15

COLORADO & SOUTHERN- *celluloid pocket mirror* shows lithograph of "Georgetown Loop" 100-125

COLORADO MIDLAND- *Cigar Cutter.* Nickel plated machine cast "Colorado Midland Chief of All Havana Cigars" on top. Measures 4 ¼" x 5 ½" 3 ¾"tall. Mfg. Erie Specialty Co. .... ◆

COTTON BELT ROUTE- *mechanical pencil* pearlized with blue logo and red highlights 15-20

COTTON BELT ROUTE- *metal clipboard* measures 4" x 6" with "Cotton Belt Logo" on clip. 60-70

DM&IR- *Letter opener*, has round handle with "DM&IR" logo & Safety First" 35-45

D&H- *outdoor thermometer* 12" round. Center logo has "Lackawanna" Antracite" around the "D&H" logo 90-100

D&H- *matchbooks* package of 6 books wrapped in original cellophane shows map on one side with D&H logo on the other 5-10

D&H CO- *paperweight* brass measures 4" x 2 ½". Reads, "The Stour Bridge Line" 1829-1929. 150-175

D&RGW- *mug* orange fire king, shows Diesel engine on one side & system map on the other, giveaway to shippers 15-20

D&RGW- *calendar* 1942 wall style measures 20" x 34". Shows steam train in Royal Gorge. 100-125

D&RGW- *ruler,* clear plastic shows color lithograph of F-Unit & reads, "Mainline Thru the Rockies" **5-10**

D&RGW- *tote bag* white vinyl souvenir. Has Mainline logo on side with streamliner train & reads, "Denver & Rio Grande Western Railroad" across the bottom **25-35**

ERIE RR- *mechanical pencil* pearlized blue & white. Shows Diesel engine over "The Heavy Duty Railroad" **30-40**

FRED HARVEY- *folding cup* aluminum.style Cast on bottom , FRED HARVEY PRICE IS 15 CENTS". **25-35**

FRED HARVEY-*china doll* Harvey Girl. Sold as a souvenir in the Fred Harvey shops. **100-125**

FRISCO- *box car matches.* Card board box in boxcar design houses approximately 30 books of matches. Box reads, "Ship It on the Frisco" **10-15**

FRISCO LINE- *advertising mirror* with logo on bottom edge of. Mirror measures 2" diameter, outside border reads, "There is something to see" Colorful lithograph with train & beautiful scenery. **100-125**

FRISCO- *Advertising piece* to announce the "Straight Shooter Route". Card board gun sits in card board leather look holster with Frisco logo in red over "VIA AVARD". **30-40**

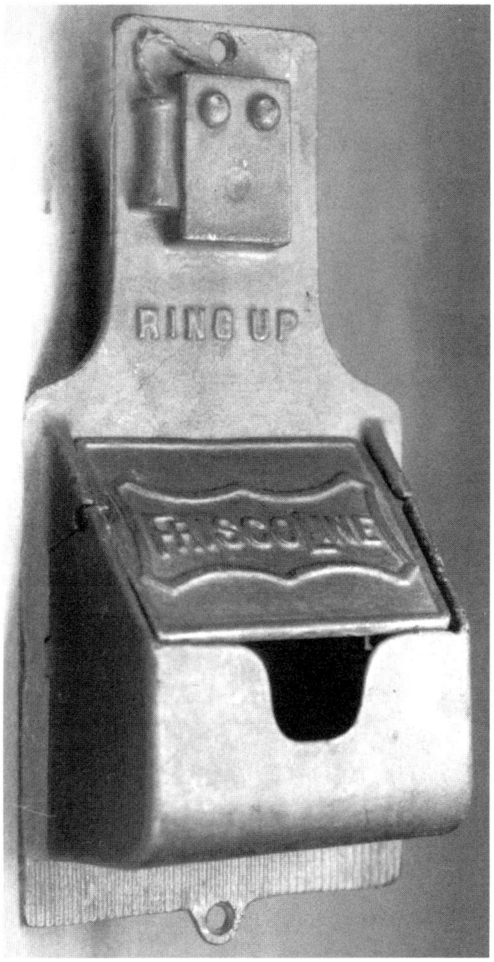

FRISCO LINES- *metal match safe.* "Frisco Lines" logo cast on pivoting lid. Match sticker along the bottom edge. Cast wall mount bell box phone on top with "RING UP" below. "Pat App'd For" on one edge. **500-550**

GNRY- *plastic swizzle sticks* with goat on top. Also found with just GN initials comes in red, green, yellow, blue, black & orange. **1-5**

GNRY- *shaving kit.* Chrome plated with GN goat logo on outside. Inside silk lining houses razor & blades. "Reads, Compliments of Great Northern Railway Route of the New Oriental Limited" **125-150**

GNRY- *mechanical pencil* pearlized advertising "The New Route of the Empire Builder" **15-20**

GNRY- *Jigsaw puzzle*, titled "Juniper Buffalo Bill & Little Young Man" or "Scalping Woman". Pictures are from original portraits by Winold Reiss **50-60**

GNRY- *advertising pinback*. Celluloid pin measures 2 ¼", reads, "Your On the Right Track With Great Northern". Shows Goat in Diesel engine. Multi colored. **10-15**

GNRY- *calendar* dated June 1930 shows colorful picture of "Little Plume" measures 11" x 21" **100-125**

GNRY- *calendar* dated August 1931 wall shows colorful picture of "Tough Bread" measures 11" x 21" **100-125**

GNRY-*Goat Stickers* shows front facing goat on red background with blue letters **1-3**

GNRY-*fingernail clippers.* Housed in yellow plastic cover that reads, "GN Employees". **5-10**

ICRR- *matches* package of 6 books wrapped in cellophane. White with orange "IC" **1-5**

ICRR- *paperweight* 3" round brass celebrating the 100 year anniversary, 1851-1951. Has high relief "IC" logo on one side system map on the other **30-35**

IOWA CENTRAL ROUTE- *match safe* pressed on tin with black logo in center. Embossed design around edge reads, "Easter 1901" **150-175**

KANSAS CITY,WYANDOTTE & NORTHWESTERN RR- *medallion* reads around outer edge of brass. "The Northwest Route" in center with arrow. "The Short Line" list of destinations on reverse **125-150**

KCS- *paperweight* two sided bean bag. Brown leather with gold letters shows "KCS LINES" logo over "Route of the Southern Bell, Streamliner Hospitality" **65-75**

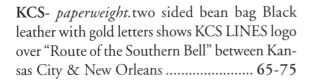

KCS- *paperweight.*two sided bean bag Black leather with gold letters shows KCS LINES logo over "Route of the Southern Bell" between Kansas City & New Orleans **65-75**

KCS- *comb* red plastic folding pocket with KCS logo **10-15**

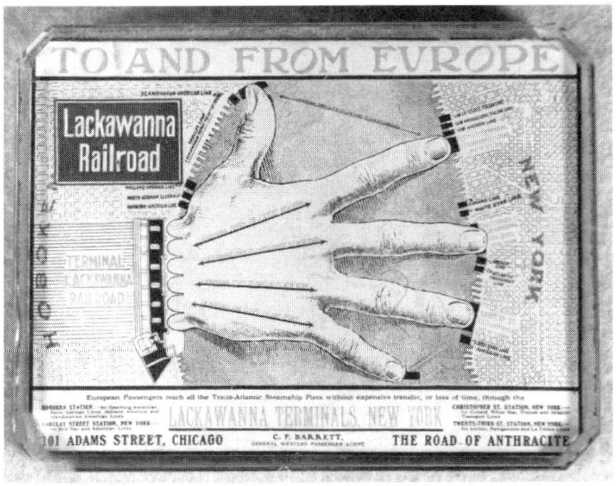

LACKAWANNA RAILROAD- *desk ornament* glass encased two sided. One side shows colorized photo of Delaware Water Gap-Lackawanna RR" Reverse has spread hand across water directing to each terminal. Beveled edges measures 4 ½" x 3 ½"...................... **100-125**

LVRR- *thermometer* circa 1940's advertising measures 6" x 2" with red & black "LV" logo on bottom edge. **75-85**

MK&T- *match safe* cast iron embossed on hinged lid reads "Missouri Kansas & Texas RY" embossed below. Underside reads, "Thos. C. Purdy V.P. & Genl. Mngr. D Miller Track Mngr. James Barker, Traffic Mngr. Gen.Pass & Tkt Agt. St. Louis, MO." **250-300**

M-K-T-*pocket knife* with celluloid cover showing lady on one side with MKT logos above & below. Reverse side reads, "The Katy Flyer" circa 1890's **150-175**

MKT-*notepad* with celluloid cover reads, "The Indian Territory & Texas" with MK&T logo. Circa 1902... **90-100**

MKT- *mechanical pencil* pearlized with red & gold highlights. Katy Logo on top of pencil "Serves the Southwest" on bottom half **15-25**

MONON ROUTE- *match safe* cast bronze alligator. Has hinged lid to house matches. Names of cities served on the head, legs & tail. Circa 1900's **450-500**

MP- *calendar.* tin perpetual wall style. Shows colorful steam engine lithograph on top. Measuring 13" x9". Bottom half houses removable month & day calendar cards. Painted green **250-300**

MP- *calendar.* tin perpetual wall style shows colorful diesel engine lithograph reads, "Route of the Eagles". Bottom half houses removable month & day calendar cards. Painted blue with silver cards **175-200**

MP LINES- *mechanical pencil* pearlized with red buzz saw logo reads, "The Eagle" **20-30**

NEW JERSEY CENTRAL/READING- *wooden cigar box.* Tag reads, "Specially Selected for Reading/New Jersey Central Dining Cars" **100-125**

NHRR- *token* aluminum 2 ¼" reads, "Compliments of Dining Car Service" **5-10**

NEW HAVEN RR- *cigarette lighter.* Side etched "New Haven RR" & signed by Patrick B. McGinnis, President. Mfg. Zippo. **20-25**

NEW ORLEANS, GREAT NORTHERN RR- *letter opener* brass engraved on handle with fancy border design on handle. Measures 8" long **35-45**

NYC- *desk ornament* shows NYC 5200 locomotive mounted on base. Dated 1928 with silver finish & felt bottom **125-150**

NYC-*wall calendar* dated 1930. Measures 25" x 26". Painting by Walter Green titled "Eastward Westward The Centuries At Buffalo Central Terminal". **125-150**

NP-"Little N'py" *advertising chalk figure.* Black waiter carrying large baked potato. Mounted on base cast "Northern Pacific" with Monad Logo. .... ◆

NP- *Brass letter opener* reads, "Route of the Big Baked Potato" **85-95**

NP- *mechanical pencil* pearlized. Shows NP Yellowstone logo **20-30**

NP- *inkwell* in design of Baked Potato. Unique item reads, "Route of the Great Big Baked Potato" on base. Single well design **450-500**

NP- *Inkwell* in design of Baked Potato. Again same as previous only with two inkwells **650-700**

NP- *tote bag* grey vinyl with Monad logo over Vista Dome North Coast Limited **15-20**

NP- *spoon* silver souvenir advertising "Route of the Great Big Baked Potato". MFg. Wallace **45-55**

NP- *plate* 8" clear glass etched "Last Spike Centennial 1883-1983, Deer Lodge Montana" around edge. Train in center drawn around map. **5-10**

QUANAH ROUTE- *sewing kit.* Matchbook design houses sewing kit giveaway. Measures 3 ½" x 3 ½" with logo on cover **10-15**

PRR-*belt buckle* cast with Keystone logo **10-15**

PRR- *paperweight* cast ornately on both sides of 5" oval **55-65**

PRR- *paperweight* cast on top of 2 ½" diameter cast iron with attached handle on top. **45-55**

PRR- *mechanical pencil* pearlized with red & black highlights. Shows engine on tracks with PRR logo **15-25**

PRR- *wall calendar* dated 1955 shows painting by Griff Tiller titled "Dynamic Progress". Shows space age Arrow train with freight train in the opposite direction on Horseshoe Curve. Measures 28 ½" x 27 ½". **100-125**

PC- *desk ornament* shows Metroliner chrome plated miniature Metro Liner mounted on tracks **15-25**

READING RY SYSTEM- *memo pad holder.* Has high relief steam engine mounted on clip that holds pad. Reading logo on both ends with copper finish **55-65**

READING RY SYSTEM- *brass desk ornament.* Engine 2100 in full relief on track. Base reads, "Reading Railway System" with logos on either side. **45-55**

ROCK ISLAND- *mechanical pencil* pearlized shows "Route of the Rockets" **30-40**

ROCK ISLAND- *mechanical pencil* pearlized with red & black diesel engine. Reads, "Travel & Ship, Route of the Rockets" with logo's on either side **35-45**

ROCK ISLAND- *paperweight* glass octagon measures 3" diameter. Shows "Great Rock Island Route" in center. "Solid Vestibule Trains" with list of cities **90-100**

ROCK ISLAND- *paperweight* round clear plastic with "Century of Service 1852-1952" celebration medal encased in center 35-45

ROCK ISLAND- *wall map* circa 1950 measures 30" x 40" with Rock Island logo in bottom left corner. 75-85

SANTA FE- *poker chips*. Red, white or blue plastic chip with embossed Santa Fe logo.Reverse side of chips reads, "When the Chips Are Down Call Santa Fe". 2-3

SANTA FE- *drink coaster*. Brass coaster with embossed logo in center and felt bottom. 10-15

SANTA FE-*perfume samples*. Small tube contains 4 different vials of perfume samples. Outside label reads, "Personality Perfumes Compliments of Santa Fe All The Way" 25-35

SANTA FE- *smoked glass tray* measures 17" oval diameter. with US map outlined in silver with either Chico drawing in sand or Santa Fe Diesel engine in corner. Several versions do exist. 25-35

SANTA FE-*mini vinyl bag*, white on blue with logo on both sides. Miniture giveaway travel bag measures 7" wide by 4" tall with zipper on top 20-25

SANTA FE- *ceramic music box* has two Santa Fe Diesel Units in the warbonnet paint scheme placed back to back on top of track. Green base reads, "SANTA FE ALL THE WAY" on both sides Music box in bottom plays "Atchison, Topeka Santa Fe" 350-400

SANTA FE- *mechanical pencil* white pearlized body with blue Santa Fe logo reads, "Ultra Modern Streamlined Trains, Southwestern & California Travel" 15-25

SANTA FE-*measuring tape*. Shows head of Chico under "SANTA FE ALL THE WAY"on chrome plated tape. Measures 1 1/2" x 1 1/2" 20-25

SANTA FE- *metal rain gauge* measures 4"x 5"in original box. Has Logo in center **20-30**

SILVERTON RR- *celluloid pinback* shows "The Rainbow Route, Through Colorado" shows colorful scene with rainbow trout on front. Pat'd 1897 .... **40-50**

SOO LINE- *magnifying glass* dome desk style. Commemorates the 75th anniversary with burgandy border **30-40**

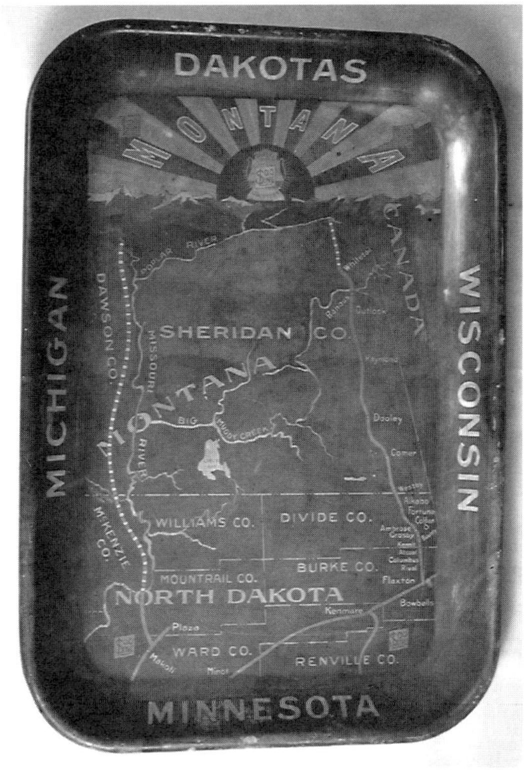

SOO LINE-*advertising tray* celebrating the building of the "Wheat Line". Shows system map. Circa 1910 measures 15" x 10 1/2" **200-250**

SP&S- *cigarette lighter* with red logo on both sides. Mfg. Noble Co. **30-40**

SP- *golf ball* with Sunset logo on side, Manufacturered by Titleist **5-10**

SOUTHERN RY- *mechanical pencil* pearlized. Shows SR logo & reads, "The Southern Serves the South". Green & white **15-25**

TEXAS & PACIFIC- *tape measure* is 2 ¾" diameter.with diamond logo showing the "4 Important Gateways, Best Passenger Service in Texas, L.S. Thorne, Vice Pres.&Gen. Mgr." Reverse side reads, "Compliments No Trouble To Answer Questions, EP Turner, Gen'l Pass. Agt. Dallas, Tex." **150-175**

UNION PACIFIC- *brass paperweight* in shape of replica of front end number plate. Cast "4000" in shield design **30-40**

UNION PACIFIC- *wooden cigar box*. Has modern UP shield logo stenciled in center **25-35**

UNION PACIFIC- *tape measure* 50 foot housed in leather case embossed Union Pacific. Mfg. Lufkin Rule Co. Measures 4" diameter **20-30**

UNION PACIFIC- *tape measure*. Safety award giveaway. Small 5ft tape with UP Shield logo **5-10**

UNION PACIFIC- *token* 1934 Aluminum advertising the Streamliner trains. **2-3**

UNION PACIFIC- *match books* housed in yellow card board stock car marked Union Pacific on the outside **5-10**

WABASH- *mechanical pencil* pearlized with flag logo. Reads, "Every Wabash Man Is A Safety Superintendent" **20-30**

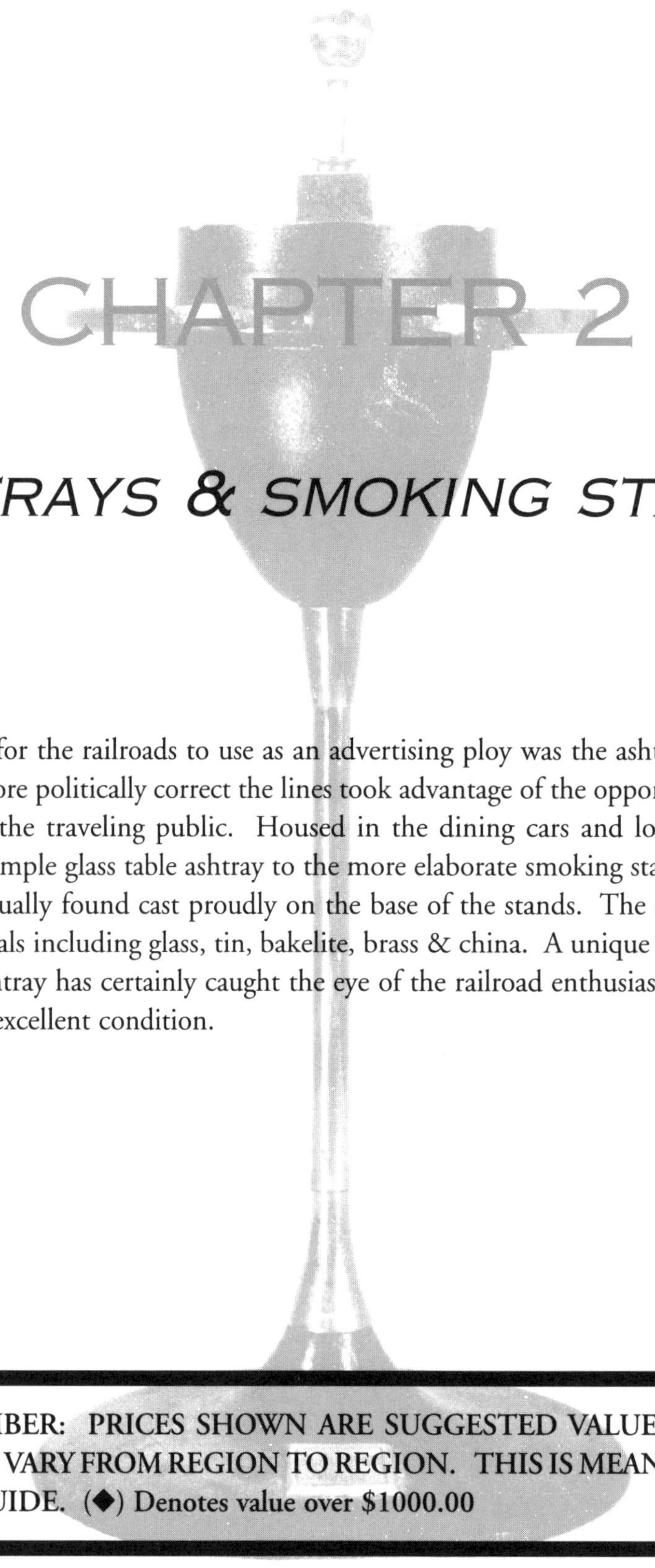

CHAPTER 2

ASHTRAYS & SMOKING STANDS

Another great source for the railroads to use as an advertising ploy was the ashtray. Back in the days when smoking was more politically correct the lines took advantage of the opportunity to display their logos and sayings to the traveling public. Housed in the dining cars and lounges you could find everything from the simple glass table ashtray to the more elaborate smoking stands where the various railroad logos were usually found cast proudly on the base of the stands. The ashtrays were made of many different materials including glass, tin, bakelite, brass & china. A unique collectible and usually easy to display the ashtray has certainly caught the eye of the railroad enthusiast. Suggested prices are for pieces in good to excellent condition.

REMEMBER: PRICES SHOWN ARE SUGGESTED VALUES ONLY. VALUES VARY FROM REGION TO REGION. THIS IS MEANT ONLY AS A GUIDE. (◆) **Denotes value over $1000.00**

ALTON RR- clear glass ashtray with 4 cigarette rests. Alton RR logo enameled in bottom **10-15**

AT&SFRY- china ashtray in California Poppy pattern. Has 4 rests. Mfg. Syracuse. **35-45**

ATLANTIC COAST LINE-enameled in bottom of clear glass ashtray with three rests. **20-25**

BURLINGTON ROUTE-smoking stand has black cast iron base with applied BR box logo. Stainless steel glass holder around top edge with cast iron ash bucket in center **325-350**

BURLINGTON ROUTE- smoked glass tray measures 9" x 7" with cattle brands surrounding Burlington Route box logo. **50-60**

CNR- green china ashtray with three rests. Cast in center "Compliments of CN" **10-15**

CHESAPEAKE & OHIO- rectangular white china ashtray Shows George Washington silhouette on side of match holder. Mfg. Buffalo china. **65-75**

CHESAPEAKE & OHIO- round white china ashtray. Shows silhouette of George Washington on side of match holder. Mfg. Buffalo china **175-200**

C&NW- logo on base of nickel finish smoking stand. Has tray for glasses. Center hinged opening to empty ashtray. Heavy base...... **350-400**

D&RGW-china ashtray with gold letters reads, "Denver Rio Grande Western Railroad" on front edge. Offered in 5 different colors including, Cobalt blue, brown, black, white & light blue. Manufacturer is Snufferette. Has slot on back side for matches, two rests & 4 snuffing holes. **100-125**

ERIE-clear glass ashtray with applied Erie logo on bottom. **5-10**

FRISCO-clear glass octagon shaped ashtray with 6 rests. Reads "Ship It On The Frisco" in red enamel on the bottom. **10-15**

FRISCO-round clear glass ashtray with applied blue & white Frisco logo reads, "5000 Miles in Nine States. **10-15**

GREAT NORTHERN-Glory of the West pattern china ashtray. Mfg. Syracuse. Bottom stamped Great Northern Ry. **100-125**

GREAT NORTHERN- Mountains & flowers pattern china ashtray with four rests. Bottom marked Great Northern Ry. Mfg. by Syracuse **75-85**

GREAT NORTHERN- Oriental pattern china ashtray. Mfg. Scammels. Bottom marked Great Northern Ry. **100-125**

GN- enameled logo applied to center bottom of clear glass ashtray with two rests **15-20**

GOLDEN STATE ROUTE- clear glass ashtray with applied colorful gold orange & white enameled logo in center bottom. **50-60**

IC- clear glass ashtray with "IC Ship & Travel" applied to center bottom **5-10**

L&N- clear glass octagon ashtray with applied red enameled L&N logo in center **10-15**

MP- Cobalt blue ashtray with gold Missouri Pacific buzzsaw logo on either side of match holder. Gold on edges as well. Manufacturer Hall **85-95**

MP- clear glass octagon ashtray with applied red enameled Buzz saw logo on bottom **5-10**

NEW HAVEN-clear glass six sided ashtray with blue enameled logo in center. Shows rocket train passing through it **10-15**

NEW HAVEN RAILROAD – glass ashtray measures 3 ½" x 3 ½" with circle logo in center reads, NHRR Dining Car Service **15-20**

NEW YORK CENTRAL- china ashtray measures 7"x7". Colorful 20th Century Limited train in center with gold highlights. **15-20**

NYNH&HRR- glass ashtray with black script logo in center. Five rests 15-20

NP-smoking stand with nickel finish. Has NP logo applied to base. Shelf for drinks and hinged lever to empty tray. Heavy cast iron base **400-450**

PRR- clear glass keystone shaped asthray. Has red enameled PRR logo in bottom with two rests. **15-20**

PC- clear round glass ashtray with green enameled PC logo in center over Penn Central Railroad. **10-15**

PULLMAN- brass smoking stand with applied Pullman on base. Attached shelf for drinks with heavy base **350-400**

RIO GRANDE- speed lettering logo in black applied to base of nickel finish smoking stand with attached shelf for drinks and lever to empty tray. 375-425

ROCK ISLAND- smoked glass ashtray with black & white Rock Island logo in center with four rests 20-25

ROCK ISLAND-logo embossed in center of brown china ashtray with white letters. Mfg. Snufferette. **100-125**

SANTA FE- small black kidney shaped ashtray with white enameled Santa Fe logo surrounded by Indian drawings. **50-60**

SANTA FE-"Turquoise Room" rectangular asthray. Blue with white & black in center with logo on bottom edge **20-25**

SANTA FE-clear glass ashtray with applied Santa Fe logo in bottom center............. **10-15**

SANTA FE- orange & black glass ashtray reads, "Santa Fe the Hi Level Way" with logo and Chico over Santa Fe train. **50-60**

SANTA FE- smoking stand with chrome finish. Has blue & silver cross logo applied to base. Shelf for drinks and hinged lever to empty tray. Heavy cast iron base **375-400**

SOO LINE- round black metal ashtray with four rests. Soo Line logo in center **10-15**

UP-clear round glass ashtray enameled letters reads, "Utah Parks, Sun Valley Idaho &Union Pacific Railroad..................................... **10-15**

UP-blue round glass ashtray enameled letters reads, "Utah Parks, Sun Valley Idaho Union Pacific Railroad..................................... **10-15**

UP-round glass ashtray with three rests. Has enameled modern shield logo in center. Comes in clear, blue, yellow & smoked glass....... **5-10**

UP-white china ashtray with modern shield logo in center with gold trim around edge and three cigarette rests **5-10**

UP- smoking stand with modern shield logo applied to base. Chrome drink shelf with ashtray in center. Knob turns on the top to empty tray. Cast iron base **275-325**

CHAPTER 3

BAGGAGE TAGS

Brass baggage tags were issued in the early days to keep track of your luggage. Unlike today where the disposible paper tag tends to be the norm, the brass tags were incised with the various railroad names and numbers. Issued often times in pairs one was attached to the luggage and the other turned in upon arrival at your destination to claim your bag. It is always a treasure to find a set of brass tags still attached to their original leather strap. It is also not unusual to find tags which have been nickle plated. Found in many different shapes and sizes a collection of baggage tags can be enjoyed for many years to come. Remember suggested prices are for tags in good to excellent condition.

REMEMBER: PRICES SHOWN ARE SUGGESTED VALUES ONLY. VALUES VARY FROM REGION TO REGION. THIS IS MEANT ONLY AS A GUIDE. **(◆) Denotes value over $1000.00**

A&LGRR- over 125 over A&WP on nickel finish brass tag with black enameled letters. Mfg. PT Foster. **45-55**

BOSTON & MAINE-brass tag #59272 in black enameled letters. Mfg. S. Robbins. **30-40**

BURLINGTON ROUTE-"Property of Chicago" in black enameled letters on brass tag with enameled BR Box logo in center. Large tag measures 2 x 2 ½". Mfg. Am.Ry. Supply. **90-100**

CENTRAL PACIFIC RR- over 22253 over LOCAL on brass tag. Mfg. WW Wilcox.... ◆

C OF G A RY CO-5642 over TERMINAL in black enameled letters on brass 2 x 2 ¾" tag. **15-20**

CB&QRR-#13152 WAY in black enameled letters on brass tag. Mfg. Hoole. **80-90**

CHICAGO GREAT WESTERN RAILWAY- under "THE PROPERTY OF" in black enameled letters on brass tag. Mfg. WW Wilcox. **150-175**

C.M.& P.S.RY- over MILWAUKEE, WIS., on brass tag with slot of top. **175-200**

CO&W- "THE CHOCTAW ROUTE" in diamond logoover 4392 on brass rectangular tag with slots on top & bottom. **250-300**

DEN & RIO G RR- Denver, COLO. On large tage measures 1 ¾" x 2 ¾". Tag reads, "Please send this check to your Gen. Baggage Office to be Returned to Gen Baggage Dept". Mfg. WW Wilcox. **250-300**

D&RGRR- LOCAL #709 rectangular style brass tag . Mfg. WW Wilcox **300-350**

DSP&PRR- Denver to Leadville, double sided brass tag. .... ◆

FJ&GRR- Gloversville and Johnstown #26. Mfg. J. Robbins. **25-30**

FJ&GRR- Fonda to Sacandaba Park. Mfg. Am.Ry. Supply **35-40**

FJ&GRR- Mayfield & Northville #7. Mfg. Am.Ry. Supply. **25-30**

FTWTH&SWRR-#4 Local. Square brass tag with black enameled letters. Mfg. MW Jones Co. **65-75**

GREAT NORTHERN RY LINE- brass tag measures 2 ¼" x 1 5/8". 7 parallel lines runs through the number 18650. MFg. WW Wilcox **200-250**

H&STJO.RR & KCSJ&CBRR- on large brass rectangular baggage tag. Reads, "Property of" over railroad names over "Return this Check" Mfg. Wilcox **250-300**

GRAND TRUNK RAILWAY SYSTEM- Slanted box logo on brass baggage check. Measures 2 ½" x 2" Has slots on top & bottom edge for leather strap **75-85**

ILL.CENT.RR- large brass tag with IC Diamond logo in circle logo on bottom. Reads, "Return This Check to Ill.Cent.RR. **45-55**

KEO&WEST RR CO- Property of the Keo & Western RR Co., Keokuk, Iowa in black enameled letters on brass tag. Measures 2 x 2 ¾" Mfg. WW Wilcox. 65-75

LIRR- East Hampton to 34th Street Via LIRR. Mfg. Am.Ry. Supply 30-40

LNA&C & L&N- Chicago to Montgomery over K-669. Mfg. WW Wilcox............ 40-50

NYP&B & NPRR- over WATCH HILL to Narrangansett Pier #1608. Mfg. J Robbins. 40-50

NYP&B & NPRR- over PROVIDENCE to Narrangansett Pier . Mfg. J Robbins. ... 40-50

NYNH&H-PB&NPRR- over Saybrook Junction to Narrangansett Pier 40-50

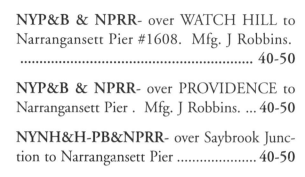

MAINE CENTRAL RR- large iron tag measures 2" x 2 ¾". Mfg. AM Goodwin. ... 45-55

MO.PAC.RY- #19942 LOCAL on brass tag. Mfg. Poole 75-85

NORTHERN PACIFIC- YELLOWSTONE PARK LINE logo in black enameled letters on brass tag measures 2" x 2 ¾". Mfg. Am.Ry. Supply Co. 150-175

NEVADA COUNTY N.G. RAILROAD- #247 in black enameled letters on shield design tag. Mfg. Am.Ry. Supply Co. 200-250

OREGON SHORT LINE RAILROAD- logo in center of brass tag measuring 2" x 2 ½". Has Property of " over logo. Mfg. WW Wilcox.................................. 300-350

OREGON PACIFIC RR- two brass tag set. One reads, "Oregon Pac RR" over Special the other reads, "Please send this check to your Gen. Baggage Office to be Returned to Gen. Baggage Dept. Oregon Pac. RR Corvallis, Or. Mfg. Hoole. **250-300**

ROCK ISLAND LINES- over local #2537 on brass tag. Mfg. Wilcox **45-55**

STJ&GIRR- over 6500 LOCAL on small brass tag. Mfg. WW Wilcox **150-200**

SANTA FE ROUTE- in box over #48 on small brass tag with scalloped edges. Slots on top and bottom edge for leather strap. Mfg. CH Hanson, Chicago **150-200**

SIERRA RY CO. OF CAL.- in black enameled letters on two tag set attached with leather strap. **250-300**

SILVERTON RR CO- #298 LOCAL on round brass tag with slot in top. Mfg. WW Wilcox **250-300**

TW&WRY- over #6430 on brass tag. Mfg. Hoole **70-80**

UPRY-over 16780 over DUPLICATE on brass tag. Mfg. Poole **150-200**

UN PAC RY- over LEADVILLE TO DENVER #4557. .... **350-400**

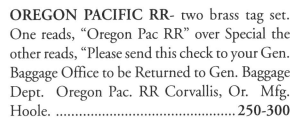

UP E DIV.- black enameled letters over Quincy & Ellsworth #170. Reads, "H&STJ. M-V.UP E DIV. Mfg. Poole. Reverse reads, "Check for Baggage Consideration of Free Carriage, its Value is agreed to be limited to $100.00. Scalloped edges **450-500**

VANDALIA RR CO-large brass tag measures 1 ¾" x 2 ¾". Reads, "Property of the Vandalia RR Co. Mfg. WW Wilcox **90-100**

CHAPTER 4

BOOKS & MANUALS

The many books and manuals available are a wonderful resource to collectors. From the Official guides which listed the many railroads that were in business to the various manuals and catalogs these books are a wealth of information for the collector. We have listed here not only the guides and catalogs but also the various rules and regulation books that can be found from the different roads. Books as well as any other collectible must be in good condition with the binding in tact and the inside pages not torn or tattered. These suggested prices are based on books in good condition.

CAR BUILDERS CYCLOPEDIA- Copyright 1931 ..... **125-140**

CAR BUILDERS CYCLOPEDIA- Copyright 1957 ..... **60-75**

CAR BUILDERS DICTIONARY- 7th edition dated 1912 ..... **250-275**

CAR BUILDERS DICTIONARY- 16th edition dated 1943 ..... **90-110**

CAR BUILDERS DICTIONARY- 18th edition dated 1949-51 ..... **75-85**

CAR BUILDERS DICTIONARY- 19th edition dated 1953 ..... **65-75**

EMD-(Electro Motive Division) Engineman's Operating Manual for Model E-3 ..... **15-20**

EMD-(Electro Motive Division) Engineman's Operating Manual for Model E-7 ..... **15-20**

EMD-(Electro Motive Division) Engineman's Operating Manual for Model E-8 ..... **15-20**

EMD-(Electro Motive Division) Engineman's Operating Manual for Model F-3 ..... **20-25**

EMD-(Electro Motive Division) Engineman's Operating Manual for Model GP-7 ..... **15-20**

EMD-(Electro Motive Division) Engineman's Operating Manual for Model GP-9 ..... **15-20**

EMD-(Electro Motive Division) Engineman's Operating Manual for Model GP-20 ..... **10-15**

EMD-(Electro Motive Division) Engineman's Operating Manual for Model SD-40-2 ..... **10-15**

GE-(General Electric) Operating Manual for Dash 8 ..... **8-12**

GE-(General Electric) Operating Manual for Class E-44 Rectifier **15-20**

GE-(General Electric)Operating Manual for Series 7 ..... **10-15**

GE- (General Electric)Operating Manual for U 25 B **15-20**

GRANTS RAILROAD & BUSINESS ATLAS- dated 1885 ..... **175-200**

LOCOMOTIVE CYCLOPEDIA- dated 1925 with 1131 pages **125-150**

LOCOMOTIVE CYCLOPEDIA- dated 1956 ..... **50-75**

MOODYS TRANSPORTATION MANUALS- 1900-1910 ..... **150-175**

MOODYS TRANSPORTATION MANUALS-1911-1919 ..... **100-125**

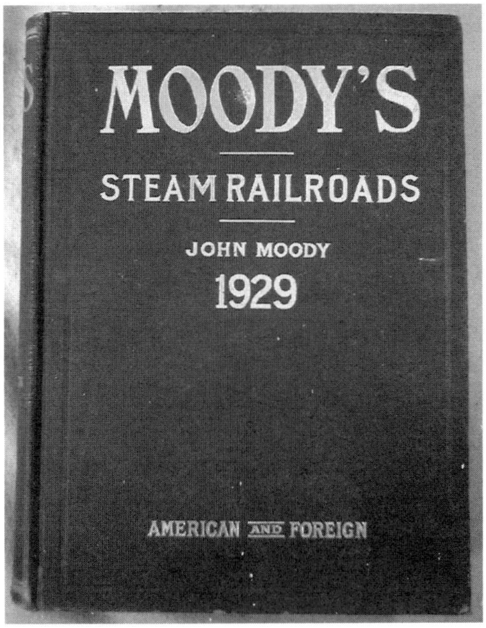

MOODYS TRANSPORTATION MANUALS-1920-1929 ..... **85-100**

MOODYS TRANSPORTATION MANUAL-1930's **75-85**

MOODYS TRANSPORTATION MANUALS-1940's **60-75**

MOODYS TRANSPORTATION MANUALS-1950's **50-60**

MOODYS TRANSPORTATION MANUALS-1960'S **40-50**

MOODYS TRANSPORTATION MANUALS-1970's 30-40

MOODYS TRANSPORTATION MANUALS-1980's 15-25

THE OFFICIAL GUIDE OF THE RAILWAYS-1900-1910 100-125

THE OFFICIAL GUIDE OF THE RAILWAYS-1911-1920 85-100

THE OFFICIAL GUIDE OF THE RAILWAYS-1920'S 75-85

THE OFFICIAL GUIDE OF THE RAILWAYS-1930's 65-75

THE OFFICIAL GUIDE OF THE RAILWAYS-1940's 55-65

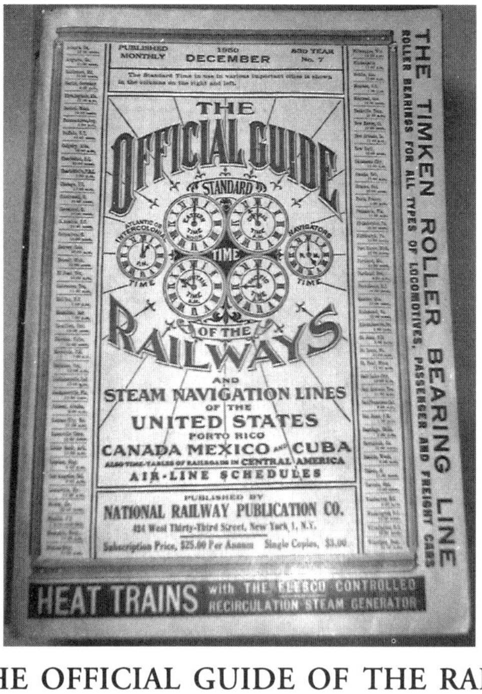

THE OFFICIAL GUIDE OF THE RAILWAYS-1950's 35-45

THE OFFICIAL GUIDE OF THE RAILWAYS-1960's 25-35

THE OFFICIAL GUIDE OF THE RAILWAYS-1970's 15-25

THE OFFICIAL GUIDE OF THE RAILWAYS-1980's 10-15

THE OFFICIAL GUIDE OF THE RAILWAYS-1990's 5-10

POOR'S MANUAL OF RAILROADS- dated 1887 200-250

POOR'S MANUAL OF RAILROADS-dated 1890 175-225

POOR'S MANUAL OF RAILROADS-dated 1902 175-200

POOR'S MANUAL OF RAILROADS-dated 1909 150-175

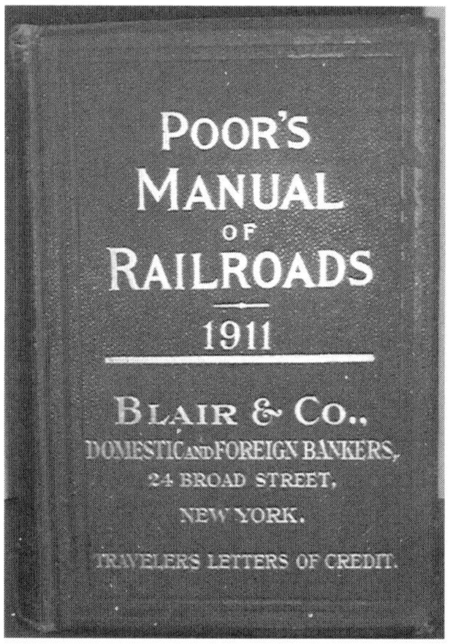

POOR'S MANUAL OF RAILROADS-dated 1911 150-175

POOR'S MANUAL OF RAILROADS-dated 1921 125-150

POOR'S MANUAL OF RAILROADS-dated 1928 125-150

POOR'S MANUAL OF RAILROADS-dated 1929 125-150

RAILWAY AGE MAGAZINES-1900-1910 includes advertising and railroad information 8-10

RAILWAY AGE MAGAZINE-1911-1920 includes advertising and various railroad info 6-8

RULE BOOKS

CNR- 1925 "Rules Governing Engineers & Fireman" **1-5**

CVRY- 1897 "Rules & Regulations 121 pages **15-20**

C&NW- 1987 "Rules & Regulations 187 pages **1-5**

CGW- 1919 "Rules & Regulations 168 pages **10-15**

CMSTP&P- 1945 "Rules & Regulations" **1-5**

D&RGRR- 1906 "Rules & Regulations" **20-25**

FRISCO- 1946 "Rules of Transportation" 220 pages **5-10**

GEORGIA RR- 1912 "Rules & Regulations" hard bound with 189 pages **10-15**

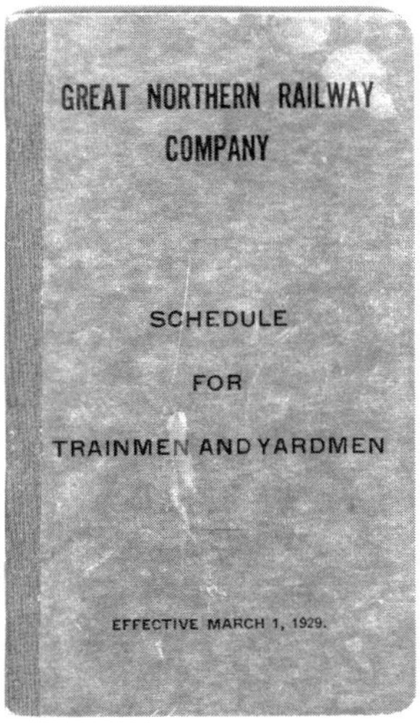

GREAT NORTHERN RY CO-Schedule for Trainman & Yardmen dated 3/1/29 ...... **10-15**

JERSEY CENTRAL LINES- 1946 "Rules & Regulations" **1-5**

MSTP&SSM- 1959 "Rules & Regulations" ... **3-5**

MP- 1959 "Rules & Regulations" with 232 pages **3-5**

NEW HAVEN RR- 1956 "Rules & Regulations" **3-5**

NYCS- 1937 "Rules & Regulations" with 165 pages **5-10**

NYO&W- 1913 "Rules & Regulations" **15-20**

N&W- **1907** "Rules & Regulations" with 128 pages **5-10**

N&W- 1938 "Rules of Transportation" **3-5**

PRR- 1925 "Rules for Engineers & Fireman" **5-10**

PRR- 1910 "Rules & Regulations" for Pennsylvania Lines west of Pittsburgh. **10-15**

READING CO- 1954 "Rules & Regulations" **1-5**

RUTLAND RR- 1957 "Rules & Regulations" **3-5**

ROCK ISLAND RR- 1940 "Uniform Code of Operating Rules" **5-10**

SANTA FE-Rules Operating Department dated Jan.5, 1975 plastic binder **1-5**

SOUTHERN RY- 1956 "Rules for Engineers & Fireman" **3-5**

UNION PACIFIC- 1907 "Rules & Regulations" with 147 pages **15-20**

UNION PACIFIC-1954 for Eastern & South Central Idaho **5-10**

WABASH- 1959 "Rules & Regulations .. **5-10**

CHAPTER 5

BREAST BADGES

There are several different categories associated with this chapter. We will first show and discuss the breast badges worn by most of the police and security divisions of the various railroads. These badges were often times very ornate and always had the name of the railroad along with the individual occupation of the wearer. Badges are a wonderful collectible as they are easy to display and enjoy. The prices have become very high for some badges and it is important to note that a large amount of the breast badges are available in reproduction form today. These badges are well made and fool very seasoned collectors. We caution you to deal only with people who will stand behind the authenticity of an item and seek professional advice when not sure. These can be very enjoyable, but of all the railroad collectibles available today these are the most vulnerable to reproduction and forgery. Remember suggested prices are for badges in good to excellent condition.

REMEMBER: PRICES SHOWN ARE SUGGESTED VALUES ONLY. VALUES VARY FROM REGION TO REGION. THIS IS MEANT ONLY AS A GUIDE. (◆) Denotes value over $1000.00

ALTON RR CO.- "*SUPERINDENDENT POLICE*". Copper on brass shield design badge with eagle perched on top. Black enamel letters. **200-250**

AT&SFRY- "*SPECIAL OFFICER*" 522 in black enameled letters on 6 point star badge with ball tips. **250-300**

ATLANTIC COAST LINE- "*PATROLMAN*" over Police Department" small nickel shield with eagle perched on top. No manufacturer shown **90-100**

BALTIMORE & OHIO- "*SERGEANT*" gold finish shield design badge Lettering is raised, with rank in black enameled letters ... **350-400**

BALTIMORE & OHIO- *"POLICE CAPTAIN"* gold finish starburst design badge with eagle perched on top. Lettering is raised around Capitol logo in center of badge **300-350**

B&ORR- *"FIRE DEPARTMENT"* #294 in design of Maltese Cross. Mfg. American Ry Supply **200-250**

BOSTON & MAINE RR-*"POLICE OFFICER"* #49 on nickel shield design badge with black enameled logo in center. Eagle perched on top **300-350**

B&MRR- *"RAILROAD POLICE"* 1 ½" diameter round badge with black enameled letters. Ornate floral design between lettering. Mfg. J. Robbins, Boston **150-175**

CANADIAN NATIONAL RYS- "*POLICE*" #645 shield design with nickel finish & black enameled letters **90-100**

CN POLICE- "*LIEUTENANT*" gold shield design badge with blue enamel letters **125-150**

CPR- "*POLICE*" small shield design badge with nickel finish and black enameled letters **100-125**

CPRY AGENT- on nickel silver shield design badge with black enameled letters **125-150**

CANADIAN PACIFIC RY- "*POLICE*" silver shield with Beaver over Canadian Pacific Ry over "Department Investigation Constable" raised letters, Mfg. Wm Scully **90-100**

CANADIAN PACIFIC RWY- "*SPECIAL SERVICE*" shield design badge with reclining beaver on top & raised letters. **150-175**

CANADIAN PACIFIC- "*NEWS AGENT*" shield design breast badge with yellow & black enamel inlay. Silver lettering. Mfg. Scully **65-75**

CB&QRR- "*SPECIAL WATCHMAN*" on five point nickel finish star design badge with black enamel letters **90-100**

CM&STPRY- "*RAILWAY POLICE*" in black enameled letters on six point star star badge with nickel finish. **350-400**

CRI&PRY- "*SPECIAL POLICE*" on six point star with nickel finish & serial number below "POLICE" **90-100**

CONCORD & MONTREAL- "*RAILROAD POLICE*" on round 1 5/8" nickel finish badge with fancy floral design between black enameled letters. Mfg. J. Robbins, Boston **350-400**

CONRAIL-*"POLICE"* silver shield design with eagle perched on top. "CONRAIL POLICE' over state seal over serial # 175-200

DL&WRRCO-"*RAILWAY POLICE*' has serial # on shield design badge with eagle perched on top. Black enamel lettering, Mfg. Am.Ry. Supply Co. 125-150

DL&WRR- "*POLICE*" shield design, nickel badge with cutout serial number #315 on bottom edge **100-125**

DELAWARE & HUDSON- "*POLICE PATROLMAN*" on nickel finish badge with black enamel inlay. Mfg. Braxmar, NY **125-150**

DTRR- "*WATCHMAN*" with serial # on shield design badge. Black enameled letters . **175-200**

DM&IR RY CO- "*SPECIAL OFFICER*" with serial # on six point star. Nickel finish with black enamel letters **90-100**

ERIE RR CO.- "*RAILROAD POLICE*" black enameled letters on nickel shield design badge. Mfg. Am.Ry. Supply Co. NY. **100-125**

ERIE RAILROAD- "*WATCHMAN*" shield design with eagle perched on top. Black enamel letters & Erie logo in center **150-175**

ERIE RAILROAD *"POLICE"* black enamled letters & logo on silver shield design badge with eagle perched on top. Mfg. Am.Ry. Sup. 100-125

ERIE RAILROAD- *"POLICE SERGEANT"* brass shield style badge with eagle perched on top. Black enamel letters & logo in center 100-125

FLA. EAST COAST RAILWAY- *"SPECIAL AGENT"* over *"POLICE"* #203 in gold letters with black enamel inlay. Gold shield badge with eagle perched on top. Most FEC badges stamped on reverse "Property of FECRY Co. Unauthorized used prohibited by law". 300-350

GNRY- *"SPECIAL POLICE"* black enameled letters on six point star design badge with ball points. Mfg. St. Paul Stamp Works or N.W. Stamp Works. 200-250

GTP- *"SPECIAL POLICE"* on shield design badge with nickle finish and serial number in center. Black enameled letters 175-200

GREAT NORTHERN RY- *"SPECIAL POLICE"* black enameled letters on round nickel plated badge with star in center. Mfg. Spokane Stamp Works. 250-300

KCTER.RY- *"SPECIAL POLICE"* on round badge with five point star in center. Outside circle reads "KCTER.RY" Kansas 1917 City Mo. 175-200

L&NRR CO- *"POLICE AGENT"* on gold shield with perched eagle on top. "AGENT" over "L&NRR CO" with Tennesee State seal in center. Police & serial # around bottom 200-225

L&NRR- *"POLICE"* six point star with serial #168 in black enameled letters 150-175

MICHIGAN CENTRAL RR CO.- *"POLICE"* shield design badge with perched eagle. Silver finish & black enamel lettering. Michigan Central RR Co. around POLICE in center. 250-300

MISSOURI PACIFIC- "*POLICE*" on five point star with applied serial #165. Colorful inlaid Illinois state seal in center. Mfg. CH Hansen, Chicago **350-400**

NEW JERSEY CENTRAL- "*RAILROAD POLICE*" black enameled logo in center of nickel starburst design badge with eagle perched on top. "Central Railroad Company of New Jersey" embossed around center. **90-100**

NEW YORK CENTRAL LINES- "*POLICE SERGEANT*" on gold starburst design badge with perched eagle. Blue enameled NYC logo in center **200-250**

NEW YORK CENTRAL LINES- "*POLICE*" blue enameled logo in center of nickel starburst design badge with eagle perched on top. Serial number applied to bottom. **90-100**

NEW YORK CENTRAL SYSTEM- "*POLICE*" silver finish starburst design badge with perched eagle. Blue enameled NYC logo in center **80-90**

NY CENTRAL RR- "*POLICE INSPECTOR*" on gold starburst design badge with perched eagle. Gold & blue enameled inlay around lettering. **125-150**

NY CITY TRANSIT- "*POLICE*" with serial number on shield design badge with nickel finish & cut out number on bottom half. **100-125**

NY CITY TRANSIT SYSTEM RR- "*WATCHMAN*" on shield design nickel finish badge with perched eagle and black enameled letters **35-45**

NYC&STLRR CO- "*NICKEL PLATE PATROLMAN*" black enameled letters on shield badge with eagle perched on top. **150-175**

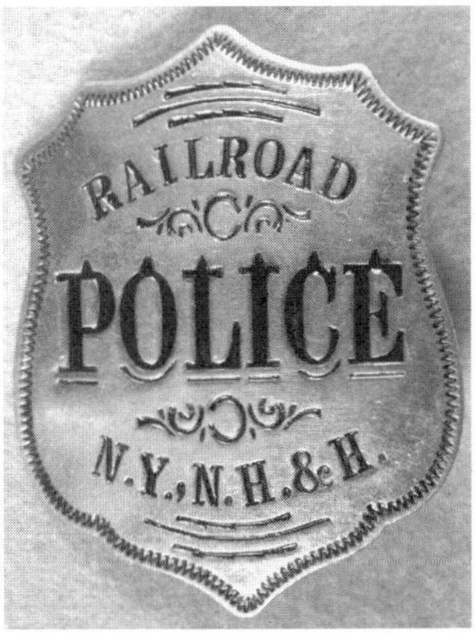

NYNH&H RAILROAD- "*POLICE*" in black enameled letters on shield design badge with fancy floral design between Railroad Police & NYNH&H. **200-250**

NYNH&H RAILROAD- "*POLICE*" on shield design badge with perched eagle. Embossed "NYNH&H" logo in center. Mfg. FG Clover **200-250**

N&WRY CO- "*POLICE PATROLMAN*" on shield design badge with perched eagle. Serial number on bottom of badge. **150-175**

NORTHERN PACIFIC RAILWAY CO-"*PATROLMAN*"#55 black enameled letters on gold finish shield design badge with eagle perched on top. Enameled red & black Monad logo in center... ◆

OSLRR- "*SPECIAL POLICE*" on round gold badge with rope design border and raised nickel finish letters. **450-500**

OSLRR-"*POLICE*" #11 black enameled letters on small shield design badge with perched eagle on top. **450-500**

PACIFIC ELECTRIC RY CO- "*POLICE AGENT*" on gold shield design badge with perched eagle. Black enameled letters. Mfg. Meyer & Wenth, Chicago. **100-125**

PRR CO- "*RAILWAY POLICE*" on nickel silver badge with ornate design in center. Black enameled "Railway Police" around the top & "PRR Co" around the bottom. Mfg. by either Am.Ry.Sup. or FG Clover................. **100-125**

PRR CO-"*RAILWAY WATCHMAN*" on shield design nickel finish badge with black enameled letters. Mfg. FG Clover **70-80**

PHILA. & READING RWY CO.- "*RAILWAY POLICE*" on round badge with five point star in center. Black enameled letters around outer edge. **175-200**

P&LERR- "*POLICE SERGEANT*" on gold shield design badge with perched eagle. Blue enameled "NYC" logo in center. Mfg. Russell Uniform, Co.................................... **300-350**

READING COMPANY- *"RAILWAY POLICE"* round design badge with starburst outer edge with perched eagle on top. Embossed streamliner engine with armoured knight in center. Serial numbered on reverse **125-150**

READING LINES- "*RAILWAY POLICE*" shield design badge with outer edge starburst & eagle perched on top. Nickel silver finish shows "READING CO" CENTRAL RR OF NJ around outside edge. "READING LINES" enameled logo in center. **175-200**

ROCK ISLAND LINES- "*SPECIAL OFFICER*" black enameled letters on 6 point star design badge. Serial numbered below designation. **90-100**

SALRY- "*POLICE*" black enameled letters on shield design badge with nickel finish & serial numbered below designation. **90-100**

SEABOARD AIRLINE-"*RAILWAY SPECIAL OFFICER"* on smaller round shield design badge with perched eagle on top. "Seaboard Airline Railway" around outer circle. "Special Officer" in center. **150-175**

SOUTHERN RY CO- "*USRS ADM GUARD*" shield design badge with nickel finish & black enameled letters. **200-250**

SOUTHERN RY SYSTEM- "*POLICE WATCHMAN*" on shield design badge with perched eagle on top. Black enameled letters around outer edge with Southern Logo in center **90-100**

SPRR- *"RAILROAD POLICE"* black enameled letters on round nickel plated badge with five point star in center. Mfg. Irvine Jachens. **175-200**

SOUTHERN PACIFIC CO.- *"RAILROAD POLICE"* #841 OREGON. Black enameled letters on six point star badge. Dated on reverse and manufactured by Irvine Jachens, SF. Made of sterling silver. .... ◆

SOUTHERN PACIFIC CO- *"SERGEANT POLICE"* black enameled letters on fancy design six point star badge made of solid gold and sterling. Mfg. Irvine Jachens, SF. .... ◆

SIRYCO- *"SPECIAL AGENT"* black enameled letters on shield design nickel finish badge with 5 point cut out star in center. Mfg. Spokane Stamp Works **700-800**

UPRR CO.- *"SPECIAL OFFICER"* on round nickel badge with five point star in center. "Special Officer, Denver, Colorado" around outside edge. "UPRRCO" in center of star. Black enameled letters. Mfg. SP Cooke, Omaha. .. **500-550**

UPRR. CO.- *"SPECIAL OFFICER"* on round nickel badge with five point star in center. "Special Officer, Omaha, Nebraska" around outside edge. UPRRCO" in center of star. Black enameled letters. Mfg. SP Cooke, Omaha. ... **500-550**

USPS RAILWAY MAIL SERVICE- shield design badge with eagle perched on top. Embossed on outer edge "Post Office Department, Railway Mail Services",US intertwined with stars in center. Nickel finish, Mfg. Am.Ry.Supply **175-200**

WABASH RY CO.- *"POLICE"* on six point star with beveled edges and black enameled letters. Nickel finish **250-300**

CHAPTER 6

BROTHERHOOD ITEMS

The unions that controlled and watched over the railroad employees were rich in their own traditions making the collectibles associated with them very desirable as well. As with the railroads themselves the unions also marked everything which makes collecting the various items even more challenging. From Union pinbacks to membership lapel pins, brotherhood lodge ribbons and china chalices used in ceremonies, the items can be very elegant and rich with history. Below you will find the various initials and their meanings. This is a sample of the more common initials found.

B OF L E	*BROTHERHOOD OF LOCOMOTIVE ENGINEERS*
B OF L F & E	*BROTHERHOOD OF LOCOMOTIVE FIREMAN & ENGINEERS*
B OF MW	*BROTHERHOOD OF MAINTENANCE OF WAY*
B OF RR B	*BROTHERHOOD OF RAILROAD BRAKEMAN*
B OF R C	*BROTHERHOOD OF RAILWAY CONDUCTORS*
B OF RR C	*BROTHERHOOD OF RAILROAD CLERKS*
B OF R T	*BROTHERHOOD OF RAILROAD TRAINMAN*
ORC	*ORDER OF RAILROAD CONDUCTORS*
ORT	*ORDER OF RAILROAD TELEGRAPHERS*

B OF A & RE- blue enamel inlay with gold letters on shield design pin with single screw post attachment **5-10**

B OF LE-Doorplate from union headquarters. BLE logo cast on the knobs as well as the top of the plate. Brass measures 11" x 3" **100-125**

B OF LE- small enameled pin with red, white & blue logo. Single screw post attachment **5-10**

B OF LE- Veterans Association pin. Gold on white with "The Bessemer Route" in center **30-40**

B OF LE- embroidered uniform patch. B of LE around outer edge, "US BLE CANADA" in center **10-15**

B OF LE- brass oval Honorary Membership badge has 4-6-0 engine cast in center. Shield hangs from the bottom. **40-50**

B OF LF&E-Convention ribbon for the Bessemer Lodge #558. Multi colored ribbon with gold train hanging from the top edge. Ribbon reverses for funeral services **15-20**

B OF LE- brass medallion dated 1863-1988 celebrating the 125th Anniversary. **5-10**

B OF LF&E- gold watch fob. Round emblem with blue background on one side, intertwined letters on reverse side. Head of knight holds the bezel. **65-75**

B OF LF&E- Ladies Society brass medallion measures 2" diameter with wreath design around enameled logo with steam engine in center. **15-20**

B OFLF&E- celluloid union pinback organized in 1873 .... **3-5**

B OF LF&E- 10year service pin. Enameled triangle logo on brass pin **5-10**

B OF LF&E- 30 year gold pin, enameled logo with curved arch & single post attachment **15-20**

B OF LRE- Brotherhood Convention Medallion dated 1916. 26th Convention held in Denver. Has two medals attached with chain, top piece has colorful Columbine flower, bottom shows Eagle perched on top of three flags. Steam engine in center flanked by two different Union logos **50-60**

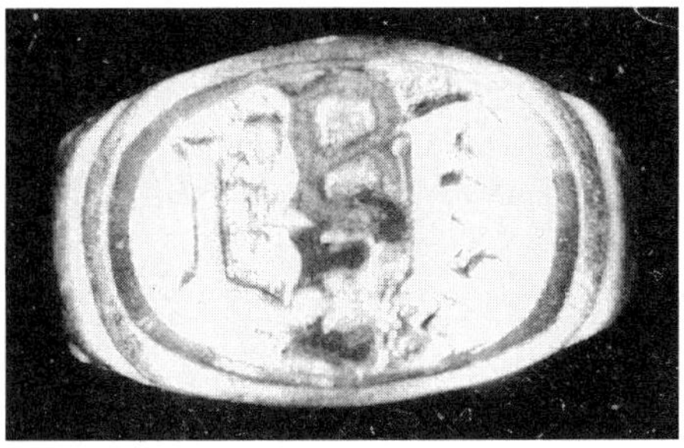

B OF LF&E-intertwined red, green white & blue enameled letters raised on 10k gold membership ring. **125-150**

B OF MW- letter opener. Small brass trowel design with wood handle. Has embossed logo and dated 1887-1951 .... **25-30**

BROTHERHOOD OF RAILWAY CARMEN OF AMERICA-written in gold on Eversharp pen & pencil set. Comes in leather case **30-35**

B OF RC-Convention ribbon for "GUEST". Green ribbon with gold medallion hanging from the bottom. Blue & white enameled inlay in center **5-10**

B OF RRC- Membership pin with enameled logo in center. Measures 7/16" diameter **3-5**

B OF RRC- large "C" around crossed pencil & quill pen with "BRR" in center. 3/8" diameter **5-10**

B OF RT- 10k gold ring with BRT logo in center. Gold leaf design on either side. **100-125**

B OF RT- watch fob has maltese cross design with round enameled logo in center. **65-75**

B OF RT- set of gold cufflinks with "BRT" enameled logo in center **10-15**

B OF RT- brass membership ID tag reads, "Accident & Health" tag used to identify wearer in case of accident. **10-15**

B OF RT-enameled membership lapel pin with red white & green enamel in pie design over 40 Years **10-15**

B OF RT- Enameled membership pin. Gold letters on colorful inlay with "T" in center of brake wheel design 5-7

B OF RT- Brotherhood Chart. Colorful and artistic poster used in the initiation ceremonies to illustrate the life of a trainman and the work of the brotherhood. Eight different scenes depict the circle of life. Measures 27" x 22" **175-200**

B OF RT-cast brass medal shows Sunburst design issued to World War Veterans who were members of the BRT. Medal reads, "For Service in the World War for Liberty and For Freedom of Nations:" **25-30**

B OF RT- gold plated pendant shows BRT over Lantern with Flags on either side. Lapel pin size the reverse shows locomotive on bridge **35-40**

B OF RT- 15 year membership pin. Gold wreath design with enameled logo in center.. **5-10**

ORC- Membership pin with red, white & green enamel inlay in pie design. Gold pictures in each piece. **3-5**

ORC- 40 or 50 year membership pin. 10 kt gold with single post attachment **10-15**

ORC- 10k gold ring. Raised intertwined letters with beautiful gold engraving on either side. **125-150**

PLEASE REMEMBER THAT VALUES SHOWN ARE SUGGESTED PRICES ONLY. THIS IS MEANT AS A GUIDE ONLY. PRICES MAY VARY FROM REGION TO REGION.

CHAPTER 7

BUILDERS PLATES & PHOTOS

Builders plates were much like a vehicle identification number on a car. Each train had a plate attached with a number that identified not only the engine but also the month & year of manufacture and the company which built the locomotive. These plates are very collectible and can be found in brass, cast iron, cast aluminum and stainless steel. During WW II brass plates were replaced with cast iron due to the shortage of brass. Plates from early locomotives are very valuable as many were scraped and melted for their metal content. Plate numbers with research can be traced and identified to a specific locomotive which helps when determining value. As with all railroad collectibles many times the plate value is based on the railroad & the locomotive it came off of. For example a Union Pacific plate off of an 0-6-0 yard switch engine is worth considerably less than a plate off of a 4-8-8-4 road engine. It is important to note that forgeries do exist. We have found one hint is to look for scale on the reverse of the plate. This was a buildup of rust from moisture, cinders and the elements which is very difficult to remove. It leaves an obvious discoloration and uneven texture to the back side of the plate. This is only one tip to help in your collecting. It is not uncommon to find a plate that has been sandblasted or chemically cleaned removing this. Plates must be in good condition. They must not be split, have pieces missing, have enlarged bolt holes or otherwise altered from their original condition.

REMEMBER: PRICES SHOWN ARE SUGGESTED VALUES ONLY. VALUES VARY FROM REGION TO REGION. THIS IS MEANT ONLY AS A GUIDE. (◆) Denotes value over $1000.00

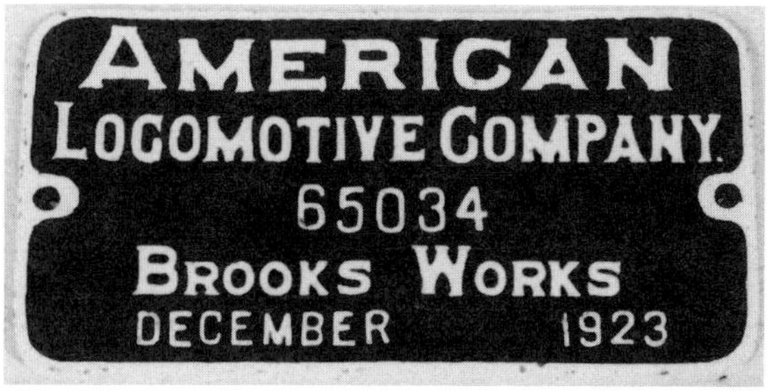

AMERICAN LOCOMOTIVE COMPANY-BROOKS WORKS -cast iron rectangular builders plate. #65034 dated December 1923. From Clinchfield RR engine #413 with a 2-8-2 wheel arrangement **375-425**

ALCO-BROOKS WORKS- cast iron rectangular builders plate #40153 dated August 1908. From Northern Pacific RR #2337 with a 2-6-2 wheel arrangement **250-300**

ALCO-BROOKS WORKS- cast iron plate #58190 dated March 1918 from ICRR #1128 with a 4-6-2 wheel arrangement **250-300**

ALCO BROOKS WORKS- cast iron plate #62889 dated January 1921 from Missoui Pacific #358 with a 4-6-0 wheel arrangement **250-300**

AMERICAN LOCOMOTIVE COMPANY/GENERAL ELECTRIC-cast iron plate #72862 dated November 1944 from New York Central S-2 #8515. Plate measures 12" x 6" **100-125**

ALCO/GE- cast iron plate #76563 dated February 1949 from Pennsylvania RR S-1 engine **100-125**

ALCO/GE- cast iron plate #79931 dated June 1952 from Pennsylvania RR RS3 engine. **100-125**

ALCO/GE-cast iron plate #75755 dated February 1948 from Union Pacific FB-1engine **100-125**

AMERICAN LOCOMOTIVE COMPANY-SCHENECTADY WORKS- cast iron plate #68337 dated June 1930 off D&RGW engine #3619 with a 2-8-8-2 wheel arrangement .... ◆

ALCO-SCHENECTADY WORKS cast iron plate #46867 dated February 1910 from Northern Pacific #1687. 2-8-2 wheel arrangement. **250-300**

BALDWIN LOCOMOTIVE WORKS-BURNHAM PARRY WILLIAMS CO round brass builders plate #11353 dated November 1890 from Denver Leadville & Gunnison Ry engine #269. .... ◆

BALDWIN LOCOMOTIVE WORKS-PHILADELPHIA- 9" round brass builders plate #51263 dated February 1919 from GNRY 0-8-0 engine #833. 350-400

BALDWIN LOCOMOTBALDWIN LOCOMOTIVE WORKS PHILADELPHIA- 9" round brass plate #46313 dated 1917 from Southern Pacific 0-6-0 engine 200-250

BALDWIN LOCOMOTIVE WORKS-PHILADELPHIA- 9" brass plate #48942 dated June 1918 off Arizona Eastern 0-6-0 engine #30 300-350

BALDWIN LOCOMOTIVE WORKS-PHILADELPHIA- 9" round brass plate #37427 dated February 1912 From NYC&HRRR 4-6-2 engine #3602 375-425

BALDWIN LOCOMOTIVE WORKS-PHILADELPHIA- 9" round plate cast 64703 dated 1942 with WWII production number L12443 off Southern Pacific cab forward AC-11 class engine 4882..........................375-425

BALDWIN LOCOMOTIVE WORKS-PHILADELPHIA- 9" round brass plate #49077 dated June 1918 off Great Northern 0-8-0 engine #814 350-400

BALDWIN LOCOMOTIVE WORKS-PHILADELPHIA- 9" round brass plate #38522 dated October 1912 off St. Louis & Southwestern 2-8-0 engine #567 400-450

BALDWIN LOCOMOTIVE WORKS-PHILADELPHIA-9" round brass plate #61156 dated January 1930 off Wabash 4-8-2 engine #2807 400-450

BALDWIN LOCOMOTIVE WORKS PHILADELPHIA-9" round brass plate 60720 dated March 1929 off D&RGW 4-8-8-4 engine #1708 800-900

BALDWIN LOCOMOTIVE WORKS PHILADELPHIA- 16 ½" round brass plate #32414 dated December 1907 off Kansas City Southern 2-8-0 700-750

BALDWIN LOCOMOTIVE WORKS WESTINGHOUSE- cast iron plate #73478 dated June 1948. Off Chicago & Northwestern 350-400

BALDWIN LOCOMOTIVE WORKS-BALDWIN LIMA HAMILTON- cast iron plate #75384 dated April 1952 off Pennsylvania RR shark nose engine #2026A..... **200-250**

BROOKS LOCOMOTIVE WORKS-14" cast iron plate #2529 dated 1895 off Butte Anaconda & Pacific 0-6-0 engine #7 .... ◆

BROOKS LOCOMOTIVE WORKS- 14" cast iron plate #2053 dated 1892 off Santa Fe 4-6-0 engine #821 .... ◆

GENERAL MOTORS/ELECTRO MOTIVE DIVISION-often referred to as "EMD" stainless steel oval plate dated December 1951; Class 0-4-4-0; Serial #15280 off Chesapeake & Ohio GP-7 engine #5774 .... **15-25**

GENERAL MOTORS/ EMD- stainless steel oval plate dated December 1965; Class 0-6-6-0; Serial #30876 off Southern SD-35 engine #3070 .... **15-25**

GENERAL MOTORS/ EMD-stainless steel oval plate dated May 1955; Class 0-4-4-0; Serial #19966 off Southern Pacific GP-9 engine #3316 .... **20-30**

GENERAL MOTORS/EMD- stainless steel oval plate dated September 1959; Class 0-4-4-0; Serial #23461 off Rock Island SW-900 engine #911 .... **30-40**

GENERAL MOTORS/EMD-stainless steel oval plate dated Febrary 1951 ; serial #13655 off PRR F7B engine #9773B **35-45**

GENERAL MOTORS/EMD- stainless steel oval plate dated August 1952; Class 0-4-4-0; Serial #24145 off Pennsylvania RR engine SW1200 #7913 .... **30-40**

GENERAL MOTORS/EMD-stainless steel oval plate dated August 1952 off PRR engine GP7 #8501 .... **45-55**

GENERAL MOTORS/EMD-stainless steel rectangular plate measures 15" x 4 ¾" dated April 21, 1945; class 0-6-6-0; off Louisville & Nashville E-7 .... **50-60**

GENERAL MOTORS/EMD-stainless steel rectangular plate #35233 dated October 1969; class 0-4-4-0; Off Southern Pacific SW-1500 engine #2540 .... **20-30**

GENERAL MOTORS/ EMD- rectangular plate dated November 1949 off Texas & Pacific F7A #8436 .... **40-50**

HK PORTER COMPANY PITTSBURGH USA- shield design brass plate dated 1918. Number 6225 off of a 0-6-0T owned by Republic Steel Corporation **200-250**

HK PORTER COMPANY PITTSBURGH USA-shield design brass plate #8210 off of a 45 ton Diesel engine owned by the South African Iron & Steel Co. **175-200**

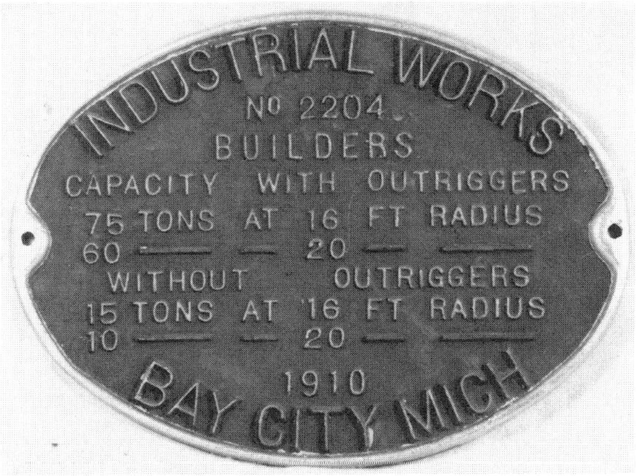

INDUSTRIAL WORKS,BAY CITY MICHIGAN-Steam crane builders plate. Large cast iron oval plate measuring 19" x 14" 75 Ton crane built in 1910 .... **250-300**

LIMA LOCOMOTIVE WORKS-diamond shaped brass plate dated January 1946 #8965 from a 2-8-2 engine #99 .... **500-550**

TRUST PLATES

DENVER & RIO GRANDE RR CO- cast iron trust plate measures 4" x 9". Reads, "Subject to D&RGRR Co First & Refunding Mortgage April 1, 1908 as First Lien". **75-85**

DENVER & RIO GRANDE WESTERN-cast iron trust plate measures 29 ½" 8". Reads, "Denver & Rio Grande Western Railroad Equipment Trust Series N Chicago Title & Trust Company, Trustee Owner & Lessor **100-125**

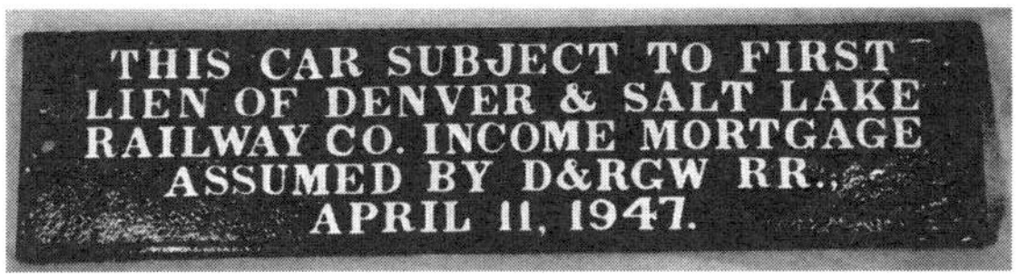

DENVER & SALT LAKE RY-cast iron trust plate measures 30 ½" x 7". Reads, "This Car Subject to First Lien of Denver & Salt Lake Railway Company Income Mortgage Assumed by D&RGWRR April 11, 1947" **100-125**

GREAT NORTHERN RY-cast iron trust plate measures 22" x 8". Reads, "Great Northern Ry First Equipment Trust of 1969 First National City Bank Trustee Owner & Lessor **75-85**

MISSOURI PACIFIC-aluminum equipment trust plate measures 36" x4" **20-30**

ROCK ISLAND LINES- aluminum trust plate dated 1964 .... **20-25**

SEABOARD COASTLINE RR-stainless steel equipment trust plate measures 8" x28" **15-25**

BUILDERS PHOTOS

The builders of railroad cars and engines supplied the railroads with beautifully framed and mounted photos of the engines and cars they purchased. These were ususally found hanging in the office of the Motive Power Superintendent or other executives. The prices suggested here are for photos found with their original framing and matting.

AMERICAN LOCOMOTIVE COMPANY- Builders photo showing Northern Pacific engine 4-6-6-4. Measures 29 ½" x 15 ½". Original framing **350-400**

AMERICAN LOCOMOTIVE COMPANY- Builders photo showing an Electric train. Measures 19 ½" x 10" in original frame ... **100-125**

BALDWIN LOCOMOTIVE WORKS-Builders photo showing Northern Pacific engine. Original frame and mat measures 27" x 15". Wheel arrangement 4-8-4. .... **250-300**

BURNHAM WILLIAMS & CO-BALDWIN LOCOMOTIVE WORKS-Builders photo showing a 2-8-0 UP engine #289 ..... **350-400**

BURNHAM WILLIAMS & CO- BALDWIN LOCOMOITVE WORKS- Builders photo showing Oregon Short Line engine #452 a 4-6-2 wheel configuration. Measures 32" x 17" **350-400**

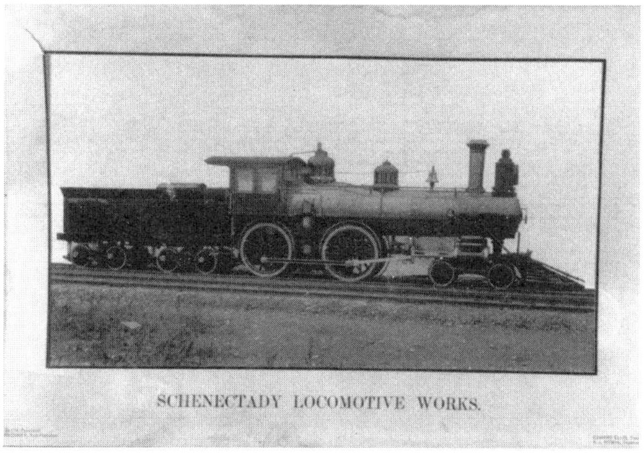

SCHENECTADY LOCOMOTIVE WORKS- Builders photo showing a 4-4-0 engine. Measures 19" x 14" unframed **250-300**

CHAPTER 8

BUTTONS & PINS

Collecting uniform buttons, pins and jewelry can give the enthusiast a wide variety of items to look for and enjoy. Uniform buttons like everything the railroads had were cast with the initials or logos of each line. Everything from letter insignia to service pins proudly displaying the devoted years spent with each road made an employees uniform his badge of courage. The following pages list not only the buttons and insignia that adorned each uniform but also some selected service pins and membership pins that were also proudly displayed.

ALTON- on gold **uniform button**. Mfg. Superior Quality 3-5

ACL- on gold **uniform button**. Mfg. Superior Quality 2-3

B&O- small gold **uniform button**, Mfg. Waterbury Co. 2-3

B&O-brass collar insignia shows cut out of Capital logo with two pin attachments. 10-15

BR- silver **uniform button**. Mfg. Waterbury Co. 2-3

BR-gold large uniform button. Mfg. Waterbury Co. 3-4

BR- lapel pin shows enameled BR box logo attached to single screw post 10-15

BR-lapel service pin. Shows enameled BR box logo over 41 Years on gold pin with single post attachment. 20-25

BR- Passenger Agent round **celluloid button pinback** with "BR" box logo in center 15-20

CNR- brass cut out **letters for collar** of uniform 2-3

CNR- brass or silver **uniform button** with embossed crown logo 1-2

CNR- ¼" oval **lapel pin** with black enameling. Mfg. Scully 10-15

CPR- gold or silver **uniform button** with reclining beaver embossed in center. Mfg. Scully 1-2

CB&Q- lapel cut out letters in rope design on single screw post attachment 10-15

C&S- gold or silver **uniform button** with intertwined C&S logo. Mfg. Waterbury Co ... 5-10

C&S- collar brass, **cut out letters** with single screw post attachment 15-20

D&RG-brass or silver **unifrom button** with intertwined D&RG in center 10-15

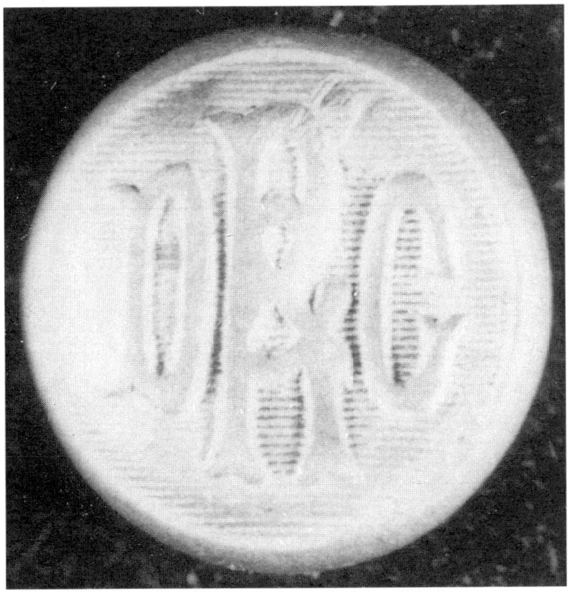

D&RG- brass or silver **uniform button with Railroad Service around edge** 10-15

D&RG- lapel pin, cut out letters with single screw post attachment 15-20

D&RGW- gold or silver **uniform button.** Mfg. Superior Quality 5-10

D&RGW- lapel pin, cut out letters with screw post attachment 10-15

D&RGW-lapel service pin shows Diesel engine over Rio Grande with single post attachment 30-40

D&RGW-_lapel service pin white enameled with gold letters with Curecanti Logo in center 40-50

ERIE- gold or silver **uniform button** 3-4

GN- celluloid **pinback**, blue & white goat logo 5-7

GN- enameled **lapel pin** with Goat logo 25-30

ICRR- gold or silver **uniform buttons** with intertwined letters. Mfg. Charles Brophy 3-5

LS&M RAILROAD CO.- Celluloid **pinback.** Green, white & blue diamond logo in center 15-20

LS&MRRCO-uniform collar pin. Diamond logo with LS&M in center & Lake Shore & Michigan Railroad Company around edge. 15-20

LEHIGH VALLEY-Veteras Association pin. Blue , red & gold enameled inlay with post attachment 20-30

L&N-uniform **service pin.** Logo in center, "Service" below. Number of stars denotes years of service........................ 20-25

MCRR-enameled membership pin has gold intertwined letters on white enamel with green enameled inlay around edge. Pioneer Association membership pin. **20-25**

MILWAUKEE ROAD- celluloid **pinback**, Milwaukee Road logo in center with "Service Club" around outer edge. Orange & red inlay **15-20**

MISSOURI PACIFIC- Buzz saw logo on small safety award **service pin.** Enamel inlay **15-20**

MP- gold or silver **uniform buttons.** Buzz saw logo on button. Mfg. Superior Quality **2-3**

MOPAC- "SAFETY CAPTAIN" on celluloid **pinback**... 5-10

MILWAUKEE ROAD-Safety **award pin.** Red enamel inlay with logo in center............ **20-25**

NEW YORK CENTRAL- gold or silver **uniform button**.. **2-3**

NYNH&H- Safety **award pin**, gold letters on green enamel with white enameled center. Screw post attachment **25-30**

N&W- safety **award pin**, gold & white enamel inlay.. **10-15**

N&W- gold or silver **uniform button** **2-3**

NORTHERN PACIFIC- Veterans Association **lapel pin.** Red & black enameled ying yang logo in center with Veterans Association around edge in gold. 30 year pin. **25-30**

NORTHERN PACIFIC- **service lapel pin** shows red & black enameled logo in center with Northern Pacific in gold on white around logo. Years of service below logo on gold wreath base. Single screw post attachment................ **25-30**

OSL- **lapel pin**, cut out letters with single screw post attachment **50-60**

PRR- lapel insignia. Cut out letters with single screw post attachment 3-4

PULLMAN- gold or silver **uniform button** 3-5

R CO- collar insignia cut out diamond logo design with two post attachments.......... 10-15

RI LINES- gold or silver **uniform buttons with star in center**... 3-5

ROCK ISLAND- lapel pin with logo in center. Gold or silver lettering with black enamel 15-20

RUTLAND RWY-25 year **service pin.** Blue enamel inlay around wreath design 50-60

RUTLAND- gold or silver **uniform button.** Mfg. Scovall 3-5

SANTA FE- lapel pin with blue & white enameled logo in center. Single screw post, gold or silver 10-15

SANTA FE- gold or silver **uniform button** with embossed logo in center 3-4

SP- gold or silver **unform button** with Sunset logo in center.. 5-7

SP- lapel pin with yellow, blue & white enameled Sunset logo in center 20-25

SP- lapel pin, silver or gold cut out letters with single post attachment 5-10

SP- 10 year Safety **pin award.** Silver letters on blue inlay with Sunset logo in center 25-30

SP- 15 year Safety **pin award,** blue inlay with Sunset logo in center 25-35

UP-lapel pin, cut out letters gold or silver 3-4

UP- red, white & blue enameled Overland Shield logo in center of 20 year **service pin** 10-15

UP- red, white & blue enameled Overland Shield logo in center of Safety First **lapel pin** 15-20

UP- Old Timers Club **service pin** 10-15

UP- gold or silver **uniform button** 3-4

UP- service pin representing "TIME INSPECTOR". Overland Shield enameled logo in center 75-85

WABASH- Veterans Association **pin** with red, white & blue enameled inlay. Logo in center 60-70

CHAPTER 9

CAP BADGES

Uniform cap badges are another wonderful and highly sought after railroad collectible. There are so many different occupations that finding and collecting all the various designations can be very challenging as well as rewarding, especially when acquiring the most illusive titles. Badges are found with either a nickle or brass finish and come in various styles as shown on the following pages. Many are hallmarked with the different manufacturers. Condition is very important when placing values on them. If a badge is bent, shows enamel loss, has surface pitting or discoloration or anything that might distract from its original condition it is worth considerably less than suggested prices listed.

REMEMBER: PRICES SHOWN ARE SUGGESTED VALUES ONLY. VALUES VARY FROM REGION TO REGION. THIS IS MEANT ONLY AS A GUIDE. (◆) **Denotes value over $1000.00**

VARIOUS STYLES

DOME

RECTANGULAR

HIGH DOME

RAISED LETTER OR EMBOSSED

CROWN

MANUFACTURERS MARKS

3 DIFFERENT AMERICAN RAILWAY SUPPLY COMPANY HALLMARKS

F.G CLOVER CO.
PREDESSESSOR
AM.RY.S.CO.

PARTRIDGE CO.
K.C., MO
SCOTFORD

IRVINE & JACHEMS
MARKET ST. S.F.

S.M. SPENCER MFG. CO. 9
CORNHILL BOSTON.

R. WOODMAN MF'R
BOSTON, MASS

SOME OF THE MORE COMMON BADGE MAKERS

AM. RY. SUPPLY
BASTIEN BROTHERS
DENVER NOVELTY COMPANY
EBY CO.
FG CLOVER
JH ROBBINS

JP COOKE
PARTRIDGE COMPANY
R. WOODMAN MF'R
SD CHILDS
WW WILCOX
WILLIAMSON STAMP COMPANY

ALLEGHENY VALLEY RY

AVRY- *"BAGGAGE MASTER"* black enameled letters on rectangular badge. Mfg. Am.Ry.Sup. **125-150**

AMTRAK

AMTRAK- *"ASSISTANT STATION MANAGER"* has enameled logo on dome style gold finish hat badge **25-35**

AMTRAK- "*CONDUCTOR*" with enameled logo on dome style gold finish hat badge **20-25**

AMTRAK- "*TRAINMAN*" with enameled logo on dome style gold finish badge **15-20**

ATLANTIC COAST LINE

ACL- "*BAGGAGE AGENT*" in black enameled letterson chrome finish dome style badge. Mfg. Am.Ry.Supply **75-85**

ACL "*CONDUCTOR*" in black enameled letters on gold finish dome style badge **50-60**

ACL- "*FIREMAN*" in black enameled letters on chrome finish dome style badge. Mfg. Am.Ry. Suppy **100-125**

ATCHISON TOPEKA & SANTA FE

AT&SFRR- "*BRAKEMAN*" black enameled letters on rectangular nickel finish badge **125-150**

AT&SFRR- "*CONDUCTOR*" black enameled letters on rectangular nickel finish badge....... **175-200**

AT&SF- "*BRAKEMAN*" black enameled letters on smaller dome style badge with fancy floral design. Nickel finish, Mfg. WW Wilcox **350-400**

BANGOR & AROOSTOOK

B&ARR- "*CONDUCTOR*" black enameled letters on brass crown style badge. Mfg. JH Robbins. **75-85**

BANGOR & AROOSTOOK- "*CONDUCTOR*" black enameled letters on rectangular style badge with gold finish. Mfg. Am.Ry.Sup. **65-75**

BANGOR & AROOSTOOK- "*PORTER*" black enameled letters on rectangular style badge with gold finish. Mfg. Am.Ry. Sup. **80-90**

BANGOR & AROOSTOOK- *"STATION AGENT"* black enameled letters on rectangular style badge with beveled edges **90-100**

BANGOR & AROOSTOOK- "*TRAINMAN*" black enameled letters on crown style badge with chrome finish. **55-65**

BELFAST & MOOSEHEAD LAKE RR

BELFAST & MOOSEHEAD LAKE RR- "*CONDUCTOR*" black enameled letters on gold finish rectangular badge. Mfg. FG Glover **200-250**

BOSTON & MAINE

BOSTON & MAINE-"*BAGGAGE MASTER*" black enameled letters on nickel finish dome style badge. Mfg. SM Spencer & Sons... **75-85**

BOSTON & MAINE- "*BRAKEMAN*" black enameled letters on nickel finish dome style badge. Mfg. SM Spencer & Sons **40-50**

BOSTON & MAINE- "*CONDUCTOR*" black enameled letters on gold finish dome style badge **60-70**

BOSTON & MAINE- "*TRAINMAN*" black enameled letters on nickel finish dome style badge **40-50**

BUFFALO ROCHESTER & PITTSBURGH

BUFFALO ROCHESTER & PITTSBURGH- "*PARLOR CAR*" enameled logo over raised "Parlor Car" on dome style nickel finish badge **200-250**

BURLINGTON CEDAR RAPIDS & NORTHERN

BCR&NRY- "*CONDUCTOR*" black enameled letters on nickel finish rectangular badge....... **175-200**

CANADIAN NATIONAL

CNR- "*CONDUCTOR*" black enameled letters on gold finish crown design badge. **40-50**

CNR- "*STEWARD*" black enameled letters on gold finish crown design badge............. **35-45**

CNR- "*TRAINMAN*" black enameled letters on nickel finish crown design badge **20-30**

CANADIAN PACIFIC

CANADIAN PACIFIC- "*NEWS AGENT*" yellow & black enameled inlay with silver letters on shield design badge with nickel finish **40-50**

CHESAPEAKE & OHIO RY

C&ORY- "*BAGGAGE AGENT*" embossed on nickel finish dome style badge. Black enameled letters with beveled edge. **65-75**

C&ORY- "*BAGGAGEMAN*" embossed on nickel finish dome style badge. Black enameled letters with beveled edge **45-55**

C&ORY- "*BRAKEMAN*" embossed on nickel finish dome style badge. Black enameled letters with beveled edge **35-45**

C&ORY- "*CONDUCTOR*" embossed on gold finish dome style badge. Black enameled letters with beveled edge. **40-50**

C&ORY- "*JANITOR*" embossed on nickel finish dome style badge. Black enameled letters with beveled edge **125-150**

C&ORY- "*PORTER*" embossed on nickel finish dome style badge. Black enameled letters with beveled edge **70-80**

C&ORY- *"STATION MASTER"* embossed on nickel finish dome style badge. Black enameled letters with beveled edge **80-90**

C&ORY- *"TRAINMAN"* embossed on nickel finish dome style badge with black enameled letters on beveled edge **35-45**

CENTRAL VERMONT

CENTRAL VERMONT- *"BAGGAGEMAN"* black enameled letters on crown design nickel badge **150-175**

CENTRAL VERMONT- *"BRAKEMAN"* black enameled letters on crown design nickel badge.. **70-80**

CHICAGO & EASTERN ILLINOIS

CHICAGO & EASTERN ILL'S RR- *"BRAKEMAN"* black enameled letters on crown style badge with nickle finish **125-150**

CHICAGO & NORTHWESTERN RY

C&NWRY- *"FREIGHT BRAKEMAN"* black enameled letters on nickel finish rectangular badge **35-45**

CHICAGO BURLINGTON & QUINCY AKA BURLINGTON ROUTE

BURLINGTON ROUTE- *"AGENT"* has box "BR" enameled logos on either side, rectangle style with nickel finish **100-125**

BURLINGTON ROUTE- *"BRAKEMAN"* black enameled letters on rectangular nickel finish badge.. **65-75**

BURLINGTON ROUTE- *"CONDUCTOR"* black enameled letters on rectangular nickel finish badge.. **75-85**

CB&QRR- *"BRAKEMAN"* black enameled letters on crown design nickel badge **65-75**

CB&QRR- *"CONDUCTOR"* black enameled letters on nickel finish rectangular badge .. **80-90**

CHICAGO GREAT WESTERN RY

CGWRY- *"BRAKEMAN"* black enameled letters on nickel finish rectangular badge **125-150**

CGWRY- *"CONDUCTOR"* black enameled letters on nickel finish rectanglar badge **175-200**

CHICAGO ROCK ISLAND & PACIFIC RY

CRI&P- *"BRAKEMAN"* embossed on pressed tin crown design badge with nickel finish **200-250**

CRI&P- "*CONDUCTOR*" embossed on pressed tin crown design badge with gold finish **250-300**

CHICAGO ST PAUL MINNEAPOLIS & OMAHA RY

CSTPM&ORY- "*BRAKEMAN*" black enameled letters on nickel finish rectangular badge **65-75**

COLORADO & SOUTHERN RY

C&SRY- "*BRAKEMAN*" black enameled letters on nickel finish rectangular badge. Mfg. Denver Novelty **150-175**

C&SRY- "*CONDUCTOR*" black enameled letters on nickel finish rectangular badge. Mfg. Denver Novelty **250-300**

COLORADO & SOUTHERN RY CO.- "*BRAKEMAN*" black enamel ornate seriff lettering on nickel finish rectangular design badge **450-500**

COLORADO & SOUTHERN RY CO- "*OPERATOR*" black enameled letters on nickel finish rectangular hat badge. Ornate seriff lettering. **750-850**

COLORADO MIDLAND RY

CMRR- "*BRAKEMAN"* black enameled letters on nickel rectangular badge **250-300**

CMRR- "*CONDUCTOR"* black enameled letters on nickel rectangular badge **300-350**

CMRY- "*BRAKEMAN*" black enameled letters on nickel rectangular badge **250-300**

COLORADO MIDLAND RR CO-"*BRAKEMAN*" black enameled letters on nickel rectangular badge **850-950**

CONRAIL

CONRAIL- "*CONDUCTOR*" high dome style with blue enameled Conrail logo. Gold finish **20-25**

CONRAIL- "*STATION MASTER*" high dome style with blue enameled Conrail logo & gold finish **25-30**

CONRAIL- "*TRAINMAN*" high dome style with blue enameled Conrail logo & gold finish **20-25**

CONRAIL- "*USHER*" high dome style with blue enameled Conrail logo & gold finish **20-25**

DELAWARE & HUDSON RR

D&H- "*CONDUCTOR*" blue enameled inlaid "D&H" logo on high fancy domed nickel finish badge.. **200-250**

D&H- "*TRAINMAN*" blue enameled inlaid "D&H" logo on high fancy domed nickel finish badge.. **175-200**

DENVER & RIO GRANDE RAILROAD

DENVER & RIO GRANDE- "*BRAKEMAN*"black enameled letters on brass or nickel finish crown design badge. Mfg. Am. Ry. Supply Co. **175-200**

DENVER & RIO GRANDE- *"BRAKEMAN"* black enameled letters on nickel finish rectangular design badge **150-175**

DENVER & RIO GRANDE- *"CONDUCTOR"* black enameled letters on brass or nickel crown design badge **300-350**

DENVER & RIO GRANDE- *"FLAGMAN"* black enameled letters on brass finish crown design badge. **500-600**

DENVER & RIO GRANDE- *"PORTER"* black enameled letters on nickel finish crown design badge **450-500**

DENVER & RIO GRANDE- *"STATION AGENT"* black enameled letters on nickel rectangular hat badge **300-350**

DENVER & RIO GRANDE WESTERN RAILROAD

DENVER &RIO GRANDE WESTERN- *"BAGGAGEMAN"* black enameled letters on rectangular hat badge **450-500**

D&RGW- *"CONDUCTOR"* with "Rio Grande Mainline Thru the Rockies" colorful enameled logo on high domed pressed tin badge with gold finish **200-250**

D&RGW- *"TRAINMAN"* with "Rio Grande Mainline Thru the Rockies" colorful enameled logo on high domed pressed tin badge with chrome finish **125-150**

D&RGW- *"Main Line Thru the Rockies"* blue & black enameled logo badge with no specific occupation **90-100**

ERIE RAILROAD

ERIE RAILROAD- *"BAGGAGE MASTER"* black enameled letters on nickel rectangular badge. Mfg. Am.Ry. Supply. **90-100**

ERIE RAILROAD- *"BRIDGEMAN"* black enameled letters on nickel rectangular badge **225-250**

ERIE RAILROAD- *"COLLECTOR"* black enameled letters on nickel rectangular badge **100-125**

ERIE RAILROAD- *"FERRY MASTER"* black enameled letters on nickel rectangular badge. Mfg. Am.Ry. Supply **225-250**

ERIE RAILROAD- "*GATEMAN*" black enameled letters on nickel rectangular badge **175-200**

ERIE RAILROAD- "*PORTER*" black enameled letters on nickel rectangular badge..... **175-200**

ERIE RAILROAD- "*STATION MASTER*" black enameled letters on nickel rectangular badge **200-250**

ERIE RAILROAD- "*TRAIN AGENT*" black enamel letters on nickel rectangular badge **175-200**

ERIE RAILROAD- "*TRAIN BAGGAGE MASTER*" black enamel letters on nickel rectangular badge **175-200**

ERIE RAILROAD- "*TRAIN PORTER*" black enameled letters on nickel rectangular badge **125-150**

FREMONT ELKHORN & MISSOURI VALLEY RAILROAD

FE&MVRR- "*BRAKEMAN*" black enamel letters on nickel rectangular badge **150-175**

FE&MVRR- "*CONDUCTOR*" black enamel letters on nickel finish rectangular badge....... **175-200**

FONDA JOHNSTOWN & GLOVERSVILLE RR

FJ&GRR- "*CONDUCTOR*" black enamel letters on dome style brass finish badge with beveled edges **175-200**

FT WORTH & DENVER CITY

FTW&DCRYCO- "*BRAKEMAN*" in black enameled letters on nickle rectangular badge **125-150**

ST LOUIS & SAN FRANCISCO RR AKA FRISCO LINES

FRISCO LINES- "*BRAKEMAN*" black enameled logo & letters on chrome finished dome style badge **100-125**

FRISCO LINES- "*CONDUCTOR*" black enameled logo & letters on gold finished dome style badge **175-200**

GRAND TRUNK WESTERN

GTW- "*BRAKEMAN*" black enameled letters on nickel rectangular badge **35-45**

GTW- "*CONDUCTOR*" black enameled letters on gold finish dome style badge with raised letters. Embossed leaf design around edges **45-55**

GREAT NORTHERN RAILWAY

GREAT NORTHERN RY- "*BRAKEMAN*" black enameled letters on nickel crown style badge **100-125**

GREAT NORTHERN RY- "*CONDUCTOR*" black enameled letters on nickel crown style badge **175-200**

KANSAS CITY SOUTHERN

KANSAS CITY SOUTHERN- "*BRAKEMAN*" black enameled letters on high dome style badge **150-175**

KANSAS CITY TERMINAL RY CO

KCTRY CO- "*USHER*" black enameled letters on high dome brass finish badge. Mfg. Partridge, Co. **65-75**

LACKAWANNA RAILROAD

LACKAWANNA RAILROAD- "*ASSISTANT AGENT*" raised letters on nickel finish rectangle with pebbled surface **70-80**

LACKAWANNA RAILROAD- "*BAGGAGE AGENT*" raised letters on nickel finish rectangle with pebbled surface **65-75**

LACKAWANNA RAILROAD- "*BAGGAGEMAN*" raised letters on nickel finish rectangle with pebbled surface **65-75**

LACKAWANNA RAILROAD- "*BRAKEMAN*" raised letters on nickel finish rectangle with pebbled surface **40-50**

LACKAWANNA RAILROAD- "*COLLECTOR*" raised letters on nickel finish rectangle with pebbled surface **75-85**

LACKAWANNA RAILROAD-"*DOORMAN*" raised letters on nickel finish rectangle with pebbled surface **80-90**

LACKAWANNA RAILROAD- "*FLAGMAN*" raised letters on nickel finish rectangle with pebbled surface **75-85**

LACKAWANNA RAILROAD- "*JANITOR*" raised letters on nickel finish rectangle with pebbled surface **80-90**

LACKAWANNA RAILROAD- "*PORTER*" raised letters on nickel finish rectangle with pebbled surface **60-70**

LACKAWANNA RAILROAD- "*STATION AGENT*" raised letters on nickel finish rectangle with pebbled surface **65-75**

LACKAWANNA RAILROAD- "*STATION MASTER*" raised letters on nickel finish rectangle with pebbled surface **90-100**

LACKAWANNA RAILROAD- "*STATION OFFICER*" raised letters on nickel finish rectangle with pebbled surface **100-125**

LACKAWANNA RAILROAD- "*TICKET SELLER*" raised letters on nickel finish rectangle with pebbled surface **75-85**

LONG ISLAND RAILROAD

LIRR- "*CONDUCTOR*" black enameled letters on nickel finish rectangular badge **40-50**

LIRR- "*TRAINMAN*" black enameled letters on nickel finish rectangular badge **35-45**

LONG ISLAND RR CO.- "*CONDUCTOR*" nickel finish on rectangular badge with nickel finish and blue & white enamel inlay **50-60**

MAINE CENTRAL OR MICHIGAN CENTRAL

MCRR- "*BRAKEMAN*" black enameled letters on nickel rectangular badge **45-55**

MCRR- "*CONDUCTOR*" black enameled letters on nickel rectangular badge **65-75**

CHICAGO MILWAUKEE ST PAUL & PACIFIC AKA MILWAUKEE ROAD

MILWAUKEE ROAD- "*CONDUCTOR*" gold letters on black background with red enameled box logo on dome style badge **100-125**

MISSOURI KANSAS & TEXAS RY

MK&TRY- "*PORTER*" raised letters on dome style badge with nickel finish **150-175**

M-K-T RY-"*BRAKEMAN*" black enameled letters on nickel finish rectangle with pebbled surface **50-60**

MINNEAPOLIS ST PAUL & SAULT STE MARIE RY CO

MSTP&SMRY CO- "*CONDUCTOR*" black enameled letters on nickel finish rectangular badge **150-175**

MISSOURI PACIFIC

MISSOURI PACIFIC- *"BRAKEMAN"* black enameled letters on nickle finish rectangular badge **40-50**

MISSOURI PACIFIC- "*CONDUCTOR*" black enameled letters on nickel finish rectangular badge **70-80**

MISSOURI PACIFIC LINES- "*CONDUCTOR*" raised letters on high dome badge with red enameled "Buzz Saw logo on top. Gold finish, pebbled surface **125-150**

MISSOURI PACIFIC LINES- "*PORTER*" with raised letters on high dome badge with red enameled "Buzz Saw" logo on top. Nickel finish, pebbled surface **200-250**

MISSOURI PACIFIC LINES- "*NEWS SERVICE*" raised letters on high dome badge with red enamelec "Buzz Saw" logo on top. Gold finish, pebbled surface **250-300**

MPRR- *"ENGINEER"* in black enameled letters on nickle rectangular badge **175-200**

MPRR- *"CONDUCTOR"* in black enameled letters on nickle rectangular badge..... **100-125**

MINNEAPOLIS & ST LOUIS RR

M&STLRR- "*BRAKEMAN*" black enameled letters on nickel rectangular badge. Mfg. Williamson Stamp Co. **125-150**

M&STLRR- "*CONDUCTOR*" black enameled letters on nickel rectangular badge. Mfg. Williamson Stamp Co. **150-175**

NEW JERSEY & NEW YORK RR

NJ&NYRR- "*COLLECTOR*" black enameled letters on gold finish rectangular badge............. **40-50**

NJ&NYRR- "*CONDUCTOR*" black enameled letters on chrome finish rectangular badge **35-45**

NEW YORK CENTRAL

NYCRR- "*CONDUCTOR*" black enameled letters on nickel finish rectangular badge... **40-50**

NEW YORK CENTRAL LINES- "*ASST. STATION AGENT*" raised letters, blue enameled logo in center of nickel finish high domed badge. "New York Central" curved above logo **90-100**

NEW YORK CENTRAL LINES- "*CONDUCTOR*" raised letters, blue enameled logo in center of nickel finish high domed badge. "New York Central" curved above logo **65-75**

NEW YORK CENTRAL LINES- "*FLAGMAN*" raised letters, blue enameled logo in center of nickel finish high domed badge. "New York Central" curved above logo **90-100**

NEW YORK CENTRAL SYSTEM- "*BAGGAGEMAN*" in raised letters, blue enameled logo in center of nickel finish high domed badge. "BIG FOUR" curved above logo **100-125**

NEW YORK CENTRAL SYSTEM- "*TRAINMAN*" in raised letters, blue enameled logo in center of nickel finish high domed badge. "MCRR" curved above logo **55-65**

NEW YORK CENTRAL SYSTEM- "*BAGGAGEMAN*" in raised letters, blue enameled logo in center of nickel finish high domed badge. "New York Central" curved above logo 65-75

NEW YORK CENTRAL SYSTEM- "*CONDUCTOR*" in raised letters, blue enameled logo in center of gold finish high domed badge. "New York Central" curved above logo 40-50

NEW YORK CENTRAL SYSTEM- "*GATEMAN*" in raised letters, blue enameled logo in center of nickel high domed badge. "New York Central" curved above logo 85-95

NEW YORK CENTRAL SYSTEM- "*PORTER*" in raised letters, blue enameled logo in center of nickel high domed badge. "New York Central" curved above logo 85-95

NEW YORK NEW HAVEN & HARTFORD RR

NYNH&HRR- "*BRAKEMAN*" black enameled letters on dome style badge with nickel finish 100-125

NYNH&HRR- "*DELIVERY CLERK*" black enameled letters on crown style badge with nickel finish 175-200

NYNH&HRR- "*GATEMAN*" black enameled letters on crown style badge with nickel finish 100-125

NYNH&HRR- '*PORTER*" black enameled letters on crown style badge with nickel finish 80-90

NYNH&HRR- "*TICKET COLLECTOR*" black enameled letters on crown style badge with nickel finish 90-100

NEW YORK RAILWAYS COMPANY

NY RAILWAYS CO.- "*CONDUCTOR*" black enameled letters on pressed tin badge 10-15

NY RAILWAYS CO.- "*EMPLOYEE*" black enameled letters on pressed tin badge 8-10

NEW YORK ONTARIO & WESTERN

NYO&WRY- *"CROSSING FLAGMAN"* black enameled letters on nickle rectangle badge. Mfg. SM Spencer, Boston, Mass. 150-175

NEW YORK SUSQUEHANNA & WESTERN

NYS&WRR- "*BAGGAGE MASTER*" black enameled letters on gold finish rectangular badge 100-125

NYS&WRR- "*CONDUCTOR*" black enameled letters on nickel finish rectangular badge 90-100

NORFOLK & WESTERN RR

N&W- "*CONDUCTOR*" cut out letters on rectangular badge with gold finish **70-80**

NORTHERN PACIFIC RAILWAY

NORTHERN PACIFIC RAILWAY- *"BRAKEMAN"* black enameled letters, nickel finish rectangular badge **65-75**

NORTHERN PACIFIC RAILWAY- "*CONDUCTOR*" black enameled letters, nickel finish rectangular badge **85-95**

NP- "*AGENT*" gold letters on rectangular black enameled brass badge. NP circular logo applied to top of badge **150-175**

NP- "*BRAKEMAN*" silver letters on rectangular black enameled badge, NP circular logo applied to top of badge **90-100**

NP- "*CONDUCTOR*" gold letters on rectangular black enameled badge. NP circular logo applied to top of badge...................... **100-125**

OREGON SHORT LINE

OSLRR- "*BRAKEMAN*" black enameled letters on nickel rectangular badge **200-250**

OSLRR- "*CONDUCTOR*" black enameled letters on nickel rectangular badge **225-275**

PENNSYLVANIA RAILROAD

PRR- "*BAGGAGEMAN*" raised letters on pebbled finish crown style brass badge with red enameled PRR Keystone logo in center. Mfg. EBY Co. **75-85**

PRR- "*CONDUCTOR*" raised letters on pebbled finish crown style brass badge with red enameled PRR Keystone logo in center. Mfg. EBY. Co. **65-75**

PRR "*STATION MASTER*" raised letters on pebbled finish crown style brass badge with red enameled PRR keystone logo in center. Mfg. EBY. Co. **90-100**

PRR- "*TRAINMAN*" raised letters on pebbled finish crown style brass badge with red enameled PRR keystone logo in center. Mfg. EBY Co. **40-50**

PENNSYLVANIA CENTRAL

PC- "*ASSISTANT STATION MASTER*" black enameled letters on pebbled finish high dome style badge with red enameled PC in center **50-60**

PC-"*ATTENDANT*" black enameled letters on pebbled finish high dome style badge with red enameled PC in center **25-35**

PC- *"CONDUTOR"* black enameled letters on pebbled finish high dome style badge with red enameled PC in center **30-40**

PC- *"STATION MASTER"* black enameled letters on pebbled finish high dome style badge with red enameled PC in center **75-85**

PC- *"TRAINMAN"* black enameled letters on pebbled finish high dome style badge with red enameled PC in center **25-35**

PC- *"USHER"* black enameled letters on pebbled finish high dome style badge with red enameled PC in center **60-70**

PORT ARTHUR ROUTE AKA KANSAS CITY SOUTHERN

PORT ARTHUR ROUTE- *"BRAKEMAN"* black enameled letters on nickel rectangular hat badge **175-200**

PORT ARTHUR ROUTE- *"CONDUCTOR"* black enameled letters on brass finish rectangular hat badge **250-300**

PULLMAN

PULLMAN- *"CONDUCTOR"* raised black enameled letters on brass pebbled finish rectangular badge **35-45**

PULLMAN- *"PORTER"* raised black enameled letters on brass pebbled finish rectangular badge.............................. **35-45**

PULLMAN CAR- *"CONDUCTOR"* raised black enameled letters on brass pebbled finish rectangular badge **75-85**

RIO GRANDE SOUTHERN RR CO

RGSRR CO- *"BRAKEMAN"* black enameled letters on nickel rectangular badge. Mfg. Denver Novelty Co. .... ◆

RGSRR CO- *"CONDUCTOR"* black enameled letters on nickel rectangular badge. Mfg. Am.Ry. Supply Co. .... ◆

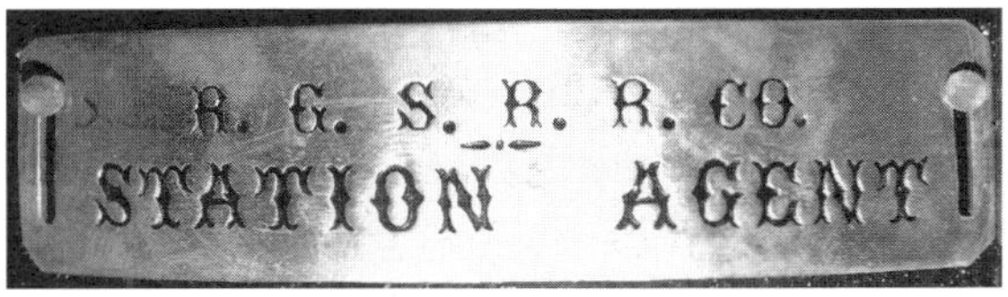

RGSRR CO- *"STATION AGENT"* fancy seriff black enameled letters on nickel rectangular badge .... ◆

RIO GRANDE SOUTHERN- *"BRAKEMAN"* black enameled letters on rectangular nickel badge. Mfg. Denver Novelty Co. .... ◆

RIO GRANDE WESTERN RY

RGWRY- *"BRAKEMAN"* black enameled letters on brass dome style badge .... ◆

RGWRY- *"CONDUCTOR"* black enameled letters on brass dome style badge .... ◆

ROCK ISLAND AKA CHICAGO ROCK ISLAND & PACIFIC

ROCK ISLAND- *"BRAKEMAN"* black enameled letters on nickel dome style badge with enameled RI logo in center. Fancy embossed leaf design on edges **65-75**

ROCK ISLAND- "*CONDUCTOR*" black enameled letters on high dome badge with brass finish. Black enameled RI logo on top center. Fancy embossed leaf design around edges 90-100

RUTLAND RAILROAD

RUTLAND RAILROAD- "*BAGGAGE MASTER*" black enameled letters on nickle finish rectangular badge 175-200

RUTLAND RAILROAD- "*BRAKEMAN*" black enameled letters on nickel finish rectangular badge 100-125

RUTLAND RAILROAD- "*STATION AGENT*" black enameled letters on nickel finish rectangular badge. Mfg. Am.Ry. Suppy Co. 150-175

RUTLAND RAILROAD- "*TRAINMAN*" black enameled letters on nickel rectangular finish badge 125-150

SANTA FE AKA ATCHISON TOPEKA & SANTA FE

SANTA FE- "*AGENT*" black enameled letters on crown style nickel finish badge; blue enameled logo in center 65-75

SANTA FE- "*BAGGAGE & MAIL HELPER*"- black enameled letters on crown style nickel finish badge; blue enameled logo in center 250-300

SANTA FE- "*BAGGAGEMAN*" black enameled letters on crown style nickel finish badge; blue enameled logo in center 100-125

SANTA FE- "*BRAKEMAN*" black enameled letters on crown style nickel finish badge; blue enameled logo in center 40-50

SANTA FE- "*CONDUCTOR*" black enameled letters on crown style nickel or brass finish badge; blue enameled logo in center 50-60

SANTA FE- "*PORTER*" black enameled letters on crown style nickel finish badge; blue enameled logo in center 85-95

SANTA FE- "*STATION AGENT*" black enameled letters on crown style nickel finish badge; blue enameled logo in center .. 125-150

SANTA FE- "*TRAIN AUDITOR*" black enameled letters on crown style nickel finish badge; blue enameled logo in center .. 300-325

SANTA FE- "*CONDUCTOR*" silver letters on fancy high domed badge with blue & white enameled Santa Fe inlaid logo; Silver & blue enameled bars between logo & occupation 125-150

SANTA FE- "*BRAKEMAN*" silver letters on fancy high domed badge with blue & white enameled Santa Fe inlaid logo; Silver & blue enameled bars between logo & occupation 90-100

SANTA FE- "*PORTER*" silver letters on fancy high domed badge with blue & white enameled Santa Fe inlaid logo; Silver & blue enameled bars between logo & occupation 125-150

SANTA FE- "*BRAKEMAN*" black enameled letters on nickel finish rectangular badge, early 125-150

SANTA FE "*CONDUCTOR*" black enameled letters on nickel finish rectangular badge 150-175

SEABOARD AIRLINE RAILROAD

SEABOARD AIRLINE- "*CONDUCTOR*" raised letters on brass finish rectangular badge with pebbled finish 60-70

SEABOARD AIRLINE- "*TRAINMAN*" raised letters on nickel finish rectangular badge........... 35-45

SOUTHERN RAILWAY

SOUTHERN- "*CONDUCTOR*" black enameled letters on nickel rectangular badge 50-60

SOUTHERN- "*FLAGMAN*" black enameled letters on nickel rectangular badge......... 60-70

SOUTHERN RY CO- "*PARCEL & MAIL CLERK*" black enameled letters on nickel dome style badge. Mfg. Am.Ry. Supply....... 175-200

SOUTHERN PACIFIC RAILROAD

SPCO- "*CONDUCTOR*" black enameled letters on brass finish rectangular badge 90-100

SPCO- "*FREIGHT BRAKEMAN*" black enameled letters on nickel rectangular badge 100-125

SPCO- "*FREIGHT CONDUCTOR*" black enameled letters on brass finish rectangular badge 125-150

SPCO- "*LOCOMOTIVE ENGINEER*" black enameled letters on brass finish rectangular badge 150-175

ST LOUIS IRON MOUNTAIN & SOUTHERN

STLIM&S- "*BRAKEMAN*" black enameled letters on nickel rectangular badge **75-100**

STLIM&S- "*CONDUCTOR*" black enameled letters on nickel rectangular badge..... **150-175**

SOO LINE AKA MINNEAPOLIS ST PAUL & SAULT STE MARIE

SOO LINE- "*BRAKEMAN*" black enameled letters on high domed badge with blue enameled logo on top. Fancy floral design around outer edge **150-175**

TEXAS MIDLAND RAILROAD

TEXAS MIDLAND RAILROAD- "*BRAKEMAN*" raised letters on nickel rectangular badge with pebbled finish **150-175**

TEXAS & PACIFIC RY

TEXAS & PACIFIC- "*BRAKEMAN*" black enameled letters on dome style badge with slotted ends & enameled red & black T&P logo on top **200-250**

TEXAS & PACIFIC RY- "*STATION BAGGAGE MASTER*" black enameled letters on high domed badge with colorful enameled "T&P" logo top center **350-400**

UNION PACIFIC RAILROAD

UNION PACIFIC- "*BRAKEMAN*" raised letters on fancy domed nickel badge with beveled edges & pebbled finish **200-250**

UNION PACIFIC- "*CONDUCTOR*" raised letters on fancy domed brass badge with beveled edges and pebbled finish **300-350**

UNION PACIFIC- "*TRAIN PORTER*" raised letters on fancy domed nickel badge with beveled edges & pebbled finish **350-400**

UNION PACIFIC- "*BRAKEMAN*" black enameled letters on nickel rectangular badge **35-45**

UNION PACIFIC- "*CONDUCTOR*" black enameled letters on brass finish rectangular badge **50-60**

UNION PACIFIC- "*ELECTRICIAN*" black enameled letters on nickel rectangular badge **200-250**

UNION PACIFIC- "*STATION AGENT*" black enameled letters on nickel rectangular badge 100-125

UNION PACIFIC- "*STATION BAGGAGEMAN*" black enameled letters on nickel rectangular badge with beveled edges 175-200

UNION PACIFIC- "*TRAIN BAGGAGEMAN*" black enameled letters on nickle rectangular badge 150-175

UNION PACIFIC- "*UNITED STATE MAIL*" black enameled letters on brass finish rectangular badge 300-350

UNION PACIFIC RR- "*BRAKEMAN*" black enameled letters on nickel rectangular badge 40-50

UNION PACIFIC RR- "*CONDUCTOR*" black enameled letters on brass finish rectangular badge 75-85

UNION PACIFIC RR- "*FIREMAN*" black enameled letters on nickel rectangular badge 250-300

UNION PACIFIC RR- "*STATION AGENT*" black enameled letters on nickel rectangular badge 125-150

UNION PACIFIC RR- "*TRUCKMAN*" black enameled letters on nickel rectangular badge 350-400

UNION PACIFIC RR- "*TRAIN BAGGAGEMAN*" black enameled letters on nickel rectangular badge 175-200

WABASH RAILWAY COMPANY

WABASH RAILWAY CO.- "*BRAKEMAN*" black enameled letters on nickel rectangular badge 65-75

WABASH RAILWAY CO- "*CONDUCTOR*" black enameled letters on nickel rectangular badge 75-85

WABASH RAILWAY CO.- "*FREIGHT YARD SEC.08 PATROLMAN*" black enameled letters on nickel dome design badge 90-100

WABASH RR- "*BRAKEMAN*" black enameled letters on nickel rectangular badge......... 65-75

WAGNER PALACE CAR COMPANY

WAGNER PALACE CAR "*PORTER*" raised letters on fancy dome style badge with beveled edges 300-350

GENERIC BADGES

The following list of badges are considered generic because they have no specific railroad names on them. The railroads used these as well to identify their employees occupations. The value is considerably less since there is no railroad designation. When found on hats they usually will be accompanied by buttons that have the railroad initials or name holding hat braid.

AGENT-black enameled letters on nickel rectangular badge 15-20

BAGGAGEMAN-black enameled letters on nickel rectangular badge 10-15

BRAKEMAN-black enameled letters on nickel rectangular badge 5-10

BRAKEMAN-skeleton cut out letters with nickel finish 3-5

CONDUCTOR-black enameled letters on gold finish rectangular badge......................... 15-20

CONDUCTOR-skeleton cut out letters with gold finish 10-15

CROSSING WATCHMAN-black enameled letters on brass rectangular badge. Mfg. Am.Ry. Sup. 25-30

ENGINEER-black enameled letters on smaller crown style badge with nickel finish 15-20

FIREMAN-black enameled letters on crown style badge. Mfg. Am.Ry. Sup................ 25-30

FLAGMAN-black enameled letters on nickel plated rectangular badge......................... 20-25

FREIGHT CONDUCTOR-black enameled letters on rectangular badge 20-25

GUARD-black enameled letters on smaller crown style badge with gold finish Mfg. Am.Ry. Sup. 20-25

INSPECTOR-raised letters on rectangular nickel finish badge with beveled edges & pebbled background 15-20

MESSENGER-black enameled letters on nickel rectangular badge. Mfg. FG Glover 20-25

MOTORMAN-black enameled letters in cursive letters on brass finish rectangular badge. Mfg. Am.Ry. Supply 15-20

NEWS AGENT- black enameled letters on smaller crown style badge. 30-40

PARLOR CAR ATTENDANT-black enameled raised letters on brass finish rectangular badge with beveled edges and pebbled background. 25-30

PORTER-black enameled letters on nickel rectangular badge. Mfg. Am.Ry. Supply 15-20

PORTER-black enameled letters on crown style badge. Mfg. Am.Ry. 20-25

SLEEPING CAR CONDUCTOR- black enameled raised letters on brass finish rectangular badge with beveled edges and pebbled background 25-30

STATION BAGGAGEMAN-black enameled letters on nickel rectangular badge. Mfg. Am.Ry. Supply. 20-25

TRAINMAN-nickel skeleton cut out letters 5-10

TRAINMAN-black enameled letters on nickel rectangular badge. Mfg. Am.Ry. Supply 10-15

TRAINMAN-raised letters on nickel finish badge with beveled edges and pebbled background 10-15

REMEMBER SUGGESTED PRICES LISTED ARE MEANT AS A GUIDE ONLY. PRICES MAY VARY FROM REGION TO REGION!!!

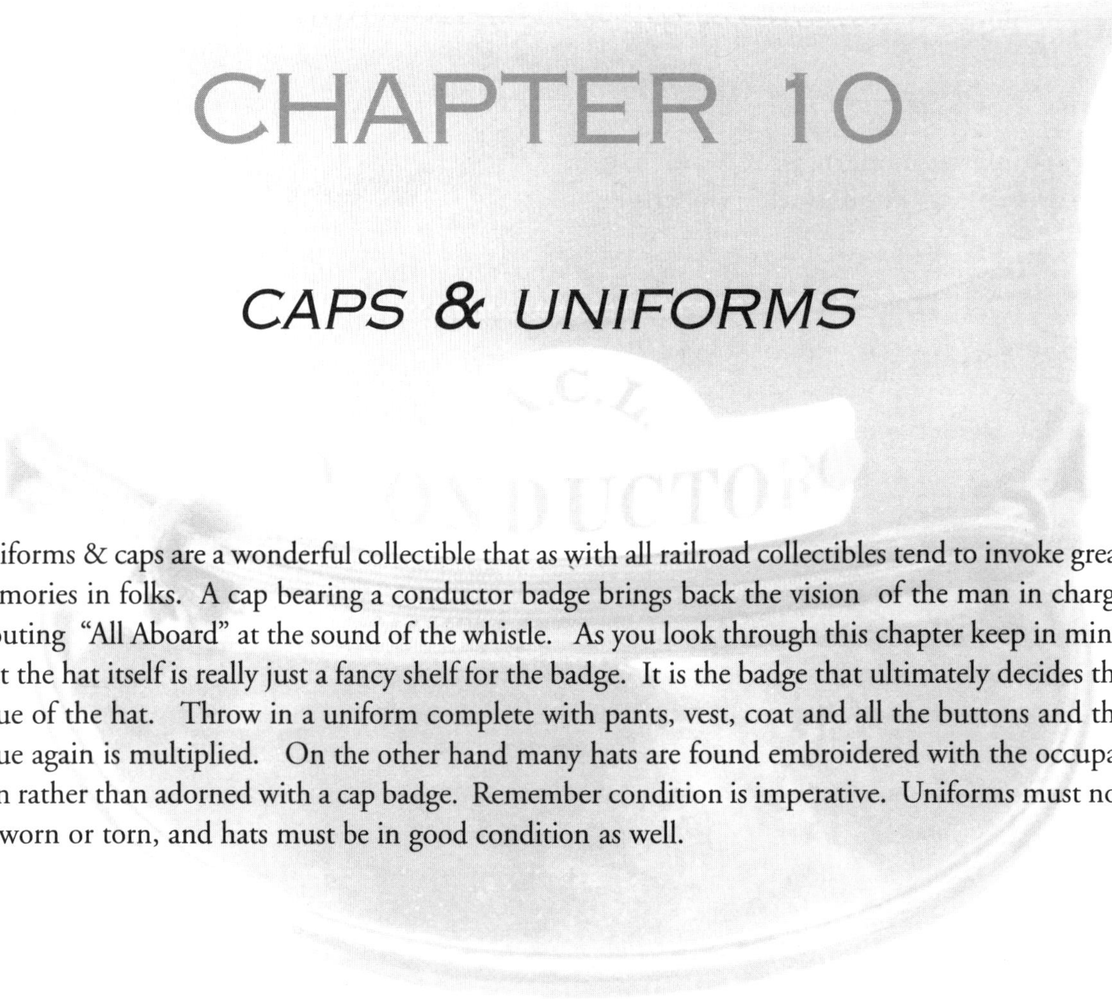

CHAPTER 10

CAPS & UNIFORMS

Uniforms & caps are a wonderful collectible that as with all railroad collectibles tend to invoke great memories in folks. A cap bearing a conductor badge brings back the vision of the man in charge shouting "All Aboard" at the sound of the whistle. As you look through this chapter keep in mind that the hat itself is really just a fancy shelf for the badge. It is the badge that ultimately decides the value of the hat. Throw in a uniform complete with pants, vest, coat and all the buttons and the value again is multiplied. On the other hand many hats are found embroidered with the occupation rather than adorned with a cap badge. Remember condition is imperative. Uniforms must not be worn or torn, and hats must be in good condition as well.

AMTRAK- *"TRAINMAN"* enameled hat badge applied to modern issue wool hat. White braid attached with two silver Amtrak buttons **35-45**

Complete uniform with hat 65-75

AMTRAK- *"CONDUCTOR"* enameled hat badge with gold braid attached by two gold buttons on modern issue wood hat........ **55-65**

Complete uniform with hat 75-85

ACL- *"CONDUCTOR"* gold domed hat badge applied to pill box style black hat with patent leather visor. Comes complete with rope braid attached by two gold ACL buttons on either side of hat **100-125**

Complete uniform with hat 200-250

BOSTON & MAINE – *"BAGGAGEMASTER"* black enameled letters on dome style badge applied to pill box style hat with leather visor. Mfg. Lamson & Hubbard **100-125**

BN- *"CONDUCTOR"* skeleton cut out letter badge below BN enameled logo badge on modern issue wool hat with leather visor **45-55**

Complete uniform with hat 90-100

CALIFORNIA ZEPHYR- embroidered patch applied to maroon maroon colored modern issue wood hat with black patent leather visor. Comes with gold rope braid applied with two gold buttons. Mfg. Schneiders. Used by Porters **100-125**

CPR- *"FREIGHT"* celluloid hat badge applied to pill box style hat **90-100**

CPR- *"TRAINMAN"* embroidered on pillbox style hat with wide black band with white borders. Mfg. Scully.................................... **45-55**

FRISCO LINES- *"CONDUCTOR"* gold domed badge on pill box style hat with patent leather visor. Gold buttons on either side **200-250**

Complete uniform with hat 300-350

FRISCO LINES- *"BRAKEMAN"* hat badge applied to pill box style hat with silver FRISCO buttons on either side 175-200

GNRY- *"CONDUCTOR"* hat with embroidered GN goat logo patch over "C-O-N-D-U-C-T-O-R" cut out badge. Gold rope braid with two gold buttons on modern issue wood hat 75-85

GTW- *"BRAKEMAN"* high domed nickel hat badge on pill box style hat with patent leather visor 75-85

GTW- *"CONDUCTOR"* high domed gold badge on pill box style hat with patent leather visor 80-90

LIRR- *"TRAINMAN"* black enameled letters on rectangular badge on grey pill box style hat 60-70

NP- *"BRAKEMAN"* cap badge with enameled logo applied to pill box style hat. Two silver buttons hold white rope braid 100-125

NP- *"CONDUCTOR"* gold cap badge with enameled logo. Pill box style hat with gold braid held by two gold buttons 150-175

PORT ARTHUR ROUTE- *"BRAKEMAN"* badge applied to pill box style hat with black patent leather visor 250-300

ROCK ISLAND- *"CONDUCTOR"* domed gold hat badge on black pill box style with gold braid attached with gold buttons 150-175

ROCK ISLAND- *"BRAKEMAN"* domed nickel hat badge on black pill box style hat with silver braid attached with two silver buttons **125-150**

RUTLAND RR- *"TRAINMAN"* nickle rectangular badge applied to black pill box style hat with black patent leather visor. Two silver Rutland buttons on either side **200-250**

SANTA FE BAND UNIFORM-Complete colorful uniform in red & blue with gold highlights. Warbonnet emblems adorn both sleeves. Belt buckle shows enameled Warbonnet logo on gold background. Hat is red & white with gold highlights and enameled Warbonnet logo hat badge. **550-600**

SANTA FE- *"CONDUCTOR"* fancy high domed enameled badge on modern issue blue wood hat with leather visor. Gold braid applied with two gold buttons. **175-200**

SANTA FE- *"BRAKEMAN"* fancy high domed enameled badge on modern issue black wool hat.with leather visor Silver attached braid with two silver Santa Fe logo buttons on either side **100-125**

SANTA FE- *"BRAKEMAN"* crown style nickel badge with enameled Santa Fe logo on dark wood modern issue hat with applied braid **65-75**

UNION PACIFIC- *"BRAKEMAN"* rectangular badge on black wool hat with silver rope braid applied with two silver UP buttons on either side **75-85**

CHAPTER 11

DEPOT & RAIL YARDS

Items from the depot and train yards are numerous. Many of these items are listed in their own separate chapters so remember that this is only a small sampling. The depot was the starting point for the traveling public so these items probably invoked great memories in collectors and enthusiasts alike. Sitting in a depot waiting for a train to arrive was an exciting time for travelers. Whether waiting patiently in a small town depot or the bustling Grand Central station the depot left a wonderful impression on the traveler as they began or ended their journies. There is a broad range of items listed here, everything from a small ticket validator to a large switch stand found in the yard. Remember that items must be in good to excellent condition to command the prices suggested here.

REMEMBER: PRICES SHOWN ARE SUGGESTED VALUES ONLY. VALUES VARY FROM REGION TO REGION. THIS IS MEANT ONLY AS A GUIDE. (◆) Denotes value over $1000.00

AT&SF- Letter box cover. Cast "AT&SF LETTER BOX" on hinged door. Measures 7 ¼" x 3 ½" **125-150**

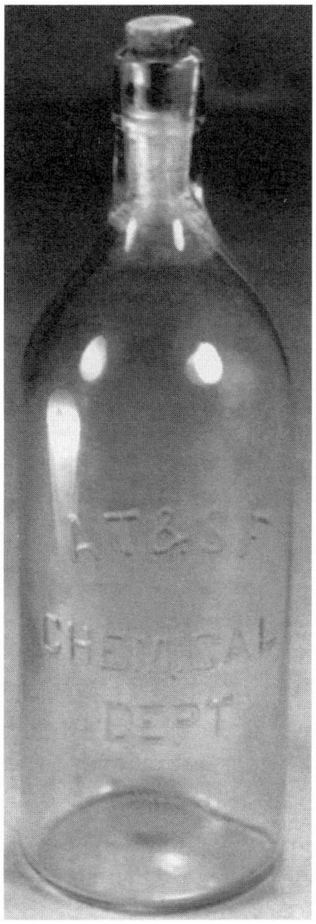

AT&SF-"CHEMICAL DEPT" embossed on side of quart size glass bottle. **100-125**

AT&SFRY CO- Coast Lines, Los Angeles Calif., ticket validator die in Cosmo machine. **175-200**

AT&SFRY CO-Coast Lines Oceanside, Calif. Ticket validator die in Hills Model A machine. **175-200**

AT&SFRR- Clement Kans wax sealer with oval brass head and wood handle. **500-550**

AT&SFRY- Mitchell Kan. Agent on round brass wax sealer with nickel handle. **350-400**

AT&SFRY-stamped on round brass tool checks with 3 digit numbers **1-2**

BURLINGTON ROUTE-porcelain sign measures 4 1/2" x 5 1/2" **200-250**

CNR- cast on top of hanging depot lamp from depot. Mfg. Bradleys Security Lamp. Black metal shade. **75-85**

CAN.PAC.RY.CO.-Kingsgate on round brass wax sealer with wood handle. **200-250**

C&ARR-brass tool check with 3 digit number **3-5**

CENTRAL PACIFIC RR-brass baggage tag with black enameled letters. Mfg. WW Wilcox .... ◆

C&ARR CO- Higginsville, MO ticket validator die in Hills Model A machine. **200-250**

C&EIRR- reflective buzzsaw logo applied to metal sign measuring 24" x 24". **50-60**

C&NW- metal wall thermometer. Reads, "Think Safety". Green on yellow. **25-35**

CB&QRR- wall map. BR logos on top corners. Map measures 34" x 46" dated 1890's. **100-125**

CK&WRR- Lovewell, Kan. AGENT on round brass wax sealer with wooden handle. **500-550**

CRR OF NJ- cast on top edge of large brass fire extinquisher. Measures 3" tall. **50-60**

CM&STPRY – Harlowton, Montana on round brass wax sealer with wood handle. ... **350-400**

CM&STPRY Seattle Wash Ticket Office on round brass wax sealer with wood handle. **350-400**

CMSTP&P-sign measuring 34"x 24". Painted metal logo sign **150-200**

CRI&P- door plate, fancy intertwined letters on top with cast leaves on the bottom ... **80-90**

CRI&PRY- Smith Center KAS Agent, on round brass wax sealer with brass handle...... **400-450**

CRI&PRY- Freight Agent, Council Bluffs, IA on round brass wax sealer with tall wood handle **400-450**

COLORADO & SOUTHERN-RY- Longmont, Co. ticket validator die in Cosmo machine. **400-450**

COLORADO & SOUTHERN RY- large depot photo shows colorful wildflowers in original frame. Mat reads flowers name and "Found Along The Line of the Colorado & Southern". Measures 15 ½" x 20 ½". **200-250**

COLORADO MIDLAND-brass dater die reads, "COLO.MID.RR GEN PASS DEPT COLORADO SPRINGS COLORADO " (photo has been reversed so it is readable) **650-700**

COTTON BELT ROUTE- metal clipboard has enameled logo on top of clip. Board measures 4" x 6". **40-50**

CRIPPLE CREEK & COLORADO SPRINGS RR- Brass dater die from Summit Colorado in Hills Model A machine. **350-400**

D&RGWRRCO- Buena Vista, Colo on validator die in Hills #7 machine. **400-450**

D&RGW- cast iron bracket with tin fuel fount & glass chimney. Iron bracket & fuel font both cast D&RGW. Used in both caboose & in the depots **175-200**

D&SLRR- counter style ticket cabinet with roll top door. Cabinet measures 18" wide by 35" tall. Mfg. Stromberg Allen & Co. Chicago. **750-800**

D.U.T.R.R.- Denver Colorado Ticket Dept. 18 on validator die in Centennial machine. **175-200**

E&THRR- over Vandalia Line on brass 1 ½" x 1" baggage tag. Mfg. WW Wilcox. **20-25**

FJ&GRR- Gloversville & Johnstown #26 on brass 1 ½" x 1 ½" baggage tag. Mfg. J. Robbins. **25-30**

GOLDEN CIRCLE RR- dater die from Independence, Colorado in Cosmo Machine **450-500**

GNRY CO- Dining Car Dept #35 on round brass wax sealer with wood handle. ... **400-450**

GREAT NORTHERN-Depot sign made of wood measuring 29" x 25 1/2" with gold letters and red outline. Goat logos in each corner **600-650**

GREAT NORTHERN RY – ENGR. DEPT. Seattle on round brass wax sealer with wood handle. **400-450**

GTR-brass depot desk lamp measures 21" tall. Mfg. HLPL Montreal. **100-125**

GC&SFRY- Hitchcock, TX on brass ticket validator die in Cosmo #2 machine. .. **175-200**

IGNRR- cast iron depot stove. Door cast IGNRR in arched letters. Measures 22" x 20" x 38". **350-400**

ICRR- Sioux Falls, SD on brass die in ticket validator machine **100-125**

ICRR-wax sealer round brass die reads, ICRR Fisher, ILL with starburst design in center **250-300**

ICRR- Neoga, ILL on brass die in ticket validator machine. **100-125**

KANSAS CITY TERMINAL RY-porcelain yellow on blue sign measures 10" x 16", reads, "Trespassing Forbidden Private Property KCTRYCO". **100-125**

MIDLAND TERMINAL MIDLAND- brass dater die & machine. (photo has been reversed so it is readable) **400-450**

MILWAUKEE ROAD- first aid kit measures 5" x 8". Metal box reads, "The Milwaukee Road State of Wash" on the lid. **20-25**

MILWAUKEE ROAD –red & white logo on fiberglass sign measuring 22" x 16". .. **100-125**

MKT- caboose stove measures approximately 38"tall cast MKT on the door. **350-400**

MKT- porcelain red white & black sign with logo in center. Measures 36" x 42". .. **400-450**

MISSOURI PACIFIC RR -Perpetual tin wall calendar. Shows Diesel engine and reads, "Route of the Eagles". Removable date cards **200-250**

MISSOURI PACIFIC- 1898 wall calendar with tear sheets. Measures 11 ½" x 14 ½" ... **200-250**

M&ORR- wax sealer brass round head with nickel handle **300-350**

MONT.CEN R'Y- Butte Depot on round brass wax sealer with toadstool handle **600-650**

NYCRR- Scarsdale NY brass dater die only, no machine. **20-25**

NYCRR- Syracuse, NY brass dater die only no machine. **20-25**

NYC- oak wall telephone attached shelf and headphone set. Front reads, "Push button to tal, Release to Listen" **100-125**

NYC SYSTEM- stretcher stenciled in large letters. Folding design measures 7 feet long with wood handles and leather straps to wrap and lock closed for storing.----------------- **100-125**

NPRY- cast on top of brass fire extinquisher measures 14". Mfg. Pyrene. -------------- **75-85**

NPRR- First Aid Kit. NP logo on top of metal box measures 5" x 8". ---------------------- **20-25**

NPRR- box full of Falcon Pen tips each marked Property of Northern Pacific. ------------- **35-45**

NPRY- wooden printers block with Monad logo. Measures 2" x 2" --------------------------- **15-20**

NPRY- "Parcel Check Room" framed sign. Measures 12 ¼" x 8 ½". ------------------- **30-40**

NPRY- printers plates for printing various forms with Monad logo. -------------------------- **5-10**

NOR.PAC.RY.CO- Kamiah, IDA on round brass wax sealer with brass toadstool handle. --------------------------------- **350-400**

NOR.PAC.RY.CO. Cleveland N.DAK. on round brass wax sealer with brass toadstool handle ----------------------------------- **350-400**

O.S.L.R.R.CO.- Tremont, Utah on brass oval wax sealer with wood handle. -------- **500-550**

PRR- cast iron wall mount bill holder. Harp shaped with 6" spike. --------------------- **40-50**

PRR- Brunswick NY on brass dater die only, no machine. --------------------------------- **30-40**

PRR-Keystone Logo on wax sealer with raised dots around edge. Wood handle----- **250-300**

PENNA RR- Newark, NJ on brass dater die only. No machine. ------------------------ **30-40**

PENNSYLVANIA SYSTEM- No. 5 pen tips full box. ------------------------------------ **20-30**

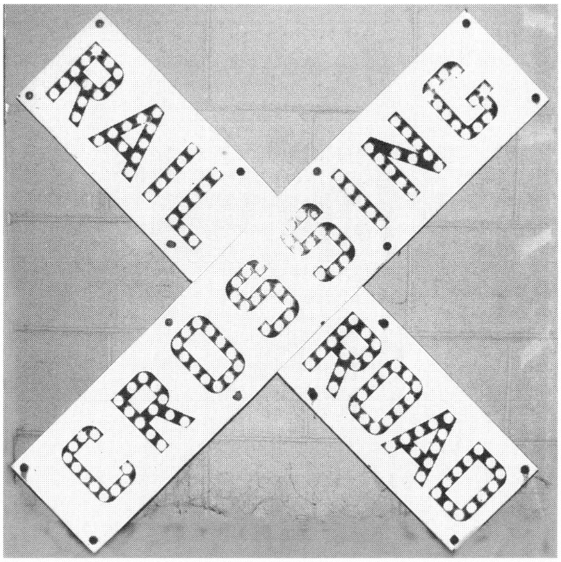

RAILROAD CROSSING SIGN-Porcelain crossbuck white with black letters and glass reflectors --------------------------------- **250-300**

ROCK ISLAND-timetable holder. Metal with Rock Island logo enameled on front, over Travel & Ship Route of the Rockets" -------- **200-250**

ROCK ISLAND LINES- small brass oval plate applied to base of ornate brass depot desk lamp with glass chimney. Mfg. A&W **200-250**

ROCK ISLAND LINES- fire extinquisher large brass style measures 24" tall. "Rock Island lines" on large attached plate on side........... **100-125**

STL&SFRY- FT Co. Hayti, MO. On brass dater die in Centennial machine........ **150-175**

ST.L.S.F.RR- Dennis Kan. AGENT on round wax sealer with brass handle. **400-450**

ST.L.SF.RR- Seymour, MO AGENT on round brass wax sealer with brass handle...... **400-450**

ST.L.&SFRRCO- White Ok IT AGENT on round brass wax sealer with nickel finish handle... **500-550**

SANTA FE- fiberglass sign white on blue with cross logo measures 30" x 30". **100-125**

SANTA FE – early porcelain sign measures 18" x 18" with logo in center **700-800**

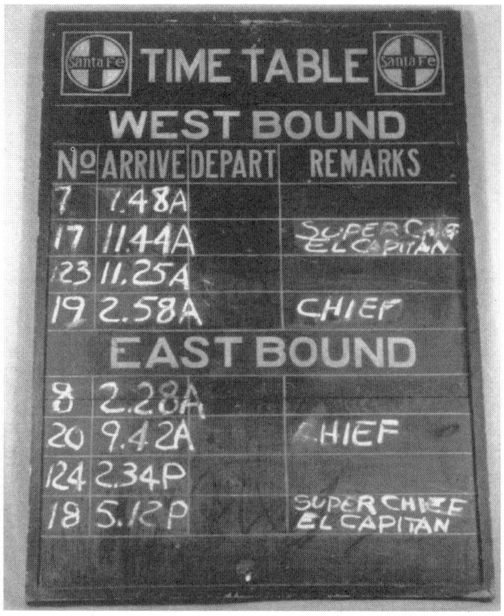

SANTA FE- schedule board white on black measures 28" x 39" with Santa Fe logos in either corner. Has columns for East Bound, West Bound, North Bound & South Bound.. **500-550**

SANTA FE Depot Clock- Beautiful school house style case manufacturered by Seth Thomas. Face has "SANTA FE RAILWAY SYSTEM". Inside of case is service tag showing depot location. .... ◆

SANTA FE RR- alcohol burner. Cast on side of brass burner used for melting sealing wax. **350-400**

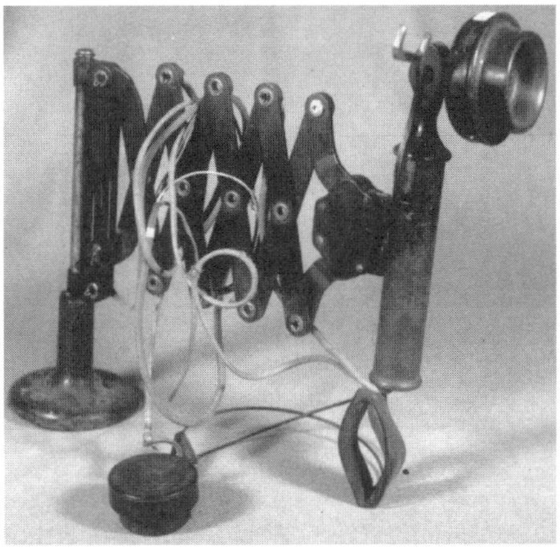

SCISSORS PHONE- depot phone attached to adjustable bracket for ease of movement around desk. Complete with ear phones and desk mount. **250-300**

SIGN- double sided porcelain flanged sign reads, "Parcels Checked in Ticket Office, 10 cents for every 24 hours". White on blue measures 5 ½" x 15". 300-350

SIGN-double sided porcelain flanged sign reads, "Postal Telegraph The International System Here". Blue on white measures 30" x 16". **100-125**

SOO LINE-brass clipboard measures 4" x 8". Top of clip reads, "SOO LINE SHIP & TRAVEL" above engine. **20-25**

SOO LINE- sign exterior shanty sign measures 4" x 33". Porcelain enameled with black letters on white background **150-175**

SOUTHERN PACIFIC- sunset logo cast on iron door knob set measures 17" x 3 ½". **175-200**

SWITCH STAND- Manufactured by Star. Measures 4ft with target **150-175**

TELEGRAPH RESONTELEGRAPH RESONATOR-triangular box with sounder and triple pivoting arm **200-250**

TELEGRAPH RESONATOR-triangular box with sounder and double pivoting arm **175-200**

TICKET CABINET- counter top style with roll top front.Has slots to house tickets and brochures. Measures approximately 18" wide & 22" tall. **300-350**

TICKET CAGE FRONT- Ornate cast iron cage front measures 30" x 40". 100-125

TICKET CAGE FRONT- Ornate brass cage measuring 27" x 30" 200-250

TICKET VALIDATOR MACHINE- missing die, Mfg. Centennial Dater 35-45

TRAIN ORDER TYPEWRITER- Only types all capitol letters, no lower case. Mfg. Royal. . 175-200

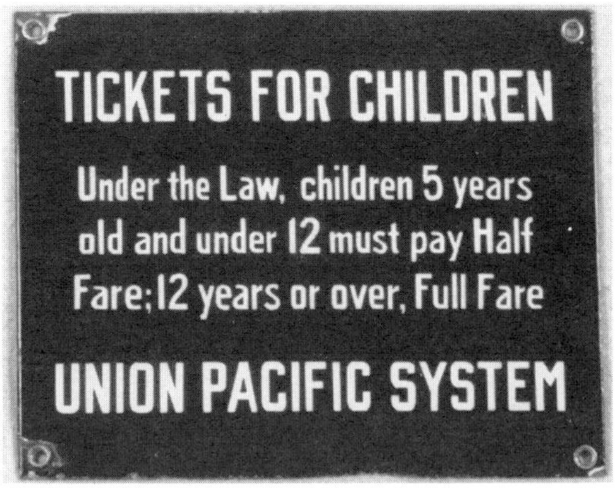
TICKETS FOR CHILDREN
Under the Law, children 5 years old and under 12 must pay Half Fare; 12 years or over, Full Fare
UNION PACIFIC SYSTEM

UNION PACIFIC SYSTEM- white on blue porcelain sign reads, "Tickets for Children Under the Law Children 5 Years Old & Under 12 Must Pay Half Fare. 12 Years or Over Full Fare" Measures 12" x 8". 250-300

UN PAC RR- Montpelier brass die in Cosmo #2 validator machine 140-150

UNION PACIFIC – brass desk ornament in shape of shield design reads, UNION PACIFIC over 4000 35-45

UNION
PACIFIC
SYSTEM
THE
OVERLAND
ROUTE

UNION PACIFIC SIGN- porcelain Overland Shield in red white & blue measures 40" x39" 700-800

UNION PACIFIC- metal timetable holder with Overland Logo enameled on the front above Travel By Train. **200-250**

UNION PACIFIC- Depot poster advertising the City of Denver train. Colorful with Streamliner train. Measures 16" x 22". **175-200**

UNION PACIFIC- black wall phone marked UPRR on the receiver. Mfg. Western Electric **150-175**

UNION PACIFIC- #864 on round brass wax sealer with brass handle **250-300**

UPRR SIGN- Porcelain sign reads, "SAFETY FIRST" measures 24" diameter with red, white & blue Overland Logo in center. UPRR on top & Safety First around the bottom. **350-400**

UPRR CO.- Caliente, NEV. On oval brass wax sealer with wood handle **400-450**

UNION STATION-El Paso, TX. On brass die in ticket validator machine. Mfg. Cosmo #2 .... **75-85**

UNION STATION- Toledo, Ohio on brass die only. Missing machine. **15-20**

VANDALIA RR CO- brass baggage tag measures 2 ½" x 2" Slot for destination card. Mfg. WW Wilcox. **50-75**

UP- door handle and backing plate with UP Shield cast on top. **100-125**

WALL PHONE- oak wood wall phone has "Push to Talk, Release to Listen" Not railroad marked **100-125**

WALL PHONE- oak wood wall phone with railroad markings **200-250**

WABASH-wax sealer, "THE WABASH CO #127" on round brass sealer with nickel handle **300-350**

WABASH RR –In center of round brass wax sealer with "DINING CAR DEPARTMENT" aound outer edge. Wood handle **400-450**

WABASH, ST LOUIS & PACIFIC RY- wax sealer with wood handle. **400-450**

WAX STICKS- embossed SOO LINE. Mfg. Princeton Sealing Wax. Box of 4 .... **25-30**

WAX STICKS- embossed B&O. Green in color box of 4 .... **25-30**

WAX MELTING TORCH- small metal torch for melting sealing wax. Mfg. Star Bros. **40-45**

WESTERN PACIFIC -porcelain logo sign measues 26" x 22 1/2" **550-600**

WESTERN UNION –'TELEGRAPH HERE" two sided flanged porcelain sign measures 16 ¾:" x 25". White on blue with black & yellow. **275-300**

WESTERN UNION-"TELEGRAPH & CABLE OFFICE" two sided porcelain flanged sign measures 12" x 24". White on blue. **175-200**

WESTERN UNION- double sided porcelain sign measures 18 ½" x 30 ¼". White on blue with arrow below writing. **100-125**

WESTERN UNION –"TELEGRAPH & CABLE" double sided flanged porcelain sign with center globe. Measures 11" x 16". Black on white **175-200**

WESTERN UNION-telegraph blank box. Metal countertop style. Front has Western Union in yellow & black **75-85**

WESTERN UNION-telegraph blank counter top box with applied blue & white porcelained enameled sign on front **300-350**

CHAPTER 12

DINING CAR CHINA

The dining car on a train was without a doubt the most enjoyable part of a persons journey. There was nothing to compare to the delight of sitting in the diner at a table adorned with the best of everything. Delicious meals served on beautiful china, silver and glassware placed on the finest linens were a treat not offered today. And to top off this wonderful scenario you would be able to watch the countryside go by while enjoying your meal. Dining car collectibles are one of the most sought after in the railroadiana hobby. A collector can amass a wonderful collection of china dishes to enjoy for many years to come. As with everything the railroads had, they marked their china with logos on the tops and bottoms of pieces. They also had many custom patterns made which were designed specifically for the railroads. On the other hand there were patterns used that were not custom or marked in any way. These patterns are referred to as stock patterns. It is difficult to prove actual railroad use, so we have chosen to only list those patterns which are custom, or specifically marked with railroad backstamps and initials. Remember as you read through this section, china must be in good to excellent condition. Showing little or no use with no chips, cracks or hairlines. As with all collectibles condition is paramount in determining values. We have shown a large percentage of the known patterns but many more do exist.

REMEMBER: PRICES SHOWN ARE SUGGESTED VALUES ONLY. VALUES VARY FROM REGION TO REGION. THIS IS MEANT ONLY AS A GUIDE. (◆) **Denotes value over $1000.00**

SOME EXAMPLES OF BACKSTAMPS & MANUFACTURERS MARKS

Bottom stamp showing Missouri Pacific railroad marks & OP Syacuse manufacturers mark.

Bottom stamp showing Santa Fe railroad marks and Syracuse manufacturers mark.

Bottom stamp showing Atlantic Coast Line Railroad mark with date of 10/47 and manufactured by Sterling China Company.

Bottom stamp showing Soo Line railroad logo and Mayer China manufacturers mark.

Top marked piece showing close up view of Denver & Rio Grande Curecanti logo.

Top marked piece showing Western Pacific Feather River Route pattern.

ABBREVIATION KEY LISTING CHINA MFG.-(MANUFACTURERS)

BSH-BAUSCHER

BUF-BUFFALO CHINA CO.

GPC-GREENWOOD POTTERY

HALL-HALL CHINA CO

HAV-HAVILAND

LAM-LAMBERTON (SCAMMELL)

MAD-MADDOX

MYR-MAYER

SGO-SHENANGO

STR-STERLING

SYR-SYRACUSE

UNP-UNION PORCELAIN WORKS

PLEASE NOTE MANY OTHER MANUFACTURERS EXIST THIS IS ONLY A SAMPLE

ALASKA RAILROAD

ALASKA RR- *Coffee cup* in **Alaska Pattern.** Blue design border with logo in center. Mfg. Sgo. **250-300**

ALASKA RR- *Ashtray* in **McKinley Pattern** with black border and logo in center. Center post houses matches with attached saucer. Mfg. Sgo. **300-350**

ALASKA-RR-*bread plate,* **McKinley pattern.** Mfg. Sgo. **100-125**

ALASKA RR-*oval* bakers dish **Talkeena Pattern** with blue design border and ARR logo in shield design. Mfg. Sgo. **150-175**

ATCHISON TOPEKA & SANTA FE AKA/ SANTA FE

AT&SFRY-*ice cream shell,* **Adobe Pattern,** tan with brown logo on top. Mfg. Syr. Bottom stamped, "Made Expressly for Santa Fe Dining Car Service". **100-125**

AT&SFRY- *bread plate,* **Adobe Pattern.** Mfg. Syr. Bottom stamped "Made Expressly for Santa Fe Dining Car Service". **75-85**

AT&SFRY- *dinner plate* **Adobe Pattern.** Not bottom stamped. Mfg. Syr. **50-60**

AT&SFRY-*fruit bowl* **Adobe Pattern.** Not bottom marked. Mfg. Syr **25-35**

AT&SFRY- *coffee cup & saucer* **Black Chain Pattern.** White with black chain design. Bottom stamped "Made Expressly For Santa Fe Dining Car Service". Mfg. Syr..........**250-300**

AT&SFRY- 9 ½" *oval platter* **Black Chain Pattern.** Bottom stamped "Made Expressly For Santa Fe Dining Car Service". Mfg. Syr..**100-125**

AT&SFRY-*dinner plate* **Bleeding Blue Pattern** has Santa Fe in script letters with blue border. Mfg. Mad. **400-450**

AT&SFRY- 9" *rectangular platter* **Bleeding Blue Pattern** has "Santa Fe" in script letters with blue border. Mfg. Mad. **300-350**

AT&SFRY-*water or milk pitcher,* **Bleeding Blue Pattern** has Santa Fe in script letters with blue border. Mfg. Lamberton, Albert Pick Chicago .... ◆

AT&SFRY- *butter pat* **California Poppy Pattern.** White china with yellow poppy floral design. Bottom stamped, "Made Expressly For Santa Fe Dining Car Service". Mfg. Syr. **100-125**

AT&SFRY- *7 ¼" bread plate* **California Poppy Pattern.** Bottom stamped, "Made Expressly For Santa Fe Dining Car Service". Mfg. Syr. **75-85**

AT&SFRY-*coffee cup & saucer* in **California Poppy Pattern.**.Not bottom stamped **100-125**

AT&SFRY-*teapot* in **California Poppy Pattern.** Mfg. Bauscher. Full bottom stamp **300-350**

AT&SFRY-*chocolate pot* in **California Poppy Pattern.** Mfg. Syr. Bottom stamped **200-250**

AT&SRY-*5" fruit bowl* in **California Poppy Pattern. Bottom stamped. Manufacturer Syracuse** **75-85**

AT&SFRY-*gravy boat* in **California Poppy Pattern.** Mfg. Bauscher. Bottom stamped "Made Expressly for Santa Fe Dining Car Service". **350-400**

AT&SFRY-*bread plate* in **California Poppy Pattern.** Mfg. Syr. Not bottom stamped. **35-45**

AT&SFRY-*10" oval platter* in **California Poppy Pattern.** Bottom stamped "Made Expressly For Santa Fe Dining Car Service. Mfg. Bauscher. **150-175**

AT&SFRY-*sugar bowl* with **California Poppy Pattern.** Tree stump design with lid. Mfg. Syr. Not bottom stamped. **150-175**

AT&SFRY-*rectangular platter* in **Columbian Pattern.** White china with scalloped edge and black decoration reads, "Santa Fe Route". Mfg. Haviland .... ◆

AT&SFRY-*dinner plate*, **Columbian Pattern.** White china with scalloped edge and black decoration reads, "Santa Fe". Mfg. Haviland ..... ◆

AT&SFRY- 8" *luncheon plate* in **Griffon Pattern** design. Black on white with gothic designs. Bottom stamped. Mfg. Bauscher 125-150

AT&SFRY- *coffee cup & saucer* in **Griffon Pattern** design.. Mfg. Syracuse. Bottom stamped 200-250

AT&SFRY-*bouillon cup* in **Griffon Pattern** design. Two handles. Bottom stamped. Mfg. Syr. 200-250

AT&SFRY-*dinner plate.* **Mimbreno Pattern.** Mfg. Syr.. Ivory china with red and reddish brown design in Indian motif. Bottom stamped, "Made Expressly For Santa Fe Dining Car Service.". 175-200

AT&SFRY-*creamer* **Mimbreno Pattern.** Mfg. Syr. Bottom stamped, "Made Expressly For Santa Fe Dining Car Service.". 300-350

AT&SFRY-*bouillon cup & saucer.* **Mimbreno Pattern..** Mfg. Syr. Bottom stamped with full bottom stamped design as shown. 250-300

AT&SFRY-*butter pat.* **Mimbreno Pattern.** No bottom stamp 25-35

AT&SFRY-*butter pat* **Mimbreno Pattern.** Mfg. Syr. Bottom stamped, "Made Expressly For Santa Fe" 75-85

AT&SFRY-*gravy boat* **Mimbreno Pattern.** Mfg. Syr. Bottom stamped 250-300

AT&SFRY-*fruit bowl* **Mimbreno Pattern.** Mfg. Syr.. Bottom stamped 100-125

AT&SFRY-*chocolate pot.* **Mimbreno Pattern.** Mfg. Syr. Bottom stamped "Made Expressly for Santa Fe Dining Car Service.". 400-450

AT&SFRY-*teapot.* **Mimbreno Pattern.** Mfg. Syr. Full Bottom stamp 550-600

AT&SFRY-*demi cup & saucer set.* **Mimbreno Pattern.** Mfg. Syr. Bottom stamped. **650-700**

AT&SFRY-*oval celery dish.* **Mimbreno Pattern** Mfg. Syr. Full bottom stamp **125-150**

AT&SFRY-*pedestal ice cream dish.* **Mimbreno Pattern** MFg. Syr. Bottom Stamped **200-250**

AT&SFRY-*7 ¾" luncheon plate* **Mimbreno Pattern.** Mfg. Syr. Full bottom stamp....... **90-100**

ATLANTA & WEST POINT

A&WP- *demi cup & saucer* **West Point Pattern.** White china with grey decoration. No manufacture shown. .... ◆

ATLANTIC COAST LINE

ACL-*butter pat.* **Carolina Pattern.** White china with grey stripes. Bottom stamped. Mfg. Str. **15-20**

ACL- *butter pat* **Flora of the South Pattern.** White china with multi colored floral design. Bottom stamped. Mfg. Buf **100-125**

ACL-*oval bakers dish* **Palmetto Pattern** white china with green decoration & logo on top. Mfg. McNichol Pottery. **175-200**

BALTIMORE & OHIO

B&O-*hot food cover* **Capitol Pattern.** Gold & black band decoration on white china with top marked gold Capitol logo. Measures 6" diameter. Mfg. Sgo. **125-150**

B&O-*cream pitcher* **Capitol Pattern** measures 4 ¼" tall. Mfg. Sgo. **150-175**

B&O-*demi cup & saucer* **Capitol Pattern.** Top marked. Mfg. Scm. **250-300**

B&O- *9" dinner plate* **Capitol Pattern.** Top marked. Mfg. Sgo **125-150**

B&O-*8 ¾" rimmed soup plate* **Capitol Pattern.** Top marked & bottom stamped "B&ORR". Mfg. Syr. **65-75**

B&O- *11 ¼" oval platter* **Capitol Pattern.** Top marked Mfg. Sgo **100-125**

B&O-_gravy boat_ **Capitol Pattern** measures 5". Mfg. Sgo. **125-150**

B&O- _13 ½" oval platter_ **Capitol Pattern.** Top marked. Mfg. Sgo. **150-175**

B&O- _pedestal ice cream dish_ **Capitol Pattern.** Top marked. Mfg. Sgo **90-100**

B&O- _coffee cup & saucer_ **Centenary Pattern.** Blue intricate scenic designs on white china Both pieces bottom stamped. Mfg. Scm. ... **125-150**

B&O-_bread plate_ **Centenary Pattern** measures 6 ¾" diameter. Mfg. Scm. **40-50**

B&O-_12" celery dish_ **Centenary Pattern.** Mfg. Scm. Design Patented. **150-175**

B&O-_cream pitcher_ **Centenary Pattern** measures 3 ½" tall. Blue design on white china. Mfg. Scm. Blue line version **125-150**

B&O- _9" dinner plate_ **Centenary Pattern.** Bottom marked. Mfg. Scm. **100-125**

B&O- _11 ½" oval platter_ **Centenary Pattern.** Bottom stamped Mfg. Scm. Design Patented. **150-175**

B&O-_double egg cup._ **Centenary Pattern.** Blue design on white china. Mfg. Shenango. **Note: Pieces found with the Shenango manufacturers marks may or may not have been used in actual dining car service Many of these pieces were sold through the B&O Museum in later years.** **10-15**

B&O- _pedestal ice cream dish_ **Centenary Pattern.** Bottom stamped. Mfg. Scm. **150-175**

B&O- _11 ½" oval platter_ **Centenary Pattern.** Bottom stamped Mfg. Scm. Design Patented. **150-175**

B&O-_14" oval platter_ **Centenary Pattern.** Bottom stamped. Mfg. Scm. Design Patented. **200-250**

B&O- _5" sauce dish_ **Centenary Pattern.** Mfg. Scm. **30-40**

B&O-_cream pitcher_ **Derby Pattern** measures 4 ¼" tall. Bottom stamped "Made for B&O H. P. Chandlee Sons Co. Baltimore" . Blue floral pattern on white china. Scalloped edge. **250-300**

BOSTON & ALBANY

B&A-*large milk pitcher* **Berkshire Pattern.** Draped border design in yellow & green with orange logo and brown letters. Side marked with logo & bottom stamped. Mfg. Syr. .. **500-550**

B&A- *rimmed 6 ¼" bowl.* **Berkshire Pattern** Top marked with logo and bottom stamped. Mfg. Syr. **90-100**

B&A-*butter pat* **Berkshire Pattern.** Top marked. No mfg. shown **100-125**

BOSTON & MAINE

B&M-*8" oval bowl.* **Bar Harbor Pattern.** White china with black & brown pinstripes and black logo. Top marked. Mfg. Mad. **350-400**

B&M-*10 ½" oval platter.* **Minuteman Pattern** has blue border with standing Minuteman in center. Mfg. Syr. **400-450**

CANADIAN NATIONAL RAILWAY

CNR- *creamer* with handle **Bonaventure Pattern.** White china with wide blue band, yellow pinstripes with logo on side. Mfg. Grindley. **45-55**

CNR- *French style teapot* **Brown Pattern.** Brown china with raised CNR in white on side. Mfg. Limoges or Hall. **100-125**

CNR- *butter pat,* **Continental Pattern.** Yellow china with brown stripes. Bottom stamped "C.N.R.". Mfg. Grindley **10-15**

CNR-*coffee cup & saucer.* **Continental Pattern.** "CNR". Bottom & top marked "C.N.R." Mfg.Grindley **40-50**

CNR-*6 ¼" bread plate* **Continental Pattern.** Top & bottom marked. Mfg. Grindley........ **10-15**

CNR- *handled creamer.* **Jasper Pattern.** White china with multi colored floral design.with gold highlights. Bottom marked "Canadian National System". Mfg. Royal Doulton 150-175

CNR-*9 ½" oval platter* **Windsor Pattern.** White china with brown logo in Maple leaf design with pinstripe. Mfg. Medalta 20-25

CANADIAN PACIFIC RAILWAY

CPR-*coffee cup & saucer* **Maple Leaf Pattern.** White china with multicolored border and top marked "Canadian Pacific". Mfg. Minton 150-175

CENTRAL VERMONT

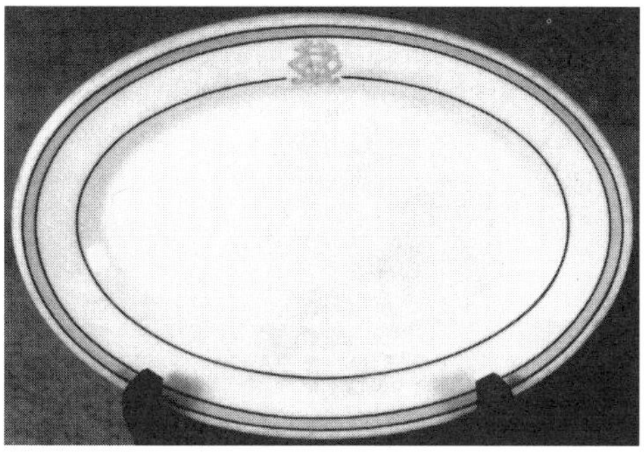

CVRY- *8" oval platter* **Palmer Pattern.** White china with black & green stripes and green intertwined logo. Mfg Myr. .... ◆

CVRY- *6" oval bakers dish* **Palmer Pattern.** Mfg. Myr. .... ◆

CHESAPEAKE & OHIO

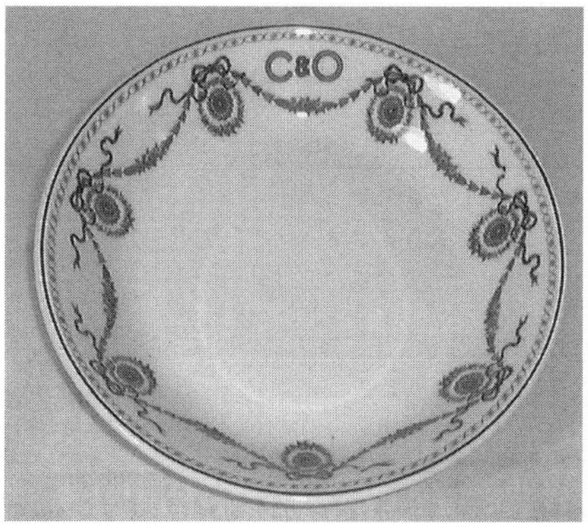

C&ORY-*8" bowl* **Charlottesville Pattern.** White china with brown & green draped design with black bows & ribbons. Mfg. Syr. 125-150

C&ORY-*9 ½" dinner plate* **George Washington Pattern.** White china with gold trim and top marked with portrait of George Washington. Mfg. Buf. 150-175

C&ORY- *handled creamer* **George Washington Pattern.** White china with gold trim. Bottom stamped C&ORY. Mfg. Buf. 75-85

C&ORY- *service plate* **George Washington Pattern.** White china with beautiful ornate wide gold edge and large portrait of George Washington in center. Mfg. Buf. 450-500

CHICAGO & ALTON

C&ARY- *bowl* **Lincoln Pattern.** White china with green & pink squares and green triangle logo. Mfg. Sgo. **300-350**

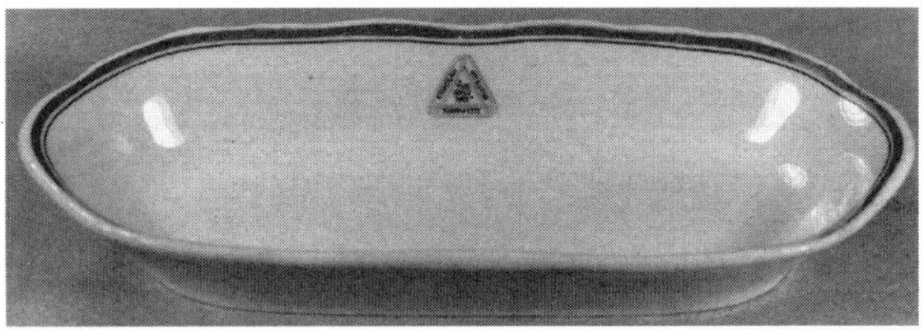

C&ARY- *oval vegetable dish* **Rutledge Pattern.** White china with gold band & black stripe. Logo gold and black triangle. Mfg. Lam. .... ◆

CHICAGO & NORTHWESTERN

C&NW- *service plate* **Flambeau Pattern.** White china with five pinstripes and multi colored streamlined train in center. "The 400" below. Mfg. Sgo. Back stamped. **450-500**

CHICAGO BURLINGTON & QUINCY

CB&Q- *ice cream shell* **Aristocrat Pattern.** White china with BR Box logo in center of black, red & gold stripes. Mfg. Syr **200-250**

CB&Q- *7 ½" bread plate* **Aristocrat Pattern.** Top marked. Mfg. Syr. **100-125**

CB&Q- *10" dinner plate* **Aristocrat Pattern.** Top marked. Mfg. Syr. **275-325**

CB&Q- *coffee cup & saucer* **Aristocrat Pattern.** White china with BR Box logo in center of black, red & gold stripe. Both pieces top marked. Mfg. Syr. **450-500**

CB&Q-*double egg cup* in **Aristocrat Pattern.** Mfg. Syr. **175-200**

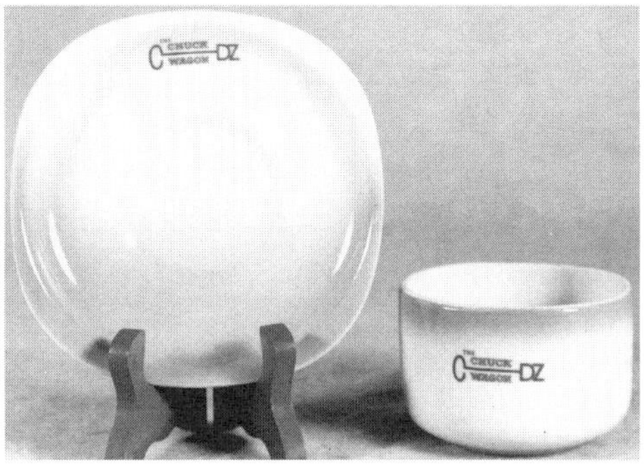

CB&Q- *bouillon cup & saucer* **Chuck Wagon Pattern.** Tan china with darker brown shading. Branding iron design in brown with grey letters reads, "Chuck Wagon" Mfg. Syr. **250-300**

CB&Q- *dinner plate* **Chuck Wagon Pattern.** Top marked. Mfg. Syr. **150-175**

CB&Q-*9 oz Boston style teapot* in **Cobalt Blue Pattern.** Gold decoration shows box logo on cobalt blue teapot. Mfg. Hall. **200-250**

CB&Q- *relish dish* **Dubuque Pattern.** Tan or ivory china with reddish brown CB inside of Q design logo Mfg. Buf. **150-175**

CB&Q- *9" dinner plate* **Dubuque Pattern.** Mfg. Buf. **200-225**

CB&Q-*double handled bouillon cup* **Dubuque Pattern.** Mfg. Buf. **100-125**

CB&Q- *cereal bowl* **Galesburg Pattern.** White china with black letters. Mfg. Greenwood Pottery. Not bottom stamped. **450-500**

CB&Q- *sugar bowl* with lid in **Galesburg Pattern.** Mfg. Greenwood Pottery. .... ◆

CB&Q-*pedestal compote* **Galesburg Pattern.** Mfg. Greenwood Pottery **700-750**

CB&Q-*ice cream shell* **Violets & Daisies Pattern.** White china with purple violets & daisy flowers Mfg. Syr. bottom stamped "CB&QRR" **175-200**

CB&Q-*butter pat* **Violets & Daisies Pattern.** . Bottom stamped "CB&QRR". Mfg. Buffalo. **90-100**

CB&Q-*double egg cup* **Violets & Daisies Pattern.** Mfg. Syr. Not bottom stamped. **75-85**

CB&Q-*9" oval platter.* **Violets & Daisies Pattern.** Not bottom stamped. Mfg. Syr. **65-75**

CB&Q- *5 ½" bread plate* **Zephyr Pattern.** Tan china with silver stripe and box logo. Bottom stamped "Made Expressly For Burlington RR". Mfg. Syr. **350-400**

CHICAGO , INDIANAPOLIS & LOUISVILLE

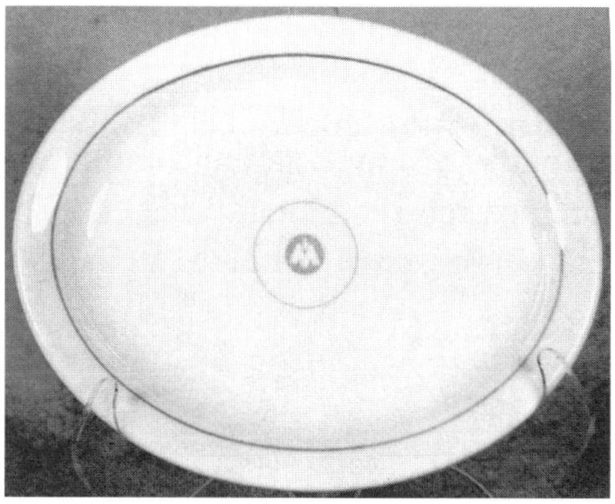

CI&L- (Monon Route) *7" oval plate* **Hoosier Pattern.** White china with red pinstripe and grey-green logo. Mfg. Sgo. **200-250**

CHICAGO MILWAUKEE & PUGET SOUND

CM&PS- *9" oval platter* **Puget Pattern.** White china with dark green stripes and logo decoration. Mfg. Mayer. **150-175**

CHICAGO MILWAUKEE & ST PAUL

CM&STP- *teapot* pattern unnamed at time of printing. Green china with embossed box logo in white on top edge. White beaded border below logo. Mfg. Lovatts Langley Wear, England. .... ◆

CM&STP-*coffee cup & saucer* **Olympian Pattern.** White fine china with gold trim. Inside of cup marked "CM&STP". Saucer marked "The Olympian". Mfg. Limoges....... **125-150**

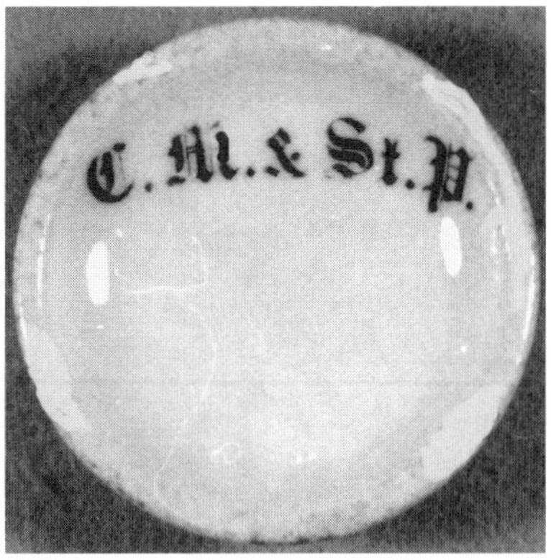

CM&STP-*butter pat* **St. Paul Pattern.** White china with maroon old English script letters "CM&STP" Mfg. Greenwood. **400-450**

CHICAGO MILWAUKEE ST PAUL & PACIFIC

CMSTP&P-*oval vegetable dish* **Galatea Pattern.** White china with blue orange & green design. Bottom stamped "Galatea" and marked "CMSTP&PRR". Mfg. Syr. **175-200**

CMSTP&P-*sugar bowl* **Galatea Pattern.** Bottom stamped Galatea & CMSTP&PRR. Mfg. Syr. **550-600**

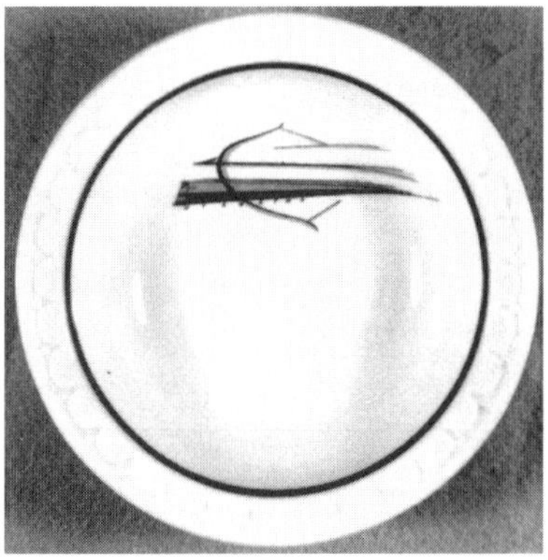

CMSTP&P-*fruit bowl* **Hiawatha Pattern.** White china with blue decoration showing streamline Hiawatha train in art deco design. Bottom stamped. "Designed Expressly for the Hiawatha". Mfg. Syr **300-350**

CMSTP&P-*bouillon cup* **Hiawatha Pattern.** Bottom stamped "Designed Expressly for the Hiawatha". Mfg. Syr **300-350**

CMSTP&P-*cake compote.* **La Crosse Pattern.** White china with green pinstripes. Bottom stamped C.M.St.P&P. Mfg. Warwick. **200-250**

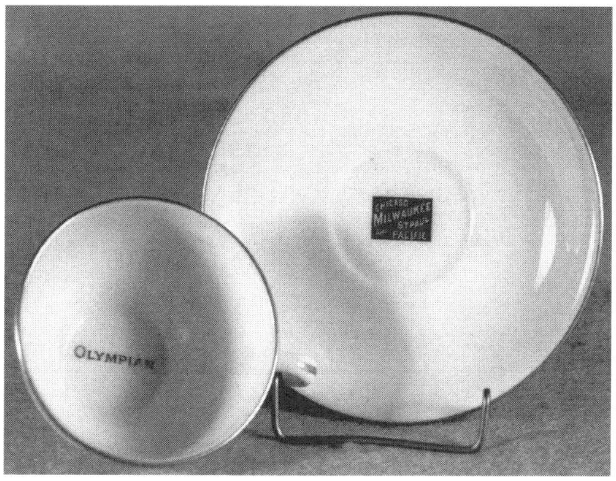

CMSTP&P- *coffee cup & saucer* **Olympian Pattern.** White china with gold box logo and trim. Mfg. Limoges. **90-100**

CMSTP&P-*double egg cup* **Peacock Pattern.** White china with multicolored floral design & peacock, not bottom stamped. Mfg. Syr. **100-125**

CMSTP&P-*butter pat* **Peacock Pattern..** Not bottom stamped. **90-100**

CMSTP&P- *8" oval platter* **Peacock Pattern. Mfg. Syr.** **50-60**

CMSTP&P-*double egg cup* **Traveler Pattern.** White china with pink design & flying geese Not bottom stamped. Mfg. Syr. **75-85**

CMSTP&P-*butter pat* **Traveler Pattern.** . Mfg. Syr **25-35**

CMSTP&P-*coffee cup & saucer* **Traveler Pattern.** No bottom stamp. Mfg. Syr.... **175-200**

CMSTP&P-*demi cup & saucer.* **Traveler Pattern.** White china with pink design & flying geese. Saucer bottom stamped "Designed Expressly For Milwaukee Road Dining Car Service". Mfg. Syr **150-175**

CMSTP&P-*fruit bowl* **Traveler Pattern.** Measures 5" diameter. Mfg. Syr. Not bottom stamped **25-30**

CMSTP&P- *oval platter* **Traveler Pattern.** Measures 8" diameter. Mfg. Syr. Not bottom stamped **40-50**

CMSTP&P- *11 ¼" service plate* **Willow Pattern.** Ornate Chinese design in red on white china plate. Bottom stamped "CMSTP&PRR". Mfg. Buf. **350-400**

CHICAGO ROCK ISLAND & PACIFIC

CRI&P-*demi set* **El Reno Pattern.** White china with red band and logo. Top marked not bottom stamped. Mfg. Sgo. .... ◆

CRI&P- *11 ½" divided dinner plate* **El Reno Pattern.** Top marked . Mfg. Sgo. **500-550**

CRI&P- *7 1/4" bread plate.* **El Reno Pattern.** Top marked, Mfg. Sgo...................... **250-300**

CRI&P- *5 ½" bread plate* **Golden Rocket Pattern.** Ivory china with brownish orange band & logo. Mfg. Sgo. **200-250**

CRI&P-*demi set* **Golden State Pattern.** White china with floral border and two oranges in center over "Golden State" Mfg. Sgo. Not bottom stamped. **450-500**

CRI&P- *9"dinner plate* **Golden State Pattern.** Mfg. Syr. **250-300**

CRI&P-*coffee cup & saucer* **Golden State Pattern.** Mfg. Sgo. Not bottom stamped.............. **300-350**

CRI&P-*sugar bowl* **Golden State Pattern.** Tree trunk style with lid. Mfg. Sgo. Not bottom stamped. **650-700**

CRI&P-*9" oval platter* **Golden State Pattern.** Mfg. Sgo. Not bottom stamped **150-175**

CRI&P-*coffee cup & saucer* **Lasalle Pattern**. White china with green pinstripes and red diamonds with intertwined RI in center. Mfg. Buf. **350-400**

CRI&P-*10" oval platter* **Princeton Pattern**. White china with green & red designed border. Top marked with intertwined "RI" in center. Not bottom marked. Mfg. Syracuse. **100-125**

CRI&P-*8" luncheon plate* in **Sage Green pattern.** White china with red Rocket train near the top and green border. Bottom stamped "CRIRR". Mfg. Buf. .... ◆

CRI&P-*demi cup & saucer* in **Sage Green pattern.** Green with red RI monogram. Top marked with RI logo and bottom stamped "CRIRR". Mfg. Buf. .... ◆

COLORADO & SOUTHERN

C&SRY- *2 ¾" creamer* with handle **Colorado Pattern.** White china with intertwined C&S logo in orange on side. Mfg. UNP. .... ◆

C&SRY- *oval bakers dish* **Colorado Pattern.** Mfg. UNP **200-250**

C&SRY- *11 ½" oval platter* **Colorado Pattern.** Mfg. UNP. **400-450**

C&SRY- *butter pat* **Forks Creek Pattern.** White china with aqua border & intertwined C&S logo. Not bottom marked Mfg. UNP .... ◆

COLORADO MIDLAND RAILWAY

COLORADO MIDLAND RY- *8" oval bowl* **Cascade Pattern**. White china with red & green stripes and red logo. Mfg. Mad. .... ◆

COLORADO MIDLAND RY- *12" oval platter* **Manitou Pattern.** White china with blue decoration and lettering. Top marked. Mfg. Syr. **850-900**

DELAWARE & HUDSON

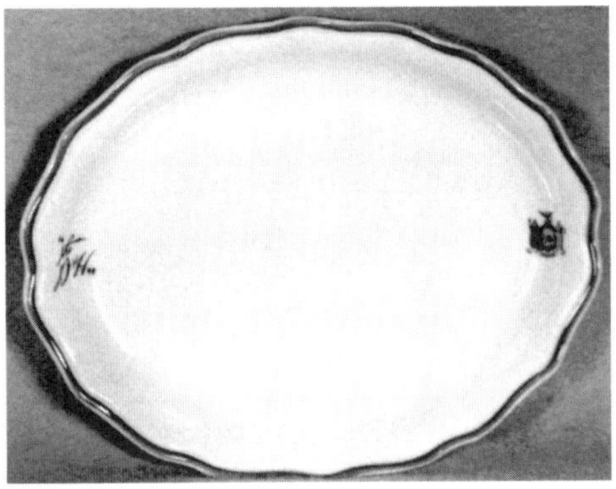

D&H-*9 ¾" oval platter* with scalloped edge. **Adirondack Pattern** White china with blue stripe & logo and multicolored state seal. Top marked. Mfg. Syr. **175-200**

D&H- *9 ¾" oval platter* in **Canterbury Pattern**. White china with D&H shield and orange & red flowers. Mfg. Syr. **175-200**

D&H- *butter pat* **Plattsburg Pattern.** White china with blue stripe and multicolored logo in center. **300-350**

DELAWARE LACKAWANNA & WESTERN

DL&W- *handled creamer* **St. Albans Pattern.** White china with green stripes and orange & blue flowers. Mfg. Syr. Bottom stamped "DL&WRR CO". **400-450**

DENVER & RIO GRANDE RAILROAD

D&RGRR-*8" pedestal compote* **Curecanti Pattern.** White china with brown & black pinstripes and Curecanti logo. Mfg. Syr. .... ◆

D&RGRR- *5 ¾"oval bakers dish* **Curecanti Pattern** in center. Mfg. Syr. 400-450

D&RGRR- *13 ½" oval platter* **Curecanti Pattern.** Mfg. Syr. 375-425

D&RGRR- *12 ¼" rectangular platter* **Curecanti Pattern.** Mfg. Syr. 350-400

D&RGRR- *demi cup & saucer* **Curecanti Pattern.** Mfg. Syr. .... ◆

DENVER & RIO GRANDE WESTERN

D&RGWRR-*creamer* **Mainline Pattern.** Side marked with logo. White china with red & gold Mainline logo. Business car use. Mfg. Str. 175-200

D&RGWRR-*coffee cup & saucer* **Mainline Pattern.** Both pieces top marked. Mfg. Str. 100-125

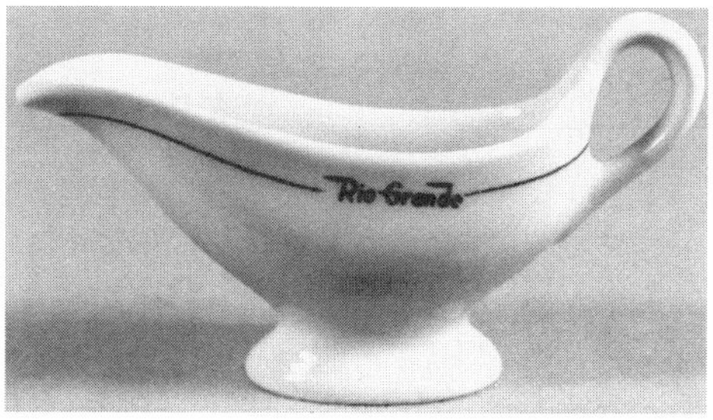

D&RGWRR- *gravy boat* **Prospector Pattern.** White china with blue stripes and "Rio Grande" speed lettering. Mfg. Syr. 175-200

D&RGWRR- *coffee cup & saucer* **Prospector Pattern.** Top marked. Dolphin style cup. Mfg. Syr. 175-200

D&RGWRR- *9" dinner plate* **Prospector Pattern.** Top marked. Mfg. Syr. 100-125

D&RGWRR *demi cup & saucer* **Prospector Pattern.** Both pieces top marked. Mfg. Syr. 250-300

D&RGWRR- *6 ¾" rimmed bowl* **Prospector Pattern.** Top marked. Mfg. Syr. 35-45

D&RGWRR- *7" oval platter* **Prospector Pattern.** Top marked. Mfg. Syr. 50-60

ERIE RAILROAD

ERIE- *15" oval platter* **Chautauqua Pattern.** White china with black diamond logo. Mfg. Greenwood Pottery 400-450

ERIE- *8 ¾" rectangular platter* **Gould Pattern.** White china with pink floral border and gold ribbon. Top marked ERIE in script letters. Mfg. Sgo. **150-175**

ERIE- *10" scalloped edge vegetable tray* **Gould Pattern.** Mfg. Limoges **175-200**

ERIE- *demi cup & saucer* **Starucca Pattern.** White china with blue pinstripes and Erie Diamond Both pieces top marked. Mfg. Syr. **400-450**

ERIE-*single egg cup* **Starucca Pattern.** Top marked No mfg.shown. **200-250**

ERIE-*coffee cup*. **Susquehanna Pattern.** White china with blue & orange colored band with Diamond logo. Mfg. Buf. **100-125**

ERIE-*10" oval vegetable dish* **Susquehanna Pattern.** Mfg. Buf. **90-100**

FLORIDA EAST COAST

FEC-*boullion cup* **Mistic Pattern.** White china with blue gray border. Mfg. Syr. Bottom stamped "FECRY" **125-150**

FEC-*creamer with handle* in **Mistic Pattern.** White china with blue gray border. Mfg. Syr. Bottom stamped "FECRY". **200-250**

FRED HARVEY

FRED HARVEY- *dinner plate* **Cactus Logo Pattern.** Tan china with brown cactus design & Fred Harvey through center. Mfg. Syr. **200-250**

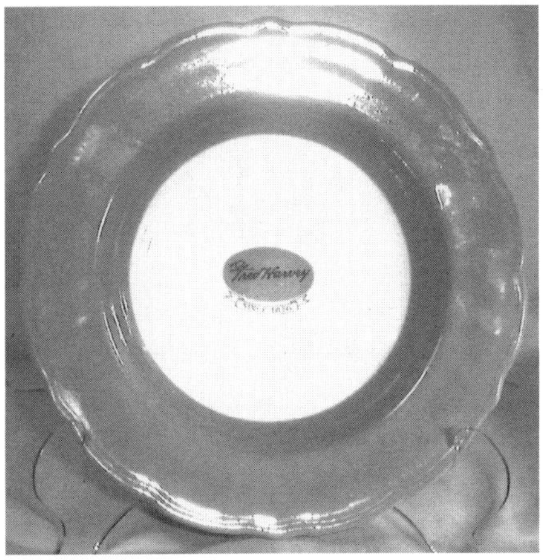

FRED HARVEY-*9 ¼" soup bowl* with scalloped edge **Gold Lion Pattern** White china with grey border & "Fred Harvey" in center. Mfg. Syr. **100-125**

FRED HARVEY- *coffee cup* **Harvey Girl Pattern.** White china with Harvey Girl in black on side. Mfg. Jackson. 100-125

FRED HARVEY-*5" cereal bowl* **Southwest Pattern.** White china with rust & black pinstripes & "FH" in center of rust colored circle. 200-250

GREAT NORTHERN RAILWAY

GNRY-*double egg cup* **Empire Pattern** Tan china with dark brown vine border. Bottom marked "GNRY" Mfg. Syr. 250-300

GNRY-*bread plate* **Empire Pattern.** Tan china with dark brown vine border. Bottom marked "GNRY". Mfg. Syr. 175-200

GNRY-*bread plate* **Glory of the West Pattern.** White china showing mountain scenes in green & gray tones. Mfg. Syr. Bottom stamped. 50-60

GNRY-*7" oval platter* **Glory of the West Pattern.** MFg. Syr. Bottom stamped......... 55-65

GNRY-*footed bowl* **Hill Pattern.** White china with intertwined GN in beige with rust outline Side marked. Mfg. Sgo. 250-300

GNRY-*8" oval platter* **Hill Pattern..** Mfg. Sgo. No bottom stamp................. 200-250

GNRY-*gravy boat* **Hill Pattern.** Side marked. No bottom stamp.......... 400-450

GNRY- *5 ¼" sauce dish* **Mountains & Flowers Pattern.** White china with with floral & mountain design.Bottom stamped "Great Northern Railway" . Mfg. Syr.............................. 35-45

GNRY-*ashtray* **Mountains & Flowers Pattern.** Bottom stamped "Great Northern Ry.". Mfg. Syr 65-75

GNRY- *7 ½" bowl* **Mountains & Flowers Pattern.** Bottom stamped. Mfg. Syr. 65-75

GNRY-*creamer* with handle **Oriental Pattern.** White china with multicolored floral pattern. Mfg. Syr Not bottom stamped 150-175

GNRY- *8"childs plate* **Rocky Pattern.** White china with multicolored costumed animals around edge. GN logo in center. Mfg. Syr. 750-850

GNRY-*childs cup* **Rocky Pattern.** Side marked with GN logo. Mfg. Syr 600-700

GNRY-*cereal bowl* **Rocky Pattern.** Side marked with GN logo. Mfg. Syr. Not bottom stamped. 600-700

GULF MOBILE & OHIO

GM&O- *teapot* **Rose Pattern.** White china with pink border & logo on side. Mfg. Syr. 700-800

GM&O- *demi cup & saucer* **Rose Pattern..** Mfg. Syr. 700-800

GM&O-*4 ½" fruit bowl* **Rose Pattern.** Top marked. Mfg. Syr. 70-80

ILLINOIS CENTRAL RAILROAD

ICRR-*coffee cup & saucer* **Coral Pattern.** White china with Salmon pink background. Mfg. Syr. Not bottom stamped. 40-50

ICRR-*6 ¼" bread plate* **Coral Pattern** Mfg. Syr. Not bottom stamped 20-30

ICRR-*fruit bowl* **Coral Pattern.** Not bottom stamped. Mfg. Syr. 20-30

ICRR- *service plate* **French Quarter Pattern. "Fan Window In Clairbourne Court, Toulouse Street"** Bottom stamped "Illinois Central System" Mfg. Bsh. **650-700**

ICRR-*service plate* **French Quarter Pattern. "Pirate Alley New Orleans"** . Mfg. Bsh. Bottom stamped "Illinois Central System" **650-700**

ICRR *service plate* **French Quarter Pattern. "Arts & Crafts Patio Royal Street New Orleans"** Not bottom stamped. Mfg. Bsh **650-700**

ICRR-*creamer* with handle **Louisiane Pattern.** White with black & orange stripes and black IC logo. Mfg. Sgo. **200-250**

ICRR-*11" oval platter* **Louisiane Pattern.** Top marked. Mfg. Bauscher. **175-200**

LEHIGH VALLEY RAILROAD

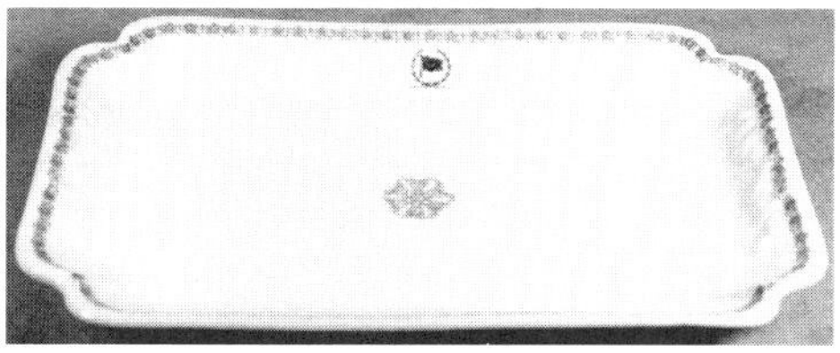

LVRR- *13 ½" rectangular platter* in **Asa Packer Pattern.** White china with blue flowers and green leaves with LV in center of wreath with flag. Bottom stamped. Mfg. Limoges .... ◆

LOUISVILLE & NASHVILLE

L&NRR-*demi cup & saucer* **Regent Pattern.** White china with multicolored band and flowers. Mfg. Syr. Not bottom stamped. **100-125**

L&NRR- *creamer* 3" tall in **Regent Pattern..** Mfg. Syr. Not bottom stamped. **40-50**

MAINE CENTRAL

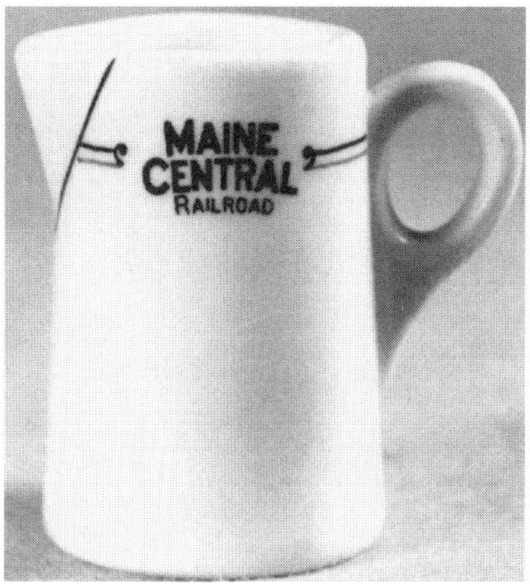

MCRR-*handled creamer* in **Kennebec Pattern.** White china with black & red pinstripes and MCRR logo in black. Mfg. Syr. **400-450**

MINNEAPOLIS ST PAUL & SAULT STE MARIE

MSTP&SSM-(Soo Line) *double egg cup* in **Logan Pattern.** White china with multicolored floral design. Bottom stamped "Soo Line". Mfg. Mayer 150-175

MSTP&SSM-(Soo Line) *handled creamer* in **Logan Pattern.** Bottom stamped "Soo Line". Mfg. Mayer.. 450-500

MSTP&SSM (Soo Line) *8" bread plate* in **Logan Pattern.** Bottom stamped. "Soo Line". Mfg. Lam. 90-100

MISSOURI PACIFIC RAILROAD

MP-*butter pat* **Bismark Pattern.** White china with black & orange pinstripes with "Missouri Pacific" in black. Mfg. Bauscher. 275-325

MP-*gravy boat* **Eagle Pattern.** White china with yellow & black stripes & black Eagle logo. Not bottom stamped. Mfg. Syr. 300-350

MP- *sauce dish* in **Eagle Pattern.** Top marked and bottom stamped "Missouri Pacific". Mfg. Syr. 25-35

MP-*7" oval platter* **Eagle Pattern.** Top marked & bottom stamped. "Missouri Pacific" Mfg. Syr. 40-50

MP-*double egg cup* **St. Albans Pattern.** White china with green stripes and blue & orange floral pattern. Bottom stamped "Missouri Pacific". Mfg. Syr. 175-200

MP-*7 ¼" bread plate* **St. Albans Pattern..** Bottom stamped "Missouri Pacific". Mfg. Syr. 75-85

MP-*11" oval platter* **St. Albans Pattern.** Bottom stamped "Missouri Pacific". Mfg. Syr. 100-125

MP-*service plate* in **State Capitols Pattern.** White china with state capitols around outer edge and Diesel engine in center. Top marked "Route of the Eagles".Bottom stamped "Missouri Pacific Lines" Mfg. Syr. **300-350**

MP- *service plate* in **State Flowers Pattern.** White china with different flowers around edge and steam engine in center. Very colorful. Top marked "Missouri Pacific Lines. Mfg. Syr. **225-275**

MP- *service plate* **Sunshine Special Pattern.** White china with colorful blossoms around edge. Top reads, "The Sunshine Special". Colorful center design. Mfg. Syr. **750-800**

NEW YORK CENTRAL

NYC- *bread plate* **Century Pattern.** White china with grey decoration. Bottom stamped New York Central. Mfg. Buf. **300-350**

NYC-*bread plate* **Century Pattern.** White china with wide grey border and decoration. Bottom stamped New York Central. Mfg. Buf. **250-300**

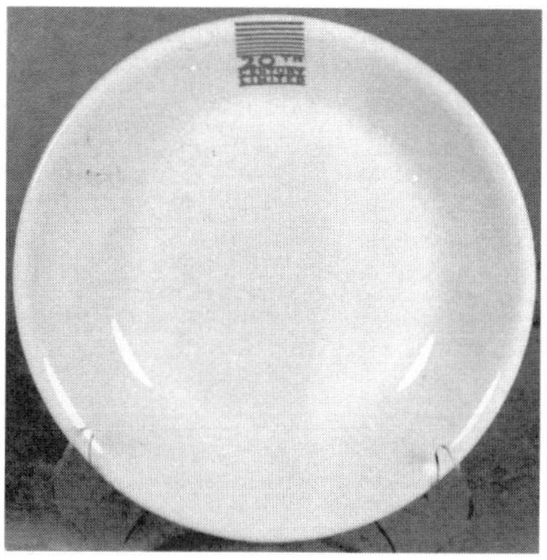

NYC- *7½" cereal bowl* **Century Pattern.** White china with grey decoration and 8 stripes. Bottom stamped New York Central. Mfg. Buf. **250-300**

NYC-*gravy boat* **Dewitt Clinton Pattern.** White china with floral design in brown & blue & gray tones. Mfg. Syr. Bottom stamped "New York Central Lines" **150-175**

NYC-*soup bowl* **Dewitt Clinton Pattern.** Mfg. Syr. Bottom stamped, New York Central Lines. ... **60-70**

NYC- *single egg cup* with pedestal base **Dewitt Clinton Pattern** .No mfg. shown. **100-125**

NYC-*creamer* with handle in **Dewitt Clinton Pattern.** Mfg. Syr. Bottom stamped. ... **65-75**

NYC-*creamer* **Hudson Pattern.** White china with green & tan vine design. Bottom stamped "New York Central Lines". Mfg. Lim. **200-250**

NYC-*10 ¼" rectangular platter* **Hudson Pattern.** Bottom stamped New York Central Lines. Mfg. Limoges **100-125**

NYC- *square butter pat* **Hudson Pattern.** Bottom stamped New York Central Lines. Mfg. Lim. **100-125**

NYC-*10 ¼" rectangular platter* **Hudson Pattern.** Bottom stamped New York Central Lines. Mfg. Lim. **100-125**

NYC-*square butter pat* **Hyde Park Pattern.** . White china with pink flowers and gold highlights. Bottom stamped New York Central Lines. Mfg. Lim. **100-125**

NYC- *handled creamer* **Hyde Park Pattern** Bottom stamped New York Central Lines. Mfg. Lim. **200-250**

NYC- *8 ¾" rectangular platter* **Hyde Park Pattern.** Bottom stamped "New York Central Lines". Mfg. Lim. **75-85**

NYC-*5 ½" bowl* **Mercury Pattern.** White china with dark brown NYC and stripes. Top marked & bottom stamped "New York Central". Mfg. Syr. **60-70**

NYC-*coffee cup & saucer* **Mercury Pattern.** Both pieces top marked & bottom stamped "New York Central". Mfg. Syr. **100-125**

NYC- *9 ½" dinner plate* **Pacemaker Pattern.** White china with gray NYC and stripes. Top marked & bottom stamped. Mfg. Syr. . **70-80**

NEW YORK CENTRAL & HUDSON RIVER

NYC&HRRR- *6 "footed bowl* **Harmon Pattern.** White china with green vine and logo. Mfg. Syr. **400-450**

NEW YORK CHICAGO & ST. LOUIS AKA NICKLE PLATE ROAD

NYC&STL (Nickel Plate) *bouillon cup* in **Bellevue Pattern.** White china with blue pinstripes and logo. Top marked. Mfg. Walker. **90-100**

NYC&STL (Nickel Plate) *9" dinner plate in* **Bellevue Pattern.** White china with blue pinstripes and logo. Top marked. Mfg. Walker **80-90**

NYC&STL (Nickel Plate) *bread plate* in **Bellevue Pattern.** White china with blue pinstripes and logo. Top marked. Mfg. Walker **50-60**

NYC&STL- (Nickel Plate) *oval bakers dish* **Cleveland Pattern.** White china with green decoration. Top marked. Mfg. Syr. **350-400**

NYC&STL-(Nickel Plate) *2" creamer* in **Fort Wayne Pattern.** White china with cobalt blue and silver band. Top marked."Nickel Plate". Mfg. Syr. **150-175**

NYC&STL-(Nickel Plate) *6 1/4" bread plate in* **Fort Wayne Pattern.** White china with cobalt blue and silver band. Top marked "Nickel Plate" Mfg. Syr. **175-200**

NYC&STL-(Nickel Plate) *demi cup & saucer in* **Fort Wayne Pattern.** White china with cobalt blue and silver band. Top marked "Nickel Plate" Mfg. Syr. .... ◆

NEW YORK NEW HAVEN & HARTFORD

NYNH&H- *beanpot* in **Beantown Pattern**. Tan & brown with black NH logo on side. **90-100**

NYNH&H-*7" plate* **Indian Tree Pattern.** White china with brown border and multicolored design around edges and center. Bottom stamped "NYNH&HRR CO". Mfg. Sgo. **65-75**

NYNH&H-*9" dinner plate.* **Indian Tree Pattern.** Bottom stamped, "NYNH&HRR.CO" Mfg. Sgo. **100-125**

NYNH&H- *11 ½" oval platter.* **Indian Tree Pattern.** Bottom stamped. "NYNH&HRR CO" Mfg. Sgo. **90-100**

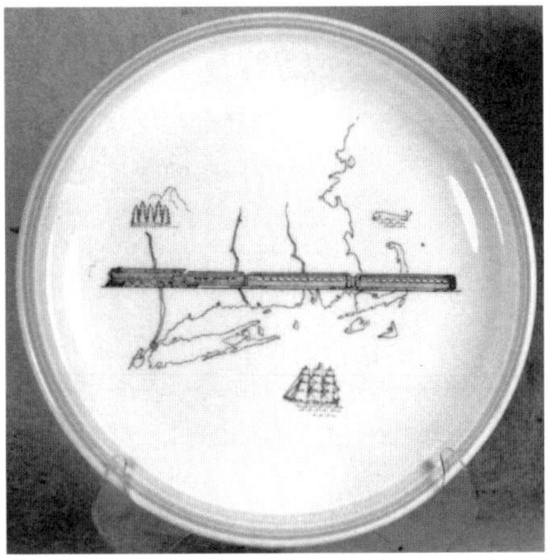

NYNH&H- *8 ½" luncheon plate* in **Merchants Pattern.** Ivory china plate with white & gray border, red map with train in center. Bottom stamped "NYNH&HRR". Mfg. Buf ... **60-70**

NYNH&H-*2 ¼" creamer* **Platinum Blue Pattern.** Light blue with white Greek figure. Side marked & bottom stamped "NYH&HRR CO" Mfg. Scm. **90-100**

NYNH&H-*bouillon cup* **Platinum Blue Pattern.** Bottom stamped "NYNH&HRR CO" Mfg. Buf. **45-55**

NORFOLK & WESTERN

N&W-*demi cup & saucer* **Cavalier Pattern.** White china with brown & green floral band & intertwined N&W Mfg. Lam. **400-450**

N&W- *bouillon cup* **Cavalier Pattern..** Not bottom marked. Mfg. Lam **40-50**

N&W- *8" oval platter* **Cavalier Pattern.** White china with brown & green floral band & intertwined N&W on top. Mfg. Lam. **90-100**

NORTHERN PACIFIC

NP-*11 1/4" oval platter* in **Garnet Pattern.** White china with purple floral band and green leaves. Backstamped with NP Monad logo. Mfg.Hav. **250-300**

NP *coffee cup & saucer* **Monad Pattern.** Saucer top marked with logo. Cup has orange & green bands no logo. Mfg. Sgo. **150-175**

NP- *7 ¼" plate* in **Monad Pattern.** Ivory china with green & orange stripes with red & black NP Monad logo on top. Mfg. Sgo. **50-60**

NP- *5" fruit bowl* **Monad Pattern.** Not bottom stamped. Mfg. Sgo. **35-45**

NP-*teapot* in **Verde Green Pattern.** Green with side marked Yellowstone Park logo in gold Mfg. Hall **400-450**

NP-*hot water pot* in **Verde Green Pattern.** Green with side marked Yellowstone Park logo in gold. Mfg. Hall **325-375**

NP-*footed compote* **Yellowstone Pattern.** Ivory china with yellow & green stripes and black Monad Yellowstone Park logo. Mfg. Sgo **400-450**

NP-*6 ½" bowl* **Yellowstone Pattern.** Ivory china with yellow & green stripes and black Monad Yellowstone Park logo. Mfg. Sgo. **100-125**

PENNSYLVANIA RAILROAD

PRR- *6 ½" rimmed bowl* **Broadway Pattern.** Base color ivory with brown stripes and multi-colored shades. Bottom stamped PRR keystone logo. Mfg. Scm. **25-35**

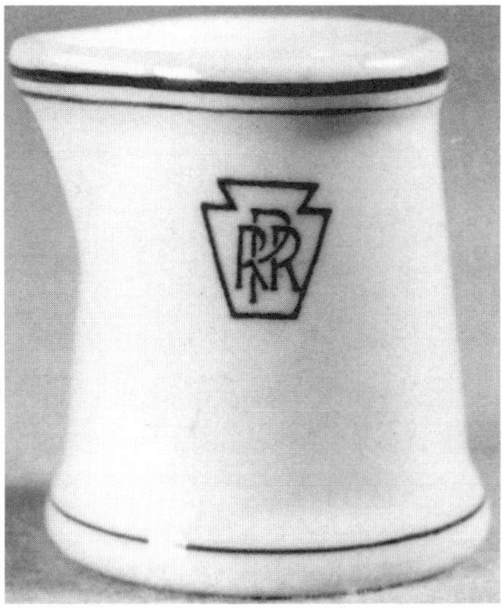

PRR-*creamer* 2 ½" in **Keystone Pattern.** Tan china with dark brown pinstripes and keystone logo on side. Mfg. Scm. **100-125**

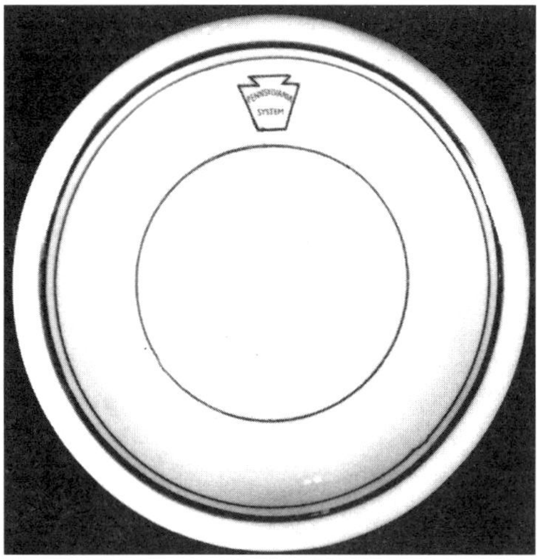

PRR- *butter pat* **Liberty Pattern.** White china with red pinstripes and red "Pennsylvania System" logo on top.Top marked, but not bottom stamped. **100-125**

PRR-*compote with pedestal base* in **Liberty Pattern.** Mfg. Syr. **175-200**

PRR-*9 ½" dinner plate* in **Mountain Laurel Pattern.** White china with green border and floral design. Bottom stamped with PRR keystone logo. Mfg. Syr. **50-60**

PRR- *pedestal compote* in **Purple Laurel Pattern.** White china with reddish brown pinstripes and multicolored floral band. Bottom stamped PRR logo. Mfg. Str. **150-175**

PITTSBURGH & LAKE ERIE

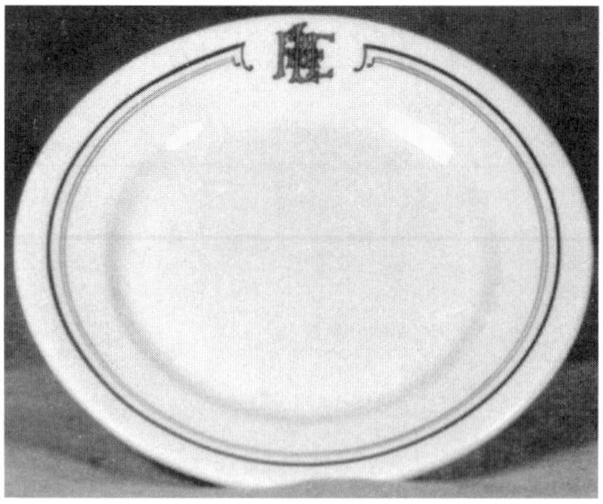

P&LE- *8 ¼" plate* **Youngstown Pattern.** White china with green & brown stripes and green intertwined letters. Mfg. Myr. **200-250**

PULLMAN

PULLMAN- *creamer with handle* **Calumet Pattern.** White china with black &red pinstripes and "Pullman" in black. Measures 4" tall. **150-175**

PULLMAN- *creamer* without handle . **Calumet Pattern.** White china with black &red pinstripes and "Pullman" in black. Measures 4" tall. **100-125**

PULLMAN-*creamer with handle* in **Indian Tree Pattern.** White china with brown border and multicolored design around edge. Side marked "PULLMAN". **100-125**

PULLMAN- *butter pat* **Indian Tree Pattern.** Top marked "Pullman" Mfg. Syr. **90-100**

PULLMAN- *pedestal egg cup* **Indian Tree Pattern.** Side marked. "Pullman". **125-150**

PULLMAN-*9" dinner plate* **Indian Tree Pattern.** Top marked "Pullman". Mfg. Syr. **200-250**

PULLMAN-*5" sauce dish* **Indian Tree Pattern.** White china with brown border and multicolored design around edge. Top marked "PULLMAN". **75-85**

PULLMAN *creamer no handle* on **Indian Tree Pattern.** Side marked "PULLMAN". ... **75-85**

PULLMAN- *cup & saucer* in **Indian Tree Pattern.** Top marked "PULLMAN". Mfg. Syr...... **250-300**

PULLMAN-*7 ½" plate* in **Indian Tree Pattern.** Top marked "Pullman". Mfg. Syr.. .... **30-40**

RICHMOND FREDERICKSBURG & POTOMAC

RF&P-*5 ½" fruit bowl* **Tri Link Pattern.** White china with orange stripes and black & orange zipper designed border with black & orange triangular RF&P logo top marked. Mfg. Syr. **350-400**

SAN PEDRO LOS ANGELES & SALT LAKE

SPLA&SL- *11 ½" oval platter* **Harriman Blue Pattern.** White china with blue vine border top marked with Salt Lake Route logo. Mfg. Mad. **375-425**

SPLA&SL-*gravy boat* in **Harriman Blue Pattern.** Top marked with Salt Lake Route logo. Mfg. Mad **500-550**

SPLA&SL- *10" oval celery dish* **Harriman Blue Pattern.** Top marked. Mfg. Mad **400-450**

SOUTHERN RAILWAY

SRY- *demi cup & saucer* **Peach Blossom Pattern.** White china with orange & blue pinstripes with brown & orange SR logo.Both pieces top marked. Mfg. Buf. **300-350**

SRY- *5 ¾" fruit bowl* **Peach Blossom Pattern.** Top marked. Mfg. Buf...................... **100-125**

SRY- *demi cup & saucer* in **Piedmont Pattern.** White with blue & yellow pinstripes. Bottom stamped "Southern Railway". Mfg. Str. ... **65-75**

SOUTHERN PACIFIC RAILROAD

SP-*9" dinner plate* **Golden State Pattern.** White china with multicolored vine design and top marked with two oranges & reads, "Golden State". Bottom stamped "Southern Pacific". Mfg. Syracuse. **450-500**

SP- *9 ¼" dinner plate* **Harriman Blue Pattern.** White china with blue decoration and logo. Mfg. Mad. **200-250**

SP- *2 ¾" handled creamer* in **Imperial Pattern.** White china with floral band and two oranges on side. Bottom stamped. Mfg. Mad. **400-450**

SP-*9 ¼" dinner plate* in **Prairie Mountain Wildflower Pattern..** Full bottom stamp "Southern Pacific Lines". Mfg. Syr. **125-150**

SP- *bouillon cup* **Prairie Mountain Wildflower Pattern.** Full bottom stamp"Southern Pacific Lines".. Mfg. Syr. **50-60**

SP- *7 ¼" bread plate* **Prairie Mountain Wildflower Pattern.** Full Bottom stamp"Southern Pacific Lines".. Mfg. Syr. **35-45**

SP- *oval divided dinner plate* **Prairie Mountain Wildflower Pattern.** White china with black pinstripe and multi colored wild flowers Full bottom stamp "Southern Pacific Lines". Mfg. Syr. **250-300**

SP- *coffee cup & saucer* in **Prairie Mountain Wildflower Pattern.** Both pieces bottom stamped "Southern Pacific Lines". Mfg. Syr. **100-125**

SP-*pedestal egg cup* **Prairie Mountain Wildflower Pattern.** Bottom stamped"Southern Pacific Lines". Mfg. Syr. **250-300**

SP- *3 ½" handled creamer* in **Sunset Pattern.** White china with green pinstripe with green & white floral band and multicolored Sunset Logo. Mfg. Sgo **250-300**

SP-*coffee cup & saucer* in **Sunset Pattern..** Large flower version. Mfg. Sgo. **350-400**

UNION PACIFIC RAILROAD

UP- *double egg cup* **Challenger Pattern.** Tan with brown & yellow lettering. Top marked "The Challenger". Mfg. Syr. **75-85**

UP-*coffee cup & saucer* **Challenger Pattern.** Top marked & bottom stamped. Mfg. Syr. **100-125**

UP-*10" dinner plate* **Challenger Pattern.** Top marked & bottom stamped. Mfg. Sgo. . **75-85**

UP-*5 ¼" fruit bowl* **Challenger Pattern.** Top marked "The Challenger". Mfg. Syr. **20-25**

UP-*9 ¾" oval platter* **Challenger Pattern.** Top marked "The Challenger". Mfg. Syr. **40-50**

UP-*10" oval platter* in **Columbine Pattern.** White china with wide black band green pinstripes with hand painted Columbine flowers. Bottom stamped with "Columbine The State Flower Colorado" Mfg. Syr. **300-350**

UP-*ice cream shell* **Columbine Pattern.**. Bottom stamped with "Columbine The State Flower Colorado". Mfg. Syracuse. **600-650**

UP- *7 ¼" bread plate* **Columbine Pattern.** Bottom stamped with "Columbine The State Flower Colorado" Mfg. Syr. **200-225**

UP-*butter pat* **Columbine Pattern.** Bottom stamped with "Columbine the State Flower Colorado" **700-800**

UP-*demi cup & saucer* **Columbine Pattern.** Both pieces bottom stamped with "Columbine the State Flower Colorado" Mfg. Syr. .... ◆

UP- *service plate* in **Cobalt Blue Service.** White china with wide cobalt blue band & gold modern UP Shield logo & stripes. Business car use. **100-125**

UP-*demi cup & saucer* **Corporate Pattern.** White china with blue & gold stripes and modern shield logo surrounded by floral design. Mfg. Sterling. Business car use **100-125**

UP-*coffee cup & saucer* **Corporate Pattern.** Mfg. Str. **65-75**

UP-*egg cup* with pedestal base in **Desert Flower Pattern.** White china with large green flowers. Bottom stamped. Mfg. Syr. **65-75**

UP-*cup & saucer* in **Desert Flower Pattern.** Bottom stamped. Mfg. Syr. **100-125**

UP-*demi cup & saucer* in **Desert Flower Pattern.** Bottom stamped. Mfg. Syr....... **175-200**

UP-*rimmed bowl* in **Desert Flower Pattern.** Bottom stamped Mfg. Syr. **35-45**

UP-*creamer* with handle in **Desert Flower Pattern.** White china with large green flowers. Bottom stamped "Union Pacific RR". Mfg. Syr. **100-125**

UP- *10 ½" dinner plate* **Desert Flower Pattern.** Bottom stamped. Mfg. Syr. **65-75**

UP *creamer with handle* in **Harriman Blue Pattern.** . White china with blue edge design & side marked with Overland Shield logo in blue. Mfg. Mad **600-650**

UP-*10 ¾" oval bowl* **Harriman Blue Pattern** Top marked with Overland Shield logo. Mfg. Mad. **150-175**

UP- *bouillon cup* **Harriman Blue Pattern.** Bottom stamped with UP Overland Shield. .. **20-30**

UP-*butter pat* **Harriman Blue Pattern.** White china with blue edge design. Bottom marked with UP Overland Shield logo. **90-100**

UP- *pedestal teacup* in **Harriman Blue Pattern.** Bottom marked with UP Overland Shield logo. Mfg. Mad **200-225**

UP-*9" dinner plate* **Harriman Blue Pattern.** Bottom marked with UP Overland logo. Mfg. Maddock. 75-85

UP- *pedestal egg cup* in **Harriman Blue Pattern.** Bottom marked with UP Overland logo Mfg. Mad. **125-150**

UP-*hot cocoa cup* in **Harriman Blue Pattern.** Bottom marked with UP Overland Shield logo. Mfg. Mad. **100-125**

UP- *butter pat* **Historical Pattern.** White china with red & blue shield and several different scenes form outer band This version has 11 different scenes around out edge. Top marked. **350-400**

UP-*butter pat* **Historical Pattern.** This version has 21 different scenes around outer edge. Top marked. Bottom stamped. Mfg. Sgo. **400-450**

UP- *7 ¼" bread plate* **Historical Pattern..** Bottom stamped "Union Pacific RR ". Mfg. Sgo. **150-175**

UP- *coffee cup & saucer* **Historical Pattern.** Both pieces top marked & bottom stamped "Union Pacific RR" . Mfg. Sgo. **450-500**

UP-*8" oval platter* **Historical Pattern.** Top marked & bottom stamped"Union Pacific RR" Mfg. Sgo. **275-300**

UP-*relish tray* **Historical Pattern.** Bottom stamped. "Union Pacific RR" Mfg. Syr.. .... **300-350**

UP- *8 ½" oval platter* **in Overland Pinstripes Pattern.** Top marked "The Overland Route". Color white china with green & red stripes and green lettering. Mfg. Mad. .... ◆

UP-*demi cup & saucer* **Portland Rose Pattern.** Ivory china with pink roses & green leaves. Bottom marked with shield that reads, "Portland Rose" over "For You A Rose In Portland Grows". Mfg. Syr. **800-900**

UP- *9" dinner plate* **Portland Rose Pattern.** Bottom marked with shield that reads,"Portland Rose" over "For You a Rose in Portland Grows" Mfg. Syr. **300-350**

UP-*pedestal ice cream or sherbert dish.* **Winged Streamliner Pattern.** White china with gold design & red or green highlights. Logo is art deco design showing streamlined train with wings Mfg. Scm. . Not bottom stamped. **40-50**

UP-*butter pat* **Winged Streamliner Pattern..** Not bottom stamped. Mfg. Syracuse. ... **20-25**

UP- *bouillon cup* **Winged Streamliner Pattern.** Not bottom stamped. Mfg. Syr. **20-30**

UP-*coffee cup & saucer* **Winged Streamliner Pattern.** Mfg. Str. 75-85

UP-*creamer with handle* **Winged Streamliner Pattern.** Mfg. Str. **100-125**

UP-*demi set* **Winged Steamliner Pattern.** Mfg. Str. **60-70**

UP-*10 ¾" dinner plate* **Winged Streamliner Pattern.** Mfg. Str. **65-75**

UP -*5" fruit bowl* **Winged Streamliner Pattern.** Mfg. Str. **20-25**

UP-*ice cream shell* **Winged Streamliner Pattern.** Mfg. Str. Not bottom stamped **40-50**

UP-*coffee cup & saucer* **Zion Pattern.** Tan china with multi colored hand painted design. Both pieces bottom stamped UPRR. Mfg. Sgo. **400-450**

UP- *7 ¼" bread plate* **Zion Pattern.** Bottom stamped UPRR. Mfg. Sgo. **200-250**

UINTAH RAILWAY

UINTAH RAILWAY-*butter pat* **Uintah Pattern.** White china with black decoration. Mfg. OPC. **350-400**

UINTAH RAILWAY- *demi cup & saucer* **Uintah Pattern.** White china with black decoration. . 700-800

UINTAH RAILWAY- *pedestal compote* **Uintah Pattern.** Mfg. OPC. 750-850

UINTAH RAILWAY- *pedestal egg cup* **Uintah Pattern.** .... ◆

VICKSBURG SHREVEPORT & PACIFIC

VS&P -*6 ¼ "rimmed bowl* **Vicksburg Pattern.** White china with rust colored stripes and Vicksburg Route logo on top edge. Mfg. Scammell 350-400

VS&P- *demi cup & saucer* in **Vicksburg Pattern.** Mfg. Scammell .... ◆

WABASH RAILWAY

WABASH- *coffee cup & saucer* in **Banner Pattern.** White china with grey border and red stripes with red & blue flag logo Mfg. Syr. 250-300

WABASH-*creamer with handle* in **Banner Pattern.** Measures 4" tall.. Mfg. Syr. 350-400

WABASH-*bread plate* **Banner Pattern.** Top marked. Mfg. Syr. 100-125

WABASH- *demi cup & saucer.* **Banner Pattern** Both pieces top marked. Mfg. Syr. 450-500

WABASH-*creamer* **Monroe Pattern.** Tan china with white & blue teardrop designs. Not bottom stamped. Mfg. Syr. 100-125

WABASH- *oval baker* **Wabash Pattern.** White china with maroon lettering. Mfg. Greenwood . 450-500

WESTERN PACIFIC RAILWAY

WESTERN PACIFIC-*gravy boat* **Feather River Route Pattern.** Tan china with red feathers and highlighted black & red "Western Pacific" lettering. Side marked. Mfg. Sgo. 250-300

WESTERN PACIFIC-*bouillon cup* **Feather River Route Pattern..** Top marked. Mfg. Sgo. 65-75

WESTERN PACIFIC –*demi cup & saucer* **Feather River Route Pattern.** Top marked. Mfg. Sgo. 300-350

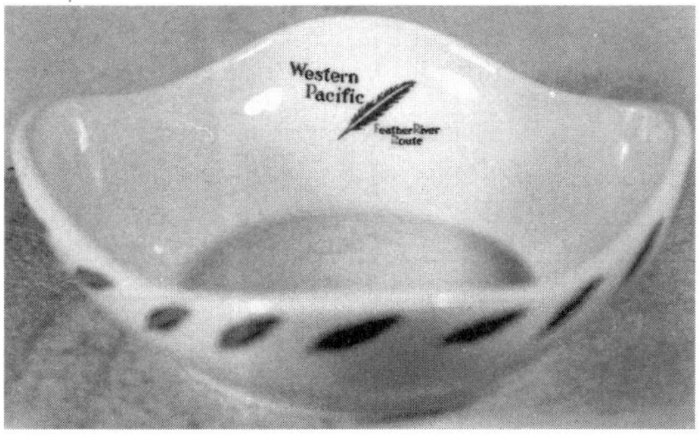

WESTERN PACIFIC- *salad bowl* **Feather River Route Pattern.** Inside marked. Mfg. Sgo. 175-200

WESTERN PACIFIC-*9 ½" dinner plate* **Feather River Route Pattern.** Top marked. Mfg. Sgo. 150-175

WESTERN PACIFIC- *hot food cover* **Feather River Route Pattern.** Side marked. Mfg. Sgo. ... 175-200

WESTERN PACIFIC- *7 ½" oval platter* **Feather River Route Pattern.** Top marked. Mfg. Sgo. 100-125

WESTERN PACIFIC- *6 ¼" bowl* **Keddie Pattern.** White china with green decoration. Mfg. Warwick 800-850

WESTERN PACIFIC- *butter pat* **Keddie Pattern.** White china with green decoration. Mfg. Warwick .... ◆

REMEMBER PRICES SHOWN ARE FOR CHINA PIECES THAT ARE IN GOOD TO EXCELLENT CONDITION. PIECES MUST NOT SHOW EXCESSIVE USE, CHIPS, CRACKS OR HAIRLINES TO COMMAND THE SUGGESTED PRICES LISTED.

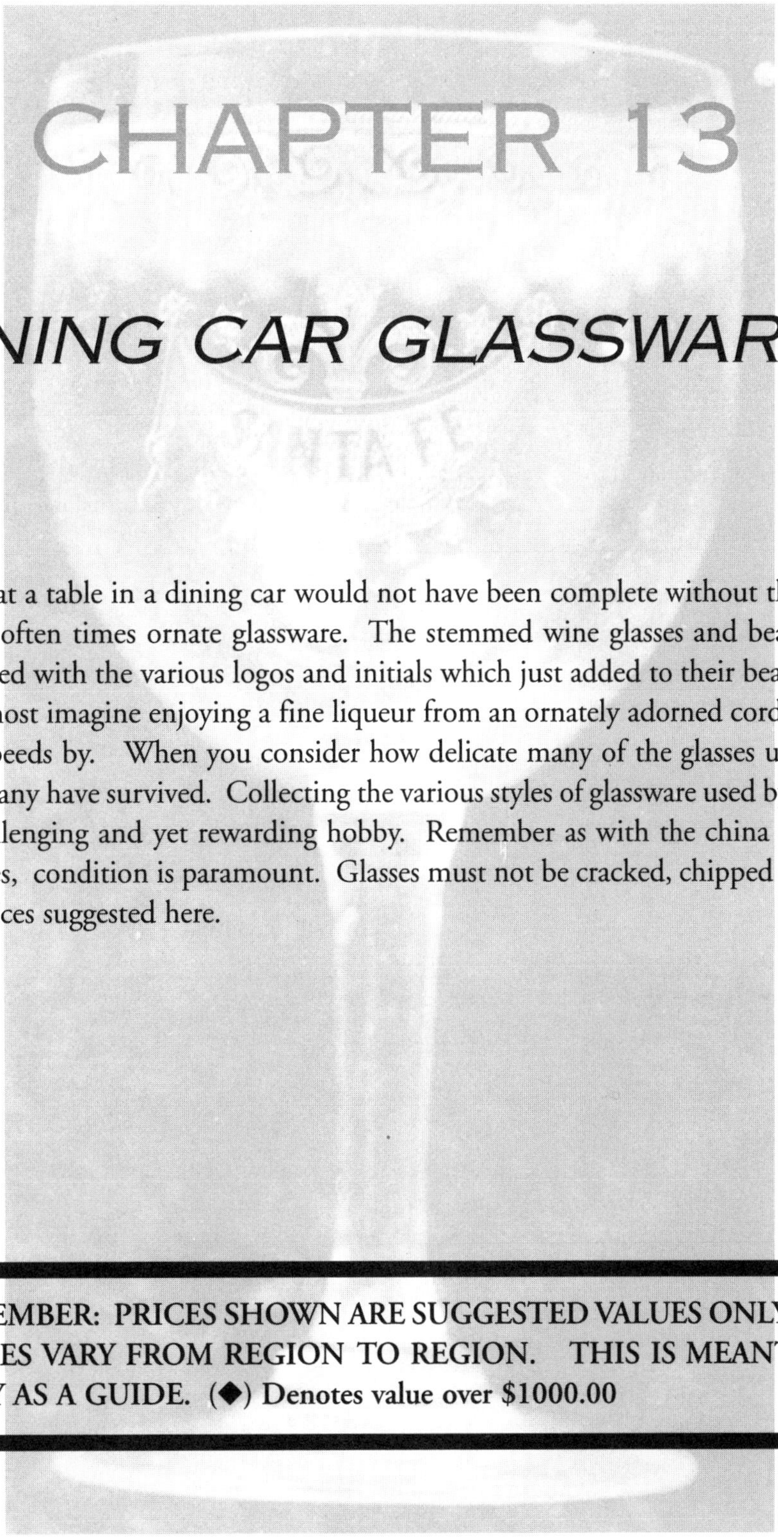

CHAPTER 13

DINING CAR GLASSWARE

The place setting at a table in a dining car would not have been complete without the addition of the beautiful and often times ornate glassware. The stemmed wine glasses and beautiful cordial glasses were adorned with the various logos and initials which just added to their beautiful appearance. One can almost imagine enjoying a fine liqueur from an ornately adorned cordial glass while the countryside speeds by. When you consider how delicate many of the glasses used were, it is amazing that so many have survived. Collecting the various styles of glassware used by the railroads can be a very challenging and yet rewarding hobby. Remember as with the china and all other railroad collectibles, condition is paramount. Glasses must not be cracked, chipped or logos worn to demand the prices suggested here.

REMEMBER: PRICES SHOWN ARE SUGGESTED VALUES ONLY. VALUES VARY FROM REGION TO REGION. THIS IS MEANT ONLY AS A GUIDE. (◆) Denotes value over $1000.00

AMTRAK

AMTRAK-*wine glass.* Stemmed glass with black enameled "Coast Starlight" logo on side........ **20-30**

AMTRAK-*wine glass.* Green stemmed glass with white enameled "Empire Builder" logo on side **20-30**

AMTRAK-*wine glass.* Green stemmed glass with white enameled "Pioneer" logo on side.................. **20-30**

ATLANTIC COAST LINE

ACL- *water glass.* Purple enameled ACL logo on side of glass **15-20**

ATCHISON TOPEKA & SANTA FE

AT&SF- *stemmed wine glass* with ornate etched "Santa Fe" in draped design. **350-400**

AT&SF-*stemmed wine glass* with etched "Santa Fe" surrounded by eight parallel lines. **100-125**

AT&SF-*water glass etched* "Santa Fe" surrounded by eight parallel lines. **55-65**

AT&SF-*stemmed wine glass* with frosted"Santa Fe" on top edge **45-55**

AT&SF-*highball glass* with fluted base. frosted "Santa Fe" on top edge **35-45**

AT&SF-*water glass* with frosted "Santa Fe" on top edge **15-20**

AT&SF-*Club soda bottle.* Green glass with enameled label with either blue or green Santa Fe Logo **100-125**

BALTIMORE & OHIO

B&O-*milk glass* with crest shows "B&O" "Linking 13 Great States" in white enamel **10-15**

BURLINGTON NORTHERN

BN- *old fashioned glass* with black enameled BN logo. **5-10**

CHICAGO & NORTHWESTERN

C&NW- *juice glass* with black enameled "C&NW" logo. **10-15**

CHICAGO BURLINGTON & QUINCY

CB&Q- *old fashioned glass* with thick base and 8 fluted sides. Embossed "Burlington Route" on inside base of glass **75-85**

CHICAGO MILWAUKEE ST PAUL & PACIFIC

CMSTP&P- *milk glass* with large frosted Milwaukee Road box logo on side. **50-60**

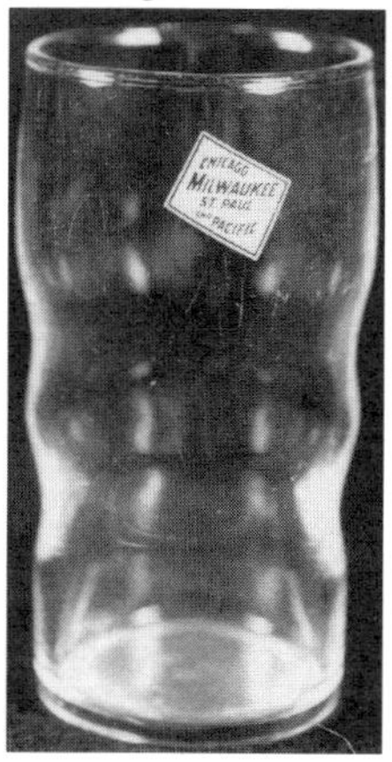

CMSTP&P-*water glass* with small frosted Milwuakee Road box logo on side **35-45**

CMSTP&P-*parfeit glass* with small frostedMilwuakee Road box logo on side **100-125**

CMSTP&P-*sherbert glass* with small frosted Milwaukee Road box logo on side......... **45-55**

CMSTP&P-*milk glass* with red & orange enameled design shows three locomotives on one side. Caption reads, "Morning Hiawatha, The Olympian, Midwest Hiawatha". Reverse reads, "Afternoon Hiawatha, Pioneer Unlimited.. **35-45**

CHICAGO ROCK ISLAND & PACIFIC

CRI&P- *cocktail glass* **8 ounce** round shaped. Has Rock Island red enameled logo with Route of the Rockets 1852 on one side Golden State and Oranges logo in gold & orange on the other **10-15**

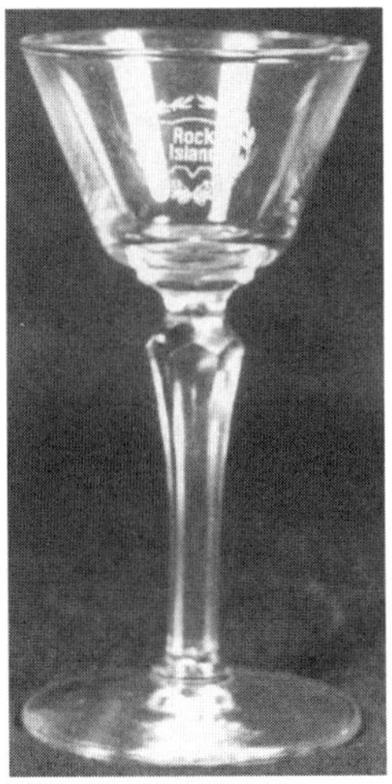

CRI&P-*stemmed wine glass* with frosted Rock Island logo inside of wreath. Tapered 6 sided stem **200-250**

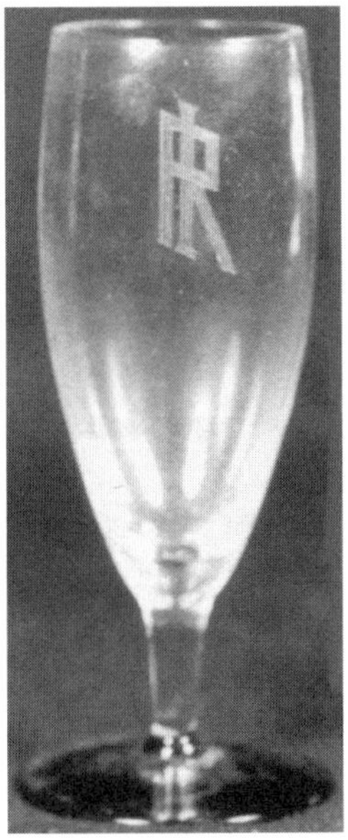

CRI&P-*stemmed wine glass* with cut "RI" monogram on clear glass with ruby red base............... **250-300**

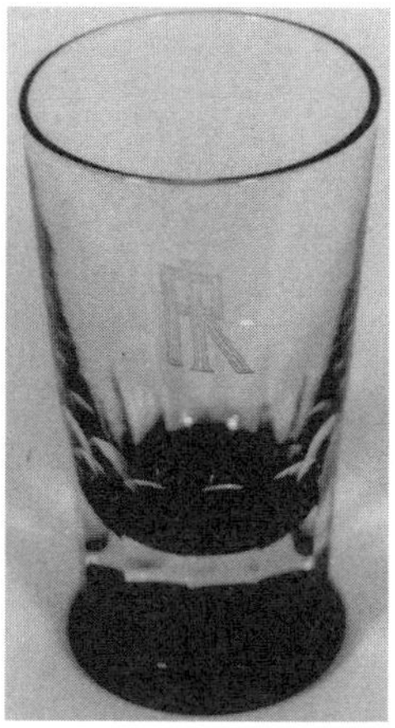

CRI&P-*glass* measures 4" tall. Has cut "RI" monogram on clear glass. Heavy red base with 13 flutes. **175-200**

COLORADO & SOUTHERN

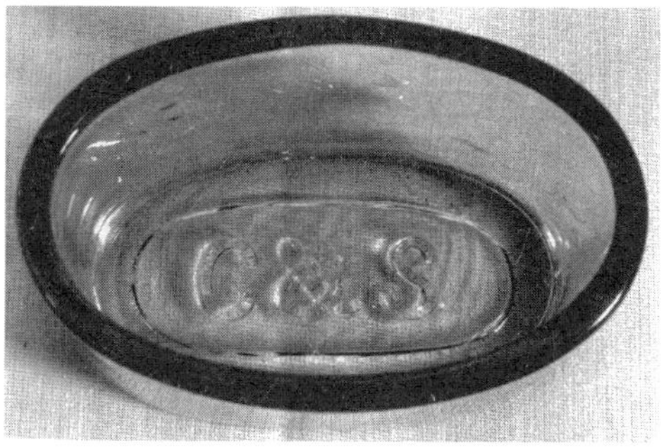

C&S- *oval master salt.* Cast "C&S" in the bottom of the glass. **200-250**

DELAWARE & HUDSON

D&H- *highball glass* with white enameled D&H logo on side **5-10**

DELAWARE LACKAWANNA & WESTERN

DL&W-*water glass* with burgundy enamled "Phoebe Show" logo on side **20-25**

DENVER & RIO GRANDE

D&RGRR- *cordial glass* measures 3 ¾" tall with etched Curecanti logo on side. Fluted sides **650-700**

D&RGRR-*highball glass* cast "D&RGRR" around inside base of glass **250-300**

DENVER & RIO GRANDE WESTERN

D&RGWRR-*water glass* with etched Curecanti logo on side **550-600**

D&RGWRR-*water carafe* bulb style with "Curecanti Logo or "Rio Grande" speed letters etched on glass. .... ◆

FRED HARVEY

FRED HARVEY- *milk bottle* ½ pint size cast "Fred Harvey Half Pint Liquid" **60-75**

GREAT NORTHERN

GREAT NORTHERN-*juice glass* with frosted GN monogram on side **40-50**

GREAT NORTHERN-*footed glass* measures 3 3/16" tall with one inch diameter goat logo on side with three parallel lines above......... **75-85**

GREAT NORTHERN-*water glass* measures 4 ¾" tall with straight sides. One inch goat logo on side with three parallel lines above.... **75-85**

GULF MOBILE & OHIO

GM&O-*high ball glass* with white enameled winged logo on side.............................. **25-30**

MISSOURI PACIFIC

MP-*milk bottle* one quart size with MP Buzzsaw logo cast on side. Reads, "Bottled on Ben Bush Farm for Missouri Pacific Lines" cast on reverse **85-95**

MP-*milk bottle* one pint size with red enameled MP Buzzsaw logo on side **45-55**

MP-*milk bottle* ½ pint size with red enameled MP Buzzsaw logo on side, Reverse reads, "Sunnymade Farm, Bismark Missouri ... **10-15**

MISSOURI KANSAS & TEXAS

MK&T-*water carafe* with etched "MKT" logo on side. Bulb style carafe **800-900**

NYC-*soda glass* has white enameled "NYC" on side **10-15**

NYC-*cordial glass* measures 4" tall "New York System" in gold logo **40-50**

NYC-*water glass* measures 5 ¼" with applied white enameled 20th Century Limited logo **45-55**

NYC-*stemmed wine glass* measures 5" tall 2 ¼" diameter. Has white enameled 20th Century Limited logo on side of glass **75-85**

NORTHERN PACIFIC

NP-*glass stir stick*, red enameled letters reads, "Route of the North Coast Limited, NP Railway" **45-55**

NP-*water glass* measures 3 7/8with red & black enameled Monad logo on bottom half of glass side **25-35**

NP-*water glass* measures 3 7/8 with red & black enameled Monad logo on top half of glass **20-30**

PENNSYLVANIA RAILROAD

PRR-*glass* roly poly style measures 2 ¼" tall. Has red & white enameled Keystone logo with diesel engine pulling freight train **15-20**

PULLMAN

PULLMAN-*glass coffee carafe* with black enameled letters. Logo on side reads, "Travel & Sleep, Safety & Comfort" around circle with Pullman car through center. Neck covered with rubber heat protector. **100-125**

PULLMAN-*highball glass* measures 3 1/6" with 8 flutes around the base. "Pullman Company" embossed in bottom of glass **30-40**

ST LOUIS SAN FRANCISCO AKA FRISCO

ST.LOUIS & SAN FRANCISCO- *glass* with blue enameled Frisco logo on side. Measures 4 ¾" tall **10-15**

ST.LOUIS & SAN FRANCISCO- *juice glass* etched on side "Frisco Lines over St. Louis – San Francisco Ry" **65-75**

SOUTHERN RAILWAY

SOUTHERN-*stemmed wine glass* green enameled design with SR monogram. Reads, "Southern Railway, Serves the South, Look Ahead, Look South. **15-20**

UNION PACIFIC

UP-*stemmed water glass* with frosted modern UP Shield logo on side **10-15**

UP-*stemmed water glass* with frosted modern UP Shield logo on side and ball in center of stem **20-25**

UP-*juice glass* with white enameled modern UP Shield logo on side **5-10**

WESTERN PACIFIC

WP-*milk glass* measures 3 7/8" with frosted Feather River Route logo on side. **20-30**

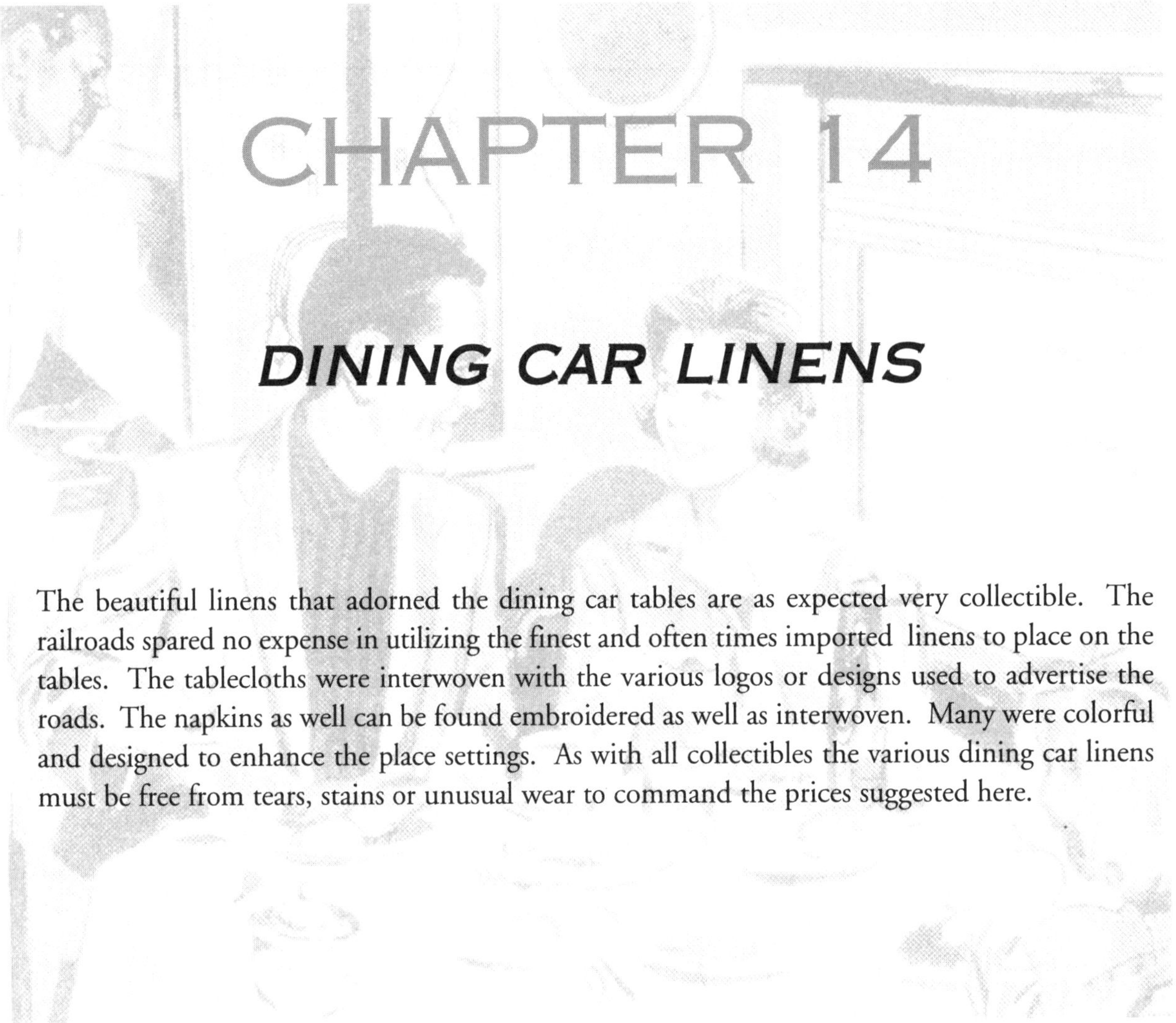

CHAPTER 14

DINING CAR LINENS

The beautiful linens that adorned the dining car tables are as expected very collectible. The railroads spared no expense in utilizing the finest and often times imported linens to place on the tables. The tablecloths were interwoven with the various logos or designs used to advertise the roads. The napkins as well can be found embroidered as well as interwoven. Many were colorful and designed to enhance the place settings. As with all collectibles the various dining car linens must be free from tears, stains or unusual wear to command the prices suggested here.

AT&SFRY dish towel with 1952 embroidered on red stripe down center Measures 16" x 17". **10-15**

AT&SFRY CO dish towel 1970 interwoven on blue stripe down center **5-10**

BR- linen napkin box logo interwoven in center of white.napkin **5-10**

CZ- tablecloth. interwoven logo in center of white linen Measures 45" x 50". **15-20**

CN- white dish towel with blue stenciled CN **5-10**

CHESAPEAKE & OHIO- interwoven in blue on white bath towel. **10-15**

CMSTP&P- box logo interwoven on both sides of white linen tablecloth measuring 35" x 36". **60-70**

GM&O- brown linen headrest cover with interwoven GM&O logo **5-10**

IC- interwoven in beige on edge of brown linen headrest cover. **5-10**

KCS- stenciled on inside hem of grey linen headrest cover. **15-20**

NYC-interwoven on top & bottom edge of white dish towel with blue letters. **5-10**

NYNH&H- interwoven logo in center of white linen napkin. **5-10**

NYNH&H- white linen napkin with embroidered NHRR on edge **3-5**

N&W- interwoven in red on center linen head rest cover. **10-15**

NPRY- cursive letters embroidered in white on corner of beige linen napkin 5-10

NP- Monad logo interwoven in center of tan & beige napkin with floral design around the edges. **20-25**

NP- Yellowstone logo interwoven in center of tan & beige napkin with floral design around the edges. **25-30**

NP- Monad logo interwoven in center of tan & beige tablecloth measuring 67 ½" x 52. .... **90-110**

NORTHERN PACIFIC RY- embroidered letters in corner of tan & beige tablecloth measuring 59"-50". **35-45**

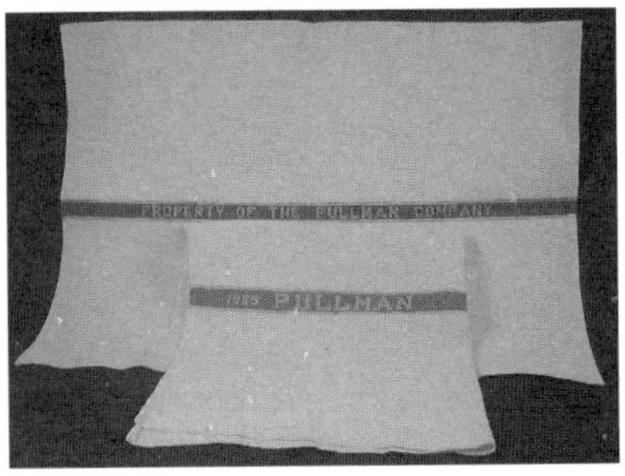

PULLMAN- white dish towel interwoven "Property of Pullman Company". **3-5**

RIO GRANDE- brown linen headrest cover with rust colored speed lettering logo **25-35**

ROCK ISLAND- beige headrest cover "Route of the Rockets" on one end, "Rock Island" on the other. **35-45**

ROCK ISLAND- headrest cover with Golden State Route over oranges interwoven on beige linen. **25-35**

SANTA FE- linen headrest cover with interwoven Santa Fe logo. Green on burgundy. **25-35**

SANTA FE- interwoven in fancy script letters on white linen napkin with floral design. **25-35**

SANTA FE interwoven in fancy script letters on white linen tablecloth with floral & leaf design around the edges. Measures 42" x 60". **55-65**

SCL- green on yellow or brown on green linen headrest cover interwoven "Seaboard Coast Line Railroad". **10-15**

UPRR-Overland Route logo stenciled in black on both ends of linen napkin. **10-15**

UPRR- white dish towel with blue stripe interwoven UNION PACIFIC in center. **5-8**

UPRR- yellow linen napkin with red UP on one end and The Streamliner with train on the other. **25-35**

UPRR- burnt orange napkin with interwoven UPRR on edge. **5-8**

UP- white linen pillowcase with stenciled UP Shield or UPRR on edge **5-8**

WABASH- beige headrest cover with embroidered maroon letters. **10-15**

WABASH- headrest cover with embroidered flag logo on edge **15-20**

REMEMBER: THIS IS ONLY A GUIDE. SUGGESTED PRICES MAY VARY FROM REGION TO REGION AND AS WITH ALL COLLECTIBLES THEY ARE ONLY WORTH WHAT SOMEONE IS WILLING TO PAY.

CHAPTER 15

DINING CAR MENUS

The menus from the various railroad dining cars can be a most enjoyable item to collect. The early menus usually had beautiful lithography and the railroads used the menus as a wonderful medium to advertise the various scenes along the line. Usually found with great photos and drawings, it is a real treat to read an early menu and find such delectable items as Russian Caviar, Yacht Club Beef & Plum Pudding priced to empty your wallet at 25 to 50 cents a serving. Childrens menus also have found a great following as the railroads tried their best to entertain the whole traveling family by offering fun and games and lively decorated menus for the small traveler. Menus must not have creases, tears or stains to command the suggested prices listed here.

ATCHISON TOPEKA & SANTA FE

AT&SF- *breakfast menu* dated 1970. From the Super Chief shows colorful scene of Indian holding Kachina doll **15-20**

AT&SF- *breakfast lunch or dinner menu's* dated in the 60's showing different Indian scenes on the covers **10-15**

AT&SF- *dinner menu* for "The Turquoise Room" dated in the 50's. Large format menu with blue cover **35-40**

AT&SF- *dinner menu* dated 1942 for "The Chief". Cover shows red lettering and reads, "Santa Fe Dining Car Service" & "Fred Harvey" **20-25**

BOSTON & ALBANY RAILROAD

BOSTON & ALBANY- *menu* dated 1934 shows NYC logo, covers breakfast, lunch & dinner with advertising. Measures 10"x 6 ½" **20-25**

CHICAGO BURLINGTON & QUINCY

BURLINGTON ROUTE- *Dinner menu* has color cover of Rocky Mountain National Park. Circa 1930's.. **20-25**

BURLINGTON ROUTE- *luncheon menu* "Chuck Wagon" dated 1970 .... **10-15**

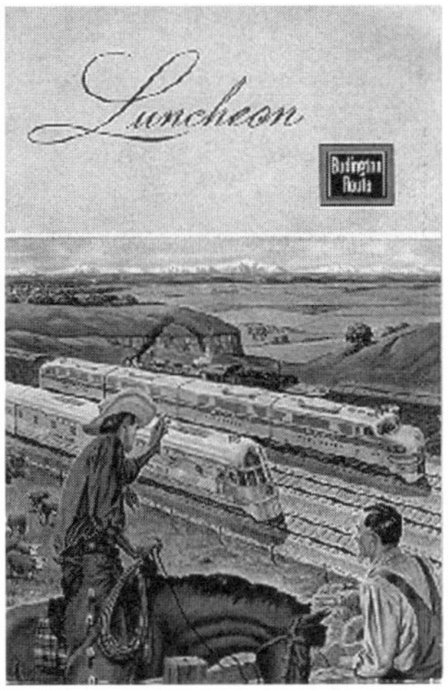

BURLINGTON ROUTE- *Lunch menu* shows scene on cover with Rancher waving at train. War issue **10-15**

BURLINGTON ROUTE-*luncheon menu* war issue celebrating the soldiers. Dated in the 40's **15-20**

CALIFORNIA ZEPHYR

CALIFORNIA ZEPHYR- *Breakfast, lunch or dinner cards* measure 8 ½" x 11". Dated in the late 60's.. **1-5**

CANADIAN NATIONAL RAILWAY

CANADIAN NATIONAL RY- *Lunch Menu* dated 1966, measures 5 ¼" x 11 ½" **1-5**

CANADIAN PACIFIC RAILWAY

CANADIAN PACIFIC RY- *childrens menu* measures 11" x 8 ¾" single two sided card with menu on one side and colorful circus scene with Beavers on reverse **5-10**

CHICAGO & ALTON RAILROAD

C&A RR- *luncheon menu* "Café Car Service Midnight". Measures 6"x8 ½". **20-25**

CHICAGO MILWAUKEE ST PAUL & PACIFIC

CHICAGO MILWAUKEE ST PAUL & PACIFIC- *dinner menu* shows sepia tone photo of "Sagebrush Point, Morrison Cave, Montana. Dated 1945 .... **20-25**

CHICAGO MILWAUKEE ST PAUL & PACIFIC- *Breakfast menu* shows "Hiawatha" on the cover dated 1956 .... **20-25**

CHICAGO MILWAUKEE ST PAUL & PACIFIC- *Dinner menu* shows "Old Faithful, Yellowstone National Park" on cover, dated 1948 .... **35-40**

CHICAGO MILWAUKEE ST PAUL & PACIFIC- *Childrens menu* shows Indian on front shaking hands with little girl. Describes childrens Indians games inside **25-35**

COLORADO MIDLAND RAILROAD

COLORADO MIDLAND RAILWAY- *dinner menu & wine list* circa 1900's. "The Midland Route Dining Car Service" **400-450**

DENVER & RIO GRANDE RAILROAD

DENVER & RIO GRANDE RR- *dinner menu* "Dining Car Service" dated 1915 opens to reveal menu on one side and Wine List on the other. Colorful lithographed cover **90-100**

DENVER & RIO GRANDE RR/ RIO GRANDE WESTERN RR- *Wine List* from Dining Car Service. Cover has lithograph of both logos intertwined in grapevine design. Circa 1900's **100-125**

DENVER & RIO GRANDE RR/ RIO GRANDE WESTERN RR- *breakfast menu* cover shows "Echo Cliffs on the Line of the Denver & Rio Grande RR" dated 1901 .... **75-85**

DENVER & RIO GRANDE WESTERN

DENVER & RIO GRANDE WESTERN- *Dinner menu* cover shows train in Royal Gorge dated 1940 .... **15-20**

DENVER & RIO GRANDE WESTERN- *dinner menu* dated 1951. Shows Mt. Timpanogos on front cover & Glenwood Canyon on reverse **20-25**

DENVER & RIO GRANDE WESTERN- *Beverage card* measures 5"x 7" with blue & white speed letter logo on cover. 1970's **1-3**

FRED HARVEY

FRED HARVEY- *Luncheon menu* shows "The Alvarado" on the cover dated February 1935 .... **45-50**

GREAT NORTHERN

GREAT NORTHERN- *Luncheon Menu* celebrating "National Apple Week" on the cover dated 1929 .... **35-45**

GREAT NORTHERN- *childrens menu* dated 1923 in booklet style houses menu for complete week. Each page shares a poem describing the jobs of the various train personel **40-50**

GREAT NORTHERN- *breakfast menu* shows colorful photo of "Cutbank Chalets, Cutbank River, Glacier National Park" **35-40**

GREAT NORTHERN- *Breakfast menu* dated 1949. Shows "Black Feet Indian" on colorful cover **20-25**

GREAT NORTHERN- *Dinner menu* dated 1947. Cover shows "Oriental Limited" **25-30**

ILLINOIS CENTRAL RAILROAD

ILLINOIS CENTRAL RR- *Luncheon menu* dated 1960. Covers shows "Chicago Shore Line" **5-10**

LEHIGH VALLEY RAILROAD

LEHIGH VALLEY RR- *Breakfast menu.* Cover shows "Route of the Black Diamond". .. **30-35**

LEHIGH VALLEY RR- *breakfast menu card.* Shows logo on bottom left corner **15-20**

LEHIGH VALLEY RR- *beverage menu* with logo in center & colorful green on orange **35-40**

LOUISVILLE & NASHVILLE RAILROAD

LOUISVILLE & NASHVILLE RR- *luncheon menu* dated 1958. Shows yellow diesel engine on the cover **5-10**

NEW YORK CENTRAL RAILROAD

NEW YORK CENTRAL *dinner menu* from the 20TH Century Limited from 1949 .... **15-20**

NORTHERN PACIFIC RAILROAD

NORTHERN PACIFIC- *breakfast menu* from the "North Coast Limited" shows Yellowstone Park Line logo on cover **10-15**

PENNSYLVANIA RAILROAD

PENNSYLVANIA RR- *dinner menu* with wine list dated 1908. Cover shows Pioneer Woman admiring coach with red PRR logo **75-85**

ST. LOUIS & SAN FRANCISCO aka FRISCO

FRISCO- *dinner menu* with logo in gold on cover of dated 1954. .... **20-25**

SILVERTON NORTHERN RAILROAD

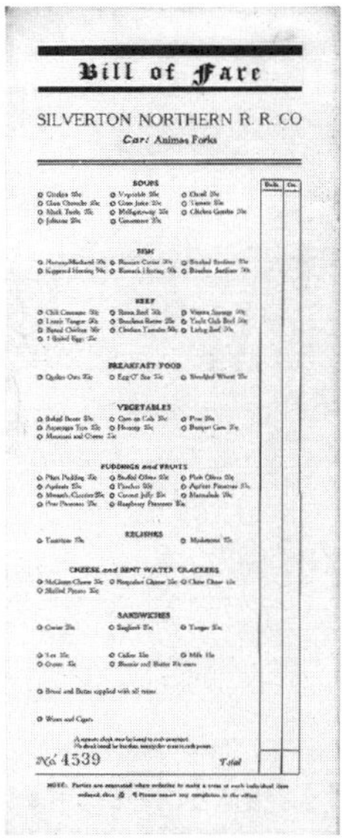
Bill of Fare
SILVERTON NORTHERN R. R. CO
Car: Animas Forks
No. 4539

SILVERTON NORTHERN- *menu card* measures 5 ½" x 13 ½" with red & blue lettering on white background **30-40**

SILVERTON NORTHERN- *wine list* measures 5 ½" x 9 ½" card again with red & blue lettering on white background. **100-125**

TEXAS & PACIFIC RAILROAD

TEXAS & PACIFIC *breakfast menu* card measures 6 ½" x 10" Circa 1960's **1-5**

UNION PACIFIC RAILROAD

UNION PACIFIC- *childrens menu* shows Overland Shield on cover circa 1930 .... **30-35**

UNION PACIFIC- *breakfast menu* for the "City of Portland" dated 1950's **10-15**

UNION PACIFIC-*luncheon menu* with wine list for the "City of Portland" dated 1950's **15-20**

UNION PACIFIC *beverage menu* listing wines and beverages available. Dated 1940's **15-20**

UNION PACIFIC-SOUTHERN PACIFIC- "The Overland Limited" breakfast menu card. Menu on one side with color scene of "Crossing the Great Salt Lake" on reverse **40-50**

UNION PACIFIC-SOUTHERN PACIFIC- "The Overland Limited" *lunch menu card.* Menu on one side with color scene of "Mormon Temple" on the reverse **40-50**

CHAPTER 16

DINING CAR SILVER

Dining car silver items, without a doubt, were the icing on the cake to a beautifully set table in a dining car. The silver was usually the very heavy, silver soldered style that could withstand the often bumpy ride offered on a train car. Embossed and engraved with the various logos and initials of the railroads the silver gave the table settings an elegant appearance. It is understandable that collecting the beautiful accent pieces has become another wonderful facet of the railroadiana hobby. Pieces that are top or side marked tend to command more than those that are only bottom marked. As with all other railroad collectibles, condition is paramount. Pieces must not show excessive marks or dents, and logos and initials must be very legible, showing little or no wear. Prices shown are for excellent to near mint condition pieces.

REMEMBER: PRICES SHOWN ARE SUGGESTED VALUES ONLY. VALUES VARY FROM REGION TO REGION. THIS IS MEANT ONLY AS A GUIDE. (◆) **Denotes value over $1000.00**

SOME EXAMPLES OF BACKSTAMPS, TOP MARKS & SIDE MARKS

Bottom marked piece with "B & O" initials. Shows Reed & Barton manufacturers mark.

Side marked piece showing applied PRR Keystone logo.

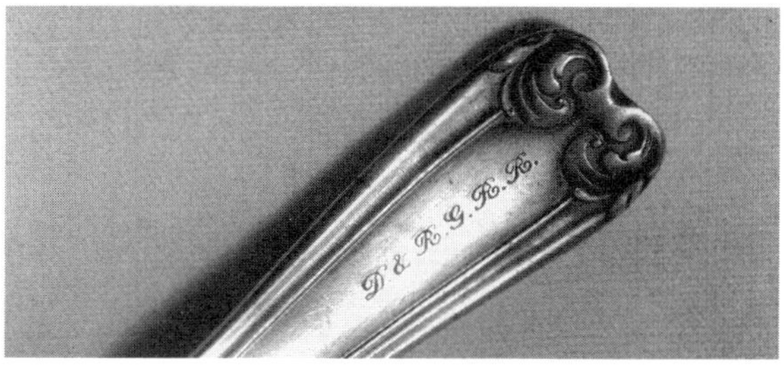

Top marked with "D&RGRR" letters in script design.

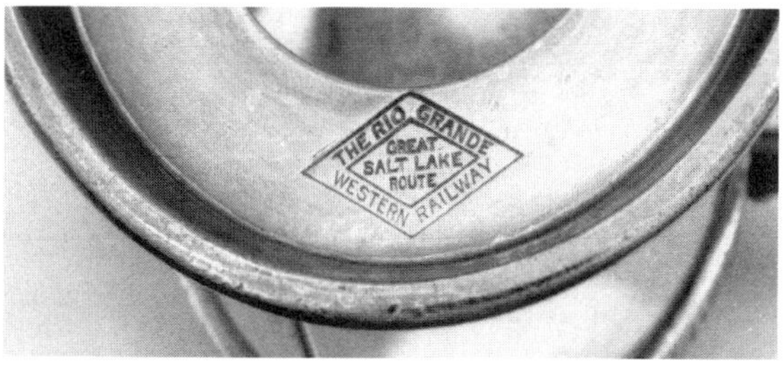

Bottom marked with " Rio Grande Western Railway Salt Lake Route" logo.

ABBREVIATION KEY LISTING SILVER MFG. (MANUFACTURERS)

CH-CH HANSON

ELKINGTON

GMCo-GORHAM

HARRISON BROTHERS & HOWSAM

IS-INTERNATIONAL SILVER

MER-MERIDIAN BROTHERS

ROGERS-ROGERS & HAMILTON

R&B-REED & BARTON

SMITH BROS

STANLEY THERMOS CO

TORONTO-TORONTO SILVER PLATE CO.

VICTOR

WALLACE

WILEY

ATCHISON TOPEKA & SANTA FE
aka SANTA FE

SANTA FE-*sugar bowl* 12 oz size with lid. Side marked "Santa Fe" in script letters and bottom stamped "Santa Fe". Mfg. R&B **150-175**

SANTA FE-*beverage glass* holder side marked "Santa Fe" in old english script. Mfg. GMCo. **250-300**

SANTA FE-*butter pat.* Top marked "Santa Fe" in old english script. Mfg. Harrison Bros. Measures 2 1/2" diamond **100-125**

SANTA FE-*butter pat.* Bottom marked "Santa Fe" in english script. Mfg. IS **25-35**

SANTA FE-*candy dish* with tab handles. Nickle plated and top marked on each handle "Santa Fe". **75-85**

SANTA FE-*coffee pot* 10 oz or 14 oz side marked with "Santa Fe" in old english script. Also bottom marked. Ribbed design. Mfg. GM Co. **250-300**

SANTA FE-*creamer* 6oz or 8 oz side marked with "Santa Fe" in old english script. Also bottom marked. Hinged lid. Ribbed design. Mfg. GM.Co. **150-175**

SANTA FE-*cruet or condiment set.* Silver frame with three fluted glass bottles. Bottom marked "Santa Fe". Mfg. IS **150-175**

SANTA FE-*finger bowl* with underliner. Top marked & bottom marked "Santa Fe" in script letters. Beautiful ornate pattern with embossed floral design. Mfg. R&B **500-550**

SANTA FE- *creamer* 6 oz size side marked with "Santa Fe" in old english script. Ribbed design. Bottom marked. Mfg. GM Co. No lid **100-125**

SANTA FE-*oval tray* measures 12 ¼" long. Top marked "Santa Fe" in script letters. Mfg. Harrison Bro. **100-125**

SANTA FE-*glass water carafe* with silver frame. Top marked "Santa Fe" in english script letters. Mfg. R&B **500-550**

SANTA FE-*glass water carafe* with silver frame. Glass has "Santa Fe" cut into it and frame top marked "Santa Fe" script letters. Mfg. R&B .... ◆

SANTA FE *knife fork or spoon.* Top marked "Santa Fe" in script letters. **Albany Pattern** Mfg. Gorham **10-15**

SANTA FE-*sugar tongs* top marked "Santa Fe" in script letters. Mfg. GMCo. **225-275**

ATLANTA & WEST POINT
aka WEST POINT ROUTE

WEST POINT ROUTE- *dinner fork* top marked A&WP. Pattern Cecil. Mfg. R&B **25-35**

ATLANTIC COAST LINE RAILROAD

ACL *teaspoon.*top marked on **Broadway pattern** Mfg. IS. **5-10**

BALTIMORE & OHIO RAILROAD

B&ORR-*soup tureen* two pint size, with ladle . Bottom marked "B&ORR". Mfg. R&B **175-200**

B&O-*soup 7" ladle* top marked on **Clovelly Pattern** Mfg. R&B. **55-65**

B&O-*sugar tongs.* Top marked, **Clovelly Pattern** Mfg. R&B. **75-90**

BOSTON & ALBANY RAILROAD

B&A- *cream pitcher.* 2 ounce size. Bottom marked "B&ARR". Mfg. R&B **75-85**

BOSTON & MAINE RAILROAD

B&M- *tureen.* 1 ½" pint side marked with B&M arrow logo. Mfg. Rogers........ **275-325**

B&M- *crumber.* Top marked with B&M arrow logo. Mfg. Rogers Bros. **250-300**

B&M *coffee pot.* Side marked with B&M arrow logo. One pint size. Mfg. Rogers **225-275**

CHICAGO BURLINGTON & QUINCY

aka BURLINGTON ROUTE

BR- *hot food cover.* Side marked with BR box logo. Mfg. R&B **175-200**

BR-*crumber.* Top marked with BR box logo. Modern B pattern............................ **110-125**

BR-*cream pitcher.* Side marked with "BR". 8 oz size with hinged lid. Bottom marked "Property of CB&QRR". Mfg. R&B **75-85**

BR-*cream pitcher.* Side marked with reverse "BR". 7 oz size with hinged lid. Mfg. R&B **85-95**

BR-*sugar bowl.* Double handles side marked with reverse "BR". Mfg. R&B. **150-175**

BR-*soup spoon*, **Belmont pattern** top marked with box logo. Mfg. R&B **15-20**

BR-*coffee pot.* 2 pint size with applied BR reverse monogram on side. Mfg. R&B **175-200**

BR- *serving spoon* top marked with BR box logo, Belmont pattern Mfg. R&B **20-30**

BR- *soup tureen* side marked with applied BR reverse monogram. One pint size, Mfg. R&B **150-175**

BR-*gingerale bottle holder* top marked with BR box logo. Mfg. R&B **150-175**

BR-*toothpick holder* side marked "BR". Bottom marked Property of the CB&QRR. Mfg. R&B **150-175**

CALIFORNIA ZEPHYR

CZ-*supreme set.* 3 pieces includes bottom , glass insert & silver pierced juice ring. Both pieces bottom marked with CZ logo. Mfg. IS **150-175**

CZ-6" *au gratin dish* with tab holders. Bottom marked with CZ logo. Mfg. IS **85-95**

CZ-*tip tray.* Small aluminum round tray with greek god Zephrus in center. Mfg. CH Hanson 35-45

CZ-5" *casserole dish* with tab handles. Bottom marked with CZ logo. Mfg. IS 65-75

CZ-*menu holder* bottom marked with CZ logo. Mfg. IS **85-100**

CZ- 9 ½" *oval tray.* Bottom marked with CZ logo. Mfg. IS **55-65**

CANADIAN NATIONAL RAILWAY

CNR- *dinner knife.* Top marked with Maple Leaf logo. Mfg.Mc.Co. **5-10**

CNR- *fish fork.* Top marked with CN logo. Mfg. IS **5-10**

CANADIAN PACIFIC RAILWAY

CPR- *cream pitcher.* Side marked with intertwined CPR. Mfg. Elkington **25-35**

CPR-9" *oval tray.* Top marked with fancy intertwined CPR. Mfg. Elkington **25-35**

CPR-*gravy boat.* Side marked with intertwined CPR. Mfg. Wiley **25-35**

CPR-*10" oval tray* top marked with fancy intertwined CPR. Mfg. Elkington **25-35**

CPR-*serving spoon.* Top marked with intertwined CPR. Mfg. Wiley. **10-15**

CPR-*sugar bowl.* Side marked with intertwined CPR . Mfg. Elkington **25-35**

CENTRAL VERMONT RAILWAY

CVRY-*soup spoon* bottom marked "Central Vermont Ry". Mfg. IS **35-45**

CVRY- *tablespoon.* Bottom marked on **Cromwell pattern** spoon. Mfg. IS **20-30**

CHICAGO & NORTHWESTERN

C&NW-*cocktail fork*- Bottom marked with C&NW SYSTEM. Mfg. IS **10-20**

C&NW-*cruet or condiment set.* Bottom marked "C&NWRY". Mfg. IS. Glass bottles with fluted sides **125-150**

C&NW-*desert fork.* Bottom marked "C&NW SYSTEM". Mfg. IS. **10-20**

C&NW- *horseradish holder* bottom marked. Original glass bottle. Mfg. R&B **125-150**

C&NW-*soup ladle.* Bottom marked with C&NWRY. Mfg. R&B **15-25**

C&NW-*syrup pitcher* with attached underliner and hinged lid. Bottom marked "C&NWRY". Mfg. R&B **125-150**

C&NW- *table knife*. Bottom marked "C&NW SYSTEM". Mfg. IS **10-20**

C&NWRY- *corn cob holders*. Pair both side marked. Mfg. R&B **100-125**

C&N WRY- *hot food cover*. Bottom marked. Measures 6 ¼" diameter. Mfg. IS. **75-85**

C&NWRY- *menu holder*. Bottom marked with two pencils holders. Mfg. IS **100-125**

C&NWRY- *pedestal ice cream dish*. Bottom marked, Mfg.IS **55-65**

C&NW- *sugar tongs*. Top marked C&NW SYSTEM. MFg IS **90-100**

CHICAGO INDIANAPOLIS &LOUISVILLE aka MONON ROUTE

MONON- *syrup pitcher* 14 oz size with MONON. Bottom stamped. Mfg. IS **250-300**

MONON-*butter pat*. Bottom marked "MONON". Dated 1947. Mfg. IS. **85-95**

CHICAGO MILWAUKEE & ST. PAUL

CM&STP- *bread plate*. 5 5/8" diameter. Bottom marked with script letters. Mfg. IS **45-55**

CM&STP-*creamer* bottom marked with script letters. 10 oz with hinged lid. Mfg. IS **50-75**

CM&STP- *knife fork or spoon* bottom marked in script letter. Mfg. IS **15-20**

CM&STP-*ice tongs* top marked. Mfg. R&B. **125-150**

CM&STP- *sugar bowl*. Bottom marked in script letters on 8 oz bowl with pedestal base. Mfg. IS **75-85**

CM&STP- *teapot* with hinged lid. One pint size. Bottom marked with script letters. Mfg. IS **90-100**

CHICAGO MILWAUKEE ST PAUL & PACIFIC

CMSTP&P- *tureen*. 20 oz size with side marked Hiawatha Logo. Top marked "Milwaukee Road" on lid. Mfg. IS **300-350**

CMSTP&P-*horse radish holder*. Side marked with Milwaukee Road logo. Original glass insert. Mfg. IS **150-175**

CMSTP&P-*Menu holder*. Side marked with Milwaukee Road logo. Two pencil holders. Pierced design. Mfg. IS..................... **175-200**

CMSTP&P-*sugar bowl*. 6 oz size with winged finial handle. Side marked "The Milwaukee Road". Mfg. IS. **150-175**

CMSTP&P-*supreme set*. Two piece set top marked "Milwaukee Road" with pierced juice ring. Bottom marked "CMSTP&P" on 6" bottom. Mfg. IS dated 1947 .... **175-200**

CHICAGO ROCK ISLAND & PACIFIC RAILWAY

CRI&PRY-*bowl* with pedestal base and single tab handle. Side marked with "Golden Rocket" logo. Bottom marked "CRI&P". Mfg. IS **175-200**

CRI&PRY-*butter pat*.square design Bottom marked "Rock Island Lines". Line & ribbon design around edge. Mfg. IS **30-40**

CRI&PRY -*cake cover* measures 5 ½" diameter. Pagoda design with pierced edge. Bottom marked "Rock Island Lines". Mfg. Gorham **60-70**

CRI&PRY *-candy or nut dish.* Footed shell design with handle. Bottom marked "Rock Island Lines". Mfg. Wallace **60-70**

CRI&PRY-*coffee pot.* Half pint size with hinged lid and pagoda style top. Bottom marked "Rock Island Lines". Mfg. Gorham. **125-150**

CRI&PRY *-creamer* 6 oz size with fluted sides and hinged lid. Bottom marked "Rock Island Lines". Mfg. Wallace **65-75**

CRI&PRY *-cruet or condiment set* silver frame holds three glass bottles with fluted sides and silver lids. Frame bottom marked "Rock Island Lines". Mfg. IS **200-250**

CRI&PRY *-crumber* bottom marked "Rock Island Lines". Mfg. Gorham. Circa 1912 .... **90-100**

CRI&PRY-*fork, knife or spoon* Bottom marked "CRI&PRY". **Claredon pattern** Mfg. R&B **25-35**

CRI&PRY *-glass water carafe* with silver frame. "Rock Island Lines" on handle. Fancy leaf design on silver frame. Mfg. Wallace. **350-400**

CRI&PRY- *hot food cover.* Measures 6" round. Top marked with "Golden Rocket" logo. Bottom marked "CRI&P". Mfg. IS **175-200**

CRI&PRY *-knife, fork or teaspoon* top marked with "Rock Island Lines" **Pattern Silhouette.** Mfg. IS **10-15**

CRI&PRY *-menu holder* side marked with applied RI logo. Two pencil holders. Mfg. Wallace **200-250**

CRI&PRY *-mustard frame* with glass insert. Bottom marked "Rock Island Lines". Mfg. Wallace. **125-150**

CRI&PRY - *gravy boat.* Bottom marked "Rock Island Lines". 3 oz size. Mfg. Wallace **90-110**

COLORADO & SOUTHERN RAILWAY

C&SRY-*oval tray* measures 10". Top marked "Colorado & Southern Railway". Mfg. R&B **250-300**

C&SRY-*soup tureen* with lid. Side marked "Colorado & Southern Railway". Mfg. R&B **275-325**

COLORADO MIDLAND RAILWAY

CMRY-*tablespoon.* Top marked "Colo. Mid Ry". Mfg. Rogers & Hamilton **75-85**

CMRY-*knife- top marked* "Colo.Mid.Ry". Mfg. Rogers & Hamilton **85-100**

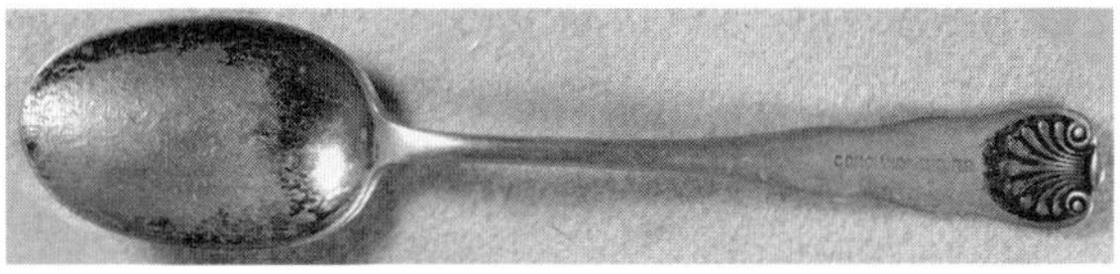

CMRY-*mustard pot.* Bottom marked "CMRY". Hinged lid with original glass insert. Mfg. R&B **225-250**

CMRY- *sugar bowl.* Bottom marked CMRY. 10oz with lid. Mfg. R&B **275-325**

CMRY- *coffee pot.* Bottom marked CMRY, with hinged lid. Mfg. R&B **350-400**

DELAWARE LACKAWANNA & WESTERN

DL&W- *sugar bowl.* 9 oz size with lid. Bottom marked "DL&WRR". Mfg. R&B **90-100**

LACKAWANNA RR- *tablespoon.* Bottom marked, Mfg. IS **15-20**

DENVER & RIO GRANDE RAILROAD

D&RGRR- *sugar bowl* with lid 12 oz size side marked with Curecanti Logo. Mfg. R&B **400-450**

D&RGRR-*coffee pot.*12 oz size with insulated handles. Side marked with Curecanti logo. Mfg. R&B **400-450**

D&RGRR- *butter pat* square design with curecanti logo in center. Mfg. R&B **175-225**

D&RGRR-*cake compote.* 10" diameter side marked "Denver & Rio Grande" in old english script. Mfg. R&B .... ◆

D&RGRR-*creamer.* 8 oz size with hinged lid. Side marked in old english script "Denver & Rio Grande". Circa 1910................. **450-500**

D&RGRR-*creamer* 8 oz with hinged lid. Bottom marked "Rio Grande Dining Car Service". Mfg. R&B. Floral band around center **225-250**

D&RGRR-*dinner fork.* Top marked with "D&RGRR" in script letters. Mfg. R&B **50-60**

D&RGRR-*ice bucket* side marked with curecanti logo. Double handled. Mfg. R&B. **800-900**

D&RGRR-*Soda spoon* with twisted shaft. Top marked "D&RGRR" in script letters. Mfg. R&B **65-75**

D&RGRR-*sugar bowl.* 9 oz size side marked in old english script "Denver & Rio Grande". Circa 1910....................................... **450-500**

D&RGRR-*sugar bowl.* 9 oz size bottom marked "Rio Grande Dining Car Service". Mfg. R&B Floral band around center. **175-200**

D&RGRR-*syrup pitcher* with hinged lid and attached underliner. Side marked with Curecanti logo. Mfg. R&B **350-400**

D&RGRR-*tablespoon.* Top marked "D&RGRR" in script letters. Mfg. R&B **45-55**

DENVER & RIO GRANDE WESTERN

D&RGWRR-*sugar bowl* 12 oz size. Side marked "Rio Grande" speed letters. Handle knotched for hanging tongs. Mfg. IS **150-175**

D&RGWRR-*butter icer.* Two piece set both bottom marked. Mfg. R&B **175-200**

D&RGWRR-*chocolate pot.* 14oz size with hinged lid. Side marked with "Rio Grande" speed letters. Mfg. IS **175-200**

D&RGWRR-*creamer* with hinged lid. Side marked with Curecanti logo. 8 oz size. Mfg. R&B **350-400**

D&RGWRR-*dinner knife* bottom marked "RIO GRANDE" in speed lettering. Mfg. IS **20-30**

D&RGWRR-*hot food cover.* 6 ¼" diameter side marked "RIO GRANDE" in speed letters. Mfg. IS **100-125**

D&RGWRR-*sugar bowl* with lid side marked with Curecanti logo.. 4 oz size. Mfg. R&B **400-450**

D&RGWRR-*sugar bowl* side marked with Curecanti Logo. 8oz size with lid. Mfg. R&B **350-400**

D&RGWRR- *sugar tongs.* Side marked on Belmont pattern tongs. MFg. R&B **250-300**

D&RGWRR- *teapot* 11 oz size with hinged lid. Side marked in "RIO GRANDE" speed lettering. Bottom stamped D&RGWRR. Mfg. R&B **150-175**

D&RGWRR- *tureen* with underliner plate. Both pieces top marked with Curecanti logo. Mfg. R&B **375-425**

EL PASO & SOUTHWESTERN

EP&SW- *teapot.* 12 oz size with hinged lid. Bottom stamped "EP&SW" Mfg. GMCo. **250-300**

EP&SW- *sugar bowl.* 12 oz side with double handles and lid. Side marked with SW Route logo. Bottom marked EP&SW. Mfg. Wallace **350-400**

ERIE RAILROAD

ERIE- *coffee pot.* 14 oz size. Bottom stamped "Lackawanna". Mfg. IS. **90-100**

ERIE-*dinner fork.* Top marked with diamond logo on **Grecian pattern** fork. Mfg. IS **25-30**

FLORIDA EAST COAST

FEC- *coffee pot.* 8 oz size bottom marked with "Florida East Coast Railway Co.". Mfg. IS. Side marked "FEC" logo. **250-300**

FEC- *nut pick* top marked with intertwined letters. Mfg. IS **40-50**

FEC-*sugar bowl.* 8 oz size bottom marked "Florida East Coast Railway Co". Mfg. IS. Side marked "FEC"logo **225-275**

FEC- *sugar tongs* top marked with intertwined letters. Grecian pattern Mfg. IS. **100-125**

FT WORTH & DENVER CITY

FW&DC-*creamer.* 7 oz size with hinged lid. Side marked "Ft Worth & Denver City Railway" in script letters. Mfg. R&B **300-350**

FRED HARVEY

FRED HARVEY-*coffee pot.* 8 oz size bottom marked "Fred Harvey". Mfg. IS. **90-100**

FRED HARVEY-*dinner fork.* **Albany pattern.** Bottom marked. Mfg. IS **10-15**

FRED HARVEY- *serving spoon.* **Carolina pattern.** Top marked "Fred Harvey. Mfg. Gorham. ... **45-50**

FRED HARVEY-*silver tray.* 9 ½" diameter bottom marked "Fred Harvey". Mfg. IS **55-65**

FRED HARVEY-*sugar bowl* with lid. 8 oz size. Bottom marked "Fred harvey" Mfg. IS **75-85**

FRED HARVEY-*tablespoon.* **Albany pattern.** Bottom marked. Mfg. IS **10-15**

GRAND TRUNK WESTERN

GTW-*butter icer* with double handle. Top marked with GTW box logo. Mfg. Toronto Silver Plate Co. **50-60**

GREAT NORTHERN RAILWAY

GN-*creamer* with hinged lid and beaded edge. Bottom stamped "Great Northern Railway". Mfg. Meridian **150-175**

GN-*sugar bowl* with lid. Beaded edge design. Bottom stamped "Great Northern Railway". Mfg. Meridian **150-175**

GN- *butter pat.* Top marked with intertwined GN logo in center. Bottom stamped "Great Northern Rwy". Mfg. IS.................... **90-100**

GULF MOBILE & OHIO

GM&O-*creamer* 8 oz size with hinged lid. Bottom marked "GM&O". Mfg. IS **150-175**

GM&O-*demi spoon.* Top marked "GM&O". **Broadway pattern.** Mfg. IS **25-35**

GM&O-*knife* top marked "GM&O". **Broadway pattern.** Mfg. IS **15-25**

GM&O- *pickle fork.* Top marked. "GM&O". **Broadway pattern.** Mfg. IS **30-40**

ILLINOIS CENTRAL

ICRR-*creamer* 7 oz size with hinged lid. Side marked with intertwined letters. Bottom stamped "ICRR". Mfg. R&B **95-110**

ICRR-*crumber* top marked with intertwined letters. Mfg. R&B............................... **75-85**

ICRR-*finger bowl* marked inside the bowl with intertwined letters. Bottom marked "ICRR". Mfg. R&B **85-95**

ICRR-*fish fork* top marked "ICRR" **pattern Windsor**. Mfg. Wallace **25-35**

ICRR-*hot food cover* measures 10" diameter. Side marked with intertwined letters. Bottom stamped "ICRR". Mfg. R&B **100-125**

ICRR- *gingerale holder.* Top marked with IC Diamond Logo. Mfg. Meridian....... **150-175**

ICRR-*oval tray* measures 10 ½" diameter. Top marked "ICRR" intertwined letters. Bottom marked "ICRR". Mfg. R&B **100-125**

ICRR- *pedestal bowl* side marked with "ICRR" intertwined letters. Measures 4 ½" tall 6 ¾" across the top with 4" base. Mfg. R&B. **100-125**

ICRR-*sugar bowl* with double handles and lid. Side marked with intertwined letters. Bottom stamped "ICRR". Mfg. R&B **100-125**

LOS ANGELES & SALT LAKE

aka SALT LAKE ROUTE

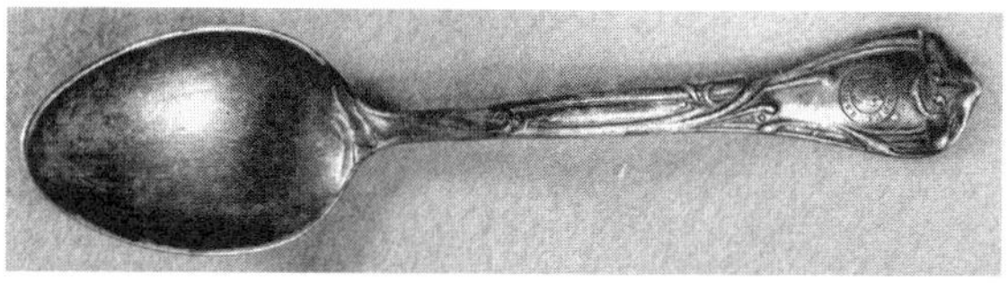

SALT LAKE ROUTE-*knife, fork or spoon* top marked with Salt Lake Route logo. **Pattern Modern Art.** Mfg. R&B. Circa 1904. .... **65-75**

SALT LAKE ROUTE-*sugar tongs* top marked with Salt Lake Route logo. **Pattern Modern Art.** Mfg. R&B **175-200**

LOUISVILLE & NASHVILLE RAILROAD

L&N- *soup spoon.* Top marked in script letters. Mfg. Rogers Bros. **25-35**

MAINE CENTRAL RAILROAD

MAINE CENTRAL-*dinner knife.* Top marked with "MC" in box logo. Mfg. IS **45-55**

MAINE CENTRAL-*dinner knife* top marked MCRR in script letters. Mfg. Meridian **45-55**

MISSOURI KANSAS & TEXAS

MK&T-*coffee pot* 8 oz size. Side marked with applied MKT logo. Bottom marked "MK&T". Mfg. GMCo. **300-350**

MK&T- *butter pat* bottom stamped "MK&T". Mfg. IS **45-55**

MK&T-*finger bowl* measures 3 ¾" diameter. Has applied MKT logo. Mfg. GMCo. **150-175**

MK&T-*teaspoon* bottom marked "MK&TRY DINING DEPT". Mfg. R&B #6 .... **35-45**

MISSOURI PACIFIC RAILROAD

MP- *bowl* measures 6" round with buzz saw logo on inside or side marked on the bowl. Bottom stamped Mfg. IS **35-45**

MP-*corn cob holders.* Both side marked "Missouri Pacific Lines". Mfg. IS. Twisted handle **70-80**

MP-*creamer* 2 oz size. Side marked with buzz saw logo and bottom marked "Missouri Pacific Lines". Mfg. IS **90-100**

MP-*menu holder* side marked with flying eagle logo. Bottom marked. Mfg. IS **125-150**

MP-*demi spoon* bottom marked "MP". Mfg. IS **25-35**

MP-*fish fork* bottom marked "Missouri Pacific Lines". Mfg. IS **15-20**

MP- *Tureen* with lid. Measures 10 oz. Side marked with buzz saw logo & bottom stamped "MP". Mfg IS. Embossed tulip floral design **100-125**

MP-*Ice cream dish* pedestal style. Side marked with Flying Eagle logo. Bottom stamped. Mfg. IS **55-65**

MP-*ice teaspoon* bottom marked "Missouri Pacific Lines". Mfg. IS **10-15**

MP-*oval tray* measures 8" diameter. Top marked with Buzz saw logo. Bottom stamped. Mfg. IS **75-85**

MP-*sauce boat* bottom stamped "MP" Mfg. IS **35-45**

MP-*soup spoon* bottom marked with "Missouri Pacific Lines". Mfg. IS **5-10**

MP-*sugar bowl* 12 oz size side marked with buzz saw logo. Bottom marked "Missouri Pacific Lines". Mfg IS **100-125**

MP-*sugar tongs* inside marked "Missouri Pacific Lines". Mfg. Roger **75-85**

NASHVILLE CHATANOOGA & ST.LOUIS

NC&STL-*sugar tongs* top marked. Sierra pattern. Mfg. IS **300-350**

NEW YORK CENTRAL

NYC-*cocoa pot* 10oz size with hinged lid. Top marked "NYC" on lid. Mfg. IS **70-80**

NYC-*cream pitcher* ½ pint size with handle. Bottom marked "NEW YORK CENTRAL". Mfg. Barbour Silver Co. **75-85**

NYC-*creamer* 8 oz size top marked "NYC" on lid. Mfg. IS **70-80**

NYC-*demi spoon* bottom marked "NYC" **Century B Pattern,** Mfg.IS **20-25**

NYC-*footed salad bowl* measures 6 1/8" diameter. Bottom marked "NYC LINES". Mfg. R&B **50-60**

NYC-*6" ladle* bottom marked "NYC" **Century B Pattern,** Mfg. IS **55-65**

NYC-*Menu holder* half moon style. Side marked "NYC". Mfg. IS **125-150**

NYC-*Menu holder* with fancy screen design. Bottom marked "NYC". Mfg. R&B **100-125**

NYC-*small jelly spoon* bottom marked "NYC". **Century B pattern** MFg. IS **15-20**

NYC-*sugar bowl* double handled with footed base. Bottom stamped "NYC LINES". Mfg. R&B **85-95**

NYC-*sugar bowl* 8 oz size with hinged lid. Top marked "NYC" on lid & bottom stamped NYC. Mfg. IS **75-85**

NYC-*glass water carafe* with silver frame marked "NYC LINES" on inside of lid. Mfg. R&B **250-300**

NYC-*butter pat or tip tray* top marked with NYC SYSTEM logo, "Quality Railroad Service" around logo. Mfg IS **65-75**

NYC-*cocktail fork* bottom marked "NYC" Mfg. IS **15-20**

NEW YORK NEW HAVEN & HARTFORD

NEW HAVEN RR-*coffee pot.* 10 oz size with hinged lid. Bottom marked "New Haven RR". Leaf design around top edge. Mfg. R&B **85-95**

NEW HAVEN RR-*demi spoon* bottom marked "New Haven RR". Mfg. Victor **20-25**

NEW HAVEN RR- *dinner fork* bottom marked "New Haven RR". Mfg. IS **10-15**

NEW HAVEN RR- *ice tongs* measure 7" long. Inside marked "New Haven RR". Bird claw ends. Mfg. R&B **95-110**

NEW HAVEN RR-*sugar tongs.* Inside marked New Haven RR. Alamo pattern. Mfg. Wallace **75-85**

NYNH&H-*soup tureen* with lid & double handled. Bottom marked "NYNH&HRR". Mfg. R&B **75-85**

NYNH&H-*creamer* 8 oz size with handle. Bottom marked "NYNH&HRR". Mfg. R&B **40-50**

NYNH&H-*oval tray* measures 12" diameter. Bottom marked "NYNH&HRR". Mfg. R&B **50-60**

NYNH&H-*sugar bowl* 11 oz size with lid. Bottom marked "NYNH&HRR". Mfg. R&B **65-75**

NYNH&H-*sugar tongs* marked inside. Mfg. Gorham **75-85**

NORTHERN PACIFIC RAILROAD

NP-*ice bowl* with pedestal base. Side marked with NPR Yellowstone Park logo. Bottom marked "NPR" in script letters. Mfg.R&B **150-175**

NP-*bakers dish* measures 6" oval. Side marked with Yellowstone Park logo. Bottom marked "Northern Pacific Ry" on underside of lid and bowl. Mfg. IS **175-200**

NP-*creamer* 8 oz size with hinged lid. Side marked with Yellowstone Park logo. Mfg. IS **150-175**

NP-*creamer* 7 oz size with hinged lid. Side marked with Monad logo. Bottom marked NPR in script letters. Pagoda style lid on pedestal base. Mfg IS **125-150**

NPR-*fish fork* top marked in script letters. **Winthrop pattern** Mfg. Gorham **25-35**

NP-*knife, fork or spoon* top marked with Monad logo. "NPR" on reverse. **Pattern Embassy.** Mfg. R&B **25-35**

NP-*knife, fork or spoon* bottom marked "Northern Pacific Railway Company". **Pattern Silhouette.** Mfg. IS **15-20**

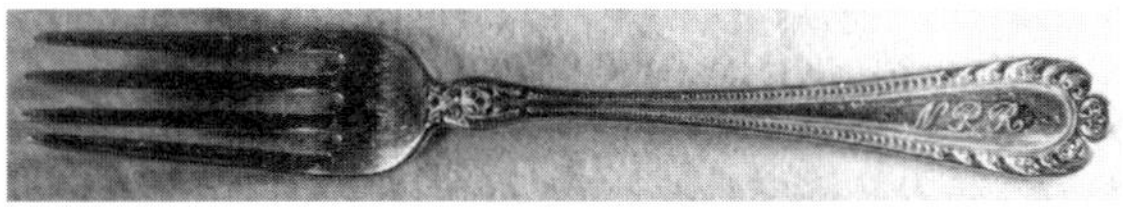

NPR-*knife, fork or spoon* top marked "NPR" in script letters on **Winthrop pattern** silverware. Mfg. Gorham **30-40**

NPR-*6" or 7" ladle* top marked with Monad logo. Bottom marked NPR. Pattern **Embassy pattern** **100-125**

NP- *sugar bowl.* Lid marked with Monad logo. Bottom marked "NPR". Pagoda style with pedestal base. Mfg. R&B **150-175**

NP-*sugar bowl.* ½ pint size. Side marked with Yellowstone Park logo. Bottom marked "NPR". Mfg. R&B **100-125**

NP-*supreme set.* Two piece set with glass insert. Top juice ring has Yellowstone Park logo. Bottom piece marked "NPR". Mfg. IS .. **100-125**

NP-*Syrup pitcher* with attached underliner. Side marked with Yellowstone Park logo. Bottom marked "NPR" Mfg. IS **100-125**

NP-*Syrup pitcher* with attached underliner. Side marked with Monad logo. Bottom marked NPR. Mfg. R&B. Pagoda style....... **275-325**

NP- *Water carafe* with cut glass Yellowstone Park logo on insert. Frame inside marked on lid "Northern Pacific Railroad".Mfg. IS .... ◆

NORFOLK & WESTERN RAILROAD

N&W-*Glass water carafe* with silver frame top marked "N&W" in fancy script letters. Patented 12/14/09. Mfg. R&B **250-300**

N&W-*teaspoon* top marked "N&W" stenciled design letters. Mfg. Wallace **5-10**

OREGON SHORT LINE

OSL-*dinner fork.* Bottom marked "OSLRR". **Pattern Avalon** Mfg. Community. Circa 1911 .... **75-85**

OSL-*teaspoon* bottom marked "OSLRR". **Pattern Avalon**. Mfg. Community. Circa 1911. .... **90-100**

PENNSYLVANIA RAILROAD

PRR-*syrup pitcher* with dripless spout. Keystone logo raised on side. Bottom stamped PRR in script letters. Mfg. IS **200-250**

PRR-*chocolate pot* 14 oz size with hinged lid. Has raised keystone logo on side. Mfg. IS **100-125**

PRR-*salt & pepper shaker set* with PRR Keystone logo in center of lid. Glass jars in octagon shape. **325-375**

PRR-*butter pat* bottom stamped "PRR". Mfg. IS **30-40**

PRR-*creamer* with hinged lid. Side marked "PRR" in script letter. Mfg. Rowley Co. **65-75**

PRR-*sugar tongs* side marked with PRR Keystone logo.**Kings pattern** Mfg. R&B **100-125**

PRR-*teaspoon* top marked "PRR" in Keystone logo. Mfg. IS **15-20**

PRR-*water carafe* with cut glass insert. "PRR" keystone logo cut into glass. Silver frame marked "PRR" on side of lid. Mfg. IS **600-650**

PERE MARQUETTE

PM-*finger bowl* side marked & bottom stamped. Mfg. Wallace **100-125**

PULLMAN

PULLMAN-*butter pat* measures 3 ½" square. Bow & lines pattern around edge. Bottom marked "The Pullman Co.". Mfg. IS ... **25-35**

PULLMAN-*creamer* 10 oz size with hinged lid. Bottom marked "The Pullman Company". Mfg. IS **65-75**

PULLMAN-*ladle* bottom marked "The Pullman Company". Pattern Cromwell. Mfg. IS **35-45**

PULLMAN-*mustard pot* silver frame with glass insert. Frame bottom marked "The Pullman Company". Mfg. IS **90-100**

PULLMAN-*oval tray* 10" diameter. Bottom marked "The Pullman Company". Mfg. IS **50-60**

PULLMAN-*thermos* side marked "PULLMAN". Mfg. Stanley Thermos. **65-75**

PULLMAN-*hot food or cake cover*. Measures 6 5/8" diameter. Ribbon & thread design. Inside marked "The Pullman Company". Mfg. IS **50-60**

QUEEN & CRESCENT ROUTE

Q&C-*creamer* 3 oz size with hinged lid. Side marked with applied Q&C box logo. Mfg. Wallace **175-200**

Q&C-*teapot* 10 oz size with hinged lid. Side marked with applied Q&C box logo. Mfg. Wallace **275-325**

Q&C-*soup tureen* 12 oz size with double handles. Side marked with applied Q&C box logo. Mfg. Wallace **275-325**

READING RAILWAY

READING LINES-*meat clever* side marked "Reading Lines" with wood handle. **75-85**

READING LINES-*butter pat* measures 3" square. Bottom stamped "Reading Co". Mfg. IS **20-30**

READING LINES-*sugar bowl* 8 oz size. Bottom marked "Reading Co.". Mfg IS **75-85**

RICHMOND FREDRICKSBURG & POTOMAC

RF&P-*menu holder.* Side marked with triangle "Richmond Washington Line" logo. Mfg. IS **200-250**

RIO GRANDE WESTERN

RIO GRANDE WESTERN-*soup tureen* with lid & double handles. Bottom marked with RGW diamond logo. Mfg. R&B...... **175-200**

RIO GRANDE WESTERN-*mustard pot* silver frame with glass insert. Frame bottom marked with RGW diamond logo. Mfg. R&B **200-250**

RIO GRANDE WESTERN-*sugar bowl* with lid. 14oz size. Bottom marked with RGW diamond logo. Mfg. R&B **175-200**

RIO GRANDE WESTERN-*knife, fork or spoon* bottom marked with RGW diamond logo. **Pattern Claredon**. Mfg. R&B **35-45**

RUTLAND RAILROAD

RUTLAND-*crumber* top marked with Rutland box logo. Mfg. IS. **300-350**

ST LOUIS & SAN FRANCISCO

FRISCO- *butter pat.* Square design. Bottom marked. Mfg. GMCo. **30-40**

FRISCO-*sugar bowl.* 11 oz size with lid. Bottom marked. Mfg. R&B **75-100**

FRISCO *tablespoon.* Bottom marked "Frisco". **Sierra pattern.** Mfg. R&B **15-20**

SEABOARD AIR LINE

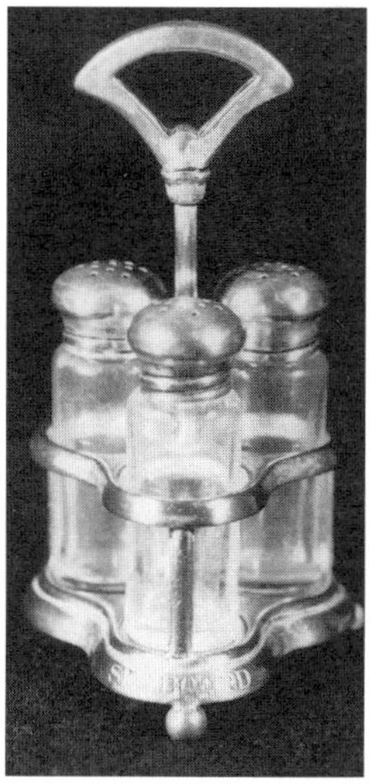

SEABOARD-*cruet or condiment set* with three glass bottles in silver frame. Frame top marked along bottom edge "Seaboard" & bottom marked "SAL #4".Mfg. IS **175-200**

SEABOARD-*cocoa pot* 10 oz size with hinged lid. Side marked "SCL". Mfg. IS **90-100**

SEABOARD-*menu holder* side marked "SEABOARD". Two pencil holders on either side. Mfg. IS. **125-150**

SEABOARD-*tureen* 32 oz size with double handles and lid. Bottom marked "SAL #28". Private car use. Mfg. IS. **150-175**

SOUTHERN RAILWAY

SRY-*creamer* 2 oz size bottom stamped "Southern Railway". Mfg. R&B. **50-60**

SRY-*finger bowl* bottom stamped "Southern Railway". Mfg. IS **40-50**

SRY-*sugar bowl* 12 oz size with lid. Side marked with arrow logo. Mfg. R&B **100-125**

SRY-*spoon fork or knife* bottom marked "Southern" **Pattern #172**. Mfg. R&B **5-10**

SRY-*sugar tongs* top marked "Southern" **Pattern Sierra**. Mfg. R&B **70-80**

SOUTHERN PACIFIC RAILROAD

SP-*butter icer*. Bottom marked "Southern Pacific". Mfg. R&B **40-50**

SP-*cash tray* measures 7" diameter. Engraved scene of passenger train in center and bottom marked "SP LINES". Mfg. R&B **200-250**

SP-*coffee pot* 10 oz size side marked with SP ball & wing logo. Bottom marked "SP Lines". Mfg. R&B **100-125**

SP-*knife fork or spoon* with Sunset logo top marked.on **Clovelly pattern** silver. Mfg. R&B **15-20**

SP-*mustard pot* with glass insert. Side marked with logo & bottom marked "Southern Pacific". Leaf & ribbon design Mfg. IS **175-200**

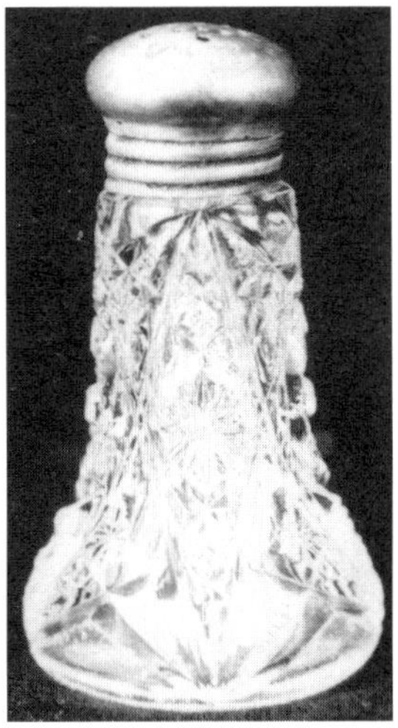

SP-*salt shaker* with cut glass base. Top marked "SPCo" in script letters. **85-95**

SP-*sherbert, ice cream cup holder*. Missing silver bowl insert. Side marked "Southern Pacific". Mfg. R&B **90-100**

SP-*sugar tongs* top marked with "Southern Pacific" Grecian Pattern. Mfg. R&B **100-125**

SP-*sugar tongs* inside marked "SPCO" in script letters. Westfield pattern. Mfg. IS **95-110**

SP-*syrup pitcher* 10 oz size with attached underliner. Side marked with Sunset logo and bottom stamped. Mfg. R&B **100-125**

SP- *teaspoon* **Renaissance pattern**. Bottom marked. MFg. **65-75**

SPOKANE PORTLAND & SEATTLE

SP&S- *soup spoon*.bottom marked "SP&SRY" **Pattern Embassy**. Mfg. R&B **20-25**

SP&S-*sugar bowl* double handled with lid. Bottom marked "SP&SRY". MFg. Grand Silver Co. **75-85**

TEXAS & PACIFIC RAILWAY

T&PRY-*beverage glass holder* side marked with T&P diamond logo. Mfg. IS **200-250**

T&PRY-*creamer* 8 oz size with hinged lid. Side marked with T&P diamond logo. Bottom stamped. Mfg. R&B **200-250**

T&PRY-*coffee pot* 10 oz size with hinged lid. Side marked with T&P diamond logo. Bottom stamped. Mfg. R&B **250-300**

T&PRY-*hot food cover* measures 9 ½" diameter. Side marked with Flying Eagle logo. Inside marked "Texas & Pacific Railway". Mfg. IS **100-125**

T&PRY- *knife, fork or spoon* bottom marked "Texas & Pacific Ry". Mfg. IS. **20-25**

T&PRY-*6" ladle* top marked with T&P in script letters. MFg. Wallace **85-95**

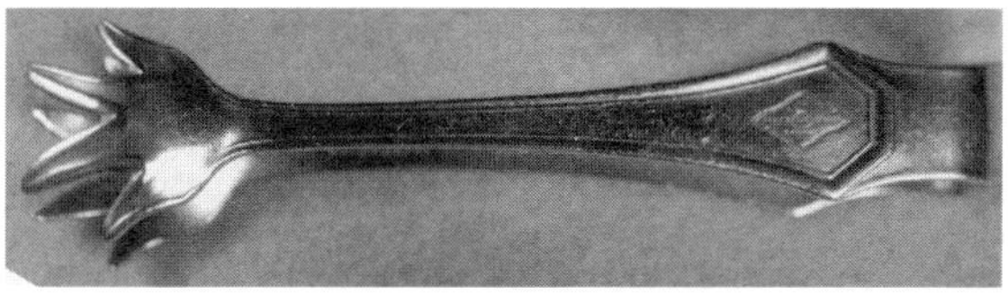

T&PRY-*sugar tongs* top marked with diamond logo.**Sierra pattern** MFg. R&B **175-200**

UNION PACIFIC RAILROAD

UP-*caster set* with salt & pepper shakers. Silver frame bottom marked "UPRR" in script letters. Mfg. IS **100-125**

UP-*butter pat* bottom marked "UPRR" in script letters. Mfg. IS **35-45**

UP-*corn cob holders* both side marked "UP SYSTEM". Mfg. R&B **65-75**

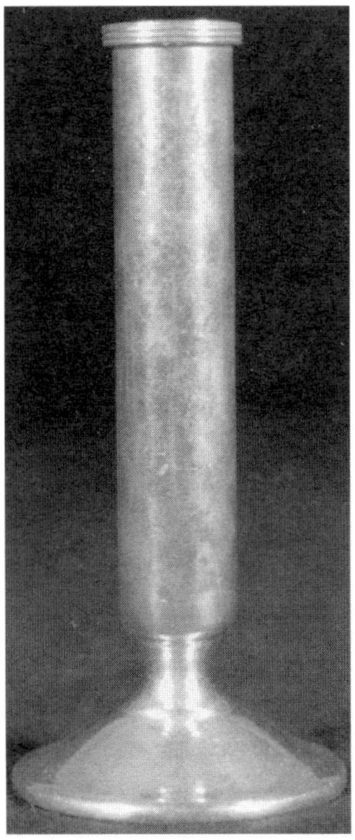

UP-*bud vase-* bottom marked "UPRR' in script letters. Mfg. IS **100-125**

UP-*chocolate pot* 10 oz size with hinged lid. Bottom marked "UPRR" in script letters. Mfg. IS **65-75**

UP-*coffee pot* 1 pint size side marked with Overland Route logo. Bottom stamped "UPRR". Mfg. R&B **175-200**

UP-*coffee pot* 64 oz size side marked with Winged Streamliner logo. Bottom marked "UPRR". Mfg. IS **300-350**

UP-*demi spoon* bottom marked "UPRR" in script letters. **Pattern Vermont** **20-30**

UP-*gravy or sauce boat* side marked with Overland Route logo, bottom stamped UP SYSTEM. Mfg. R&B **125-150**

UP-*hot food cover* top marked with Overland Route logo, also bottom marked UP SYSTEM. Mfg. R&B **125-150**

UP- *ice bucket* bottom marked "UPRR" in script letters. Mfg. R&B **60-70**

UP-*knife fork or spoon* in **Savoy pattern**. Bottom marked "UPRR" in script letters. Mfg. IS **10-15**

UP-***menu holder*** bottom marked "UPRR" in script letters. Mfg. IS **90-110**

UP-*mustard pot* side marked with Overland Route logo with original glass insert. Mfg. IS **150-175**

UP-*oval tray* top marked with Overland Route logo. 9" size. Leaf & ribbon design around outer edge. Mfg. R&B **100-125**

UP-*soup tureen* 20 oz size with lid. Bottom marked "UPRR" in script letters. MFg. IS **65-75**

UP-*soup tureen* 1 pint size with attached underliner. Side marked with "Overland Route" logo. Bottom marked "UPRR". Mfg. R&B **125-150**

UP-*syrup pitcher* with attached underliner. Side marked with Overland Route logo. Bottom marked UP SYSTEM. MFg. R&B ... **125-150**

UP-*underliner tray* measures 5 ¼" round bottom marked "UPRR" in script letters. Mfg. IS **30-40**

UP- *water carafe.* Ribbed design glass insert in silver frame top marked with "Overland Shield" logo. Inside of lid marked "UPRR". Mfg. R&B **500-550**

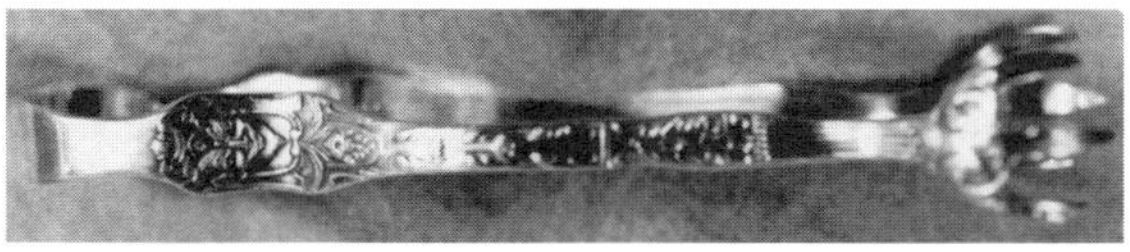

UP-*sugar tongs* inside marked "UPRR" in script letters. **Renaissance pattern.** Mfg. **200-250**

UP-*mustard pot with ladle.* Bottom marked "UPRR" in script letters. Mfg. IS **85-95**

UP-*tray* measures 6 " diameter. Top marked with Overland Route logo. Rope & ribbon design around edge. Mfg. IS **75-85**

UP-*tureen* one pint size side marked with Overland Route logo, bottom stamped UP SYSTEM. MFg. R&B **125-150**

UINTAH RAILWAY

UINTAH-***syrup pitcher*** with attached underliner. Side marked "UNITAH RAILWAY". Mfg. Rogers **250-300**

UINTAH- *knife, fork or spoon* top marked "UNITAH RY" in script letters. **Pattern Windsor.** Mfg. Rogers **55-65**

WABASH RAILROAD

WABASH- *water carafe.* Wabash Flag logo cut into glass. Silver frame inside marked "Wabash". Mfg. IS .... ◆

WESTERN PACIFIC

WESTERN PACIFIC-*fish fork* bottom marked with WP Feather River Route logo. Mfg. Is **35-45**

CHAPTER 17

EXPRESS

The various express companies that serviced the railroads are very much a large collectible part of the railroad hobby. Express items including employee badges, wax sealers, locks & keys & signs are unique and desirable in their own way. Signs of course adorned all the depots pointing the way for the traveling public to send their valuables as well as handle their financial needs while on the road. There were many Express Companies around the country servicing not only the major railroads but also industry & business. The most famous of course would have to be Wells Fargo & Company Express one of the first which certainly helped settle the west. Great history goes with many of these companies making the hobby of collecting more exciting & fulfilling. As with all the other collectibles condition is paramount. Signs with heavy porcelain loss are certainly worth less than those that have been well preserved. All items must be in good condition to command the prices suggested here.

REMEMBER: PRICES SHOWN ARE SUGGESTED VALUES ONLY. VALUES VARY FROM REGION TO REGION. THIS IS MEANT ONLY AS A GUIDE. **(◆) Denotes value over $1000.00**

ADAMS EXPRESS COMPANY

AD EX CO-*brass switch key* tapered barrel double ring key **300-350**

AD EX CO-*brass lock* heart shaped. Cast down panel "AD.EX.CO." **500-550**

ADAMS EXPRESS COMPANY- oval or round brass *wax sealer* with wood or nickel handle from "Anytown USA". *Photo has been reversed to make it legible* **100-125**

ADAMS EXPRESS CO.- *metal strong box.* Measures 12" x 12" x 16" and weighs approximately 75 pounds. **300-350**

ADAMS EXPRESS COMPANY-*call card.* Cardboard sign two sided measures 13 ½" x 19 ½". Orange background with gold lettering & metal frame **450-500**

ADAMS EXPRESS COMPANY- *rate cutter.* Brass measures 6 ½" x 1 ½". **90-100**

ADAMS EXPRESS COMPANY-*porcelain sign* red, green & white reads, "MONEY ORDERS SOLD HERE". **400-450**

AMERICAN EXPRESS COMPANY

AM.EX.CO. *brass lock* heart shaped cast down panel "AM.EX.CO". No manufacturer shown **350-400**

AM.EX.CO-*brass lock* heart shaped with iron shackle. Cast down panel AM,EX,CO. Manufactured by Climax **300-350**

AM.EX.CO.- *wax sealer* oval or round brass base with metal bulb or wood handle. With "Anytown USA" designation **100-125**

AMERICAN EXPRESS CO.- *oval brass wax sealer* with nickel or wood handle from "Anytown USA". Photo has been reversed to make it easier to read **90-100**

AMERICAN EXPRESS CO- *paperweight* celebrating the 100 year anniversary dated 1850-1950 Clear with gold & red inlaid logo in center **30-40**

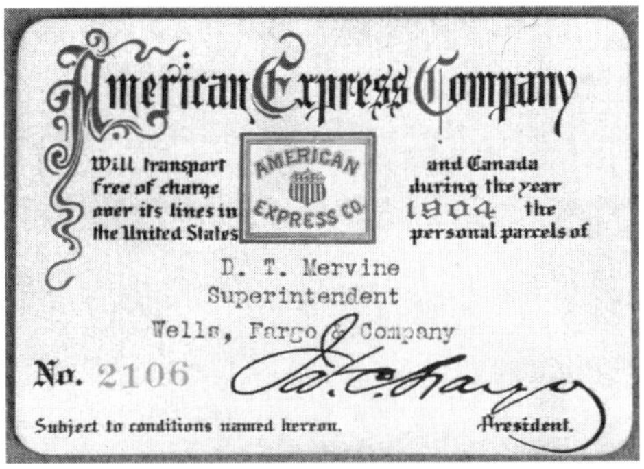
American Express Company
Will transport free of charge over its lines in the United States and Canada during the year 1904 the personal parcels of
D. T. Mervine
Superintendent
Wells, Fargo & Company
No. 2106
Subject to conditions named hereon. President.

AMERICAN EXPRESS COMPANY-*parcel pass* dated 1904 black on white with red, white & blue logo in center. **20-30**

AMERICAN EXPRESS COMPANY- *porcelain sign* "MONEY ORDERS SOLD HERE" Double sided blue on white with flanged edge measures 17" x 13" **350-400**

AMERICAN EXPRESS COMPANY-*porcelain sign* reads, "MONEY ORDERS, FOREIGN CHECKS, TRAVELERS CHEQUES, LETTERS OF CREDIT, TELEGRAPHIC TRANSFERS" white on blue double sided with flanged edge **400-450**

AMERICAN EXPRESS COMPANY- *counter scale* 24 pound marked on both sides. **125-150**

AMERICAN RAILWAY EXPRESS

AM.RY.EX.- *lead seal press.* Iron pliers like tool measures 9 ½" long. Mfg. J. Brooks. **25-35**

AM.RY.EX.- *steel lock* stamped on body & shackle. Comes with marked AM. EX. Co. key. Mfg. Corbin. **45-55**

AMERICAN RAILWAY EXPRESS–*call card.* Cardboard with metal frame sign measures 12" x 12" Green with red & white letters **100-125**

AMERICAN RAILWAY EXPRESS- *wax sealer* round or oval brass with wood or metal handle and issued in "Anytown USA". *Photo has been reversed to make it legible* **100-125**

AMERICAN RAILWAY EXPRESS AGENCY- *cap badge* with light blue enamel inlay **90-100**

AMERICAN RAILWAY EXPRESS AGENCY-*celluloid badge* diamond shaped with logo & #2253. Aluminum frame. Mfg. Bastien. **75-85**

AMERICAN RAILWAY EXPRESS- *sign* porcelain three piece design with words on each. Green with yellow brown & orange letters & shading **250-300**

AMERICAN RAILWAY EXPRESS AGENCY- *cap badge* with green enamel inlay. **75-85**

CANADIAN NATIONAL EXPRESS COMPANY

CAN. NAT'L EXPRESS CO- *wax sealer* round brass seal with wood handle............... **150-175**

CANADIAN NATIONAL EXPRESS-*call card* measures 12" x 12". Plastic two sided... **10-15**

CANADIAN PACIFIC EXPRESS COMPANY

CANADIAN PACIFIC EXPRESS-*cap badge* shows reclining beaver on top of shield badge with serial number **175-200**

CANADIAN PACIFIC EXPRESS- *wax sealer* round or oval wax sealer with wood or nickel handle. Serial number in center........ 150-175

DENVER & RIO GRANDE EXPRESS

DENVER & RIO GRANDE EXPRESS-*parcel pass* dated 1902 with diamond logo in top left corner. 300-350

NATIONAL EXPRESS COMPANY

NATIONAL EX. CO.-*wax sealer* oval brass from Lennon , Mich. or "Anytown, USA". *Photo has been reversed to be readable* 175-200

NORTHERN EXPRESS COMPANY

NORTHERN EXPRESS- *call card* made of card-board with metal frame measures 12 ¾" diamond with Monad logo in center 700-750

PACIFIC EXPRESS COMPANY

PACIFIC EX CO- *wax sealer* round brass style with brass handle. "Anytown USA". *Photo has been reversed*...................................... 175-200

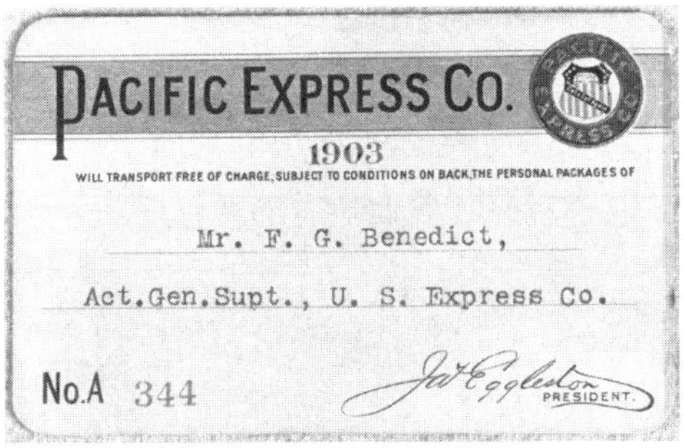

PACIFIC EXPRESS COMPANY- *parcel pass* dated 1909 black on blue 15-25

PACIFIC EXPRESS COMPANY-*brass lock* six lever style with face cast "Pacific Express Company". .... ◆

RAILWAY EXPRESS AGENCY

REA- *porcelain sign* modern diamond logo measuring 36" x 36". Red & white 150-175

REA- *porcelain sign* modern diamond logo measuring 12" x 12". Red & white 50-75

REA- *counter rack* small wooden style diamond logos applied to side of with 9 slots. Measures 5" x 13 x 13. 25-35

REA-*porcelain sign* "Packages Received Here" two sided with flanged edge and red & white logo. Measures 14" x 16" 350-400

REA-*Clipboard* with enameled REA logo over world map over Railway Express Agency. Measures 4 ½" x 9" 70-80

REA- *porcelain sign* older diamond logo on measuring 36"x 36". Red/ white & black 300-350

REA AIR EXPRESS- *porcelain sign* diamond logo red & white measures 36" x 36" 450-500

REA EXPRESS-*oval wax sealer* "Public Charlotte, NC" wood handle 75-85

RAILWAY EXPRESS AGENCY *porcelain sign* with arrow design. Yellow on white .. 150-175

RAILWAY EXPRESS AGENCY- *book* "Directory of Offices" dated 1951. Soft bound with 125 pages 10-15

RAILWAY EXPRESS AGENCY - *tin sign* reads, "Fast Dependable Through Service" with card board backing. Measures 13 ¼" x 19". **375-425**

RAILWAY EXPRESS AGENCY-*celluloid sign* "A Century of Service 1839-1939" Colorful sign with stagecoach, pony express rider, plane & train **700-750**

RY.EX.AGY- *drivers supply box* wooden, stenciled on top "RY.EX.AGY" . Measures 12" x12" x 9". Slots for labels, sealers & company forms. **150-175**

RY.EX.AGY.- *steel lock* with RY.EX.AGY. marked key. Mfg. Corbin **30-40**

RY.EX.AGY- *canvas bag.* stenciled on side "RY.EX.AGY." Measures 13" x 8" **7-10**

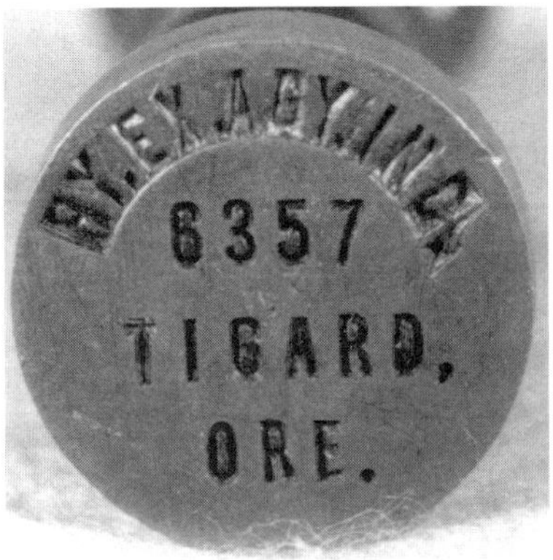

RY.EX.AGY. INC- *wax sealer* round or oval brass with wood or nickel handle from "Anytown USA" **90-100**

RY.EX.AGY.INC.- *wax sealer* reads, "Messenger" on round or oval with serial # **45-55**

RAILWAY EXPRESS AGENCY - *porcelain sign* diamond logo from side of baggage wagons. Measures 8" x 8" **100-125**

RAILWAY EXPRESS AGENCY- *cap badge*, diamond logo with red inlay **65-75**

RAILWAY EXPRESS AGENCY- *porcelain sign* measures 12" x 72" with yellow letters on black background **300-350**

RAILWAY EXPRESS AGENCY INCORPORATED- *porcelain sign* measures 12" x 72" with yellow letters on black background **275-300**

RAILWAY EXPRESS AGENCY-*call card* measures 12" x 12". Made of celluloid, double sided 75-85

<u>*SOUTHEASTERN EXPRESS COMPANY*</u>

SOUTHEASTERN EXPRESS CO.- *wax sealer* round brass with wood handle and serial number in center 250-300

<u>*UNITED STATES EXPRESS COMPANY*</u>

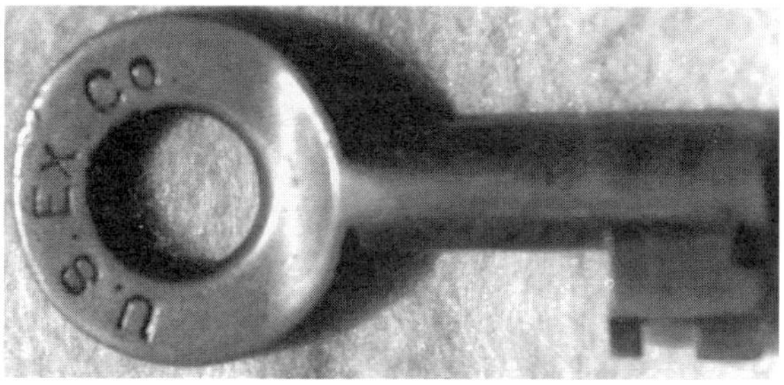

US EX CO.-*brass key* switch style with no manufacturer shown 150-175

US EXPRESS COMPANY- *parcel pass* dated 1896 black on white 15-25

US EX CO-*brass lock* stamped US EX CO on the shackle. Heart shaped lock with hole for lead sealer 200-250

UNITED STATES EXPRESS- *Employee breast badge* in small shield design with black enameled letters 250-300

<u>*WELLS FARGO & COMPANY EXPRESS*</u>

WF&CO.EXP.- 1912 *parcel frank.* Yellow on black 30-40

WF&CO-*padlock,* iron lock cast "WF&CO" down panel. Mfg. Climax with hole for lead sealer 500-550

WF&CO-*brass key* tapered barrel double ring with no manufacturer shown. 275-300

WELLS FARGO & CO'S EXPRESS-*cap badge.* Diamond celluloid logo applied to nickle badge 650-700

WF&CO-*padlock* brass lock cast "WF&CO" down panel. No manufacturer shown. Hole for lead seal **700-750**

WELLS FARGO & CO.-*porcelain sign*, 2 sided diamond logo in red, white & blue. Measures 21" x 21". **400-450**

WELLS FARGO & CO'S EXPRESS- *wax sealer* round or oval brass with metal toadstool or wood handle "Anytown USA" **200-250**

WELLS FARGO-*rate cutter* brass with black enameled letters. Lists money order rates **100-125**

WELLS FARGO & CO- *brass sign* "Travelers Checks For Sale Here" measures 4 ½" x 8" with gold chain for hanging. **250-300**

WESTERN EXPRESS COMPANY

WESTERN EX. CO- *wax sealer* round brass with brass toadstool handle **300-350**

CHAPTER 18

KEYS

It is amazing to consider that a small brass or steel padlock key could be valuable. But let us assure you they are very much worth taking a second look at. It is also interesting to note that a key does not have to have a lock to be valuable. They are very collectible on their own. The keys we are referring to are the ones used by the railroads to lock the switch stands in the train yards as well as many of the outer buildings. The keys were marked with the individual railroads initials and often times serial numbered which is how the railroads would issue the keys to their employees. Values for keys are determined not only by the condition of the key but more importantly by the railroad initials and of course the time period in which the railroad was in business. The most commonly seen key is the switch key. These were used to lock the padlocks on the various switch stands found in the train yards or along the line. Many different employees would have had keys for these padlocks, so the lock as well as the cut for the key were the same, to allow access by many different people. As a result it is still possible to find matching locks & keys even today. Many of the keys you will find will have other initials which indentify their specific purpose. For example an "S" on a key specifies "SWITCH" which is the most commonly found key. On the following pages we have listed some of the designations and their respective definitions. It is important to know the era in which a particular road was in business. If you find a key with initials from a road that was gone by the 1880's and the initials are on a modern issue key, it should immediately send up a red flag. Remember keys must be in good to excellent condition to command the suggested prices shown here.

REMEMBER: PRICES SHOWN ARE SUGGESTED VALUES ONLY. VALUES VARY FROM REGION TO REGION. THIS IS MEANT ONLY AS A GUIDE. (◆) **Denotes value over $1000.00**

KEY ABBREVIATIONS

BCC .... BAGGAGE CAR CELLAR
C .... CAR
DCC .... DINING CAR CELLAR
ED .... EASTERN DIVISION
HC .... HAND CAR
IH .... ICE HOUSE
MC .... MAIL CAR
M OF W .... MAINTENANCE OF WAY
OB .... OIL BOX
PH .... PUMP HOUSE
RT .... REPAIR TRACK
R&B .... ROADWAY & BRIDGE
SCALE .... (SPELLED OUT)
SIGNAL .... (SPELLED OUT)
SY .... STOCK YARD
S .... SWITCH
TB .... TOOL BOX
TH .... TOOL HOUSE
TR .... TOOL RACK
WD .... WESTERN DIVISION
WS .... WATER SERVICE

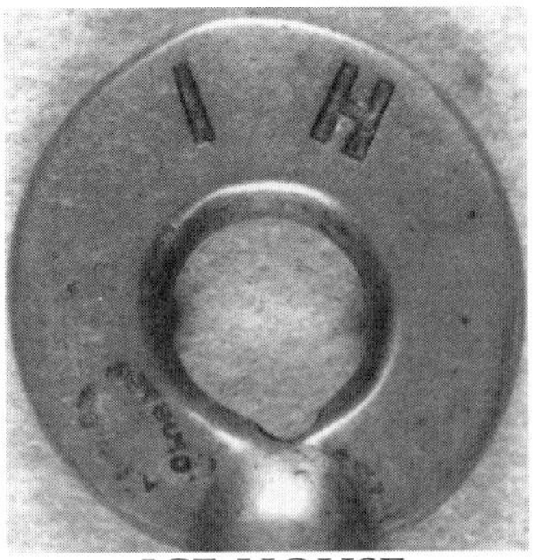

ICE HOUSE

TOOL HOUSE

SIGNAL (SPELLED OUT)

SWITC H

STOCK YARD

KEY MANUFACTURERS

Below we have shown some of the more commonly seen manufacturers marks. This is only a sample of the makers. Please note: It is not uncommon to find a key without a makers mark.

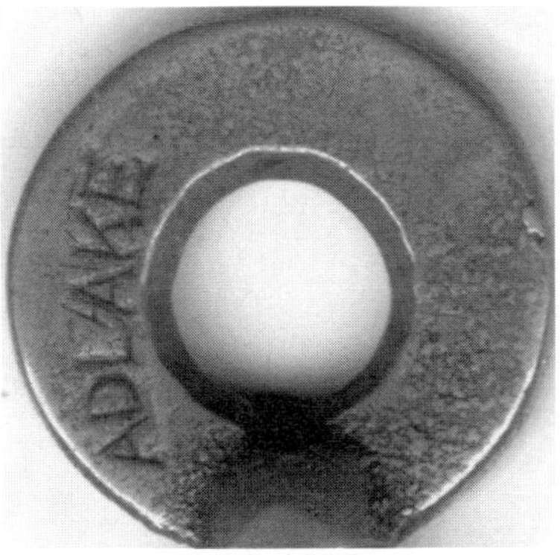

ADLAKE

ADLAKE

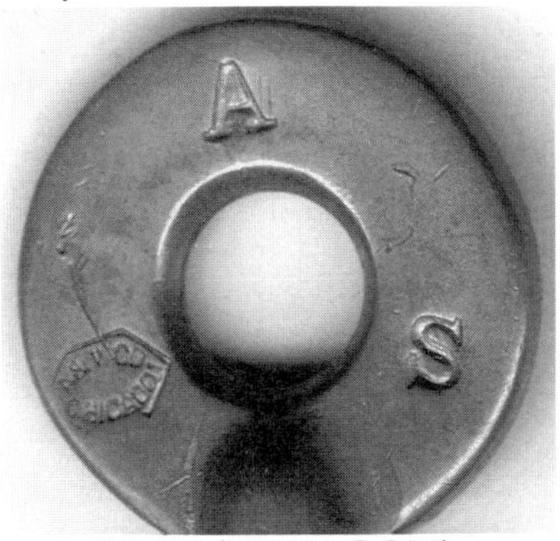

A&W (HEXAGON)

A&W (OVAL)

W. BOHANNAN

FRAIM (KEYSTONE)

FRAIM (BANNER)

FS HDW (FS HARDWARE)

HANDLAN-BUCK MFG. CO

M.M.BUCK & CO

SHERBURNE & CO.

SLAYMAKER

KEY STYLES & TIME FRAMES

It is important to learn the style of keys as well as the time period in which the key was issued. When possible this can be important in determining authenticity. Some examples are shown below. Again this is only a sample, further study is necessary to insure your confidence in collecting keys.

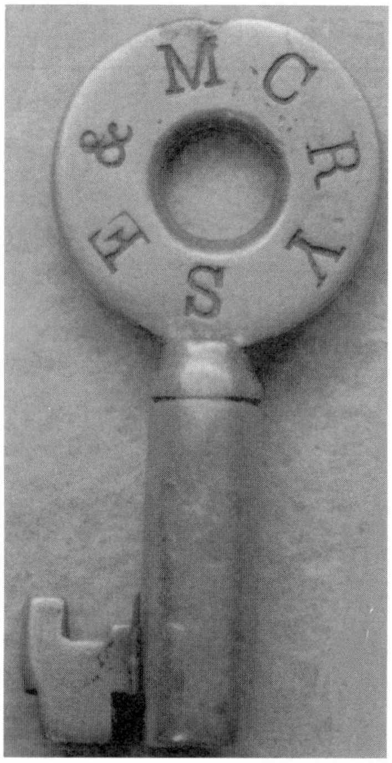

LATE 1800'S SINGLE RING TAPERED BARREL

1890'S TAPERED BARREL SERIF LETTERS

1890'S TAPERED BARREL RING HILT

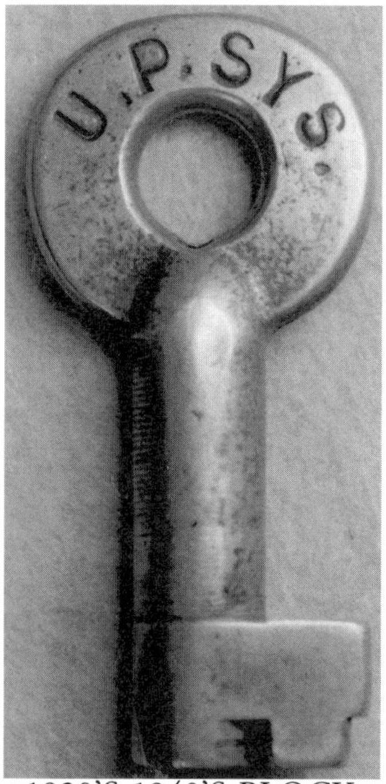

1920'S-1940'S BLOCK LETTERS

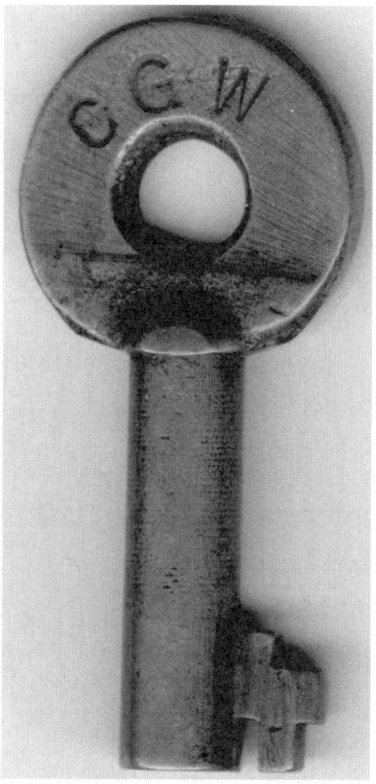

40'S TO PRESENT

STEEL OILER STYLE

AC&Y-(Akron Canton & Youngstown) reverse serial #935. 40-50

AGSRR-(Alabama Great Southern) Manufacturer is A&W in oval. "S" on reverse 90-110

A&SRR-(Albany & Susquehanna) serial #456. Mfg. Manufacturer A&W in oval......... 20-30

ARR-(Alaska)Manufacturer is Adlake 40-50

ALTON RR- no manufacturers marks, circa 1930's 50-60

A&LM- (Arkansas & Louisana Midland) "A 182" serial number on reverse. Manufacturer is Adlake 45-55

A&NRR- (Atchison & Nebraska)"C" on reverse, tapered barrel single ring key 275-325

AT&SFRR- (Atchison Topeka & Santa Fe)"S" on front of hilt on early tapered barrel key 125-150

AT&SFRR- (Atchison Topeka & Santa Fe) Manufacturer is Bohannan on single ring key 125-150

AT&SFRR- (Atchison Topeka & Santa Fe) "TOOL HOUSE" stamped on hilt reverse 100-125

AT&SFRR- (Atchison Topeka & Santa Fe) single ring tapered barrel key. Manufacturer is SB Co. These keys are a smaller style key marked with either #1, #2, #3, #4, or #5 100-125

AT&SFRY- (Atchison Topeka & Santa Fe)serial #11760 on reverse, Mfg. Adlake........... 15-20

AT&SFRYD-(Atchison Topeka & Santa Fe)no manufacturer newer key 10-15

AWP WA GA-(serial #1005. Manufacturer Adlake 30-40

ACL-(Atlantic Coast Line)serial #20709. Manufacturer Adlake 10-15

A&PRR- (Atlantic & Pacific)"S" tapered barrel key 250-300

B&ORR- (Baltimore & Ohio) serial #22083. Manufacturer Adlake.......................... 10-15

B&ORR CO.- (Baltimore & Ohio) "S" serial #81994. Manufacturer FS Hardware.... 10-15

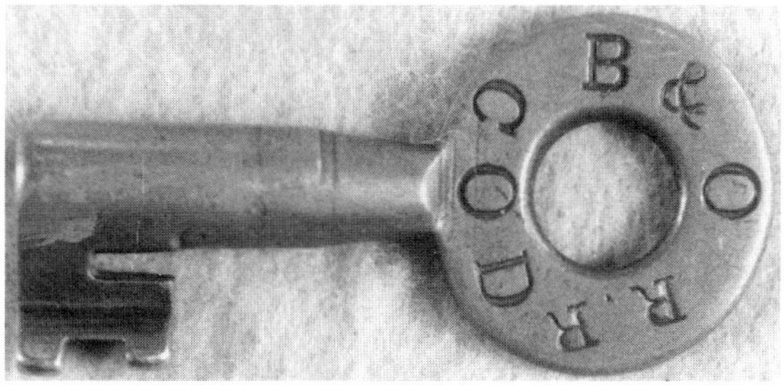

B&ORR COD-(Baltimore & Ohio) Tapered barrel double ring key......................... 90-100

B&O- (Baltimore & Ohio) Manufacturer Slaymaker 10-15

B&O- (Baltimore & Ohio) "A9513" serial numbered. Manufacturer FS Hardware 10-15

B&OLSTA- Manufacturer FS Hardware. No serial number shown............................ 20-25

B&OCTT RR- "S" on reverse. Manufacturer A&W in oval....................................... 20-30

B&A- (Boston & Albany)Manufacturer Adlake 10-15

BELT- serial #7972, Manufacturer Adlake ... 10-15

B&LERR- (Bessemer & Lake Erie) serial #6865. Manufacturer Slaymaker 55-65

B&MRR- (Boston & Maine) tapered barrel, manufacturer is Sherburne 90-100

B&MRR- (Boston & Maine) serial #3414 with no manufacturer listed......................... 15-20

B&MRR- (Boston & Maine) "S4511" on reverse. Manufacturer is Bohannan 40-50

B&MRR- (Boston & Maine) "C" on reverse. Manufacturer is Bohannan 45-50

BCR- serial #4848. Manufacturer Adlake 10-15

B&MRRR- (Burlington & Missouri River) "DS" reverse "S" NEB. Mfg. JF Wollensak, single ring key.................................. 300-350

B&MRRR-NEB-(Burlington & Missouri River Nebraska) steel key. Manufacturer A&W in oval 125-150

BCR&MRR- (Burlington Cedar Rapids & Minnesota) "S" on reverse, tapered single ring key.. 300-350

BCR&NRR- (Burlington Cedar Rapids & Northern) "S" on reverse of this early tapered key.. 200-250

BN INC- (Burlington Northern Inc.)manufacturer Adlake..................... 10-15

BURLINGTON ROUTE- large letters on this early tapered key.................................. 75-85

BURLINGTON ROUTE- small letters manufacturer is A&W in hex 25-35

BURLINGTON ROUTE- small letters manufacturer is Adlake................................. 15-25

BURLINGTON ROUTE- steel key, manufacturer is A&W in oval 20-30

BA&P- (Butte Anaconda & Pacific)"S" on reverse. No manufacturers listed............. 25-35

CNR- (Canadian National) "S"raised letters. Mfg. Mitchell 10-15

CPR- (Canadian Pacific) "S" Mfg. Mitchell **10-15**

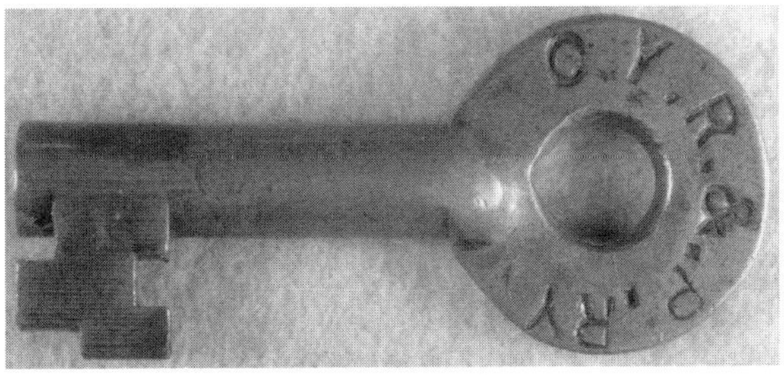

CYR&PRY- (Cananea Yaqui River & Pacific) "S" Mfg. A&W **175-200**

CRR OF GA-(Central RR of Georgia) single ring key with "S 425" on reverse. Mfg. Bohannan **100-125**

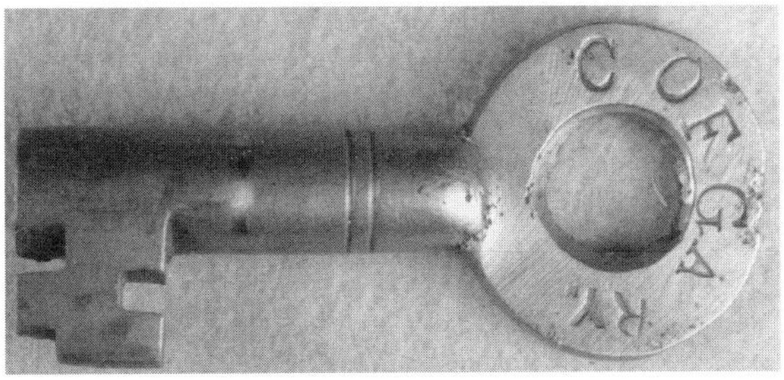

C OF GA RY- (Central of Georgia) serial #417 double ring key. Manufacturer is Climax **125-150**

CRR OF IO- (Central of Iowa)"S" on reverse of this tapered key with no listed manufacturer **225-275**

CRR OF NJ- (Central of New Jersey) serial #17157. Manufacturer is FS Hardware ... **40-50**

CRR OF NJ- (Central of New Jersey)serial #13819. Manufacturer is Slaymaker **35-45**

CVRR- (Central Vermont) manufacturer Fraim **30-40**

CVRR- (Central Vermont) manufacturer A&W in oval **35-45**

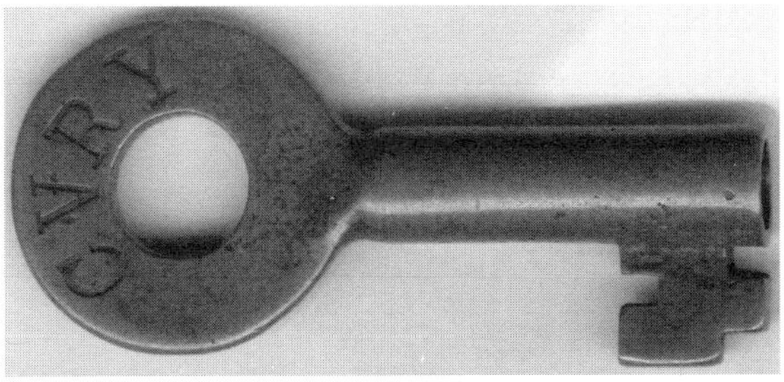

CVRY- (Central Vermont) large letters. Unknown manufacturer **40-50**

C&O- (Chesapeake & Ohio) serial #4179, Mfg. Adlake **10-15**

C&ORY-(Chesapeake & Ohio) serial #19772, Mfg. Slaymaker **15-20**

C&ARR- (Chicago & Alton) serial #8350 "S". Manufacturer is A&W in oval **25-35**

C&ARR- (Chicago & Alton) serial #7156 "S". Manufacturer Adlake **15-25**

C&EI- (Chicago & Eastern Illinois) "F 5584" manufacturer Adlake **15-25**

C&EIRR- (Chicago & Eastern Illinois) "S" manufacturer A&W in oval **25-35**

C&EIRR- (Chicago & Eastern Illinois) "S" 2201. Steel key **20-30**

C&GTRR-(Chicago & Grand Trunk) Manufacturer A&W hex early key **125-150**

C&IM- (Chicago & Illinois Midland) serial #857. Manufacturer is Adlake **15-25**

C&NERY- (Cisco & Northeastern) "S" tapered barrel. Mfg. Handlan Buck **175-200**

C&NWRR- (Chicago & Northwestern) "S" Manufacturer is A&W in oval **25-35**

C&NWRR- (Chicago & Northwestern) "S" Manufacturer is Bohannan **30-40**

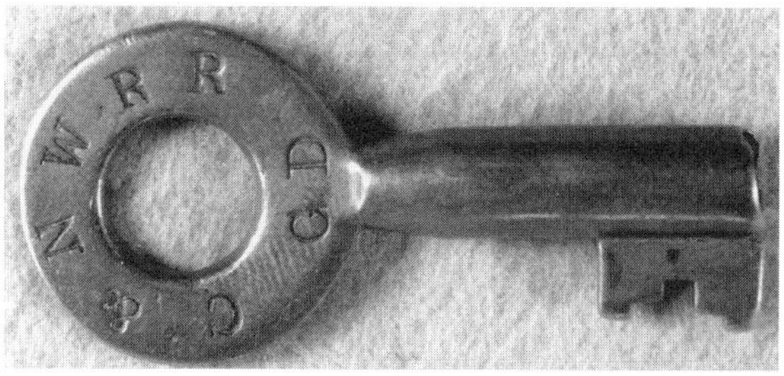

C&NWRR-(Chicago & Northwestern) "GD"(Galena Division) seriff letters tapered barrel key **100-125**

C&NWRY- (Chicago & Northwestern) "S" Manufacturere is Adlake **10-15**

C&NW- (Chicago & Northwestern)large hilt, manufacturer Adlake **10-15**

C&WIRR-(Chicago & Western Indiana) "S 375" on reverse. Manufacturer is A&W in oval.. **30-40**

C&WI-(Chicago & Western Indiana) serial #7369. Manufacturer is Adlake **20-30**

CB&Q- (Chicago Burlington & Quincy) large tapered barrel key **75-85**

CB&QRR- (Chicago Burlington & Quincy) serial #3945. Manufacturer is A&W in oval **50-60**

CGW RY- (Chicago Great Western) serial #2110 Manufacturer is A&W in oval ... **45-55**

CK&NRR- (Chicago Kansas & Nebraska) "S" manufacturer is A&W in hex. Early key **175-200**

CK&NRR- (Chicago Kansas & Nebraska)"HC" manufacturer A&W in hex design **125-150**

CM&STPRR- (Chicago Milwaukee & St Paul) Mfg. Loeffelholz **20-30**

CM&STPRR- (Chicago Milwaukee & ST. Paul) "BCC" Manufacturer Loeffelholz **40-50**

Key front mark

Key reverse mark

CM&STPRR- (Chicago Milwaukee & ST. Paul) "DCC" Manufacturer Loeffelholz **40-50**

CM&STPRR- (Chicago Milwaukee & ST. Paul) "RT". Manufacturer Loeffelholz **40-50**

CM&STP- (Chicago Milwaukee & ST. Paul) "MC" on reverse of this double bit smaller style key **75-85**

CM&STP-(Chicago Milwaukee & ST. Paul) "MC" on reverse of this double bit tapered barrel smaller style key **100-125**

CM&STPRY- (Chicago Milwaukee & ST. Paul) small letters "S" on reverse of this steel key **15-25**

CMSTP&P- (Chicago Milwuakee St Paul & Pacific) Mfg. FS Hardware **15-25**

CMST on front **P&PRR** on reverse.(Chicago Milwaukee St Paul & Pacific) Manufacturer is Adlake **10-15**

CRI&PRR (Chicago Rock Island & Pacific) "S" early tapered key. **90-100**

CRI&PRR- (Chicago Rock Island & Pacific)"S" Mfg. A&W in oval **15-25**

CRI&PRR- (Chicago Rock Island & Pacific)"HC". Mfg. A&W in oval **30-40**

CRI&PRR- (Chicago Rock Island & Pacific)"RT" Mfg. A&W in oval **75-85**

CRI&PRR- (Chicago Rock Island & Pacific) "SCALES" manufacturer is A&W in oval **80-90**

CRI&P- (Chicago Rock Island & Pacific)"IH" Mfg. A&W oval **75-85**

CRI&P- (Chicago Rock Island & Pacific) manufacturer Adlake **15-20**

CRI&P- (Chicago Rock Island & Pacific)"PH" Mfg. Adlake.. **75-85**

CRI&P- (Chicago Rock Island & Pacific)"TH" Mfg. Adlake.. **40-50**

CRI&P-(Chicago Rock Island & Pacific) small steel oiler key. Mfg. is Corbin **50-60**

CSF&CRR- (Chicago Santa Fe & California) "S" on reverse of this early tapered key........... **250-300**

CSTP&KCRR- (Chicago St. Paul & Kansas City) early tapered key....................... **250-300**

CSTPM&ORR- (Chicago St Paul Minneapolis & Omaha) "S" "ED" (EASTERN DIVISION) **40-50**

CSTPM&ORY-(Chicago St Paul Minneapolis & Omaha) "S" "WD" (Western Division) **40-50**

CSTPM&ORY-(Chicago St Paul Minneapolis & Omaha) "S" Mfg. Slaymaker............ **50-60**

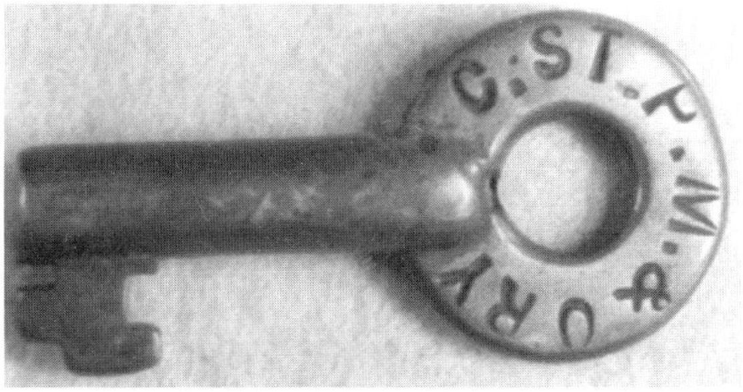

CSTPM&ORY- (Chicago St Paul Minneapolis & Omaha)"S" Mfg. A&W in oval **50-60**

CO&GRY- (Choctaw Oklahoma & Gulf) double ring early key **200-250**

CCC&STL-(Cleveland Cinncinati Chicago & St Louis) serial #X381. Mfg. A&W in oval 25-35

C&OWRY- (Clinton & Oklahoma Western) serial #135. Manufacturer is FS Hardware 100-125

C&DMRR- (Chilicothe & Des Moines) "S" on reverse of early tapered key 325-375

C&GRY-(Columbia & Greenville) Mfg. Adlake 75-85

C&SRY- (Colorado & Southern) Large seriff letters 175-200

C&SRY- (Colorado & Southern) "S 910" Mfg. A&W oval 75-85

C&SRY- (Colorado & Southern) steel key. Mfg. A&W oval 225-275

C&S- (Colorado & Southern)Mfg. Adlake .. 40-50

C&WRY- (Colorado & Wyoming) "S" on reverse. Tapered key manufactured by Handlan Buck 90-100

C&W- (Colorado & Wyoming) Mfg. Adlake, newer key 20-30

CMRR-(Colorado Midland) Single ring, tapered barrel key. Manufacturer is SB Co. Smaller style keys marked with either #1, #2, #3, #4 or #5. 150-175

CMRR-(Colorado Midland) serial #1250. No mfg. listed 175-200

CMRR- -(Colorado Midland) "S" single ring key. Manufacturer is Bohannan 200-250

CMRY- -(Colorado Midland) "S" early tapered key 225-275

CMRY- -(Colorado Midland) "S1511" on reverse. Manufacturer is Fraim 175-200

CMRY- -(Colorado Midland) "S 880". Manufacturer A&W hex 175-200

CS&CCDRY- (Colorado Springs & Cripple Creek District) "S182". Manufacturer is A&W in hex 175-200

CC&CS- (Cripple Creek & Colorado Springs) steel key, no mfg. 100-125

CRRR- (Connecticut River) early tapered key 90-100

D&H- (Delaware & Hudson) serial #229. Mfg. FS Hdw. 15-20

DL&W-(Delaware Lackawanna & Western) Manufacturer Fraim 15-25

D&RG- (Denver & Rio Grande)"S" large seriff letters 100-125

D&RG- (Denver & Rio Grande) "A2385" small seriff letters **65-75**

D&RGRR-(Denver & Rio Grande) single ring tapered barrel key. Manufacturer is Bohannan **200-250**

D&RGRR- (Denver & Rio Grande)large seriff letters with "S" on reverse **100-125**

D&RGRR-(Denver & Rio Grande) "S" F 4565. Manufacturer is A&W in oval **65-75**

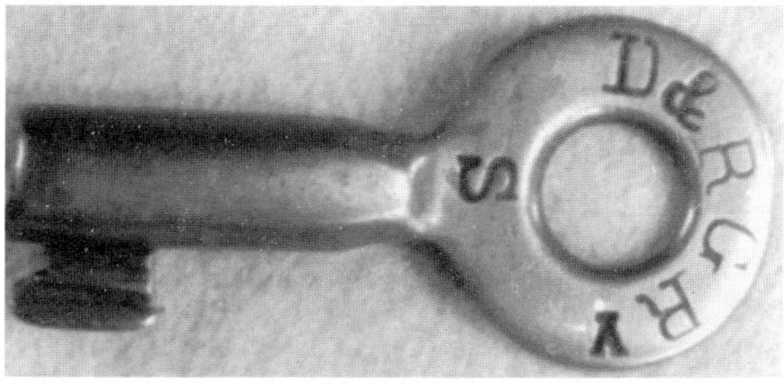

D&RGRY- (Denver & Rio Grande) "S" on front. Serial #227. Early tapered barrel key **250-300**

D&RGW- (Denver & Rio Grande Western) serial #1907. Mfg. Adlake **15-25**

D&RGWRR- (Denver & Rio Grande Western) serial #11721. Mfg. Adlake **25-35**

D&SL- (Denver & Salt Lake) serial #3213. Mfg. Adlake **50-60**

DNW&PRR- (Denver Northwestern & Pacific) steel key. Manufacturer is A&W in oval **175-200**

DNW&PRR- (Denver Northwestern & Pacific) Mfg. A&W in oval **225-275**

DSP&PRR- (Denver South Park & Pacific) early tapered key. Manufacturer is MM Buck .... ◆

DMURY- (Des Moines Union) serial #152. Mfg. Adlake **15-20**

DMU-(Des Moines Union) Mfg. Adlake newer key **10-15**

D&TSL-(Detroit & Toledo Shore Line) serial #S475, Mfg. Adlake **20-30**

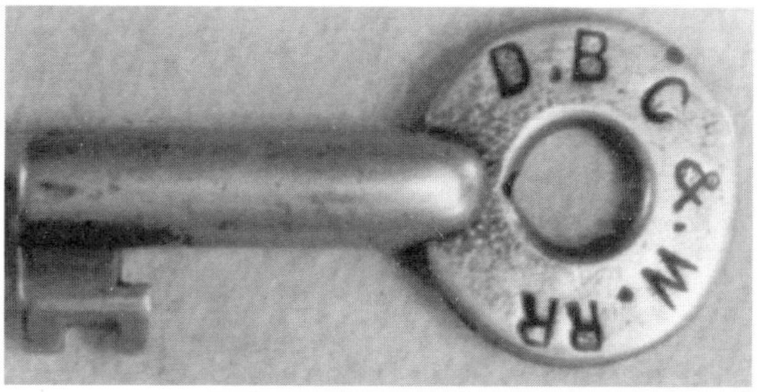

DBC&WRR- (Detroit Bay City & Western) serial #150,manufacturer is A&W in oval **125-150**

DT&I-(Detroit Toledo & Ironton) serial #4800. Mfg. Adlake **20-30**

DTRR- (Detroit Terminal) manufacturer Adlake **15-20**

D&MRR- (Duluth & Manitoba) tapered barrel single ring key. Manufacturer is JL Howard **125-150**

DM&IR- (Duluth Missabe & Iron Range) serial #1775. Mfg. Adlake **15-20**

DM&NRY- (Duluth Missabe & Northern) "MC" double bit smaller style key **175-200**

DW&P- (Duluth Winnipeg & Pacific) no manufacturer **65-75**

EJ&E- (Elgin Joliet & Eastern) serial #22885. Mfg. Adlake **15-25**

EJ&ERR- (Elgin Joliet & Eastern) "S2690". Manufacturer is A&W in oval **65-75**

EP&NE RY- (El Paso & Northeastern) "S" Mfg. MM Buck. Tapered barrel key **300-350**

EP&SW- (El Paso & Southwestern) "ED" (Eastern Division) serial #S593, Manufacturer Bohannan **200-250**

EP&SW-(El Paso & Southwestern) large letters, no mfg. **100-125**

EP&SWRY-(El Paso & Southwestern) "ED" (Eastern Division) tapered key. Mfg. Handlan Buck **200-250**

<E> (Erie) **Diamond Logo**- Mfg. Adlake...... **20-30**

ERIE- "S" Mfg. Fraim **15-25**

ERIE RR-(Erie) manufacturer FS Hdw. **20-30**

ERR- (Erie) early tapered barrel. Manufacturer is T. Slaight **100-125**

EL- (Erie Lackawanna) serial #7412. Mfg. Adlake **10-20**

E&MCRY- (Everett & Monte Cristo) large seriff letters, tapered barrel single ring key **375-425**

F&PMRY- (Flint & Pere Marquette) single ring tapered barrel key **150-175**

FL&CCRR CO- (Florence & Cripple Creek) "S" tapered barrel double ring key. **350-400**

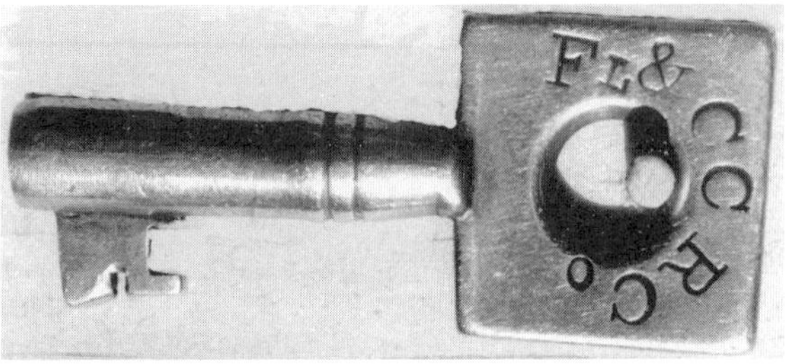

FL&CCRR CO- (Florence & Cripple Creek) "S" square hilt tapered barrel double ring key **600-650**

FEC- (Florida East Coast) manufacturer Adlake **10-15**

FECRY-(Florida East Coast) serial #5450, manufacturer Adlake **20-30**

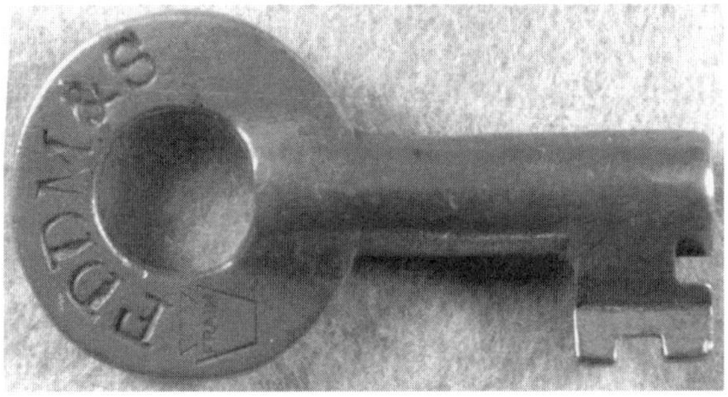

FTDDM&S-(Ft Dodge Des Moines & Southern) serial #88. Manufacturer is Fraim in Keystone **75-85**

FTDDM&S- (Ft Dodge Des Moines & Southern) large hilt, no mfg. **30-40**

FTS&W- (Ft. Smith & Western) "S" Mfg. A&W oval **75-85**

FTS&WRR-(Ft Smith & Western) Mfg. OM Edwards **150-175**

FW&DC- (Ft Worth & Denver City) Mfg. Adlake **30-40**

FTW&DCRY-(Ft Worth & Denver City) early tapered barrel "S" on reverse............. **100-125**

FW&DCRY-(Ft Worth & Denver City) "S" Mfg. A&W hex **85-95**

FWSYCO- (Ft Worth Stock Yard) serial #30 .... **50-60**

F&KRR-(Frankfort & Kokomo) early tapered key **175-200**

FE&MVRR- (Fremont Elkhorn & Missouri Valley) "S" single ring, manufacturer is Bohannan **100-125**

FRISCO- Mfg. Adlake **15-20**

FRISCO- large seriff letters. Manufacturer is Slaymaker **20-30**

FRISCO- "CAR" large seriff letters....... **65-75**

FRISCO- "RT" Mfg. Fraim **60-70**

FRISCO- "TB" Mfg. Fraim **85-95**

GR&IRR- (Grand Rapids & Indiana) serial #880S. Early tapered barrel key **100-125**

GB&WRR-(Green Bay & Western) serial #2610. Mfg. Adlake **50-60**

GTR- (Grand Trunk) steel key **25-35**

GTR-(Grand Trunk) brass key. No manufacturer **20-30**

GTRY- (Grand Trunk) "S" on reverse. Mfg. Adlake **20-30**

GTW- (Grand Trunk Western) Mfg. Adlake, newer key **10-15**

GTW- (Grand Trunk Western) 'S" cast on hilt. Mfg. RM Co. **15-20**

GNRY- (Great Northern) serial #E2550. Mfg. Slaymaker **40-50**

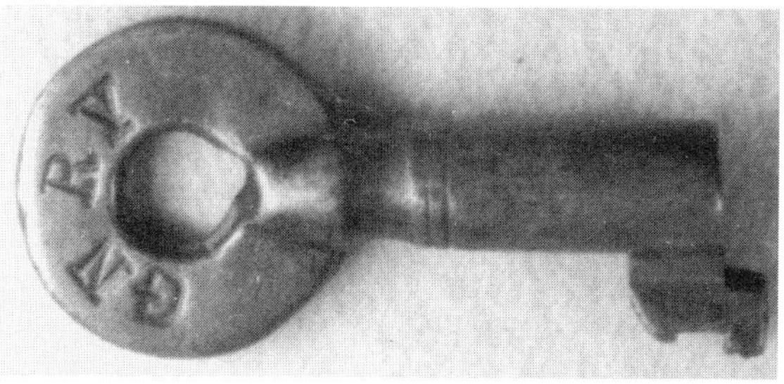

GNRY- (Great Northern) "S" early double ring tapered barrel key **200-250**

GNRY- (Great Northern) 'S" short barrel no mfg. **20-30**

GWRY- (Great Western)serial #1277 .. **30-40**

GC&SFRY-(Gulf Colorado & Santa Fe) Mfg. Adlake **45-55**

GC&SFRY- (Gulf Colorado & Santa Fe) early tapered barrel key. Mfg. SB Co. These are smaller style keys marked with either #1, #2, #3, #4 or #5. .... **100-125**

GM&ORR- (Gulf Mobile & Ohio) serial #9025 .... **25-35**

H&STJRR- (Hannibal & St. Joseph) early tapered barrel single ring key **200-250**

HBLRR- (Harbor Belt Line) serial #938. Mfg. Slaymaker **25-35**

HVRR- (Hocking Valley) serial #2249. Mfg. FS Hardware.. **65-75**

H&TC- (Houston & Texas Central) "S" Mfg. A&W in oval **65-75**

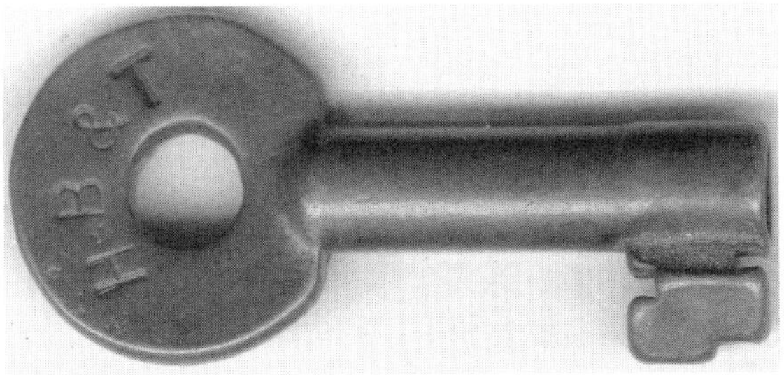

HB&T- (Houston Belt & Terminal) Mfg. Adlake **15-25**

HE&WTRY-(Houston East & West Texas) serial #405. Mfg. Fraim keystone **125-150**

ICRR- (Illinois Central) serial #K 10. Mfg. Fraim **15-25**

ICRR- (Illinois Central) serial #30550. Mfg. A&W in oval **15-25**

ICRR- (Illinois Central) serial #92650. Mfg. Adlake **10-15**

ICGRR- (Illinois Central Gulf) Mfg. Adlake **10-15**

IHB- (Indiana Harbor Belt) large hilt, Mfg. Adlake **10-15**

I&GNRR- (International Great Northern) serial #245 .... **25-35**

I&STLRR- (Indianapolis & St. Louis) serial #990 S". Mfg. Bohannan **125-150**

INRY- (Iowa Northern) "S" on reverse. Mfg. A&W in oval **70-80**

ITRR- (Illinois Terminal) reverse 1290 Mfg. Adlake **20-30**

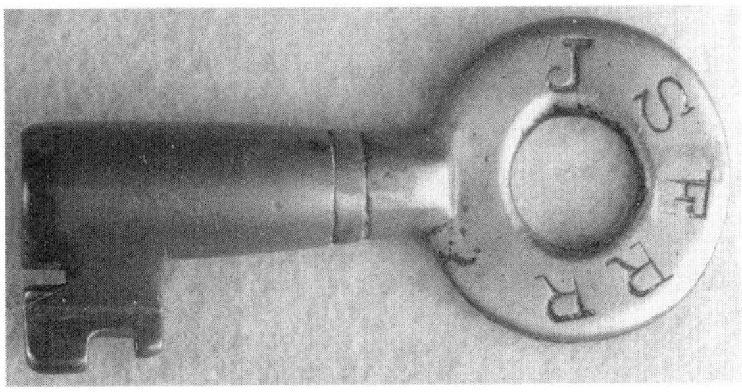

JSERR- (Jacksonville Southeastern) "S575". Tapered barrel double ring key **100-125**

JCL- (Jersey Central Lines) serial #24730 ... **15-25**

K&IT- (Kansas & Indiana Terminal) serial #2450. Mfg. Adlake **30-40**

KCFS&GRR-(Kansas City Ft. Scott & Gulf) "S" tapered barrel **200-250**

KCFS&MRR- (Kansas City Ft. Scott & Memphis) early tapered barrel **125-150**

KCKV&W- (Kansas City Kaw Valley & Western) "S" Mfg. A&W hex **125-150**

KCM&ORR- (Kansas City Mexico & Orient) reverse 770. Mfg. Adlake **125-150**

KCM&ORY- (Kansas City Mexico & Orient) Mfg. A&W oval **125-150**

KCP&GRR- (Kansas City Pittsburgh & Gulf) "S" single ring. Manufacturer Bohannan **200-250**

KCSRYCO- (Kansas City Southern) steel key. No manufacturer shown **25-35**

KCSRY- (Kansas City Southern) steel key ... **25-35**

KCS- (Kansas City Southern) large seriff letter **25-30**

KCS- (Kansas City Southern) "C" on reverse. 'S71". Smaller style key with oval hilt.. **25-30**

KCT-(Kansas City Terminal) serial #1977. Mfg. Adlake **10-15**

KO&G- '(Kansas Oklahoma & Gulf) "S" no manufacturer listed **90-100**

KPRW- (Kansas Pacific) tapered barrel. Manufacturer is MM buck **350-400**

KPRR- (Kansas Pacific) "S" single ring. Manufacturer is Bohannan **250-300**

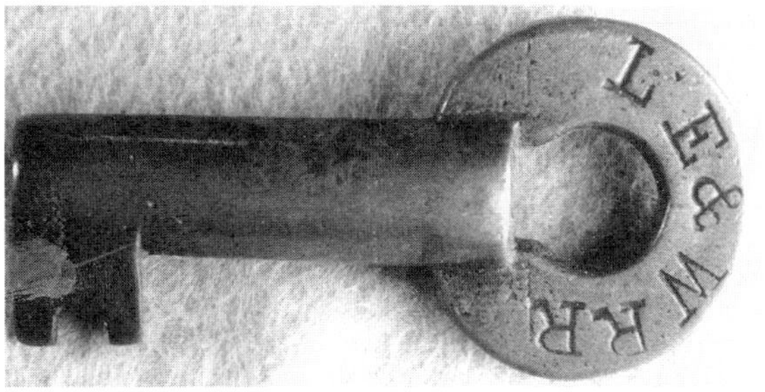

LE&WRR- (Lake Erie & Western) reverse "C" serial #510. .... **65-75**

LS&MS- (Lake Shore & Michigan Southern) large seriff letters. "S" **35-45**

LS&MSRR- (Lake Shore & Michigan Southern) "S" tapered key **75-85**

LS&MSRR- (Lake Shore & Michigan Southern) "S" Mfg. A&W hex **65-75**

LS&MSRR-(Lake Shore & Michigan Southern) steel oiler style key **25-35**

LS&I- (Lake Superior & Ishpeming) large steel oiler type key **20-30**

LVRR- (Lehigh Valley) "C 4977 S" manufacturer is A&W in oval **40-50**

LVRR- (Lehigh Valley) "S" serial #A11719 ....**35-45**

LVRR- (Ligonier Valley) serial #175. Manufacturer is GW Nock, tapered barrel, double ring **175-200**

LIRR- (Long Island) steel key. Mfg. Climax **35-45**

L&NRR- (Louisville & Nashville) serial #11590. Mfg. Fraim **15-20**

L&NRR- (Louisville & Nashville) serial #6557. Mfg. Slaymaker **10-15**

LA&SL- (Los Angeles & Salt Lake) serial #2701 "S". Manufacturer is A&W in hex **85-95**

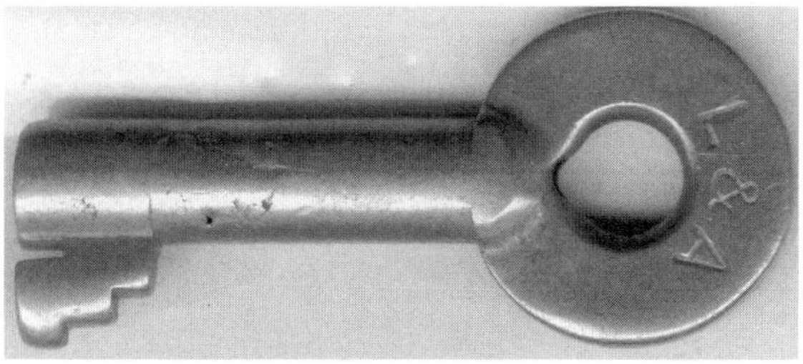

L&A-(Louisiana & Arkansas) serial #6901. Manufacturer Adlake **40-50**

L&A- (Louisiana & Arkansas) serial #6750. Mfg. Slaymaker **50-60**

L&A- (Louisiana & Arkansas) serial #5795. Mfg. Fraim **55-65**

LH&STL-(Louisville Henderson & St. Louis) manufacturer Adlake **50-60**

LA&T-(Louisiana Arkansas & Texas) Manufacturer Adlake **50-60**

LH&GRY- (Lufkin Hemphill & Gulf) Reverse "S 58". Mfg. A&W in oval. **300-350**

MCRR- (Maine Central)"C" on reverse, Mfg. Bohannan **70-80**

MCRR- (Maine Central) "S" on reverse, Mfg. Bohannan **30-40**

M&NERY- (Manistee & Northeastern) "S" Mfg. A&W oval **75-85**

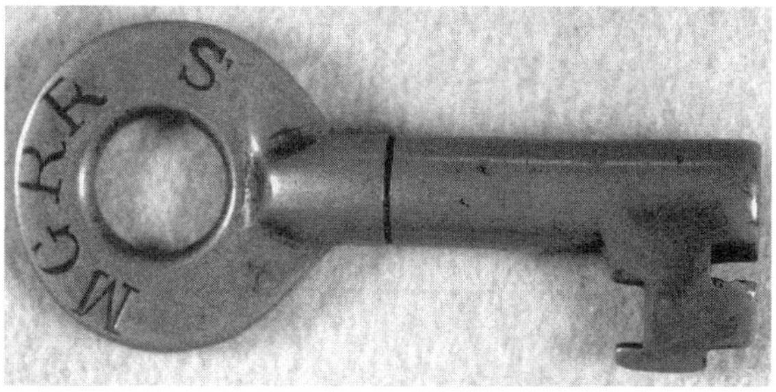

MGRR- (Manassas Gap) "S" single ring Mfg. Bohannan **100-125**

MC&CLRR- (Mason City & Clear Lake) reverse Mfg. Fraim **125-150**

MTRY- (Midland Terminal) Manufacturer Adlake **65-75**

MVRR- (Midland Valley) Mfg. FS Hardware **30-40**

MVRR- (Midland Valley)"S" Mfg. Adlake **30-40**

MVRR- (Midland Valley) Mfg. A&W in oval **50-60**

MVRR- (Midland Valley) "C" Mfg. A&W in hex **45-55**

MCRR- (Michigan Central) "S" on reverse. Mfg. Bohannan **45-55**

MNRY- (Milwaukee Northern) "S" Mfg. is A&W in oval **85-95**

M&STL- (Minneapolis & St. Louis) no manufacturer listed **20-30**

M&STLRY- (Minneapolis & St. Louis)Manufacturer Fraim **75-85**

M&STLRR- (Minneapolis & St. Louis) "S" tapered barrel **125-150**

MD&W- (Minnesota Dakota & Western) Manufacturer Adlake **80-90**

MTRYCO-(Minnesota Transfer) Mfg. Fraim **25-35**

MSTP&SSM- (Minneapolis St Paul & Sault Ste. Marie) "WC" (Wisconsin Central) mfg. Slaymaker **75-85**

MSTP&SSM- (Minneapolis St Paul & Sault Ste. Marie)no manufacturer.................. **40-50**

MSTP&SSMRR- (Minneapolis St Paul & Sault Ste. Marie)reverse "CD" Mfg. A&W in oval **40-50**

M&ORR- (Mobile & Ohio) serial #5049 .... **45-55**

MK&TRY- (Missouri Kansas & Texas) serial #12100. Tapered barrel single ring key .. **85-95**

MK&TRY- (Missouri Kansas & Texas) serial #2546. Mfg. Slaymaker **20-30**

MK&TRR- (Missouri Kansas & Texas) Manufacturer Adlake **10-15**

MOPAC-(Missouri Pacific) "REP TRACK" on reverse manufacturer is Slaymaker **40-50**

MOPAC- (Missouri Pacific) serial #1005. Mfg. Adlake **10-15**

MOPAC RR- -(Missouri Pacific)**steel key "S 4754"** **20-30**

MO PAC-(Missouri Pacific) reverse "MW" . Manufacturer unknown 10-15

MOPRR- -(Missouri Pacific)steel key "A 16055" manufacturer is A&W in oval **20-30**

MPRR- -(Missouri Pacific) serial #13550. Mfg. Adlake **10-15**

MPMW- -(Missouri Pacific Maintenance of Way) key. Mfg. FS Hardware **10-15**

MP&T&P- (Missouri Pacific & Texas & Pacific) serial #68465 .... **20-30**

MRR- (Monongahela) Mfg. Slaymaker. **50-60**

NC&STL- (Nashville Chatanooga & St. Louis) Mfg. Adlake.. **25-35**

NC&STLRY-(Nashville Chattanooga & St. Louis) serial #A1755. Manufacturer is Fraim **50-60**

NY&LB- (New York & Long Branch) serial #A887. Mfg. FS Hardware **35-45**

NY&LB- (New York & Long Branch) Mfg. Adlake **15-20**

NY&LB-(New York & Long Branch)single ring tapered barrel. Manufacturer is Gladstone Bros. **90-100**

NYCRR- (New York Central) serial #3722. Mfg. Bohannan **30-40**

NYCRR- (New York Central) serial #1559. Mfg. A&W hex **20-30**

NYCS-(New York Central System) Manufacturer Adlake **10-15**

NYCS-(New York Central System)manufacturer Fraim **15-20**

NYCS- (New York Central System) "S" single ring Mfg. Bohannan **30-40**

NYCS- (New York Central System) "TH" no mfg. shown **20-30**

NYCS-(New York Central System) large steel oiler type key **15-20**

NYC&STLRR- (New York Chicago & St. Louis) "S" 1605. Manufacturer is A&W in hex **35-45**

NYNH&H- (New York New Haven & Hartford) Manufacturer is Adlake................ **15-20**

NYNH&HRR- (New York New Haven & Hartford)steel Mfg. Adlake **15-20**

NYNH&HRR- (New York New Haven & Hartford) small steel key. Manufacturer is Eagle **15-20**

NYLE&WRR- (New York Lake Erie & Western) "S" early tapered barrel key. Mfg. Slaight **150-175**

NYO&W-(New York Ontario & Western) serial #13425. Mfg. Adlake **30-40**

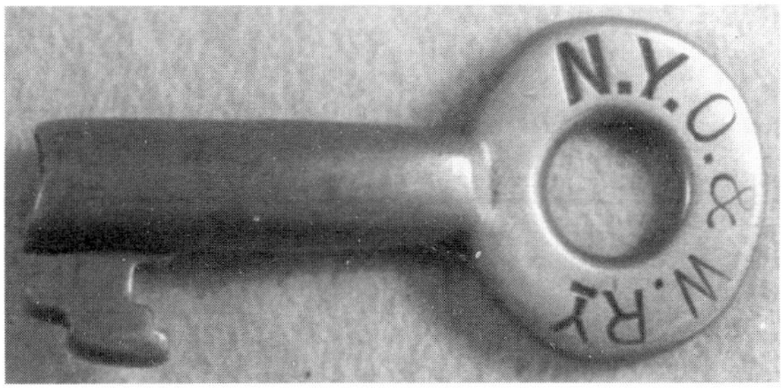

NYO&WRY-(New York Ontario & Western) tapered barrel....................................... **90-100**

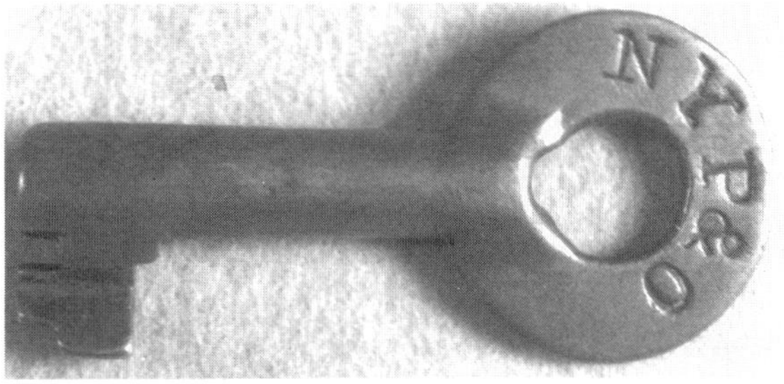

NYP&O- (New York Pennsylvania & Ohio) "S" mfg. Fraim **100-125**

NKP- (Nickel Plate) serial #9025. Mfg. Adlake **10-15**

NSRR- (North Shore) serial #10. Mfg. Adlake **15-20**

N&W-(Norfolk & Western) serial #4250 Mfg. Adlake **10-15**

N&WRY- (Norfolk & Western) serial #50400. Mfg. Slaymaker **25-35**

N&WRY- (Norfolk & Western) serial # 16486. Mfg. Adlake... **15-20**

NP- (Northern Pacific) Manufacturer Adlake **10-15**

NPRR- (Northern Pacific) early single ring key. Manufacturer is Bohannan **125-150**

NPRR- (Northern Pacific) "S" Mfg. Loeffelholz **150-175**

NPRR- (Northern Pacific) "S" serial #A495. Early tapered barrel key 150-175

NPRR- (Northern Pacific)Mfg. Fraim 40-50

NPRR- (Northern Pacific) "S" Mfg. A&W in hex 35-45

NPRY-(Northern Pacific) Mfg. Adlake 15-20

OHIO RIV.RR- reverse B189. Double ring tapered barrel key 350-400

OCRR- (Old Colony) "S" manufacturer is Loeffelholz. Ring barrel early key 75-85

OCRR- (Old Colony) "S" manufacturer Bohannan, tapered barrel single ring 75-85

OCRR- (Ohio Central) serial #95. "S" Manufacturer is William Page & Co. 250-300

OR&N- (Oregon Railroad & Navigation) serial #2255 S. Manufacturer is A&W in oval 50-60

OR&NCO-(Oregon Railroad & Navigation) Single ring.Mfg. Bohannan. Serif letters 65-75

OR&NCO- (Oregon Railroad & Navigation) serial #667. "R&B" on reverse. Mfg. A&W in oval 60-70

OR&NCO- (Oregon Railroad & Navigation) serial #662. "SPECIAL" on reverse. Mfg. A&W in oval 60-70

OSL-(Oregon Short Line)"S" serial #9950. Manufacturere is A&W in oval 40-50

OSL- CS 72 SIGNAL DEPT. -(Oregon Short Line) small steel oiler style key 60-70

OSLRR- -(Oregon Short Line) "SPECIAL" on reverse. Mfg. A&W in oval 75-85

OSLRR- -(Oregon Short Line) "S" serial #1405. Mfg. Adlake 50-60

OSLRR- -(Oregon Short Line) CS 21 R&B on reverse. Mfg. A&W in oval 60-70

OSLRR- -(Oregon Short Line) CS 2 serial #14550. Mfg. A&W in oval 50-60

OWRR&NCO- (Oregon Washington Railroad & Navigation) "S" serial #9801. Mfg. A&W in oval 75-85

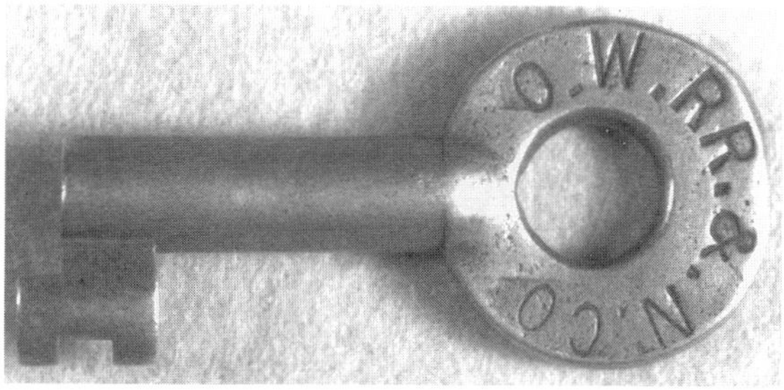

OWRR&NCO- (Oregon Washington Railroad & Navigation) "SPECIAL" Mfg. A&W in oval 90-100

OWRR&NCO- "CS3" (Oregon Washington Railroad & Navigation) on reverse 80-90

OWRR&NAV-(Oregon Washington Railroad & Navigation) serial #435S. Manufacturer is Adlake 45-55

O&CCRR- (Ozark & Cherokee Central) "S". Mfg. Bohannan 175-200

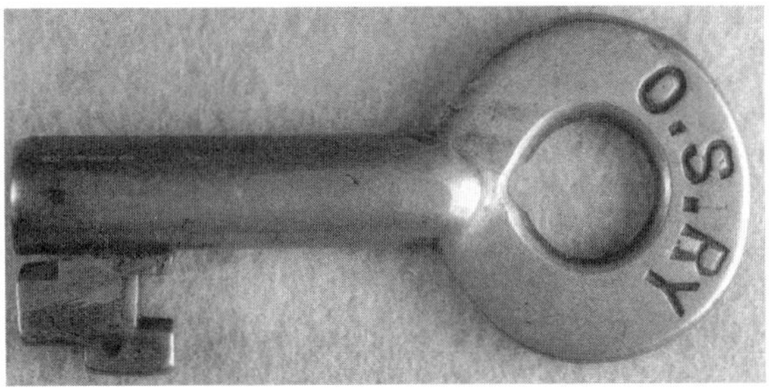

OSRY- (Ozark Southern) "S" Mfg. A&W in oval 150-175

PVCRRCO- (Pajaro Valley Consolidated) "S" serial #476. Manufacturer is A&W in hex 100-125

PERYCO- (Pacific Electric) serial #13595. Mfg. Adlake 25-35

PGE- (Pacific Great Eastern) serial #1251. Mfg. Adlake 25-35

PANHANDLE- "S" serial #455 40-50

PANHANDLE- #1565. Single ring, manufacturer is Bohannan 65-75

PMRR- (Pere Marquette) reverse Mfg. A&W in oval serial #1987 40-50

PMRR- (Pere Marquette) Mfg. Adlake 15-20

PRR- (**Pennsylvania**) serial #375 S. Mfg. A&W hex 25-35

PRR-(**Pennsylvania**)erial #3695 S. Mfg. Adlake 15-20

PRR- (**Pennsylvania**)knobby hilt Mfg. Fraim or Slaymaker 30-40

PENNA CO- (**Pennsylvania**) "E5626" manufacturer is A&W in hex 35-45

PENN SYS-(Pennsylvania System) Manufacturer is A&W in oval 65-75

PR-SL- (Pennsylvania Reading Seashore Line) knobby hilt. Mfg. Slaymaker 55-65

PCRR- (Pennsylvania Central) large hilt. Mfg. Adlake 10-15

P&PU- (Peoria & Pekin Union) #5060 Mfg. Adlake 30-40

P&PURR- (Peoria & Pekin Union) #2380 Mfg. Adlake 35-45

P&PURY- (Peoria & Pekin Union) serial #2518. Mfg. Adlake 35-45

PD&ERR- (Peoria Decatur & Evansville) single ring early key **175-200**

P&R- (Philadelphia & Reading) serial #D825. Mfg. Adlake **15-20**

P&LERR- (Pittsburgh & Lake Erie) serial #120. Manufacturer is A&W in oval **25-35**

P&WV- (Pittsburgh & West Virginia) Mfg. Adlake **40-50**

PCC&STL- (Pittsburgh Cincinnati Chicago & St. Louis) Mfg. Adlake **15-20**

PCC&STLRR- (Pittsburgh Cincinnati Chicago & St. Louis) "S" serial #T477. Mfg. A&W in oval **35-45**

PCC&STLRR- (Pittsburgh Cincinnati Chicago & St. Louis) Manufacturer is A&W in hex **65-75**

QA&P- (Quanah Acme & Pacific) Mfg. A&W in oval **100-125**

QA&PRY- (Quanah Acme & Pacific) large seriff letters. Reverse "S" **275-325**

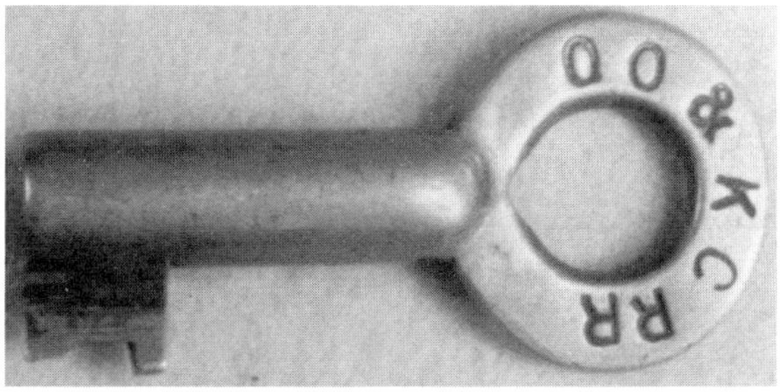

QO&KCRR- (Quincy Omaha & Kansas City) serial #315 S. Manufacturer is A&W in oval **200-250**

QO&KC- (Quincy Omaha & Kansas City) serial #125 S on reverse. Large seriff letters. **200-250**

QO&KCRY- (Quincy Omaha & Kansas City) serial #430. Manufacturer is Fraim **200-250**

R CO- (Reading Company) serial #F2995, Mfg. Fraim **10-15**

RDG CO- (Reading Company) "S 13337" . **15-20**

RF&P- (Richmond Fredricksburg & Potomac) Manufacturer Adlake **20-25**

RGSRR- (Rio Grande Southern) "S" Mfg. Bohannan **350-400**

RRI & STLRR- (Rockford Rock Island & St. Louis) tapered barrel. Mfg. MM Buck **350-400**

RS&P- (Roscoe Snyder & Pacific) Mfg. Adlake **25-35**

RRR-(Rutland Railroad) double ring early tapered key. Mfg. Sherburne **175-200**

RUT RR-(Rutland) serial #5651. Manufacturer is Bohannan **85-95**

RUT RR- (Rutland) serial #2760. Manufacturer is A&W in oval **90-100**

STJ&GIRR-(St. Joseph & Grand Island) steel key. Serial #1270 S. Mfg. A&W in oval **100-125**

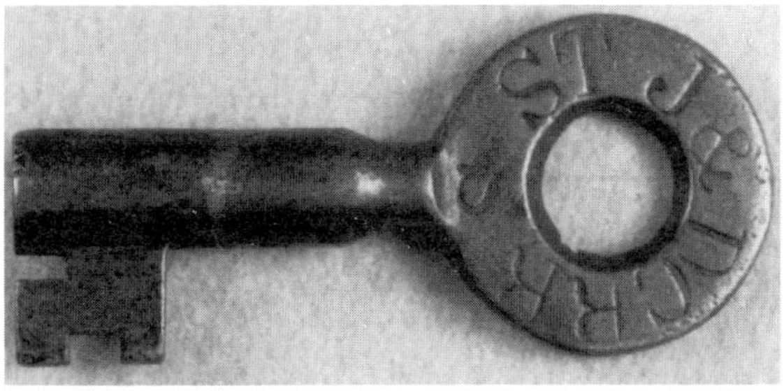

STJ&DCRR- (St.Joseph & Denver City) large seriff letters on this early tapered barrel key **350-400**

STL&H- (St. Louis & Hannibal) reverse Mfg. Handlan Buck. "S" tapered key **175-200**

STLIM&SRR- (St. Louis Iron Mountain & Southern) "S 475" Manufacturer Bohannan **175-200**

STLM&S- (St Louis Morehouse & Southern) steel key with large seriff letters and "S" on reverse **75-85**

STL&SF- (St. Louis & San Francisco) "S" on reverse large seriff letters **25-35**

STL&SFRY- (St. Louis & San Francisco) "S" Mfg. A&W hex **30-40**

STL&SFRY- (St. Louis & San Francisco) "S" tapered barrel. Mfg. Ritchie & Sons **100-125**

STL&SERW- (St. Louis & Southeastern) reverse "S" Mfg. MM Buck, single ring tapered barrel **300-350**

STL&SWRY- (St. Louis & Southwestern) "S" serial #4560. Tapered barrel early key **90-100**

STL&SWRY- (St. Louis & Southwestern) "S 8270". Tapered barrel key. Mfg. Handlan Buck. Also found marked "RR" **100-125**

STL&SWRY- (St. Louis & Southwestern) "S" Mfg. Slaymaker **25-35**

STLSWRYCO- (St. Louis & Southwestern)small steel hilt with solid brass barrel **35-45**

SSW (St. Louis & Southwestern) serial #5128. Mfg. Adlake, brass barrel with nickel hilt **25-35**

STLK&WRR- (St. Louis Keokuk & Western) "S" tapered barrel **175-200**

STLB&M- (St Louis Brownsville & Mexico) serial #4855. Mfg. Adlake **90-100**

SLR-(Salt Lake Route) Manufacturer Fraim Keystone **60-70**

SD&ARY-(San Diego & Arizona) Manufacturer A&W in oval **100-125**

SD&AE- (San Diego & Arizona Eastern) Manufacturer Adlake **45-55**

SD&AE CS-24-(San Diego & Arizona Eastern) Manufa cturer Adlake **90-100**

SR&RLRR-(Sandy River & Rangely Lakes) "S" on reverse. Large serif letters. Manufacturer Bohannan **400-450**

SFN&C- (San Francisco Napa & Calistoga) manufacturer Adlake **85-95**

SPLA&SL- (San Pedro Los Angeles & Salt Lake) large hilt. Serial #6770. No Manufacturer shown **75-85**

SL&ORY- (Salt Lake & Ogden) serial #915, Mfg FS Hardware **90-100**

SSRY- (South Shore) mfg. Adlake **125-150**

SANTA FE- "S 59023". Manufacturer is A&W in oval or hex **20-30**

SANTA FE- "SIGNAL" on reverse. Manufacturer is A&W in oval **250-300**

SANTA FE- "SY" Mfg. A&Win oval **70-80**

SANTA FE- "TH" Mfg. A&W oval **70-80**

SANTA FE- "IH" Manufacturer is A&W in oval **250-300**

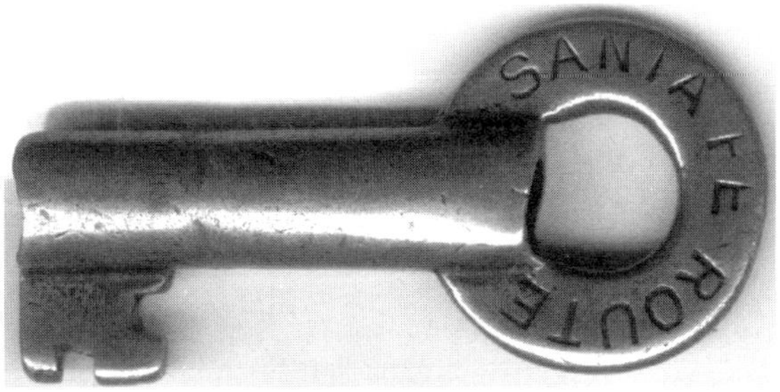

SANTA FE ROUTE- "S 6465", Mfg. A&W in hex **50-60**

SANTA FE ROUTE- "TH" Manufacturer is A&W in hex **85-95**

SF ROUTE- (Santa Fe Route) Manufacturer SB CO. **45-55**

SF ROUTE- (Santa Fe Route)"S 41810" on reverse **45-55**

SF ROUTE- (Santa Fe Route) Mfg. FS Hardware **45-55**

SEABOARD- Mfg. Slaymaker **45-55**

SALRR- (Seaboard Airline) serial #44900 ..... **20-30**

SALRY- (Seaboard Airline) serial #20450. Mfg. Adlake **10-15**

SCL- (Seaboard Coast Line) serial #3021. Mfg. Adlake **15-20**

SCLRR- (Seaboard Coast Line) Manufacturer Adlake **15-20**

SOO LINE- "S 5021". Mfg. Adlake **25-35**

SOO LINE- large letters. Mfg. Adlake **25-35**

SPC- (South Pacific Coast) reverse Mfg. Fraim 50-60

SORY- (Southern) "SR" on reverse 15-20

SOURY- (Southern) serial #24290. Mfg. Yale 10-15

SOURY- (Southern) Manufacturer Adlake 10-15

SRR- (Southern) "ES" or "WS", Manufacturer is Fraim 20-30

SP- (Southern Pacific) early tapered barrel key with ring hilt 90-100

SPCO CS 4- (Southern Pacific)"S" on reverse. Mfg. A&W 15-20

SPCO-CS 24- "R&B" (Southern Pacific) Mfg. A&W 20-30

SPCO-CS 44 – "SPECIAL". (Southern Pacific) Mfg. Adlake.. 15-20

SPCO-CS 45- (Southern Pacific)Mfg. Slaymaker 20-30

SPCO CS 47- (Southern Pacific)large hilt. Mfg. Adlake 15-20

SPCO- (Southern Pacific) "S" Mfg. A&W hex 20-30

SPCO- (Southern Pacific)steel oiler type key. "FREIGHT" on reverse......................... 65-75

SPCO- (Southern Pacific)steel oiler type key. "SWITCH" on reverse 50-60

SPCO-(Southern Pacific)steel oiler type key. "72" marked on reverse 40-50

SP LINES- (Southern Pacific Lines)Mfg. Adlake 25-35

SP LINES- (Southern Pacific Lines) "S" mfg. A&W in hex... 50-60

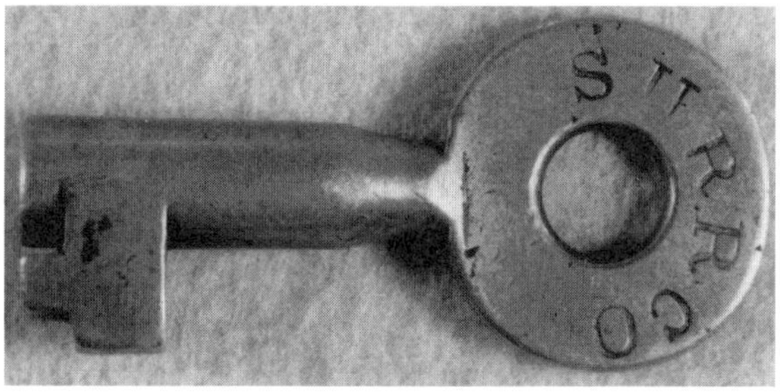

SURRCO- (Southern Utah) Reverse "S" tapered barrel Mfg. Handlan Buck 300-350

SP&S- (Spokane Portland & Seattle) Mfg. Adlake **25-35**

SP&SRY- (Spokane Portland & Seattle) "S" Mfg. A&W in oval **75-85**

SP&SRY- (Spokane Portland & Seattle) steel key with no manufacturer shown **75-85**

TERY- (Tacoma Eastern) reverse #45. No mfg. listed **30-40**

TENN RY- (Tennesee) Mfg. Slaymaker **35-45**

TC- (Tennessee Central) serial #5266 ... **25-35**

TMRR- (Tennesee Midland) Mfg. Bohannan...................................... **100-125**

T&P- (Texas & Pacific) serial #19225. Mfg. Adlake **15-20**

T&P-(Texas & Pacific) Manufacturer Slaymaker... **25-35**

T&PRR- (Texas & Pacific)serial #1995 S. Mfg. A&W hex **30-40**

TMRR- (Texas Midland) reverse "S" Mfg. Bohannan **90-100**

TO&ERR-(Texas Oklahoma & Easter) tapered barrel seriff letters. "S" on reverse. Mfg. Handlan Buck **175-200**

TSERR- (Texas Southeastern) reverse 740 S. Mfg. Adlake.. **25-35**

TRRA- (Terminal Railroad Assoc.) Mfg. A&W in oval **10-15**

TSRY-(Tidewater Southern) Mfg. Adlake **150-175**

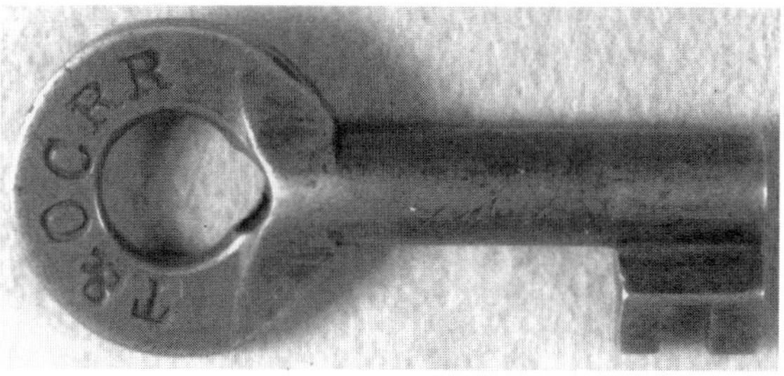

T&OCRR-(Toledo & Ohio Central) serial # "S 705". Manufacturer is Bohannan...... **65-75**

T&OCRR- -(Toledo & Ohio Central) steel key, serial #S 5097 .... **45-55**

TP&W- (Toledo Peoria & Western) everse 1369. Mfg. Adlake........................... **20-30**

TSL&KCRR- (Toledo St Louis & Kansas City) "S" Mfg. MM Buck. Early tapered key **125-150**

TSTL&WRR-(Toledo St. Louis & Western) serial #990. Steel oiler type key. Mfg. Corbin **55-65**

TSTL&WRR- (Toledo St. Louis & Western) reverse 3386. Mfg. Fraim keystone **30-40**

TW&W- (Toledo Wabash & Western) "S" early tapered barrel key with no mfg. shown **100-125**

T&GRY- (Tonopah & Goldfield) serial #A20 S". Early tapered barrel key **200-250**

T&BVRY- (Trinity & Bravos Valley) serial #533 .... **65-75**

T&BVRY- (Trinity & Bravos Valley) Mfg. Slaymaker **90-100**

TH&B- (Toronto Hamilton & Buffalo) steel key **65-75**

TH&B- (Toronto Hamilton & Buffalo) Mfg. unknown **50-60**

UP-serial (Union Pacific) #14910. Mfg. Adlake **15-20**

UP- (Union Pacific) "SCALES" Mfg. FS Hardware **80-90**

UP- (Union Pacific) "2" on front. Small tapered barrel key with R&B cut **40-50**

UPRR- (Union Pacific) "S" serial #1410. Early tapered barrel key **125-150**

UPRR- (Union Pacific)serial #7510. Mfg. A&W in hex or oval **25-35**

UPRR- (Union Pacific)Mfg. Slaymaker **30-40**

UPRR- (Union Pacific)CS 1 "S" on reverse. Mfg. A&W in oval **60-70**

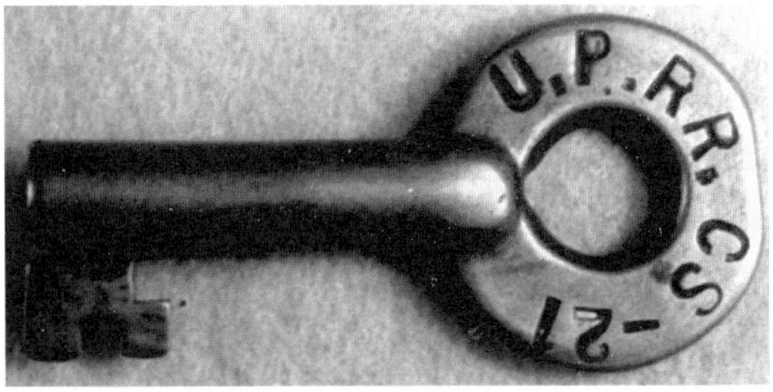

UPRR- (Union Pacific)CS 21 "R&B" on reverse, Mfg. Adlake **35-45**

UPRR- (Union Pacific) "TOOL RACK" on reverse **50-60**

UP&MPC- (Union Pacific Motive Power & Car) Mfg. FS Hardware......................... **20-30**

UP SYS- (Union Pacific System)no manufacturer shown **90-100**

UNION PACIFIC- "SWITCH" early tapered double ring key **250-300**

UTAH RY- Mfg. Adlake **65-75**

VRR- (Virginian) "S877" large hilt ... **275-300**

VGN-(Virginian) serial #4510. Mfg. Slaymaker **50-60**

V&TRR-(Virginia & Truckee) early ring barrel key. Manufacturer Bohannan **450-500**

WRR- (Wabash) serial #715 S. Steel key manufacturer is A&W in oval **20-30**

WRR- (Wabash) Mfg. Slaymaker **20-30**

WAB- serial #3621. Mfg. Adlake **15-25**

WAB RR- Mfg. MM Buck tapered barrel single ring **125-150**

WABASH- Mfg. Slaymaker **20-30**

WABASH RR- reverse 1657. Mfg. Fraim **20-30**

WSTL&PRR- (Wabash St. Louis & Pacific) serial #2721. Steel key. Manufacturer is Bohannan **125-150**

WBT&SRY- (Waco Beaumont Trinity & Sabine) early tapered key **200-250**

W&OVRY- (Warren Ouachita Valley) "S" tapered barrel. Manufacturer Handlan Buck **150-175**

WPRR- (Western Pacific) serial #4728 S. Mfg. Adlake **20-30**

WPRY- (Western Pacific) serial #2540 S. Manufacturer is A&W in oval **50-60**

W&LE- (Wheeling & Lake Erie) tapered barrel ring key **85-95**

W&LE- (Wheeling & Lake Erie) reverse 9297, Mfg. Adlake **20-30**

WP&YR- (White Pass & Yukon) no manufacturer shown **70-80**

WMRR- (Western Maryland) serial #3650. Mfg. Fraim **35-45**

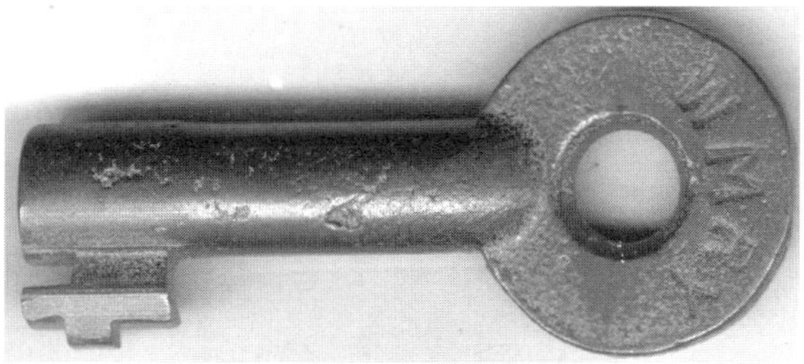

WMRY-(Western Maryland) serial #11174. Mfg. Adlake newer key **10-15**

WCRY-(Wisconsin Central) serial #2540 S. Manufacturer is Adlake **25-35**

WIS&MICH- (Wisconsin & Michigan) ring hilt, tapered **350-400**

Y&MV- (Yazoo & Mississippi Valley) Manufacturer Adlake **30-40**

Y&N-(Youngstown & Northern) Manufacturer Fraim **30-40**

COACH CABOOSE & MISCELLANEOUS

Coach & caboose keys also are quite collectible and can be quite unique in their design. Although not as valuable as some of the switch keys, these items can be very rewarding to collect and enjoyable to display. Remember as with all collectibles the keys must be in good condition. They must not be bent, damaged, cracked and the letters must be legible for the values listed to apply.

B&LERR- brass 3 rings, tapered solid barrel key **60-70**

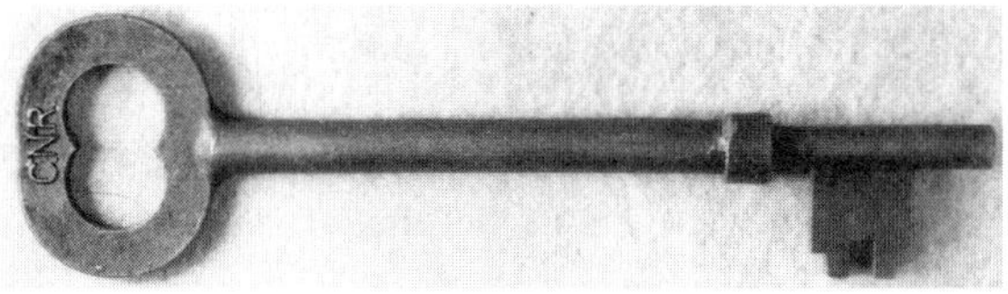

CNR-brass solid barrel, Mfg. Mitchell **5-10**

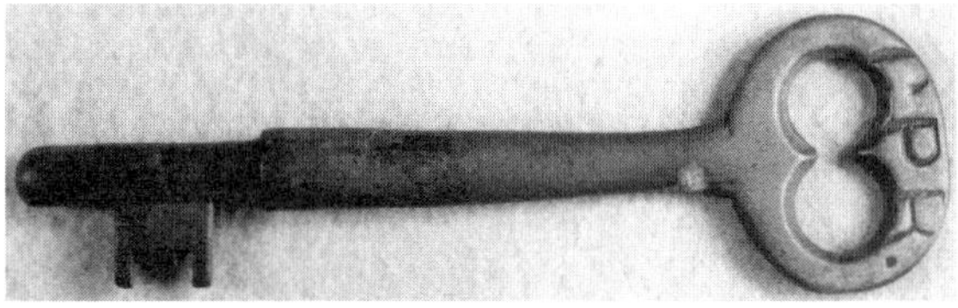

CPR- brass solid barrel, Mfg. Mitchell **5-10**

CB&Q- solid barrel, Mfg. Adlake **20-30**

D&RG- steel solid barrel **30-40**

D&RGW- steel solid barrel **20-30**

GTR- brass solid barrel **15-20**

IC-brass solid barrel **20-30**

L&NRR- 3 rings, tapered hollow barrel key early **20-30**

NYLE&W- "PH" Manufacturer Slaight & co. **35-45**

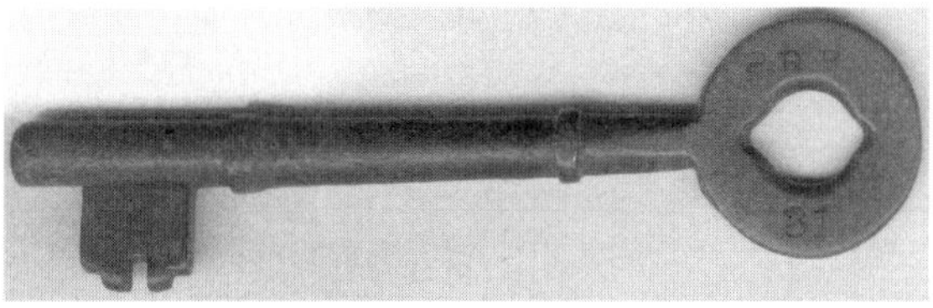

PRR- serial #31. Solid double ring key **30-40**

PINTSCH GAS KEY-Used to turn the gas on for the lighting in the coaches **20-30**

SLSF- solid barrel. Mfg. Adlake **15-20**

SP-solid barrel, Mfg. Adlake **15-20**

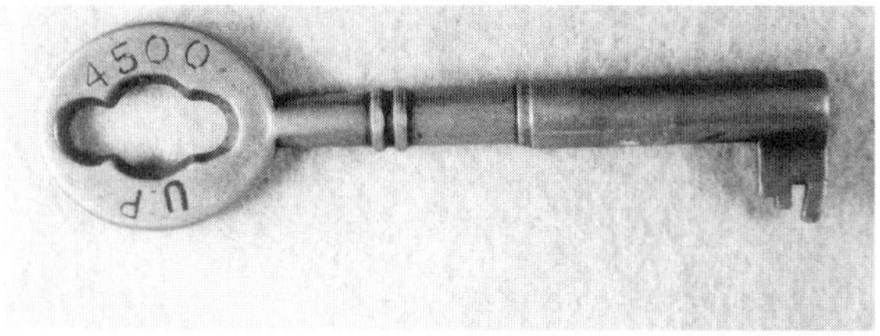

UP-serial #4500. Double ring hollow barrel **30-40**

UP-solid barrel, Mfg. Adlake **20-30**

UP- "COM S" (Commissary) Manufacturer Adlake **25-35**

WABASH RR- solid barrel brass key **15-20**

WRR-serial #5306. Solid Barrel **15-20**

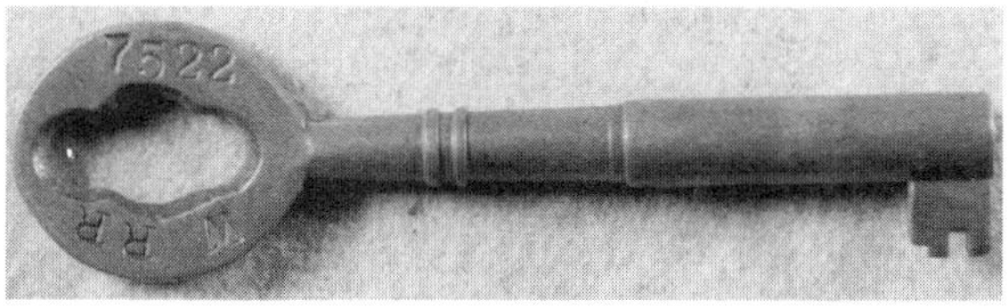

WRR- hollow barrel, double ring **35-45**

CHAPTER 19

LANTERNS SHORT GLOBE

The short globe lanterns made their appearance in the 1920's replacing their taller counterpart. Marketed as more efficient and of course cheaper for the railroads to produce, this was the first step toward the end of the kerosene lantern which lasted into the 1960's. You will find the lanterns marked on the dome as well as the shoulder of the frame. They come with clear, amber, red, blue or green globes. Globes were not always marked, but certainly a globe found railroad marked whether etched or embossed is always more valuable.

Lantern values are determined not only by condition, but globe color and how it is railroad marked. As well as the part of the country it is from. For instance, a short globe lantern with a marked clear embossed globe from an east coast line such as New York Central will not command as much as a lantern from the west coast like Atchison Topeka & Santa Fe with a clear embossed globe. There are many reasons for this but the most obvious would be availability. Lanterns need to be complete with kerosene font and burner as well as the globe to command the prices suggested.

Note: Globe Manufacturers & their abbreviations:

CNX-Corning Manufacturing Company

ADLAKE KERO- Adlake Manufacturing Company

K in circle-Kopp Glass Company

MANUFACTURERS & STYLES

Adams & Westlake No. 200 or 250

Adlake Kero

Armspear Manufacturing Co.

Dietz Vesta New York, USA

Dressel Arlington NJ

Handlan St. Louis

Dome Marked
"ROCK ISLAND LOGO"

Dome Marked
"D&RGWRR"

Dome Marked
"M&STLRR"

ATCHISON TOPEKA & SANTA FE aka SANTA FE

AT&SF-on shoulder of flat top Handlan frame with clear etched "AT&SF" globe **75-85**

AT&SF-on shoulder of flat top Handlan frame with clear etched "AT&SF" cnx globe **85-95**

AT&SF- on shoulder of flat top Handlan frame with clear cast "AT&SFRy" globe **100-125**

AT&SF-on shoulder of flat top Handlan frame with clear unmarked "Adlake Kero" globe **55-65**

AT&SFRY- on dome of Adlake 200 or 250 frame with clear etched "AT&SF" cnx globe **75-85**

AT&SFRY- on dome of Adlake 200 or 250 frame with red etched "AT&SF" cnx globe **90-100**

AT&SFRY- on dome of Adlake 200 or 250 frame with amber etched "AT&SFRY" cnx globe **150-175**

AT&SFRY- on dome of Adlake 200 or 250 frame with green etched "AT&SF" cnx globe **175-200**

AT&SFRY- on dome of Adlake 200 or 250 frame with clear unmarked cnx globe **60-70**

AT&SFRY- on shoulder of Adlake Kero frame with clear etched "AT&SF" globe **65-75**

AT&SFRY- on shoulder of Adlake Kero frame with red etched "AT&SF" cnx globe .. **75-85**

AT&SFRY- on shoulder of Adlake Kero frame with clear cast "AT&SFRY" cnx globe **100-125**

AT&SFRY- on shoulder of Dressel frame with amber etched "AT&SF" globe also cast "Adlake Kero" **125-150**

AT&SFRY- on shoulder of Dressel frame with red cast "AT&SFRY" Adlake Kero globe **125-150**

ATLANTIC COAST LINE RAILROAD

ACLRR-on shoulder of 1925 Armspear frame with clear unmarked ADLAKE KERO globe....... **60-70**

ACLRR-on shoulder of 1925 Armspear frame with clear etched "ACL" cnx globe **85-95**

BALTIMORE & OHIO RAILROAD

B&ORR- on dome of Adlake Kero 250 frame with clear unmarked cnx globe **45-55**

B&ORR- on dome of Adlake Kero 250 frame with red unmarked ADLAKE KERO globe **55-65**

B&ORR- on dome of Adlake Kero 250 frame with clear cast "B&ORR" cnx globe **65-75**

B&ORR- on dome of Adlake Kero 250 frame with red cast "B&ORR" cnx globe **85-95**

B&ORR-on dome of Adlake Kero 250 frame with clear etched "B&ORR" cnx globe **60-70**

BELT RAILWAY OF CHICAGO

BELT- on shoulder of Adlake Kero frame with clear unmarked globe **55-65**

BOSTON & ALBANY RAILROAD

BOSTON & ALBANY- on shoulder of Dietz Vesta frame with red cast "B&A" Dietz Vesta globe 75-85

B&A-on shoulder of Dressel frame with clear unmarked globe **50-60**

BOSTON & MAINE RAILROAD

B&M-on shoulder of Dietz Vesta frame with clear etched "B&MRR" globe **50-60**

BOSTON & MAINE- on shoulder of Dietz Vesta frame with clear Dietz Vesta globe **40-50**

BOSTON & MAINE- on shoulder of Dietz Vesta frame with blue unmarked globe 75-85

BUFFALO ROCHESTER & PITTSBURGH RR

BR&P- on shoulder of Dietz Vesta frame with clear etched "BR&PRY" Dietz globe 75-85

BURLINGTON ROUTE

aka CHICAGO BURLINGTON & QUINCY

BR-on shoulder of Kero or Dressel frame with clear etched "BR" globe 65-75

BR- on shoulder of Kero or Dressel frame with red etched "BR" cnx globe 75-85

BR-on shoulder of Kero or Dressel frame with amber etched "BR" cnx globe **100-125**

BR- on shoulder of Kero or Dressel frame with green etched "BR" cnx globe **150-175**

BR- on shoulder of Kero or Dressel frame with clear unmarked ADLAKE KERO cnx globe **50-60**

CANADIAN NATIONAL RAILWAY

CNR-on shoulder of Adlake Kero frame with clear cast "CNR" cnx globe **50-60**

CNR-on shoulder of Hiram Piper frame with clear etched "CNR" globe **40-50**

CNR-on shoulder of Hiram Piper frame with amber unmarked "ADLAKE KERO" globe **50-60**

CANADIAN PACIFIC RAILWAY

CPR-on shoulder of Hiram Piper frame with clear cast "CPR" globe **50-60**

CPR-on shoulder of Hiram Piper frame with red unmarked cnx globe **40-50**

CENTRAL VERMONT RAILWAY

CVRY-on dome of Adlake Kero 250 frame with clear unmarked "ADLAKE KERO" globe **60-70**

CHESAPEAKE & OHIO RAILWAY

C&ORY-on dome of Adlake Kero 250 frame with clear etched "C&O" globe **65-75**

C&ORY- on dome of Adlake Kero 250 frame with red etched "C&O" globe **75-85**

C&ORY-on dome of Adlake Kero 250 frame with amber etched "C&O" globe **100-125**

C&ORY-on dome of Adlake Kero 250 frame with clear unmarked globe **50-60**

CHICAGO & ALTON RAILROAD

CHICAGO & ALTON RR- on shoulder of Adlake Kero frame with green etched "C&ARR" cnx globe **150-175**

CHICAGO & EASTERN ILLINOIS RY

C&EIRY- on dome of Adlake Kero 250 frame with clear cast "C&EI" cnx globe **90-100**

C&EIRY- on dome of Adlake Kero 250 frame with red cast "C&EI" cnx globe **100-125**

C&EIRY-on dome of Adlake Kero 250 frame with clear unmarked globe **60-70**

CHICAGO & NORTHWESTERN RY

C&NWRY- on shoulder of Adlake Kero frame with clear etched "C&NWRY" cnx globe **65-75**

C&NWRY-on shoulder of Adlake Kero frame with red etched "C&NWRY" cnx globe **85-95**

C&NWRY-on shoulder of Adlake Kero frame with amber etched "C&NWRY" cnx globe **100-125**

C&NWRY-on shoulder of Adlake Kero frame with clear unmarked cnx globe **50-60**

CHICAGO & WESTERN INDIANA RR

C&WIRR-on dome of Adlake Kero 250 frame with clear unmarked cnx globe **70-80**

C&WIRR-on dome of Adlake Kero 250 frame with red unmarked ADLAKE KERO globe **80-90**

CHICAGO BURLINGTON & QUINCY RAILROAD aka BURLINGTON ROUTE

CB&QRR-on dome of Adlake Kero 250 frame with clear etched "CB&Q" cnx globe **90-100**

CB&QRR-on dome of Adlake Kero 250 frame with red etched "CB&Q" cnx globe **100-125**

CB&QRR-on shoulder of Adlake Kero frame with clear etched "BR" globe **80-90**

CB&QRR-on shoulder of Adlake Kero frame with red etched "BR" globe **90-100**

CB&QRR- on shoulder of Adlake Kero frame with clear unmarked cnx globe **65-75**

CHICAGO GREAT WESTERN RY

CGWRY- on shoulder of Dressel frame with red unmarked "ADLAKE KERO" globe **60-70**

CGWRY- on shoulder of Dressel frame with clear unmarked cnx globe **50-60**

CHICAGO MILWAUKEE & ST PAUL RY

CM&STPRY- on dome of Adlake Kero 250 frame with clear etched "CM&STPRY" globe **75-85**

CM&STPRY-on dome of Adlake Kero 250 frame with red etched "CM&STPRY" globe **85-95**

CHICAGO MILWAUKEE ST PAUL & PACIFIC

CMSTP&P-on shoulder of Adlake Kero or Dressel frame with clear etched "CMSTP&P" globe **60-70**

CMSTP&P-on shoulder of Adlake Kero or Dressel frame with red etched "CMSTP&P" globe **75-85**

CMSTP&P-on shoulder of Adlake Kero or Dressel frame with amber etched "CMSTP&P" globe **100-125**

CMSTP&P-on shoulder of Adlake Kero or Dressel frame with green etched "CMSTP&P" globe **125-150**

CMSTP&P-on shoulder of Adlake Kero or Dressel frame with clear unmarked globe **50-60**

CHICAGO ROCK ISLAND & PACIFIC RY

CRI&P-on shoulder of Dressel frame with clear unmarked cnx globe **65-75**

CRI&P-on shoulder of Dressel frame with red etched "CRI&P" cnx globe **100-125**

CLEVELAND CINCINNATI CHICAGO & ST LOUIS RR

CCC&STL-on shoulder of Dietz Vesta frame with clear unmarked Vesta globe **40-50**

CCC&STL-on shoulder of Dietz Vesta frame with red unmarked globe **60-70**

COLORADO & SOUTHERN RAILWAY

C&SRY- on dome of Adlake Kero 200 or 250 frame with clear unmarked cnx globe **175-200**

DELAWARE & HUDSON RAILROAD

D&HRR- on shoulder of Dressel frame with clear etched "D&HRR" globe **65-75**

D&HRR-on shoulder of Dressel frame with red etched "D&HRR" globe **85-95**

D&HRR- on shoulder of Dressel frame with amber etched "D&HRR" globe **100-125**

D&HRR- on shoulder of Dressel frame with clear unmarked ADLAKE KERO globe **50-60**

DENVER & RIO GRANDE RAILROAD

D&RGRR- on dome of Kero 200 frame with a clear unmarked "ADLAKE KERO" globe **200-250**

DENVER & RIO GRANDE WESTERN RR

D&RGWRR-on dome of Kero 200 or 250 frame with clear etched "D&RGW" cnx globe **100-125**

D&RGWRR-on dome of Kero 200 or 250 frame with red etched "D&RGW" cnx globe **125-150**

D&RGWRR-on dome of Kero 200 or 250 frame with amber etched "D&RGW" cnx globe **175-200**

D&RGWRR-on dome of Kero 200 or 250 frame with green etched "D&RGW" cnx globe **300-350**

D&RGWRR-on shoulder of Adlake Kero or Dressel frame with clear etched "D&RGW" globe also etched "SAFETY FIRST" ... **90-100**

D&RGWRR-on shoulder of Adlake Kero or Dressel frame with red etched "D&RGW" globe also etched "SAFETY FIRST" **100-125**

D&RGWRR-on shoulder of Adlake Kero or Dressel frame with amber etched "D&RGW" globe also etched "SAFETY FIRST" **125-150**

D&RGWRR-on shoulder of Adlake Kero or Dressel frame with clear unmarked "ADLAKE KERO" globe **65-75**

DENVER & SALT LAKE RAILWAY

D&SLRY-on shoulder of Adlake Kero frame with clear unmarked ADLAKE KERO globe **200-250**

DULUTH MISSABE & IRON RANGE

DM&IRRY-on shoulder of Adlake Kero frame with clear unmarked ADLAKE KERO globe **80-90**

DM&IRRY-on shoulder of Adlake Kero frame with red unmarked cnx globe **90-100**

ERIE RAILROAD

ERIE RR-on dome of Adlake Kero 250 frame with clear etched "ERIE RR" cnx globe **90-100**

ERIE <E> diamond logo on dome of Adlake Kero frame with clear etched <E> diamond logo globe **90-100**

ERIE-<E>diamond logo on dome of Adlake Kero frame with red etched <E> diamond logo globe **100-125**

ERIE-<E>diamond logo on dome of Adlake Kero frame with clear cast "ERIE" cnx globe **100-125**

ERIE-<E>diamond logo on dome of Adlake Kero frame with red cast "ERIE" cnx globe **125-150**

ERIE-<E> diamond logo on dome of Adlake Kero frame with clear unmarked globe **50-60**

FLORIDA EAST COAST RY

FECRY-on shoulder of Adlake Kero frame with clear unmarked ADLAKE KERO globe **70-80**

FECRY-on shoulder of Adlake Kero frame with red unmarked ADLAKE KERO globe **80-90**

FT WORTH & DENVER CITY

FW&DC-on dome of Adlake Kero 250 frame with clear unmarked ADLAKE KERO globe **100-125**

FtW&DC-on shoulder of Adlake Kero frame with clear unmarked globe .. **90-100**

FtW&DC-on shoulder of Adlake Kero frame with red unmarked globe **100-125**

GRAND TRUNK WESTERN

GTW-on shoulder of Adlake Kero frame with clear unmarked cnx globe **50-60**

GREAT NORTHERN RAILWAY

GNRY-on shoulder of Armspear 1925 frame with clear cast "GNRY" globe **90-100**

GNRY-on shoulder of Armspear 1925 frame with red cast "GNRY" globe **100-125**

GNRY-on shoulder of Dressel frame with clear unmarked cnx globe................ **50-60**

GNRY-on shoulder of Dressel frame with red unmarked cnx globe **60-70**

GULF COLORADO & SANTA FE RY

GC&SFRY-on dome of Kero 250 frame with clear cast "GC&SFRY" globe **200-250**

GC&SFRY-on dome of Kero 250 frame with red cast "GC&SFRY" globe **250-300**

GC&SFRY-on dome of Kero 250 frame with clear unmarked globe **100-125**

GULF MOBILE & OHIO RR

GM&ORR-on shoulder of Dressel frame with clear unmarked globe **50-60**

GM&ORR-on shoulder of Dressel frame with red unmarked globe **60-70**

HOCKING VALLEY RAILROAD

HVRY-on dome of Kero 250 frame with clear etched "HV" globe **75-85**

HVRY-on dome of Kero 250 frame with red etched "HV" globe **90-100**

HVRY-on dome of Kero 250 frame with clear unmarked ADLAKE KERO globe **50-60**

ILLINOIS CENTRAL RAILROAD

ICRR-on dome of Kero 250 frame with clear cast "ICRR" globe **60-70**

ICRR-on dome of Kero 250 frame with red cast "ICRR" globe **75-85**

ICRR-on shoulder of Adlake Kero frame with amber etched "ICRR" globe **100-125**

ICRR-on shoulder of Adlake Kero frame with clear etched "ICRR" globe **50-60**

ICRR-on shoulder of Adlake Kero frame with clear unmarked cnx globe **40-50**

INDIANA HARBOR BELT

IHB-on shoulder of Adlake Kero frame with clear unmarked globe **50-60**

IHB-on shoulder of Adlake Kero frame with red unmarked globe **60-70**

KANSAS & INDIANA TERMINAL

K&IT-on shoulder of Dressel frame with clear unmarked globe **50-60**

K&IT-on shoulder of Dressel frame with red unmarked globe **60-70**

LEHIGH VALLEY RAILROAD

LVRR-on shoulder of Adlake Kero frame with clear cast "LVRR" globe **90-100**

LVRR-on shoulder of Adlake Kero frame with red cast "LVRR" globe **100-125**

LVRR-on shoulder of Adlake Kero frame with clear unmarked cnx globe **60-70**

LONG ISLAND RAILROAD

LIRR-on shoulder of Armspear 1925 frame with clear unmarked cnx globe **50-60**

LIRR-on shoulder of Armspear 1925 frame with red unmarked cnx globe **60-70**

LIRR-on shoulder of Kero frame with clear etched "LIRR" cnx globe **65-75**

LIRR-on shoulder of Kero frame with red etched "LIRR" cnx globe **75-85**

LIRR-on shoulder of Kero frame with amber etched "LIRR" cnx globe **90-100**

LOUISVILLE & NASHVILLE RAILROAD

L&NRR- on shoulder of flat top Handlan frame with clear cast "L&NRR" also cast 1925 .... **50-60**

MAINE CENTRAL RAILROAD

MAINE CENTRAL-on shoulder of Dietz Vesta frame with clear unmarked globe **40-50**

MAINE CENTRAL-on shoulder of Dietz Vesta frame with blue unmarked Dietz Vesta globe **90-100**

MINNEAPOLIS & ST. LOUIS RAILROAD

M&STLRR-on dome of Kero 250 frame with clear etched "M&STLRR" cnx globe **100-125**

M&STLRR-on shoulder of Dressel frame with clear etched "M&STL" globe **70-80**

M&STLRR-on shoulder of Dressel frame with red etched "M&STL" globe **90-100**

MISSOURI KANSAS & TEXAS RAILROAD

MKT-on dome of Kero 250 frame with clear etched "MK&T" globe **65-75**

MKT-on dome of Kero 250 frame with red etched "MK&T" globe **75-85**

MKT-on dome of Kero 250 frame with amber etched "MK&T" globe **100-125**

MKT-on dome of Kero 250 frame with green etched "M-K-T" globe **125-150**

MKT-on shoulder of Dressel frame with clear etched "MKT" cnx globe **60-70**

MKT-on shoulder of Dressel frame with red etched "MKT" cnx globe **75-85**

MISSOURI PACIFIC RAILROAD

MOPAC-on shoulder of flat top Handlan frame with 4 ¼" clear etched "MOPAC" globe **50-60**

MOPAC-on shoulder of flat top Handlan frame with 4 ¼" red etched "MOPAC" globe ... **70-80**

MORGANS LOUISIANA & TEXAS RR

ML&TRR-on dome of Kero 250 frame with clear unmarked globe **125-150**

NEWBURG & SOUTH SHORE RR

N&SSRY-on shoulder of Armspear 1925 frame with clear unmarked cnx globe **55-65**

NEW YORK CENTRAL SYSTEM

NYCS-on shoulder of Adlake Kero frame with clear unmarked cnx globe **40-50**

NYCS-on shoulder of Adlake Kero frame with red unmarked cnx globe **45-55**

NYCS-on shoulder of flat top Handlan frame with red etched 4 ¼" "NYCS" globe **40-50**

NYCS-on shoulder of Dietz 999 frame with clear unmarked globe **40-50**

NYCS-on shoulder of Dietz Vesta frame with clear cast "NYCS" Vesta globe **50-60**

NYCS-on shouder of Dressel frame with clear unmarked globe **40-50**

NEW YORK CENTRAL RAILROAD

NYCRR-on dome of Kero 250 frame with red unmarked globe **45-55**

NEW YORK CENTRAL-on shoulder of Dietz Vesta frame with clear cast "NEW YORK CENTRAL" Vesta globe **40-50**

NEW YORK CENTRAL LINES

NYCL-on shoulder of Dietz Vesta frame with clear cast "NYC LINES" globe **40-50**

NEW YORK CHICAGO & ST LOUIS

NYC&STLRR-on dome of Adlake Kero 200 or 250 frame with clear etched "NYC&STL" globe **65-75**

NYC&STLRR- on dome of Adlake Kero 200 or 250 frame with red etched "NYC&STL" globe **75-85**

NEW YORK NEW HAVEN & HARTFORD

NYNH&H-on shoulder of Dietz Vesta frame with clear etched "NYNH&H" globe ... **50-60**

NYNH&H-on shoulder of Dietz Vesta frame with red etched "NYNH&H" globe **70-80**

NYNH&H-on shoulder of Dressel frame with clear unmarked globe **40-50**

NICKLE PLATE aka NEW YORK CHICAGO & ST LOUIS

NKP-on shoulder of Kero frame with clear etched "NKP" globe **65-75**

NKP-on shoulder of Kero frame with red etched "NKP" globe **80-90**

NKP-on shoulder of Kero frame with amber etched "NKP" globe **100-125**

NKP-on shoulder of Kero frame with heavy cast iron base & clear unmarked globe **50-60**

NKP-on shoulder of Kero frame with heavy cast iron base & red unmarked globe **60-70**

NORFOLK & WESTERN

N&WRY-on shoulder of Adlake Kero frame with clear unmarked globe **40-50**

N&WRY-on shoulder of Dressel frame with clear unmarked globe **40-50**

N&WRY-on shoulder of 1925 Armspear frame with heavy cast iron base & clear unmarked cnx globe **60-70**

NORTHERN PACIFIC

NPRY-on shoulder of Adlake Kero frame with clear etched "NPRY" globe **60-70**

NPRY-on shoulder of Adlake Kero frame with red etched "NPRY" globe **75-85**

NPRY- on shoulder of Adlake Kero frame with amber etched "NPRY" globe **100-125**

NPRY-on shoulder of Adlake Kero frame with green etched "NPRY" globe **150-175**

NPRY-on shoulder of Adlake Kero frame with clear cast "NPRY" cnx globe.............. **100-125**

NPRY-on shoulder of Adlake Kero frame with red cast "NPRY" cnx globe **125-150**

NPRY-on shoulder of Adlake Kero frame with clear unmarked cnx globe **50-60**

OREGON SHORT LINE

OSL-on shoulder of Dietz Vesta frame with clear etched "OSLRR" globe **200-250**

PACIFIC ELECTRIC RAILROAD

PAC ELEC RR-on dome of Kero 250 frame with clear etched "PAC ELEC RR" globe **90-100**

PAC ELEC RR-on dome of Kero 250 frame with red etched "PAC ELEC RR" cnx globe **100-125**

PERY-on shoulder of Adlake Kero frame with clear etched "PERY" cnx globe **75-85**

PANHANDLE & SANTA FE

P&SF-on dome of Adlake Kero 250 frame with clear unmarked cnx globe **200-225**

PENNSYLVANIA RAILROAD

PRR-Keystone logo on shoulder of Dressel frame with clear unmarked globe **40-50**

PRR-Keystone logo on dome of flat top Handlan frame with 4 ½" clear etched "PRR" Keystone logo globe **45-55**

PRR-Keystone logo on dome of flat top Handlan frame with 4 ½" red etched "PRR" Keystone logo globe **55-65**

PRR-Keystone logo on shoulder of 1925 Armspear frame with clear cast "PRR" Keystone logo globe **65-75**

PRR-Keystone logo on dome of Adlake Kero frame with clear etched logo globe **60-70**

PENN-CENTRAL

PC- logo on dome of Adlake Kero frame with clear unmarked globe **40-50**

PC- logo on dome of Adlake Kero frame with red unmarked globe **50-60**

PITTSBURGH & LAKE ERIE RR

P&LERR- on shoulder of Dietz Vesta frame with clear unmarked Vesta globe **40-50**

P&LERR-on shoulder of Dietz Vesta frame with red unmarked Vesta globe **50-60**

PITTSBURGH & WEST VIRGINIA

P&WVRYCO-on shoulder of Dietz Vesta frame with red unmarked Vesta globe **90-100**

READING RAILWAY

READING LOCO DEPT- on shoulder of Dressel frame with heavy cast iron base. Comes with clear unmarked globe **60-70**

ROCK ISLAND AKA CHICAGO ROCK ISLAND & PACIFIC

ROCK ISLAND- logo on dome of Adlake Kero frame with clear cast "RI LINES" globe **90-100**

ROCK ISLAND- logo on dome Adlake Kero frame with red cast "RI LINES" globe **100-125**

ROCK ISLAND-logo on dome of Adlake Kero frame with clear etched "RI LINES" globe **70-80**

ROCK ISLAND-logo on dome of Adlake Kero frame with red etched "RI LINES globe **90-100**

ROCK ISLAND-logo on dome of Adlake Kero frame with amber etched "RI LINES" globe **100-125**

ROCK ISLAND –logo on dome of Adlake Kero frame with green or blue etched "RI LINES" globe **175-200**

ROCK ISLAND-logo on dome of Kero 200 or 250 frame with blue etched "RI LINES" globe **250-300**

ROCK ISLAND –logo on dome of Kero 200 or 250 frame with red unmarked globe **90-100**

RUTLAND RAILROAD

RUTLAND RR-on shoulder of Adlake Kero frame with clear unmarked globe **80-90**

RUTLAND RR-on shoulder of Adlake Kero frame with red unmarked globe.......... **90-100**

RUTLAND RR-on shoulder of Adlake Kero frame with clear etched "RUTLAND RR" cnx globe **100-125**

RUTLAND RR-on shoulder of Adlake Kero frame with red etched "RUTLAND RR" cnx globe **125-150**

ST LOUIS & SAN FRANCISCO RY

SL&SFRY-on dome of Adlake 250 frame with red etched "STL&SF" globe **100-125**

ST LOUIS & SOUTHWESTERN RY

STL&SWRY-on shoulder of Adlake Kero frame with clear unmarked globe **60-70**

SEABOARD AIR LINE

SAL-on shoulder of 1925 Armspear frame with clear cast "SALRY" cnx globe **90-100**

SAL- on shoulder of 1925 Armspear frame with red cast "SALRY" cnx globe **100-125**

SOO LINE aka MINNEAPOLIS ST PAUL & SAULT STE MARIE

SOO LINE- on shoulder of 1925 Armspear frame with clear unmarked globe **75-85**

SOO LINE-on shoulder of Dressel frame with amber etched "SOO LINE" cnx globe **100-125**

SOO LINE- on shoulder of Adlake Kero frame with green etched "SOO LINE" cnx globe **150-175**

SOO LINE-on shoulder of Adlake Kero frame with clear unmarked cnx globe **50-60**

SOUTHERN RAILWAY

SOUTHERN RY-on shoulder of Adlake Kero frame with clear etched "SOUTHERN RY" globe **65-75**

SOUTHERN RY-on shoulder of Adlake Kero frame with red unmarked globe............ **60-70**

SOUTHERN PACIFIC COMPANY

SPCO- on dome of Kero 250 frame with clear cast "SPCO" cnx globe **100-125**

SPCO-on dome of Kero 250 frame with red cast "SPCO" cnx globe **125-150**

SPCO- on shoulder of Adlake Kero frame with clear cast "SPCO" cnx globe **90-100**

SPCO- on shoulder of Adlake Kero frame with red cast "SPCO" cnx globe **100-125**

SPCO- on shoulder of Adlake Kero frame with clear unmarked globe **50-60**

TEXAS & PACIFIC RAILWAY

T&PRY- on shoulder of Adlake Kero frame with clear unmarked globe **70-80**

T&PRY- on shoulder of Adlake Kero frame with red unmarked globe **80-90**

TRINITY & BRAVOS VALLEY RAILWAY

T&BVRY- on shoulder of 1925 Armspear frame with clear unmarked globe **125-150**

UNION PACIFIC

UP- on dome of Kero 200 or 250 frame with clear etched "UP" or "UPRR" globe **80-90**

UP- on dome of Kero 200 or 250 frame with red etched "UP" or "UPRR" globe...... **90-100**

UP-on dome of Kero 200 or 250 frame with amber etched "UP" or UPRR" globe **125-150**

UP-on dome of Kero 200 or 250 frame with green etched "UP" or "UPRR" cnx globe **150-175**

UPRR- on shoulder of Adlake Kero frame with clear etched "UPRR" globe **70-80**

UPRR-on shoulder of Adlake Kero frame with red etched "UP" globe **80-90**

UPRR-on shoulder of Adlake Kero frame with clear unmarked cnx globe **65-75**

UPRY-on shoulder of Adlake Kero frame with clear unmarked cnx globe **70-80**

WABASH RAILROAD

WABASH RR-on shoulder of Dietz Vesta frame with clear unmarked globe **40-50**

WABASH RR-on shoulder of Dietz Vesta frame with red etched "WABASHRR" globe .. **65-75**

WABASH RR-on shoulder of Dietz Vesta frame with blue cast "WABASH RR" Dietz Vesta globe **175-200**

WABASH-on shoulder of Dressel frame with clear etched "WABASH RY" globe **75-85**

WABASH- on shoulder of Dressel frame with red etched "WABASH RY" globe **90-100**

WESTERN PACIFIC RAILROAD

WPRR-on dome of Kero 200 or 250 frame with clear unmarked globe **75-85**

WPRR-on shoulder of Adlake Kero frame with red unmarked globe **65-75**

BATTERY OPERATED

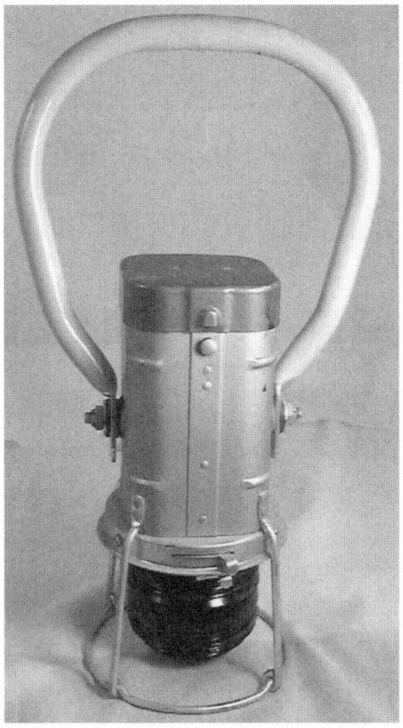

BATTERY SIGNAL LAMP-Manufacturered by Just Rite Mfg. Co. Blue attached lens cap. **15-25**

BATTERY SIGNAL LAMP-Manufactured by Conger Lantern Co. No railroad marking **10-15**

REMEMBER: PRICES LISTED ARE SUGGESTED VALUES ONLY. THIS IS ONLY A GUIDE. PRICES VARY FROM REGION TO REGION.

GLOBES ONLY

Lantern globes are a commodity due to the fact that the globe was usually the most vulnerable to destruction. Finding a frame with the wrong globe or minus the globe altogether is not uncommon. The most often seen colors are clear and red with amber, green & blue being more desirable. Globes embossed with the railroad name or initials command premium prices. Most short globe lanterns had acid etched railroad markings, making an embossed globe a better investment. Most commonly seen makers are Adlake Kero, Corning with the CNX logo, Kopp with a K in a circle. Remember globes must be in good to excellent condition with no chips or cracks to command the suggested prices.

AT&SF- (Atchison Topeka & Santa Fe) clear etched on 3 ¼" Adlake Kero globe **20-30**

AT&SF- (Atchison Topeka & Santa Fe) red etched 3 ¼" Adlake Kero globe **35-45**

AT&SF-(Atchison Topeka & Santa Fe) amber etched 3 ¼" Adlake Kero globe **75-85**

AT&SFRY-(Atchison Topeka & Santa Fe)clear etched 3 ¼" cnx globe **20-30**

AT&SFRY-(Atchison Topeka & Santa Fe) red etched 3 ¼" cnx globe **35-45**

AT&SFRY-(Atchison Topeka & Santa Fe) clear cast 3 ¼" Adlake Kero globe **40-50**

AT&SFRY-(Atchison Topeka & Santa Fe) red cast 3 ¼" Adlake Kero globe **75-85**

ACL- (Atlantic Coast Line) clear etched 3 ¼" Adlake Kero globe **25-35**

B&O-(Baltimore & Ohio) clear etched 3 ¼" Adlake Kero globe **15-20**

B&ORR- -(Baltimore & Ohio) clear cast 3 ¼" Adlake Kero globe **25-35**

B&ORR- -(Baltimore & Ohio) red cast 3 ¼" Adlake Kero globe **35-45**

BR-(Burlington Route) amber etched on 3 ¼" cnx globe **60-70**

BR- (Burlington Route) clear etched on 3 ¼" cnx globe 15-20

BR-(Burlington Route) red etched on 3 ¼" cnx globe 20-30

C&O-(Chesapeake & Ohio) clear etched on 3 ¼" Adlake Kero globe 15-25

C&EIRR- (Chicago & Eastern Illinois) red etched on 3 ¼" Adlake Kero globe 30-40

C&NW-(Chicago & Northwestern) clear etched on 3 ¼" Adlake Kero globe 15-20

C&NW-(Chicago & Northwestern) red etched on 3 ¼" Adlake Kero globe 20-30

C&NW—(Chicago & Northwestern)amber etched on 3 ¼" Adlake Kero globe 60-70

CMSTP&PRR- (Chicago Milwaukee St Paul & Pacific) clear etched on 3 ¼" cnx globe 15-20

CMSTP&PRR-(Chicago Milwaukee St Paul & Pacific)red etched on 3 ¼" cnx globe 20-30

D&H. (Delaware & Hudson) clear etched on 3 ¼" Adlake Kero globe 15-20

D&RGWRR- (Denver & Rio Grande Western)red etched 3 ¼" "Safety First" cnx globe 45-55

D&RGWRR- (Denver & Rio Grande Western) clear etched 3 ¼" "SAFETY FIRST" cnx globe 35-45

D&RGWRR- (Denver & Rio Grande Western)amber etched 3 ¼" Adlake Kero cnx globe 75-85

ERIE- clear etched 3 ¼" Adlake Kero globe .. 15-20

GC&SFRY-(Gulf Colorado & Santa Fe) clear cast 3 1/4" Adlake Kero globe 100-125

GC&SFRY- (Gulf Colorado & Santa Fe) red cast 3 ¼" Adlake Kero globe 150-175

HV- (Hocking Valley) clear etched 3 ¼" Adlake Kero globe 10-15

HV- (Hocking Valley) red etched 3 ¼" Adlake Kero globe 15-25

ICRR- (Illinois Central) amber etched 3 ¼" Adlake Kero 35-45

I-GNRR- (International Great Northern) clear etched 3 ¼" Adlake Kero globe 20-30

LVRR- (Lehigh Valley) red cast 3 ¼" globe ... 80-90

L&NRR- (Louisville & Nashville) clear cast 3 ¼" globe cast "1925" 25-35

L&NRR- (Louisville & Nashville) green etched 3 ¼" globe cast "1925" 90-100

NYCS- (New York Central System) clear cast 4 ¼" Dietz Vesta globe 15-20

NYCS- (New York Central System) clear etched 4 ¼" Handlan St. Louis globe **10-15**

NYCS- (New York Central System) red etched 4 ¼" Handlan St. Louis globe **15-20**

NEW YORK CENTRAL- clear cast on 4 ¼" Dietz Vesta globe **15-20**

NYC&STL- (New York Chicago & St. Louis) amber etched 3 ¼" Adlake Kero globe .. **65-75**

NPRY-(Northern Pacific) 3 1/4" amber etched Adlake Kero globe **90-100**

PERY- (Pacific Electric) red etched 3 ¼" Adlake Kero globe **20-30**

PRR- (Pennsylvania) Keystone logo clear etched on 3 ¼" Adlake Kero globe **10-15**

PRR- (Pennsylvania) Keystone logo clear cast on 3 ¼" Adlake Kero globe **20-30**

RI LINES- (Rock Island Lines) clear etched 3 ¼" Adlake Kero globe **15-20**

RI LINES- (Rock Island Lines) red etched 3 ¼" Adlake Kero globe **25-35**

RI LINES- (Rock Island Lines) clear cast 3 ¼" Adlake Kero globe **40-50**

SP CO- (Southern Pacific) red cast 3 ¼" Adlake Kero globe **30-40**

UP-(Union Pacific) clear etched 3 ¼" Adlake Kero globe **10-15**

UP-(Union Pacific) red etched 3 ¼" Adlake Kero globe **20-30**

UNMARKED- clear 3 ¼ Adlake Kero or cnx globe **10-15**

UNMARKED- red 3 ¼" Adlake Kero or cnx globe **15-25**

UNMARKED- amber 3 ¼" Adlake Kero or cnx globe **30-40**

UNMARKED –green or blue 3 ¼" Adlake Kero or cnx globe **50-60**

UNMARKED-clear 4 1/4" Dietz Vesta globe **10-15**

UNMARKED-red 4 1/4" Dietz Vesta globe **15-25**

UNMARKED-cobalt blue 4 1/4" Dietz Vesta globe **40-50**

CHAPTER 20

LANTERNS TALL GLOBE

The hobby of collecting railroad lanterns is most definitely one of the more popular aspects of railroadiana. The early lanterns were beautiful and quite fragile as many were made without any sort of wire guard to protect the glass. These lanterns which started appearing in the 1850's are often times referred to as fixed globes because the globes were cemented in place. They were most prevelent in the northeast part of the country. Styles slowly started to change in the 1870's with the introduction of lanterns with removable globes. Most are referred to today as the brass top style with bell bottom or wire bottom frames. In the early 1900's lanterns again were becoming more efficient with the introduction of drop in fuel pots which allowed for flame control while the fuel container was still in place. Although the lantern styles still continued to change it was in the 1920's that its short globe cousin was introduced on the scene. Lanterns with colored embossed marked globes are the most desirable with red & clear being the more common colors found. Etched & wheel cut globes are also found. On the following pages we have tried to show the various styles available. It is important to note that although we have listed a tremendous amount of information here there are literally thousands of different railroad lanterns that can be found with different railroad markings. Remember lanterns must not be rusted, pitted, bent or otherwise altered from their original state to command the prices suggested here. Globes must not be cracked or chipped.

REMEMBER: PRICES SHOWN ARE SUGGESTED VALUES ONLY. VALUES VARY FROM REGION TO REGION. THIS IS MEANT ONLY AS A GUIDE. (◆) **Denotes value over $1000.00**

Below are the more commonly seen lantern styles. Remember many more exist, we have shown only a sample here.

Circa 1860's fixed globe lantern with no wire guards & wrist bale.

Fixed globe lantern with wire guard and wrist bale.

Circa 1880's brass top bell bottom lantern with twist off bell and double wire guard.

1895 Adams & Westlake double wire flat vertical frame with wire bottom and twist off fuel pot.

1913 Adlake Reliable bell bottom lantern with single wire guard and fixed bell. Drop in fuel container.

1913 Adlake Reliable wire bottom lantern with drop in fuel container and single wire guard.

ATCHISON TOPEKA & SANTA FE

AT&SFRR- on bell of brass top bell bottom single wire guard lantern frame with clear cast "AT&SFRR" globe & twist off bell .... ◆

AT&SFRY- on bell of unmarked Adams & Westlake style frame. Fixed bell bottom single wire guard with clear cast "SANTA FE" logo globe **250-300**

AT&SFRY-on bell of unmarked Adams &Westlake style fixed bell bottom single wire guard frame with red cast "SANTA FE" logo globe **400-450**

AT&SFRY- on shoulder of 1909 Adams & Westlake fixed bell bottom single wire guard frame with clear cast "AT&SFRY" globe **250-300**

AT&SFRY-on bell of unmarked Adams & Westlake style fixed bell bottom single wire guard frame with red cast "AT&SFRY" globe **325-375**

ARIZONA EASTERN

AERR- on shoulder of 1913 Adlake Reliable single wire guard frame with clear unmarked globe.. **300-350**

ATLANTIC COAST LINE

ACLRR- on shoulder of 1913 Adlake Reliable single wire guard frame with clear unmarked globe.. **175-200**

BALTIMORE & OHIO RR

B&ORR- on shoulder of 1895 Adams & Westlake double wire guard frame with twist off pot & clear unmarked globe **150-175**

B&ORR- on shoulder of 1913 Adlake Reliable single wire guard frame with clear cast "B&O" Capitol logo globe **175-200**

B&ORR LOCO- on shoulder of 1913 Adlake Reliable single wire guard frame with clear cast "B&O" Capitol logo globe also etched "LOCO" on reverse **200-250**

B&ORR LOCO- on shoulder of 1913 Adlake Reliable single wire guard frame with red cast "B&O" Capitol logo cnx/Corning globe **250-300**

BOSTON & ALBANY RR

B&ARR- on shoulder of Dietz #6 double wire guard frame with clear cast "B&ARR" 6" globe.. **175-200**

BOSTON & LOWELL RR

B&LRR- on shoulder of brass top bell bottom single wire guard lantern with red unmarked globe and twist off glass fount **350-400**

BOSTON & MAINE RR

B&M- clear wheel cut fixed globe single wire guard lantern. Circa 1870's style with wrist bale . **450-500**

B&MRR- on shoulder of 1913 Reliable single wire guard frame with clear cast "B&MRR" globe **90-100**

BOSTON & WORCHESTER

B&W- clear wheel cut globe in fixed globe lantern with wrist bale **500-550**

BUFFALO & SUSQUEHANNA

B&SRR- on shoulder of Dietz Steel Clad double wire guard frame with clear unmarked globe **150-175**

BUFFALO ROCHESTER & PITTSBURGH

BR&PRY- on shoulder of Dietz bell bottom double wire guard frame with clear cast "BR&PRY" globe **175-200**

BURLINGTON & MISSOURI RIVER RAILROAD OF NEBRASKA

B&MR -NEB- on shoulder of 1892 Adams & Westlake wire bottom frame with single wire guard & twist off fuel container with clear cast "B&MRRR on extended base on globe...... ◆

BURLINGTON CEDAR RAPIDS & NORTHERN

BCR&N- on shoulder of 1892 Adams & Westlake single wire guard frame with twist off pot & clear unmarked globe **350-400**

BURLINGTON ROUTE

BURLINGTON ROUTE- on shoulder of 1913 single wire guard Adlake Reliable frame with clear cast "BURLINGTON ROUTE" cnx/Corning globe **100-125**

BURLINGTON ROUTE- on shoulder of 1913 single wire guard Adlake Reliable frame with red cast "BURLINGTON ROUTE" cnx/Corning globe **175-200**

BURLINGTON ROUTE- on shoulder of Handlan Buck double wire guard frame with twist off fuel pot. Comes with clear cast "BURLINGTON ROUTE" extended base globe **250-300**

BURLINGTON ROUTE- on shoulder of 92 Adams & Westlake single wire guard frame with twist off pot. Comes with red cast "BURLINGTON ROUTE"extended base **450-500**

BURLINGTON ROUTE- 1889 MM Buck frame double wire guard with twist off fuel pot. Comes with clear cast "BURLINGTON ROUTE" extended base globe **350-400**

CANADIAN PACIFIC RAILWAY

CPRY-on shoulder of ET Wright single wire guard frame with clear cast "CPR" extended base globe **125-150**

CPRY- on shoulder of ET Wright single wire guard frame with red cast "CPR" extended base globe **200-250**

CPRY- on shoulder of ET Wright single wire guard frame with green cast "CPR" extended base globe **600-700**

CAROLINA CLINCHFIELD & OHIO RY

CC&ORY- on shoulder of Keystone Casey single wire guard frame with clear unmarked extended base globe **250-300**

CENTRAL VERMONT

CVRR- on shoulder of 1873 brass top bell bottom Adams & Westlake single wire guard frame with clear unmarked globe **300-350**

CVRR- on shoulder of Railroad Signal Lamp & Lantern Co. double wire guard frame with twist off fuel container & clear unmarked globe **125-150**

CVRY- on shoulder of 1913 Armspear frame double wire guard with clear cast "CVRY" globe .. **150-175**

CVRY-on shoulder of Defiance Lantern Co. frame. Double wire guard with twisted verticals & clear cast globe........................ **300-350**

CHICAGO & ALTON RAILROAD

C&ARR- on shoulder of 1897 Adams & Westlake double wire guard frame with twist off pot. Comes with clear etched "C&ARY" extended base globe **125-150**

CHICAGO BURLINGTON & QUINCY

CB&QRR-on shoulder of brass top wire bottom 1873 Adams & Westlake single wire guard frame with green cast "CB&QRR" globe .... **t**

CHICAGO & NORTHWESTERN RY

C&NWRY- on shoulder of 1909 Adams & Westlake double wire guard frame. Comes with clear cast "C&NWRY" cnx/Corning globe **100-125**

C&NWRY- on shoulder of 1913 Adlake Reliable single wire guard frame with clear cast "C&NWRY" cnx/Corning globe **90-100**

C&NWRY- on shoulder of 1913 Adlake Reliable single wire guard frame with red cast "C&NWRY" cnx/Corning globe **125-150**

CHICAGO & INDIANA SOUTHERN

C&ISRY-on shoulder of 1895 Adams & Westlake double wire guard frame with clear cast "C&ISRR" globe................................ **300-350**

CHICAGO GREAT WESTERN

CGWRY- on shoulder of 1909 Adams & Westlake double wire guard frame with clear cast "CGWRR" cnx/Corning globe **350-400**

CHICAGO MILWAUKEE & ST PAUL RY

CM&STPRY-on 1895 Adams & Westlake brass top bell bottom double wire guard frame with twist off bell. Comes with clear cast "CM&STPRY" corning globe **175-200**

CM&STPRY- on 1895 Adams & Westlake brass top bell bottom double wire guard frame with twist off bell. Comes with red cast "CM&STPRY" globe **250-300**

CM&STPRY- on 1895 Adams & Westlake brass top bell bottom double wire guard frame with twist off bell. Comes with green etched "CM&STPRR" or "CM&STP" globe **400-450**

CM&STPRY- on 1913 Reliable single wire guard frame with clear cast "CM&STPRY" cnx/Corning globe **90-100**

CM&STPRY- on 1913 Reliable single wire guard frame with red cast "CM&STPRY" cnx/Corning globe **100-125**

CM&STPRY- on shoulder of round top Handlan single wire guard frame with clear cast "CM&STPRY" cnx/Corning globe **85-95**

CM&STPRY- on shoulder of round top Handlan single wire guard frame with red etched "CM&STPRY" cnx/Corning globe **90-100**

CHICAGO ROCK ISLAND & PACIFIC RR

CRI&PRR- on shoulder of 1889 Adams & Westlake single wire guard frame with twist off pot. Comes with clear etched "CRI&PRR" extended base globe **250-300**

CRI&PRR- on shoulder of 97 Adams & Westlake double wire guard frame with twist off pot. Comes with clear wheel cut "CRI&P" extended base globe **150-175**

CHICAGO ST PAUL MINNEAPOLIS & OMAHA RR

CSTPM&ORR- on shoulder of 1892 Adams & Westlake double wire guard frame with clear cast "CSTPM&ORR" extended base globe **500-550**

CSTPM&ORR- on shoulder of 1892 Adams & Westlake double wire guard frame with red cast "CSTPM&ORR" extended base globe **700-800**

CSTPM&ORR- on shoulder of 1895 Adams & Westlake double wire guard frame. Comes with clear cast "NORTHWESTERN LINE" logo globe **250-300**

CSTPM&ORR- on shoulder of 1897 Adams & Westlake double wire guard frame with twist off pot. Comes with red cast "NORTHWESTERN LINE" logo globe 375-425

CMSTPM&ORR- on shoulder of 1909 Adams & Westlake "THE ADAMS" double wire guard frame with red cast "NORTHWESTERN LINE" logo globe 300-350

CMSTPM&ORR- on shoulder of 1913 Reliable single wire guard frame with red cast "NORTHWESTERN LINE" logo globe 350-400

CLEVELAND CINNCINNATI CHICAGO & ST LOUIS

CCC&STLRY- on shoulder of 1912 Adlake Reliable double wire guard frame with clear cast "CCC&STLRY" cnx/Corning "SAFETY FIRST" globe 100-125

CCC&STLRY- on shoulder of 1912 Adlake Reliable double wire guard frame with red cast "CCC&STLRY" cnx/Corning globe ... 175-200

CCC&STLRR- on shoulder of Handlan Buck fixed bell bottom double wire guard frame. Comes with clear cast "CCC&STLRR" cnx/Corning globe 125-150

CINNCINNATI NEW ORLEANS & TEXAS PACIFIC RY

CNO&TPRY- on shoulder of 95 Adams & Westlake double wire guard frame with twist off pot. With clear unmarked globe 175-200

COLORADO & SOUTHERN RY

C&SRY- on 1895 Adams & Westlake double wire guard fixed bell frame. Comes with clear cast "C&SRY" extended base globe .... ◆

C&SRY- on Star Headlight double wire guard frame with clear cast "C&SRY" extended base globe .... ◆

C&SRY- on 1895 Adams & Westlake double wire guard fixed bell frame with clear etched "C&SRY" globe 250-300

C&SRY- on 1909 Adams & Westlake "THE ADAMS" double wire guard frame with clear etched "C&SRY" globe 250-300

C&SRY- on National Brass double wire guard frame with clear cast "C&SRY" extended base globe .... ◆

C&SRY OR C&SRR- on 1913 Reliable single wire guard frame with CE "C&SRY" or "C&SRR" cnx/Corning globe 225-275

C&SRY OR C&SRR- on 1913 Reliable single wire guard frame with clear unmarked globe 150-175

COLORADO MIDLAND RAILROAD

COLO. MID. RR- on shoulder of double wire guard Handlan Buck frame with clear cast "CMRR" extended base globe .... ◆

COLO. MID RR- on shoulder of double wire guard Handlan Buck frame with red etched "CMRY" extended base globe **650-750**

COLO.MID RR- on shoulder of double wire guard Handlan Buck frame with blue etched "CMRY" extended base globe .... ◆

COLO.MID. RR- on shoulder of round top single wire guard Handlan Buck frame with clear unmarked globe **500-600**

CMRY- on shoulder of 1897 Adams & Westlake double wire guard frame with twist off pot. Comes with clear cast "CMRR" extended base globe .... ◆

CMRY- on shoulder of 1897 Adams & Westlake double wire guard frame with twist off pot. Comes with clear etched "CMRY" extended base globe **550-650**

CMRY- on shoulder of brass top wire bottom Prier Brass Mfg. single wire guard frame with CC "CMRR" extended base globe .... ◆

CMRR- on shoulder of brass top bell bottom CT Hamm frame with clear cast "CMRR" extended base globe .... ◆

COLORADO SPRINGS & CRIPPLE CREEK DISTRICT RY CO

CS&CCDRYCO- on shoulder of 95 or 97 Adams & Westlake double wire guard frame with clear unmarked globe **800-900**

CONCORD & MONTREAL RAILROAD

C&MRR-on shoulder of Steam Gauge Lamp & Lantern Co. frame with clear cast "C&MRR" extended base globe **350-400**

DELAWARE & HUDSON

D&HRR- on 1913 Reliable double wire guard frame with clear cast "THE D&H" script logo globe **200-250**

D&H CO- on shoulder of 1913 Reliable single wire guard frame with red cast "THE D&H" script logo globe **250-300**

D&H CO- on shoulder of #39 Railroad bell bottom double wire guard lantern with twist off bell & clear cast "THE D&H" in fancy script letters logo globe. **250-300**

<u>DENVER & RIO GRANDE RR</u>

D&RGRR- on bell of brass top bell bottom MM Buck double wire guard frame with red cast "D&RGRR" extended base globe......... ◆

D&RGRR-on round or flat top Handlan single wire guard frame Comes with clear cast"D&RG" SAFETY FIRST mellon style globe... **250-300**

D&RGRR- on round or flat top Handlan single wire guard frame with clear etched "D&RGRR" mellon style globe **175-200**

D&RGRR- on round or flat top Handlan single wire guard frame with clear unmarked globe **125-150**

D&RGRR-on shoulder of Handlan Buck double wire guard frame with clear cast D&RGRR extended base globe .... ◆

D&RGRR-on shoulder of Handlan Buck double wire guard frame with clear unmarked globe... **250-300**

D&RGRR-on shoulder of 1895 Adams & Westlake double wire guard frame with twist off pot. Comes with clear cast "D&RGRR" extended base globe **900-1000**

D&RGRR- on shoulder of 1895 Adams & Westlake double wire guard frame with clear unmarked globe................................ **175-200**

D&RGRR-on shoulder of 1909 Adams & Westlake "THE ADAMS" double wire guard frame with clear cast "D&RGRR" Corning style globe... **500-600**

D&RGRR- on shoulder of 1909 Adams & Westlake "THE ADAMS" double wire guard frame with red etched "D&RG" Corning globe **300-350**

DENVER & RIO GRANDE WESTERN

D&RGW-on shoulder of flat top Handlan single wire guard frame with clear etched "D&RGW" SAFETY FIRST Corning globe **175-200**

D&RGW- on shoulder of flat top Handlan single wire guard frame with red etched "D&RGW" cnx/Corning globe **250-300**

D&RGW- on shoulder of flat top Handlan single wire guard frame with amber etched "D&RGW" cnx/Corning globe **350-400**

DENVER & SALT LAKE RR

D&SLRR- on shoulder of 1913 Reliable single wire guard bell bottom or wire bottom frame with clear etched "D&SLRR" cnx/Corning globe **350-400**

DENVER NORTHWESTERN & PACIFIC

DNW&P- on shoulder of 1909 Adams & Westlake "THE ADAMS" double wire guard frame. Comes with clear etched "DNW&P" globe **700-800**

DENVER SOUTH PARK & PACIFIC

DSP&PRR- on bell of brass top bell bottom MM Buck double wire guard frame with clear unmarked extended base globe .... ◆

DENVER TEXAS & GULF

DT&GRR-on bell of brass top bell bottom MM Buck double wire guard frame with clear unmarked extended base globe .... ◆

DETROIT TOLEDO & IRONTON

DT&I- on shoulder of 1903 Keystone Casey single wire guard frame with clear etched "DT&IRY" globe **375-425**

DULUTH & IRON RANGE

D&IR- on shoulder of 1897 Adams & Westlake double wire guard frame with twist off pot. Comes with clear etched "D&IRRR" cnx/Corning globe **350-400**

EL PASO & NORTHEASTERN

EP&NERY- on shoulder of 1897 Adams & Westlake double wire guard frame with twist off pot. Comes with clear unmarked globe **325-375**

EL PASO & SOUTHWESTERN

EP&SW- on shoulder of 1913 Reliable single wire guard frame with clear etched EP&SW cnx/ Corning globe **225-250**

EP&SW- on shoulder of 1913 Reliable single wire guard frame with clear cast "EP&SW" cnx/ Corning globe **375-425**

ELGIN JOLIET & EASTERN

EJ&ERR- on shoulder of 1895 Adams & Westlake double wire guard frame with twist off pot. Comes with clear cast "EJ&ERR" extended base globe **200-225**

EJ&ERY- on 1913 Reliable single wire guard frame with clear unmarked globe **100-125**

ERIE RAILROAD

ERIE- on shoulder of Armspear frame with clear unmarked globe **75-85**

ERIE- on shoulder of Armspear frame with clear cast "ERR" globe **100-125**

ERIE RR-on shoulder of #39 Railroad wire bottom frame with red cast "ERR CO" globe **125-150**

ERIE RR- on shoulder of 1895 Adams & Westlake double wire guard twist off frame with clear cast "ERRCO" globe **125-150**

FITCHBURG RAILROAD

FITCHBURG RR- in large letters spelled out on lid &bell of double wire guard frame & glass font. Comes with 6" clear cast "FRR" globe **450-500**

FLORENCE & CRIPPLE CREEK

F&CCRR-on shoulder of 1909 Adams & Westlake "THE ADAMS" double wire guard frame with clear unmarked globe .... ◆

F&CCRR- on shoulder of 1913 Reliable single wire guard frame with clear cast "F&CC" extended base globe .... ◆

F&CCRR- on shoulder of Star Headlight double wire guard frame with clear cast "F&CC" extended base globe .... ◆

FT SMITH & WESTERN

FTS&WRR- on shoulder of round top Handlan frame with clear unmarked globe **250-300**

FT WORTH & DENVER

FW&D-on shoulder of 1912 Reliable double wire guard frame with clear cast "FW&D" globe **400-450**

FT WORTH & DENVER CITY

FW&DCRY- on shoulder of 97 Adams & Westlake double wire guard frame with twist off pot. Comes with clear cast "FW&DC" cnx/ Corning globe **475-525**

FW&DCRY- on dome of 1923 Reliable single wire guard frame with clear unmarked globe. **200-250**

FW&DCRY-on dome of 1923 Reliable single wire guard frame with red cast "FW&DC" cnx/ Corning globe **550-600**

FW&DCRY-on shoulder of Star Headlight double wire guard frame with clear unmarked globe **450-500**

FRISCO - (ST LOUIS SAN FRANCISCO)

FRISCO- on shoulder of round top Handlan Buck single wire guard frame with red cast "FRISCO" cnx/Corning globe **250-300**

FRISCO- on round top or flat top Handlan single wire guard frame with clear cast "FRISCO" cnx/Corning globe **175-200**

FRISCO- on shoulder of Star Headlight double wire guard frame with clear cast "FRISCO" SAFETY FIRST globe **200-250**

FRISCO SYSTEM- on bell & shoulder of MM Buck or Handlan Buck frame with clear cast "FRISCO SYSTEM" globe **600-700**

GRAND TRUNK RAILWAY

GRAND TRUNK- on shoulder of 95 Adams & Westlake bell bottom frame with twist off bell. Comes with clear cast "GTRY" extended base globe **150-175**

GTR- on shoulder of ET Wright single wire guard frame with clear cast "GTR" cnx/Corning globe **100-125**

GTW- on shoulder of 1923 Adlake Reliable single wire guard frame with clear cast "GTW" cnx/Corning globe **100-125**

GREAT NORTHERN RAILWAY

GNRY- on shoulder of 1913 Adlake Reliable single wire guard frame with clear cast "GNRY" cnx/Corning globe **100-125**

GNRY-on shoulder of 1913 Adlake Reliable single wire guard frame with red cast "GNRY" cnx/Corning globe **300-350**

GNRY- on shoulder of 1897 Adams & Westlake double wire guard frame with twist off pot. Comes with clear cast "GNRY" cnx/Corning globe **200-250**

GNRY- on shoulder of 1897 Adams & Westlake double wire guard frame with twist off pot. Comes with red cast "GNRY" cnx/Corning globe **400-450**

GREAT WESTERN

GWRY- on shoulder of 1912 Adlake Reliable double wire guard frame with red etched "GWRY" cnx/Corning globe **400-450**

GWRY- on shoulder of 1913 Adlake Reliable single wire guard frame with clear etched "GWRY" cnx/Corning globe **300-350**

GULF COLORADO & SANTA FE RY

GC&SFRY- on shoulder 1913 Adams & Westlake fixed bell style single wire guard frame. With clear cast "GC&SFRY" cnx/Corning globe **500-550**

GC&SFRY- dome of 1923 Adlake Reliable single wire guard frame with clear cast "GC&SFRY" cnx/Corning globe **475-525**

HOCKING VALLEY RAILROAD

HVRR- on shoulder of 97 Adams & Westlake double wire guard frame with red cast "HVRY" cnx/Corning globe **250-300**

HVRY- on shoulder of Keystone Casey double wire guard frame with clear cast "HVRY" cnx/ Corning globe **200-250**

HVRY- on shoulder of 97 Adams & Westlake double wire guard frame with clear unmarked globe **100-125**

HOUSTON BELT & TERMINAL RAILROAD

HB&TRR-on shoulder of 1913 Reliable single wire guard frame with clear unmarked globe **90-100**

ILLINOIS CENTRAL RAILROAD

ICRR- on shoulder of round top Handlan single wire guard frame with clear cast "ICRR"cnx/ Corning globe **90-100**

ICRR- on shoulder of 1873 Adams & Westlake brass top bell bottom single wire guard frame. Comes with clear cast extended base globe **675-725**

ICRR-on shoulder of 1913 Adlake Reliable single wire guard frame with clear cast "ICRR" cnx/Corning globe.............................. **90-100**

ICRR- on shoulder of 1913 Adlake Reliable single wire guard frame with red cast "ICRR" cnx/Corning globe............................ **125-150**

INTERNATIONAL & GREAT NORTHERN

I&GNRR-on shoulder of 89 Handlan Buck double wire guard frame with twist off pot. Comes with clear unmarked globe **200-250**

I&GNRR- on shoulder of 1913 Adlake Reliable single wire guard frame with clear etched "I&GN" cnx/Corning globe **125-150**

INDIANA HARBOR BELT

IHBRR- on shoulder of 1913 Adlake Reliable single wire guard frame with clear etched "IHBRR" cnx/Corning globe **100-125**

IHBRR-on shoulder of 1913 Adlake Reliable single wire guard frame with red etched "IHBRR" cnx/Corning globe **125-150**

IOWA CENTRAL RAILWAY

ICRY or IACRY-(Iowa Central) on shoulder of Armspear double wire guard frame with clear cast "IACRY" extended base globe **500-550**

KENTUCKY & INDIANA TERMINAL

K&ITRR-on shoulder of flat top Handlan single wire guard frame with clear cast "K&ITRR" cnx/Corning globe **125-150**

KANSAS CITY MEXICO & ORIENT

KCM&O- on shoulder of 1923 Adlake Reliable single wire guard frame with clear unmarked globe **300-350**

KCM&ORR- on dome of 1923 Adlake Reliable single wire guard frame with clear unmarked globe **250-300**

KANSAS CITY NORTHWESTERN

KCNWRR- on shoulder of 1913 Adlake Reliable single wire guard frame with clear unmarked globe **450-500**

KANSAS CITY SOUTHERN RY

KCSRY- on shoulder of 1913 Adlake Reliable single wire guard bell bottom frame with clear etched "KCSRY" cnx/Corning globe **125-150**

KCSRY- on shoulder of 1913 Adlake Reliable single wire guard bell bottom frame with red cast "KCSRY" cnx/Corning globe **200-250**

KCSYCO- on shoulder of 89 Handlan Buck double wire guard frame with twist off pot. Comes with clear etched "KCSYCO" extended base globe **250-300**

KANSAS CITY TERMINAL RY

KCTRY- on shoulder 1913 Adlake Reliable single wire guard frame with clear cast "KCTRY" cnx/Corning globe **125-150**

LAKE SHORE & MICHIGAN SOUTHERN

LS&MSRY- on shoulder of 1913 Adlake Reliable single wire guard frame with clear unmarked globe **75-85**

LS&MSRY- on shoulder of 95 Adams & Westlake double wire guard frame with twist off pot. Comes with clear cast "LS&MSRY" extended base globe **150-175**

LS&MSRY- on shoulder of Adams & Westlake brass top bell bottom single wire guard frame with clear cast "LS&MSRY" extended base globe...................... **500-550**

LEAVENWORTH KANSAS & WESTERN

LK&W- on shoulder of 89 Handlan Buck double wire guard frame with twist off pot and clear unmarked globe .... ◆

LEHIGH VALLEY RAILROAD

LVRR- on shoulder of 1913 Armspear double wire guard frame with clear cast "LVRR" cnx/Corning globe **125-150**

LVRR- on shoulder of 1913 Armspear double wire guard frame with red cast "LVRR" cnx/Corning globe **150-175**

LOUISIANA & ARKANSAS RAILWAY

L&ARY- on shoulder of 1913 Adlake Reliable single wire guard frame with clear etched "L&A" globe **200-250**

LOUISVILLE & NASHVILLE RAILROAD

L&NRR- on shoulder of 1913 Armspear double wire guard with clear cast "L&NRR" cnx/Corning or mellon globe **100-125**

L&NRR- on shoulder of 1913 Armspear double wire guard frame with clear unmarked globe **75-85**

LOUISVILLE HENDERSON & ST LOUIS

LH&STLRY- on shoulder of 1913 Reliable single wire guard frame with clear cast "LH&STLRY" cnx/Corning globe.... **250-300**

MICHIGAN OR MAINE CENTRAL

MCRR- on shoulder of 1913 Adlake Reliable single wire guard frame with clear cast "MCRR" cnx/Corning globe.............................. **90-100**

MCRR- on shoulder of 1913 Adlake Reliable single wire guard frame with red cast "MCRR" cnx/Corning globe............................ **100-125**

MIDLAND VALLEY RAILROAD

MVRR- on shoulder of round top Handlan single wire guard frame with clear unmarked globe.. **90-100**

MINNEAPOLIS & ST. LOUIS RAILROAD

M&STLRR- on shoulder of 1923 Reliable double wire guard frame with clear cast "M&STLRY" SAFETY ALWAYS cnx/Corning globe.. **200-250**

M&STLRR- on shoulder of 1913 Armspear double wire guard frame with twist off pot & clear cast "M&STLRY" cnx/Corning globe........................ **225-275**

MISSOURI KANSAS & TEXAS RAILROAD

MK&TRR- on shoulder of Handlan Buck brass top wire bottom double wire guard frame with clear cast MK&TRY extended base globe **550-600**

MK&TRR- on shoulder of round or flat top Handlan single wire guard frame with clear etched "MK&TRY" mellon style globe **90-100**

MK&TRR- on shoulder of round or flat top Handlan single wire guard frame with red etched "MK&TRY" globe **125-150**

MK&TRR- on shoulder of round top Handlan Buck double wire guard bell bottom frame with clear cast "MKT" cnx/Corning globe **200-250**

MISSOURI PACIFIC RAILROAD

MPRR- on bell of brass top bell bottom MM Buck double wire guard frame with clear cast "MP" extended base globe................. **350-400**

MOPAC- on bell of brass top bell bottom MM Buck double wire guard frame with clear cast "MP" extended base globe................ **275-325**

MOPAC- on bell of brass top bell bottom MM Buck double wire guard frame with red cast "MP" extended base globe................. **400-450**

MOPAC- on bell of Handlan Buck double wire guard frame with twist off bell. Comes with clear cast "MP SAFETY FIRST" cnx/Corning globe **90-100**

MOPAC- on bell of Handlan Buck double wire guard frame with twist off bell. Comes with red cast "MP SAFETY FIRST" cnx/ Corning globe **125-150**

MOPAC- on bell of Handlan Buck double wire guard frame with twist off bell and amber cast "MP" cnx/Corning globe **450-500**

MOPAC- on shoulder of round top Handlan single wire guard frame with clear cast "MP SAFETY FIRST" cnx/Corning globe **90-100**

MOPAC- on shoulder of round top Handlan single wire guard frame with red cast "MP" cnx/ Corning globe **100-125**

MOPAC- on shoulder of round top Handlan single wire guard frame with clear unmarked globe **65-75**

MISSOURI OKLAHOMA & GULF RY

MO&GRY- on shoulder of round top Handlan single wire guard frame with clear unmarked globe **175-200**

NASHVILLE CHATTANOOGA & ST. LOUIS

NC&STLRY- on shoulder of 1913 Adlake Reliable single wire guard frame with clear cast "NC&STLRY" cnx/Corning globe ... **300-350**

NEW YORK CENTRAL RAILROAD

NYCRR- on shoulder of 1913 Adlake Reliable single wire guard frame with clear cast "NYCRR" cnx/Corning globe **70-80**

NYCRR- on shoulder of 1913 Adlake Reliable single wire guard frame with red cast "NYCRR" cnx/Corning globe **90-100**

NEW YORK CENTRAL- on shoulder of Deitz bell bottom double wire guard frame with clear cast "NEW YORK CENTRAL" 6" globe **75-85**

NEW YORK CENTRAL- on shoulder of Deitz bell bottom double wire guard frame with red cast "NEW YORK CENTRAL" 6" globe **100-125**

NEW YORK CENTRAL- on shoulder of Deitz bell bottom double wire guard frame with amber cast "NEW YORK CENTRAL" 6" globe **450-500**

NEW YORK CENTRAL- on shoulder of Deitz bell bottom double wire guard frame with green cast "NEW YORK CENTRAL" 6" globe **550-600**

NEW YORK CENTRAL- on shoulder of Deitz bell bottom double wire guard frame with unmarked globe **55-65**

NEW YORK NEW HAVEN & HARTFORD

NYNH&HRR- on shoulder 97 Adams & Westlake double wire guard frame with twist off pot. Comes with clear cast "NYNH&HRR" globe **100-125**

NYNH&HRR- on shoulder of 1913 Adlake Reliable single wire guard frame with clear cast "NYNH&HRR" cnx/Corning globe .. **90-100**

NYNH&HRR- on shoulder of Adams & Westlake #100 single wire guard frame with clear cast "NYNH&HRR" #100 globe........ **90-100**

NEW YORK ONTARIO & WESTERN

NYO&W- on shoulder of 1913 Adlake Reliable bell bottom single wire guard frame with 6" extended base "NYO&W" globe **550-600**

NORFOLK & WESTERN RAILWAY

N&WRY- on shoulder of 97 Armspear double wire guard frame with twist off pot. Comes with clear cast "N&W" cnx/Corning globe **175-200**

NORTHERN PACIFIC RAILROAD

NPRR- on shoulder of 97 Adams & Westlake double wire guard frame with twist off pot. Comes with clear cast "NPRR" extended base globe **325-375**

NPRR- on shoulder of 97 Adams & Westlake double wire guard frame with clear cast "NPRR" cnx/Corning globe **225-275**

NPRY- on shoulderof 1913 Armspear double wire guard frame with twist off pot. Comes with clear cast "NPRR" cnx/Corning globe **125-150**

OLD COLONY RAILROAD

OCRR- on shoulder of Deitz bell bottom double wire guard frame with 6" red unmarked globe **175-200**

OREGON RAILROAD & NAVIGATION

OR&NCO- on shoulder of 97 Adams & Westlake frame with clear cast "OR&N" extended base globe **500-550**

OR&NCO- on shoulder of 1909 Adams & Westlake double wire guard frame with clear unmarked extended base globe **200-250**

OREGON SHORT LINE

OSL- on shoulder of 1909 Adams & Westlake double wire guard frame with clear cast "OSL" cnx/Corning globe **200-250**

OSL- on shoulder of 1913 Adlake Reliable single wire guard frame with clear unmarked globe **100-125**

OSL- on shoulder of 1913 Adlake Reliable single wire guard frame with clear cast "OSL" cnx/ Corning globe **200-250**

OREGON WASHINGTON RAILROAD & NAVIGATION COMPANY

OWRR&NAV.CO- on shoulder of round top single wire guard Handlan frame with clear cast "OWRR&NCO" globe **300-350**

OWRR&NCO- on shoulder of 1913 Adlake Reliable single wire guard frame with clear cast "OWRR&NCO" globe **300-350**

PACIFIC ELECTRIC RAILWAY

PERY- on shoulder of 1913 Adlake Reliable single wire guard frame with clear unmarked globe **75-85**

PERY- on shoulder of 1909 Adams & Westlake double wire guard frame with red etched "PERY" cnx/Corning globe **150-175**

PENNSYLVANIA RAILROAD

PRR- on shoulder of Keystone Casey single wire guard frame with clear cast "PRR" cnx/Corning globe **85-95**

PRR- Keystone logo on shoulder of Keystone Casey frame with red cast "PRR" Keystone logo cnx/Corning globe **125-150**

PRR- on shoulder & bell of brass top bell bottom frame with clear cast "PRR" extended base globe **450-500**

PENNSYLVANIA LINES- on shoulder of 95 Adams & Westlake double wire guard bell bottom lantern with twist off bell. Comes with clear cast "PENNSYLVANIA LINES" globe **125-150**

PENNSYLVANIA LINES- on shoulder of 1913 Adlake Reliable single wire guard frame with clear cast "PRR" cnx/Corning globe...... **75-85**

PERE MARQUETTE

PERE MARQUETTE- on shoulder of 95 Adams & Westlake double wire guard frame with twist off pot. Comes with clear cast "PERE MARQUETTE" cnx/Corning globe **200-250**

PHILADELPHIA & READING

P&RRR- on shoulder of 97 Adams & Westlake double wire guard frame with twist off pot. Comes with clear cast "P&RRR" cnx/Corning globe **100-125**

P&RRR- on shoulder of 97 Adams & Westlake double wire guard frame with twist off pot. Comes with red cast "P&RRR" cnx/Corning globe **150-175**

P&RRR- on shoulder of RR Signal Lamp & Lantern double wire guard frame with 6" red cast "P&RRY" globe **250-300**

PITTSBURGH & LAKE ERIE

P&LERR- on shoulder of round top Handlan single wire guard frame with clear cast P&LERR cnx/Corning globe **100-125**

PITTSBURGH CINCINNATI CHICAGO & ST. LOUIS RAILWAY

PCC&STLRY- on shoulder of round top Handlan single wire guard frame with red etched "PCC&STLRY" globe **150-175**

PCC&STLRY- on shoulder of round top Handlan single wire guard frame with clear unmarked globe **90-100**

RICHMOND FREDRICKSBURG & POTOMAC

RF&P- on shoulder of 1912 double wire guard Reliable frame. Frame also may have "W-S". Comes with red unmarked cnx/ Corning globe 100-125

RIO GRANDE SOUTHERN RAILROAD

RGSRR- on shoulder of 1889 Adams & Westlake single wire guard frame with twist off pot and blue unmarked extended base globe .... ◆

RIO GRANDE WESTERN RAILWAY

RGWRY- on shoulder of 1889 MM Buck double wire guard frame with twist off pot & clear cast "RGWRY" extended base globe ... ◆

RGWRY- on shoulder and bell of brass top bell bottom MM Buck double wire guard frame with twist off bell. Comes with clear unmarked globe .... ◆

RGWRR- on shoulder of Adams & Westlake single wire guard frame with twist off pot and clear unmarked globe .... ◆

ROCK ISLAND LINES aka CHICAGO ROCK ISLAND & PACIFIC

ROCK ISLAND LINES- on 1909 Adams & Westlake double wire guard frame with clear cast "ROCK ISLAND LINES" cnx/ Corning globe 150-175

ROCK ISLAND LINES- on 1913 Reliable single wire guard frame with clear cast "ROCK ISLAND LINES" cnx/Corning globe 125-150

ROCK ISLAND LINES- on 1913 Reliable single wire guard frame with red cast "ROCK ISLAND LINES" cnx/Corning globe 175-200

ROCK ISLAND LINES- on 1913 Reliable single wire guard frame with amber cast "ROCK ISLAND LINES" cnx/Corning globe .... ◆

ROCK ISLAND LINES- on shoulder of round top Handlan double wire guard frame with clear cast "ROCK ISLAND LINES" cnx/Corning globe 125-150

ROCK ISLAND SYSTEM- on shoulder of 95 Adams & Westlake double wire guard frame with clear cast "ROCK ISLAND SYSTEM" extended base globe 300-350

ROCK ISLAND SYSTEM- on shoulder of 95 Adams & Westlake double wire guard frame with red cast "ROCK ISLAND SYSTEM" extended base globe 500-550

ROCK ISLAND SYSTEM- on shoulder of 95 Adams & Westlake double wire guard frame with green cast "ROCK ISLAND SYSTEM" extended base globe .... ◆

ROCK ISLAND SYSTEM- on shoulder of 95 Adams & Westlake double wire guard frame with clear unmarked globe 150-175

RUTLAND RAILROAD

RRR-on shoulder of Deitz #6 double wire guard bell bottom frame with clear etched "RUTLAND RR" extended base globe 300-350

RUTLAND RR- on shoulder of 1912 Adlake Reliable double wire guard bell bottom frame with clear cast "RUTLAND RR" cnx/Corning globe 500-550

RUTLAND RR- on shoulder of 1912 Adlake Reliable double wire guard bell bottom frame with red cast "RUTLAND RR" cnx/Corning globe 600-650

RUTLAND RR- on shoulder of 1912 Adlake Reliable double wire guard bell bottom frame with clear etched "RUTLAND RR" cnx/Corning globe 200-250

RUTLAND RR- on shoulder of 1912 Adlake Reliable double wire guard bell bottom frame with red etched "RUTLAND RR" cnx/Corning globe 300-350

ST JOSEPH & GRAND ISLAND RY

STJ&GIRY- on shoulder of brass top wire bottom Handlan Buck DOUBLE WIRE GUARD frame. Comes with clear cast "STJ&GIRY" globe .... ◆

STJ&GIRY-on shoulder of 1909 Adams & Westlake bell bottom double wire guard frame with clear etched "STJ&GI" cnx/Corning globe 400-450

ST LOUIS & SOUTHWESTERN RR

STL&SWRR- on shoulder of round top Handlan single wire guard frame with clear unmarked globe 175-200

STL&SWRR- on shoulder of round top Handlan single wire guard frame with clear cast "COTTON BELT ROUTE" logo globe 500-550

STL&SWRR- on shoulder of round top Handlan single wire guard frame with clear cast "THE COTTON BELT" in small letters on top edge of cnx/Corning globe 250-300

ST LOUIS KANSAS CITY & COLORADO

STLKC&CRR- on shoulder of 1889 Handlan Buck double wire guard frame with twist off pot. Comes with clear unmarked globe .... ◆

SAN PEDRO LOS ANGELES & SALT LAKE aka SALT LAKE ROUTE

SLR- on shoulder of round top Handlan single wire guard frame with red unmarked cnx/Corning globe **175-200**

SPLA&SLRR- on shoulder of 1897 Adams & Westlake double wire guard frame with twist off pot. Comes with clear unmarked globe **300-350**

SPLA&SLRR-on shoulder of 1897 Adams & Westlake double wire guard frame with twist off pot. Comes with clear cast "SPLA&SLRR" globe .... ◆

SAN ANTONIO & ARANSAS PASS

SA&AP- on shoulder of round top Handlan double wire guard frame with clear unmarked globe **150-175**

SANTA FE -(ATCHISON TOPEKA & SANTA FE)

SANTA FE- on shoulder of 1895 Adams & Westlake double wire guard frame with twist off pot. Comes with clear cast "SANTA FE" extended base logo globe **550-650**

SANTA FE- on bell of single wire guard frame with no manufacturers mark. Comes with red cast "SANTA FE" logo cnx/Corning globe **400-450**

SANTA FE- on bell of single wire guard frame with no manufacturers mark. Comes with clear cast "SANTA FE" logo cnx/Corning globe **250-300**

SANTA FE- on bell of single wire guard frame with no manufacturers mark. Comes with clear unmarked globe **100-125**

SANTA FE- on bell of single wire guard frame with no manufacturers mark. Comes with red etched "SANTA FE" logo cnx/Corning globe **200-250**

SANTA FE- on shoulder of 1909 Adams & Westlake single wire guard globe with clear cast "SANTA FE" logo globe **250-300**

SANTA FE ROUTE- on shoulder of 1889 MM Buck double wire guard frame with twist off pot. Comes with clear cast "SANTA FE ROUTE" extended base globe .... ◆

SANTA FE ROUTE-on shoulder of 1897 Adams & Westlake double wire guard frame with twist off pot. Comes with clear cast "SANTA FE ROUTE" extended base globe .... ◆

SANTA FE ROUTE- on shoulder of 1897 Adams & Westlake double wire guard frame with twist off pot. Comes with clear unmarked globe **400-450**

SANTA FE PRESCOTT & PHOENIX

SFP&P-on shoulder of 1889 Handlan Buck double wire guard frame with twist off pot. Comes with clear cast "SFP&P" extended base globe .... ◆

SFP&P- on shoulder of 1889 Handlan Buck double wire guard frame with twist off pot and unmarked extended base globe .... ◆

SOUTHERN RAILWAY

S RY- on shoulder of Railroad Signal Lamp & Lantern Co. double wire guard frame with clear cast "SRY" cnx/Corning globe **100-125**

SOUTHERN RY- on shoulder of 1913 Adlake Reliable single wire guard frame with clear cast "SOUTHERN RY" cnx/Corning globe **125-150**

SOUTHERN RY-on shoulder of 1913 Adlake Reliable single wire guard frame with clear unmarked cnx/Corning globe **85-95**

SOUTHERN PACIFIC COMPANY

SP-on shoulder of 1909 Adams & Westlake double wire guard frame with clear cast "SPCO" cnx/Corning globe **125-150**

SPCO- on shoulder of 1892 Adams & Westlake single wire guard frame with twist off pot. Comes with clear cast 6" "SPCO" globe **500-550**

SPCO- on shoulder of 1892 Adams & Westlake single wire guard frame with twist off pot. Comes with clear unmarked extended base globe **200-250**

SPCO- on shoulder of 1913 Adlake Reliable single wire guard frame with clear cast "SPCO" cnx/Corning globe **90-100**

SPOKANE PORTLAND & SEATTLE

SP&S- on shoulder of 1909 Adams & Westlake double wire guard frame with clear etched "SP&S" cnx/Corning globe **125-150**

TENNESEE CENTRAL RAILROAD

TCRR-on shoulder of 1913 Adlake Reliable single wire guard frame with clear cast "TCRR" cnx/Corning globe **300-350**

TERMINAL RAILROAD ASSOCIATION OF ST. LOUIS

TRRA OF STL- on shoulder of round top Handlan single wire guard frame with clear unmarked globe **75-85**

TRRA OF STL- on shoulder of round top Handlan single wire guard frame with red cast "TRRA of STL" globe **150-175**

TEXAS & NEW ORLEANS

T&NO- on shoulder of 1913 Adlake Reliable single wire guard frame with clear unmarked globe **100-125**

T&NO- on shoulder of 1913 Adlake Reliable single wire guard frame with red cast "T&NORR" globe **300-350**

T&NO- on shoulder of 1909 Adams & Westlake double wire guard frame with clear etched "T&NO" globe **125-150**

TEXAS & PACIFIC

T&P- on dome of 1923 Reliable single wire guard frame with clear etched "T&P" globe **100-125**

T&PRY- on shoulder of round top Handlan single wire guard frame with clear etched "T&PRY" globe................**100-125**

TOLEDO & OHIO CENTRAL

T&OCRY- on shoulder of 1913 Adlake Reliable bell bottom single wire guard frame with clear unmarked globe **100-125**

TOLEDO ST LOUIS & KANSAS CITY

TSTL&KCRR- on shoulder of 1889 MM Buck double wire guard frame with twist off pot. Comes with clear unmarked globe **400-450**

TOLEDO ST LOUIS & WESTERN

TSTL&W-on shoulder of Handlan Buck double wire guard frame with clear cast "TSTL&WRR" extended base globe...**400-450**

TSTL&W- on shoulder of 1912 Adlake Reliable double wire guard frame with clear unmarked globe...................................**150-175**

TSTL&W- on shoulder of 1912 Adlake Reliable double wire guard frame with clear cast "TSTL&WRR" cnx/Corning globe **300-350**

TONOPAH & GOLDFIELD

T&GRR- on shoulder of 95 Armspear double wire guard frame with twist off pot. Comes with clear unmarked extended base globe............ ◆

UNION PACIFIC RAILWAY

UPRW- on shoulder of brass top wire bottom Adams & Westlake single wire guard frame with clear unmarked globe .... ◆

UPRW- on shoulder of brass top wire bottom single wire guard frame with clear cast "UPRW" extended base globe .... ◆

UNION PACIFIC RAILROAD

UNION PACIFIC- on shoulder of 1892 Adams & Westlake single wire guard frame with twist off pot. Comes with clear cast "UNION PACIFIC" extended base globe..............**550-600**

UNION PACIFIC- on shoulder of 1895 Adams & Westlake double wire guard frame with clear cast "UNION over PACIFIC" globe **300-350**

UNION PACIFIC- on shoulder of 1897 Adams & Westlake double wire guard frame with clear unmarked globe................................**100-125**

UNION PACIFIC- on shoulder of 1909 Adams & Westlake double wire guard frame with clear cast "UNION PACIFIC" Overland Shield logo globe **325-375**

UNION PACIFIC- on shoulder of 1909 Adams & Westlake double wire guard frame with red cast "UNION PACIFIC" Overland Shield logo globe **500-550**

UNION PACIFIC- on shoulder of 1913 Adlake Reliable single wire guard frame with clear unmarked globe **75-85**

UNION PACIFIC- on shoulder of 1913 Adlake Reliable single wire guard frame with red etched "UNION PACIFIC" Overland Shield logo globe **200-250**

UNION PACIFIC- on shoulder of 1913 Adlake Reliable single wire guard frame with clear cast "UNION PACIFIC" Overland Shield logo globe **275-325**

UNION PACIFIC- on shoulder of 1913 Adlake Reliable single wire guard frame with red cast "UNION PACIFIC" Overland Shield logo globe **500-550**

UNION PACIFIC-on shoulder of 1913 Adlake Reliable single wire guard frame with clear cast "UNION PACIFIC" either in a panel or UNION over PACIFIC in a box. **350-400**

UNION PACIFIC- on shoulder of round top Handlan Buck double wire guard frame with clear cast "UNION PACIFIC" Overland Route shield logo globe **300-350**

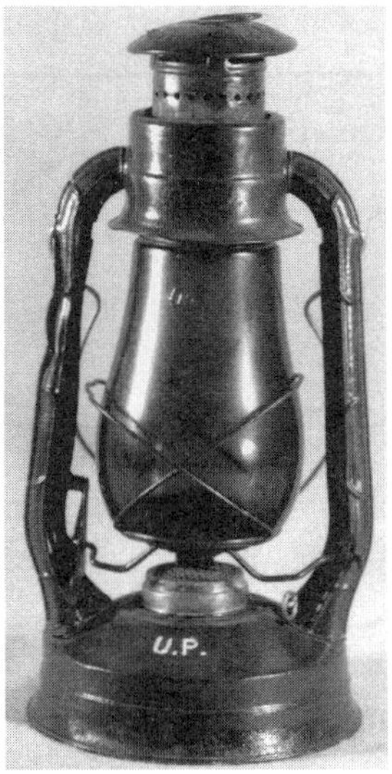

UP- on base of Dietz #2 barn style lantern with cobalt blue unmarked globe **75-85**

UP- on base of Dietz #2 barn style lantern with cobalt blue 6" etched "UP" globe **150-175**

UNION PACIFIC DENVER & GULF

UPD&GRR- on shoulder of 1892 Adams & Westlake double wire guard frame with twist off pot. Comes with clear unmarked globe ...... ◆

UPD&GRY- on shoulder of Steam Gauge & Lantern Co. double wire guard frame with clear cast "UPD&G" extended base globe .... ◆

UNITED RAILWAYS

UNITED RYS- on shoulder of flat top Handlan single wire guard frame with unmarked cnx/Corning globe **60-70**

VIRGINIA & TRUCKEE

V&TRR-on shoulder of brass top bell bottom Adams & Westlake single wire guard frame with clear unmarked extended base globe .... ◆

V&TRR- on shoulder of 1897 Adams & Westlake double wire guard frame with twist off pot. Comes with clear unmarked extended base globe .... t

WABASH RAILROAD

WABASH RR- TRANS DEPT on bell of brass top bell bottom Handlan Buck double wire guard frame with clear cast "WSTL&P" extended base globe **650-700**

WABASH RR- on shoulder of 1913 Adlake Reliable single wire guard frame with clear cast "WABASH" flying flag logo cnx/Corning globe **250-300**

WESTERN MARYLAND

WMRY- on shoulder of 1909 Adams & Westlake double wire guard frame with clear cast "WMRY" cnx/Corning globe **150-175**

WMRY-on shoulder of 1913 Adlake Reliable single wire guard frame with clear unmarked globe **80-90**

WESTERN PACIFIC RAILROAD

WPRY OR WPRR-on shoulder of 1913 Adlake Reliable single wire guard frame with clear unmarked globe **100-125**

INSPECTORS LANTERNS

ATCHISON TOPEKA & SANTA FE

AT&SFRY-raised letters on top of handle on Dietz Acme Mfg. Co. frame with clear unmarked globe **75-85**

CHICAGO MILWAUKEE & ST PAUL RY

CM&STPRY- raised letters on top of handle on Dietz Acme Mfg. Co. frame with clear unmarked globe **65-75**

DELAWARE & HUDSON

D&HCO-on oval brass plate applied to base of Dietz frame. Comes with clear unmarked globe **70-80**

ILLINOIS CENTRAL RAILROAD

ICRR-raised letters on top of handle on Dietz Acme Mfg. Co. frame with clear unmarked globe **50-60**

LEHIGH VALLEY RAILROAD

LVRR- raised letters on top of handle on Dietz Acme Mfg. Co. frame with clear unmarked globe **80-90**

NEW YORK CENTRAL SYSTEM

NYCS-raised letters on top of handle on Dietz Acme Mfg. Co. frame with clear unmarked globe **50-60**

PENNSYLVANIA RAILROAD

PRR-Keystone logo raised on top of handle on Dietz Acme Mfg. Co. frame with clear unmarked globe **65-75**

ROCK ISLAND LINES- raised letters on top of handle of Dietz Acme Mfg. Co. frame with clear unmarked globe **80-90**

SANTA FE

SANTA FE-raised letters on top of handle on Dietz Acme Mfg. Co. frame with clear unmarked globe **75-85**

SANTE FE ROUTE

SANTE FE ROUTE-on brass tag applied to base of Deitz Mfg. Frame with clear cast "SANTA FE ROUTE" globe **500-550**

SOUTHERN PACIFIC COMPANY

SPCO-raised letters on top of handle on Dietz Acme Mfg. Co. frame with clear unmarked globe **70-80**

WABASH RAILWAY

WABASH RY-raised letter on top of handle on Dietz Acme Mfg. Co. frame with clear unmarked globe **60-70**

UNMARKED INSPECTORS LANTERN

UNMARKED DIETZ LANTERN-no railroad markings **40-50**

LANTERN GLOBES

Finding lanterns complete with globes is very rewarding. Finding lanterns with marked globes embossed or etched just makes your find obviously more complete. Tall globes measure from 5" tall to 6" tall with a few varying sizes in between. Globes are found in clear, red, green, amber & cobalt blue. Collectors prefer embossed or raised letters on globes. Much like their short cousin clear & red marked globes are more common. While the amber, green or blues are more sought after. Below we have shown the three most common styles of globes for the tall frames.

Barrel or mellon style globe

Corning globe has CNX logo embossed on top edge

Extended base globe usually found in earlier frames

AT&SFRY-(Atchison Topeka & Santa Fe) clear cast 5 3/8" cnx globe 150-175

AT&SFRY- (Atchison Topeka & Santa Fe)red cast 5 3/8" cnx globe 250-300

AT&SFRY-(Atchison Topeka & Santa Fe)clear cast on one side "SANTA FE" cross logo on the opposite side of this 5 3/8" cnx globe 375-425

B&ORR—(Baltimore & Ohio) clear cast 5 3/8" barrel or mellon style globe 35-45

B&ORR- -(Baltimore & Ohio) clear cast on 5 ¼" cnx globe 35-45

B&O- -(Baltimore & Ohio) Capitol logo clear cast on 5 3/8" cnx globe 100-125

B&O- -(Baltimore & Ohio) Capitol logo red cast on 5 3/8" cnx globe 150-175

B&LERR-(Bessimer & Lake Erie) red cast 5 3/8" extended base globe 150-175

B&ARR-(Boston & Albany) clear cast 6" extended base globe 65-75

B&MRR-(Boston & Maine) clear cast 5 3/8" cnx globe 30-40

B&MRR-(Boston & Maine) red cast 5 3/8" cnx globe 60-70

BURLINGTON ROUTE-clear cast in box on 5 ½" cnx globe 50-60

BURLINGTON ROUTE- red cast in box on 5 ½" cnx globe 100-125

BURLINGTON ROUTE- clear cast in box on 5 ½" extended base globe 150-175

B&M NEB.-(Burlington & Missouri River of Nebraska) clear cast on 5 ¼" extended base globe ◆

B&MRRR of NEB- .-(Burlington & Missouri River of Nebraska)red cast on 5 ¼" extended base globe .... ◆

CRR OF NJ- (Central Railroad of New Jersey) clear etched on 5 3/8" cnx globe 30-40

C&EIRR-(Chicago & Eastern Illinois) clear cast 5 1/4" extended base globe. Etched "Safety First" on reverse 90-100

C&NWRY—(Chicago & Northwestern)clear cast on 5 3/8" cnx globe 65-75

CM&STPRY-(Chicago Milwaukee & St. Paul) clear cast on 5 ½" cnx globe 40-50

CM&STPRY—(Chicago Milwaukee & St. Paul)red cast on 5 ½" cnx globe 75-85

CM&STPRY--(Chicago Milwaukee & St. Paul)clear cast on 5 ¼" extended base globe 100-125

CHICAGO PEORIA & ST. LOUIS- diamond logo etched on clear 5 ¼” barrel or mellon style globe **250-300**

CHICAGO PEORIA & ST. LOUIS- diamond logo etched on red 5 ¼” barrel or mellon globe **350-400**

COTTON BELT- clear cast in small letters on top edge of 5 3/8” cnx globe **60-70**

D&H CO- (Delaware & Hudson) clear cast in fancy script letters on 5 ½” cnx globe **100-125**

D&RG- (Denver & Rio Grande) clear cast 5 3/8” mellon also cast “Safety First” on reverse **125-150**

D&RGRR-(Denver & Rio Grande) clear etched 5 3/8” mellon or barrel type globe **65-75**

COTTON BELT ROUTE- logo clear cast on 5 3/8” cnx globe **350-400**

D&H CO.- (Delaware & Hudson) red cast in fancy script letters on 5 ½” cnx globe **175-200**

D&RGRR-(Denver & Rio Grande) clear cast 5 1/4” extended base globe **750-850**

D&RGRR- (Denver & Rio Grande) red cast 5 ¼” extended base globe .... ◆

ERR CO- (Erie) clear cast 5 3/8" cnx globe .. **50-60**

ERR CO- (Erie) red cast 5 3/8" cnx globe **75-85**

EP&SW-(El Paso & Southwestern) clear cast on 5 1/4" cnx globe **250-300**

FTW&DCRY- (Ft Worth & Denver City) clear etched on 5 ½" cnx globe **75-85**

FRISCO- clear cast 5 ¼" cnx globe also etched "Safety First" on reverse **100-125**

GTR- (Grand Trunk) clear cast 5 ½" extended base globe **70-80**

GNRY- (Great Northern) amber etched 5 ¼" cnx globe also etched "Safety First on reverse .. **300-350**

GB&WRR- (Green Bay & Western) clear etched 5 3/8" cnx globe **150-175**

HVRY- (Hocking Valley) red cast 5 ¼" cnx globe **125-150**

ICRR- (Illinois Central) clear cast 5 ½" extended base globe **75-85**

ICRR- (Illinois Central) clear cast 5 3/8" cnx globe **35-45**

ICRR- (Illinois Central)red cast 5 3/8" cnx globe **80-90**

LS&MSRY- (Lake Shore & Michigan Southern) clear cast 5 3/8" cnx globe **65-75**

LS&MSRY-(Lake Shore & Michigan Southern) clear cast 5 1/4" extended base **125-150**

LS&MSRY-(Lake Shore & Michigan Southern) red cast 5 1/4" extended base **200-250**

LS&MSRY-(Lake Shore & Michigan Southern) green cast extended base globe........... **750-800**

L&NRR- (Louisville & Nashville) clear cast 5 3/8" mellon or barrel type globe......... **75-85**

MCRR- (Maine Central) or (Michigan Central) clear cast 5 ½" cnx globe **75-85**

MCRR- (Maine Central) or (Michigan Central) red cast 5 ½" extended base.............. **150-200**

MP- (Missouri Pacific) clear cast with SAFETY FIRST on 5 3/8" cnx globe **40-50**

MP- (Missouri Pacific) red cast with SAFETY FIRST on 5 3/8" cnx globe **60-70**

MP-(Missouri Pacific) clear cast extended base globe.. **100-125**

MP-MIssouri Pacific) red cast 5 1/4" extended base globe **175-225**

NC&STLRY- (Nashville Chattenooga & St. Louis) clear fancy etched design between railroad tracks. 5 3/8" mellon or barrel type globe **300-325**

NYCRR- (New York Central) clear cast 5 3/8" cnx globe **30-40**

NYLE&WRR- (New York Lake Erie & Western) clear cast 6" barrel style globe **90-100**

NPRY-(Northern Pacific) 5" clear cast extended base globe **750-850**

NPRR-(Northern Pacific)5 1/4"clear cast extended base globe **250-300**

NPRR-(Northern Pacific) 5 3/8" clear cast cnx globe **80-90**

OSL- (Oregon Short Line) clear cast 5 ¼" extended base globe **650-750**

OSL- (Oregon Short Line) clear cast 5 3/8" cnx globe **100-125**

PERY- (Pacific Electric)"Safety First" clear etched on 5 3/8" cnx globe **45-55**

PERY- (Pacific Electric) "Safety First" red etched on 5 3/8" cnx globe **90-100**

PRR- (Pennsylvania) clear cast 5 3/8" extended base globe **45-55**

PRR- (Pennsylvania) red cast 5 3/8" extended base globe **75-85**

PRR-(Pennsylvania) clear cast 5 ½" cnx globe **35-45**

PRR- (Pennsylvania) red cast 5 ½" cnx globe **55-65**

PENNSYLVANIA LINES- clear cast 5 3/8" mellon globe **35-45**

PENNSYLVANIA LINES- clear etched 5 3/8" mellon globe **20-30**

PC&STL-(Pittsburgh Cincinnati & St. Louis) 5 1/4" wheel cut globe for fixed globe Kelly brass lantern **200-250**

PCC&STLRY- (Pittsburgh Cincinnati Chicago & St. Louis) clear cast 5 ½" cnx globe **45-55**

RI LINES- (Rock Island Lines) box logo clear cast 5 3/8" cnx globe **80-90**

RI LINES- (Rock Island Lines) box logo red cast 5 3/8" cnx globe **100-125**

RI SYSTEM- (Rock Island System) box logo clear cast 5 ¼" extended base globe ... **225-275**

SANTA FE- clear cast logo on 5 3/8" cnx globe **125-150**

SANTA FE- red cast logo on 5 3/8" cnx globe **300-350**

SP CO-(Southern Pacific) clear cast 5 3/8" cnx globe **65-75**

SP CO- (Southern Pacific) red cast 5 3/8" cnx globe **90-100**

SP&S- (Spokane Portland Seattle) clear etched on 5 ¼" cnx globe **50-60**

T&PRY- (Texas & Pacific) clear etched on 5 3/8" mellon type globe **40-50**

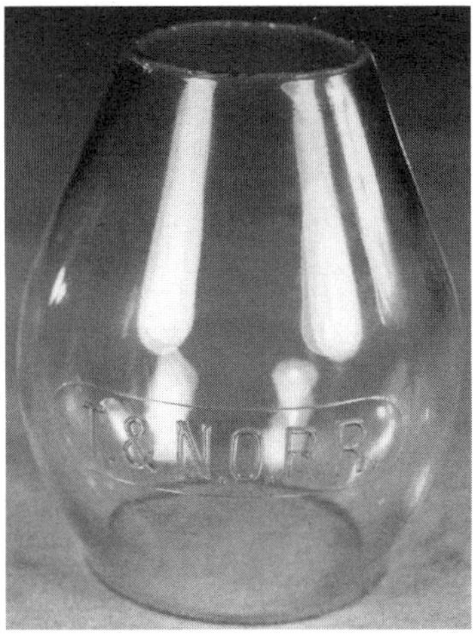

T&NORR- (Texas & New Orleans) clear cast 5 3/8" cnx globe **125-150**

T&OCRY- (Toledo & Ohio Central) clear cast 5 ½" extended base globe **150-175**

UNION PACIFIC- Overland Shield clear cast on 5 3/8" cnx globe **200-250**

UNION over PACIFIC-in box clear cast on 5 3/8" cnx globe **250-300**

UNION PACIFIC- in panel clear cast on 5 3/8" cnx globe **250-300**

WABASH- clear etched 5 ¼" cnx globe **40-50**

WABASH- Flying Flag logo clear cast on 5 3/8" cnx globe **125-150**

UNMARKED- clear 5 ¼", 5 3/8" or 5 ½" cnx or extended base globe **20-30**

UNMARKED- red 5 ¼", 5 3/8" or 5 ½" cnx or extended base globe **35-45**

UNMARKED- amber 5 ¼" ,5 3/8" or 5 ½" cnx or extended base globe **60-70**

REMEMBER PRICES LISTED ARE FOR LANTERNS & GLOBES IN GOOD TO EXCELLENT CONDITION. SUGGESTED PRICES ARE MEANT AS A GUIDE ONLY. PRICES MAY VARY FROM REGION TO REGION.

CHAPTER 21

LANTERNS PRESENTATION

Conductors or presentation lanterns are a wonderful railroad collectible. A gift to celebrate retirement or to otherwise reward a special deed these beautiful lanterns were often engraved with the recipients name on either the globe or the frame. These lanterns are most often found nickle plated over brass as well as just brass or even silver plated. The globes are found clear as well as two color globes in either green over clear, red over clear and blue over clear. The two color globe styles are the more desirable especially when found fancily engraved with floral designs around the recipients name. Manufacturers marks can be found usually on the bottom side of the lantern. As with all collectibles lanterns must be in pristene condition to command the prices suggested here. Lanterns must not have fatigue cracks or plating loss. Be bent or have missing parts and globes must not be chipped or cracked.

REMEMBER: PRICES SHOWN ARE SUGGESTED VALUES ONLY. VALUES VARY FROM REGION TO REGION. THIS IS MEANT ONLY AS A GUIDE. **(◆) Denotes value over $1000.00**

ADAMS & WESTLAKE- nickel plated brass bell bottom frame with 1864 Patent date. Comes with clear unmarked globe **400-500**

ADAMS & WESTLAKE- nickel plated brass bell bottom frame with "PULLMAN" in raised letters on bell. Globe is etched "P CO" or "PPC CO" **400-500**

ADAMS & WESTLAKE- nickel plated brass bell bottom frame with 1864 patent date. Comes with green over clear globe etched with recipients name in fancy wreath design .... ◆

CT HAMM- #3 brass wire bottom frame with green over clear wheel cut globe with the recipients name, beautiful & ornate .... ◆

CT HAMM- #39 brass lantern frame with clear unmarked globe **500-600**

CM&STPRY-embossed on bell of nickel plated Adams & Westlake frame. Patented 1864 this lantern comes with a clear etched "CM&STPRR" globe .... ◆

DAYTON MFG.- nickel plated brass bell bottom frame with clear unmarked globe **400-450**

HANDLAN BUCK- #3 brass bell bottom frame with green over clear unmarked globe .. **750-850**

KELLY LAMP CO.- nickel plated brass wire bottom frame with clear unmarked globe **400-500**

MM BUCK- silver plated brass bell bottom frame with blue over clear wheel cut globe .. ◆

MEYROSE MFG.- nickel plated brass bell bottom frame with clear unmarked globe **500-600**

POST & CO.- nickel plated brass bell bottom frame with clear unmarked globe **500-600**

PARMELEE & BONNELL-brass presentation lantern with clear wheel cut globe showing recipients name in wreath .... ◆

WM WESTLAKE- 1865 patent on nickel plated brass bell bottom frame with clear globe etched with name in fancy wreath design .... ◆

STEAM GAUGE & LANTERN CO.- nickel plated brass bell bottom frame with green over clear etched globe .... ◆

WM WESTLAKE-on1866 patent on silver plated wire bottom frame with clear wheel cut globe.. ◆

PRESENTATION GLOBES

The values listed below are for unmarked globes in varying sizes. Globes must not be chipped or cracked

CLEAR - 150-175

GREEN OVER CLEAR.................... 350-400

RED OVER CLEAR 450-550

COBALT BLUE OVER CLEAR...... 650-750

MARKED PRESENTATION GLOBES

The values listed below are for wheel cut or engraved globes in varying sizes. Globes must not be chipped or cracked.

CLEAR 250-350

GREEN OVER CLEAR.................... 500-600

RED OVER CLEAR 650-750

COBALT BLUE OVER CLEAR................ ◆

REMEMBER SUGGESTED PRICES ARE MEANT AS A GUIDE ONLY.
VALUE VARY FROM REGION TO REGION.

CHAPTER 22

LIGHTS SWITCH, CLASS, MARKER & MISCELLANEOUS

The switch lights were used by the railroads in the yards to direct the trains along the tracks. These lights are by far the most recognizable railroad collectible. Folks tend to see a switch light in a store and it immediately brings back memories of riding the train. These lights are one of the few items that continue to hold value even when they are not specifically railroad marked. This is due to the fact that they were used exclusively by the railroads. On the other hand when they are marked is when the values can soar, again depending upon which initials or marks the light might have. You can still buy brand new today from the original manufacturers kerosene operated switch lights. The irony to this is that they are often times more expensive to buy brand new than to purchase an original old light that was actually used. The caboose marker lights are the most collectible in this category. They adorned the back of the caboose. The railroad classification lights were used on the front of the engines to specifiy the purpose of the train. Lenses in these are usually clear with interior colored lenses, usually green but also found red that were flipped to change the status of the train. These also are very collectible. Many of these were originally kerosene but are often times found modified to electric which was done by the railroads in later years. Also in this category are semphore lights which were used on signal arms. These are found most often with clear lenses. Remember condition is important. Lights must be in good to excellent condition to command the prices suggested here.

BELOW ARE THE MOST COMMONLY FOUND STYLES AS WELL AS A LIST OF THE MOST COMMONLY FOUND MANUFACTURERS. NOTE: IT WAS NOT UNCOMMON FOR THE MAJOR ROADS TO MANUFACTURE THEIR OWN LIGHTING. WHICH EXPLAINS LIGHTS FOUND WITHOUT A MANUFACTURERS MARK

HANDLAN CABOOSE OR REAR END MARKER

ADLAKE SEMAPHORE

ELECTRIC CLASSIFICATION LIGHT

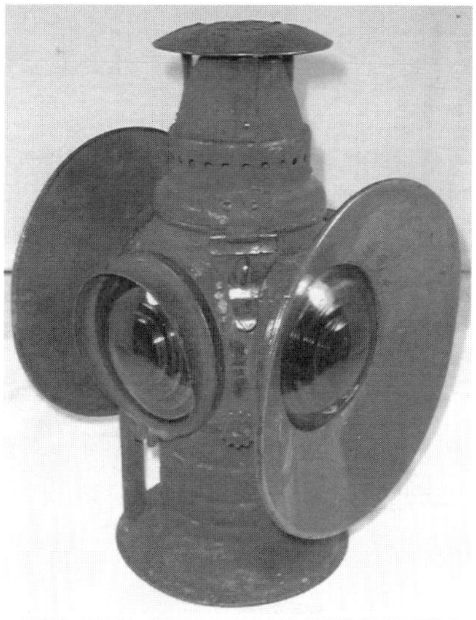

ADLAKE SWITCH LIGHT WITH DAY TARGETS

ADLAKE SWITCH LIGHT WITH BELL BOTTOM

ADLAKE SWITCH LIGHT WITH FORK BASE

<u>MOST OFTEN SEEN MANUFACTURERS</u>

ADAMS & WESTLAKE

ADLAKE

ARMSPEAR

DRESSEL

HANDLAN

HIRAM PIPER

PETER GRAY

PYLE NATIONAL

AC&YRR- (Akron Canton & Youngstown) steam engine classification light. Mfg. Adams & Westlake. Inside has green lens that changes with flipper. **200-250**

ADLAKE- cannonball style switch light with reflective lenses. Some found with stone guard to protect the lenses. **40-50**

ADLAKE- electric cannonball style switch light, model no. 1162. Cast aluminum body with cast iron switch stand base. Found with different color lense combinations such as two green & two red or two blue & two amber **75-85**

ADLAKE- or PYLE NATIONAL small electric caboose marker light. Three amber & one red lens or three green & one red **50-60**

ADLAKE-or PYLE NATIONAL small electric caboose marker light set. Comes with three amber & one red or three green & one red lense **150-175**

BN INC- (Burlington Northern) switch light. Square top Adlake light with porcelain day targets. Two red and two green lenses. Complete with fuel font **175-200**

BR- (Burlington Route) on applied plate on top edge of square top Adlake switch light. Two green & two red lenses complete with fuel container **250-300**

CNR-(Canadian National) cast on side of switch light. Mfg. Hiram Piper. Two green & two amber lenses complete with fuel container **100-125**

CPR- (Canadian Pacific) cast on side of switch light. Mfg. Hiram Piper. Two green & two amber lenses, complete with fuel container 125-150

CPR-(Canadian Pacific) caboose light. Mfg. Hiram Piper. Three green & one red lens. Complete with mounting bracket & fuel container 175-200

C OF V-(Central of Vermont) on applied plate on side of square top Adlake switch light. Two red & two green lenses complete with fuel container 250-300

C&ORY-(Chesapeake & Ohio) on applied plate on side round top Handlan switch light. Has two red & two green porcelain day targets. Complete with fuel container. 250-300

C&NWRR-(Chicago & Northwestern) marked on side of round top Handlan caboose marker light with three green and one red lens. Complete with fuel container... 225-275

CB&QRR- (Chicago Burlington & Quincy) marked on applied plate on side of square top Adlake switch light with two green and two red lenses. Complete with fuel container. 250-300

CB&QRR- (Chicago Burlington & Quincy) LEFT on applied plate on side of round top Handlan caboose marker light. Bell bottom style with three green lenses & one red lens. Complete with fuel container 300-350

CM&PSRR- (Chicago Milwaukee & Puget Sound) marked on side of semaphore light. Mfg. Adlake with two clear lenses 90-100

CM&STPRY-(Chicago Milwaukee & St. Paul) marked on side of switch light with fluted top. No manufacturer shown. Comes with two green & two red lenses, complete with fuel container ... 200-250

CM&STPRY- (Chicago Milwaukee & St. Paul) steam engine classification light. Complete with green flippers in side 200-250

CMSTP&P- (Chicago Milwaukee St Paul & Pacific) on shoulder of square top Adlake switch light. Comes with two red & two amber lenses complete with fuel container 200-250

CRI&PRY-(Chicago Rock Island & Pacific) on applied plate of side of Adlake square top switch light. Two red & two green lenses. Complete with fuel container 300-350

D&H-(Delaware & Hudson) Embossed on bottom edge of class light with fluted dome. Two clear lenses. Mounting bracket marked "LEFT SIDE". Green filters on the inside 450-500

D&RGW-(Denver & Rio Grande Western) applied plate across top of square top Adlake or Handlan switch light. Two amber and two green lenses complete with fuel container 275-325

D&RGWRY- (Denver & Rio Grande Western) on applied plate on side of steam engine classification lights. Mfg. Handlan. These are referred to as the nautical style lights with one clear & one green radial lens. Usually found electried which was done by the railroad. **500-550**

FRISCO- (St. Louis & San Francisco) on applied plate on door of Handlan round top switch light. Two amber and two green lenses. Complete with fuel container **175-200**

GTW- (Grand Trunk Western) on applied plate on side of square top Adlake switch light. Two green & two amber lenses complete with fuel container **200-250**

GN #4-or #5 (Great Northern) on applied plate on side of square top Adlake switch light. Two red & two green lenses complete with fuel container **225-275**

MK&TRR- (Missouri Kansas & Texas) on applied plate on side of Handlan switch light. Two green & two red lenses. Complete with fuel container **200-250**

MK&T- (Missouri Kansas & Texas) on applied plate on side of Adlake square top switch light with bell bottom and mounting tubes on the side. Two red & two green lenses. Complete with fuel container and pyrex chimney **225-275**

MKT- (Missouri Kansas & Texas) on applied plate of side of Dressel round top caboose marker complete with bracket. One red and 3 green lenses. . **275-325**

MOPAC-(Missouri Pacific) on applied plate on side of Handlan switch light. Two green & two amber lenses. Complete with fuel container **225-275**

NCBRR-(Nevada Copper Belt) embossed on side of Adlake switch light with fluted top. Comes with two red and two green lenses. Complete **500-550**

OSL- - (Oregon Short Line) on shoulder of semaphore light with single green lens. Mfg. Handlan. Complete with fuel container **100-125**

OSL- LEFT- (Oregon Short Line) cast on shoulder of round top Adlake caboose marker with bracket. One large red & three green lenses. Complete with fuel container **250-300**

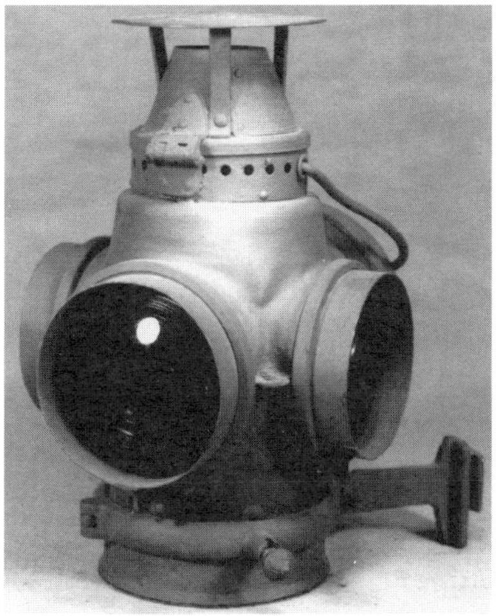

SANTA FE- on applied plate on side of flat top Adlake style caboose marker light with dual mounting brackets. Three amber & one red lens. Pinch fuel container removes from the bottom. **175-225**

SANTA FE- on applied plate of side of flat top Adlake style switch light. Comes with three blue and one amber lens. Complete with pinch fuel container which removes from the bottom. Has two mounting tubes on side. **150-175**

SL&SFRR- (St Louis & San Francisco) embossed on side of Adlake semaphore light with single red lens. Complete with fuel container **90-100**

STL&SW-(St. Louis & Southwestern) on applied plate of side of caboose marker light. Mfg. Handlan. With three green and one red lens. Complete with mounting bracket and fuel container **250-300**

SP- (Southern Pacific) RIGHT cast on shoulder of round top Adlake caboose marker Three green and on red lens. Complete with fuel font **250-300**

T&NORR-(Texas & New Orleans) marked on side of Adlake caboose marker with three green and one red lens. Complete with fuel container and mounting bracket **250-300**

SWITCH LIGHT- unmarked manufactured by Adlake, Handlan or Dressel. Complete with all lenses in tact and fuel container. **175-225**

UPRR-(Union Pacific) marked on side of square top Adlake or Handlan switch light. Comes with two red and two green lenses. Complete with fuel container **225-275**

UPRR- (Union Pacific) marked on side of Adlake caboose marker light. Three green and one large red lens. Complete with fuel container and mounting bracket **275-325**

CHAPTER 23

LOCKS
BRASS HEART SHAPED

The locks were plentiful that were used by the railroads. Security was a must of course so everything had to be protected. Obviously, one of the more important sites for that was the switch stands in the yards and along the route. Switch stands were placed next to a section of track so that the track could be moved to change the direction of the train. A switch might be placed to send a train into a siding area so another engine could pass, or to send a train onto a whole new section of track thus changing its direction. Because of this it is certainly understandable that they would need to stay locked at all times. On the other hand they also needed to be accessible by many different personel. So each railroad had their own key cut which enabled many different employees to access the locks. The railroads stamped their initials on the shackle or body of the lock. They also had locks that were embossed with the initials or logos. These are the most sought after. They can be quite beautiful and ornate. Found in their original aged state a lock with its own natural patina is much more desirable than one that has been highly cleaned or polished. This can actually devalue a lock. Remember locks must not be damaged, with broken shackles or key covers. Letters must not be overly worn and shackles cannot be frozen. Dents & dings can also hurt the value.

REMEMBER: PRICES SHOWN ARE SUGGESTED VALUES ONLY. VALUES VARY FROM REGION TO REGION. THIS IS MEANT ONLY AS A GUIDE. (**◆**) **Denotes value over $1000.00**

A&WPRR- (Atlantic & West Point) stamped on shackle of brass heart shaped lock. "C" on reverse. **25-35**

AT&SF- (Atchison Topeka & Santa Fe) stamped on shackle of heart shaped switch lock. Mfg. A&W in hex **40-50**

AT&SFRR-(Atchison Topeka & Santa Fe) stamped on shackle of heart shaped switch lock. "Mfg. Bohannan. "S" on reverse **85-95**

AT&SFRR- (Atchison Topeka & Santa Fe) stamped on shackle of heart shaped switch lock. Mfg. Bohannan. "TH" on reverse ... **125-150**

AT&SFRR- (Atchison Topeka & Santa Fe) stamped on shackle of heart shaped switch lock. Mfg. Bohannan. "SY" on reverse **150-175**

AT&SFRR- (Atchison Topeka & Santa Fe) stamped on shackle of small heart shaped lock. "#1, #2, #3, #4 or #5" stamped on reverse. Mfg. SB Co. **100-125**

AT&SF over RR- (Atchison Topeka & Santa Fe) cast down panel on brass heart shaped switch lock. Mfg. Post & Co. .... ◆

B&OSWRY- (Baltimore & Ohio Southwestern) fancy cast on front of brass heart shaped lock. Mfg. Union Lock & Hdw **450-500**

B&O L STA- (Baltimore & Ohio Local Station) incised on plate applied to left side of key cover. Brass heart shaped lock, manufactured by Dayton, Mfg. **50-60**

B&O over RR- (Baltimore & Ohio) incised on plate applied to left side of key cover. Brass heart shaped lock manufacturered by FS Hdw **35-45**

B&ARR- "S" (Boston & Albany) stamped on body of brass heart shaped switch lock. Mfg. Ritchie & Sons **40-50**

B&MRR- (Boston & Maine) incised down panel of brass heart shaped switch lock. Mfg. Bohannan. "S" on reverse **40-50**

B&MRR- (Boston & Maine) incised down panel of brass heart shaped switch lock. Mfg. Bohannan. "C" on reverse **45-55**

B&MRR- (Boston & Maine) cast down panel of brass heart shaped lock. Pebbled finish. **200-250**

B&MRR- (Boston & Maine) stamped on shackle of brass heart shaped switch lock. Mfg. OM.Edwards. **35-45**

B&MRR- (Boston & Maine) stamped on shackle of iron heart shaped switch lock with brass shackle. Mfg. Sherburne **30-40**

B&MRRR-(Burlington & Missouri River) stamped on shackle of brass heart shaped switch lock. Mfg. Bohannan **250-300**

BA&PRY- (Butte Anaconda & Pacific) incised down panel of brass heart shaped lock. **90-100**

CPRR OF CAL- (Central Pacific RR of California) stamped on body of large brass heart shaped switch lock. **150-175**

C&ORY- (Chesapeake & Ohio) cast down panel on brass heart shaped switch lock. Key cover cast "To Get Key Out Close Lock" **200-250**

C&ARR-(Chicago & Alton) stamped on shackle of brass heart shaped switch lock. "S"on reverse. Mfg. Union Brass................. **100-125**

C&NWRR- (Chicago & Northwestern) stamped on shackle of brass heart shaped switch lock. "S" on reverse. Mfg. Slaymaker.... **40-50**

C&NWRR- (Chicago & Northwestern) stamped down panel of brass heart shaped switchlock. Mfg. Slaymaker. "S" on reverse. **125-150**

CB&KCRY- (Chicago Burlington & Kansas City) stamped on shackle of brass heart shaped switch lock. Mfg. Union Brass. **450-500**

CM&STPRR- (Chicago Milwaukee & St Paul) cast down panel of brass heart shaped lock. Reverse key cover cast "Baggage Car Cellar" **350-400**

CM&STPRR- (Chicago Milwaukee & St Paul) cast down panel of brass heart shaped lock. Reverse panel stamped "DCC". **250-300**

CM&STPRR- (Chicago Milwaukee & St Paul) cast down panel of brass heart shaped lock. Reverse key cover cast "Repair Track" **250-300**

CM&STPRR- (Chicago Milwaukee & St Paul) cast down panel of brass heart shaped lock. Reverse key cover cast "Freight Car" **250-300**

CM&STPRR-(Chicago Milwaukee & St Paul) cast down panel of brass half heart shaped lock. Mfg. Loeffelholz **65-75**

CM&STPRY- (Chicago Milwaukee & St Paul) "US Mail Car" cast on body of smaller heart shaped brass lock. **700-800**

CMSTP&PRR or RY (Chicago Milwaukee St Paul & Pacific) Stamped on shackle of brass heart shaped switch lock. Mfg. Hansel **20-30**

CMSTP&PRR- (Chicago Milwaukee St Paul & Pacific) cast down panel of brass heart shaped lock. Mfg. SB Co. "S" on reverse...... **100-125**

CMSTP&PRR- (Chicago Milwaukee St Paul & Pacific) cast down panel of brass half heart shaped switch lock. Mfg. Loeffelholz..... **60-70**

CRI&PRR- (Chicago Rock Island & Pacific) stamped on shackle of brass heart shaped switch lock. "S" on reverse. Mfg. Hansl. Mfg. **25-35**

CRI&PRR- (Chicago Rock Island & Pacific) stamped on shackle of brass heart shaped switch lock. "RT" stamped on reverse. Mfg. Hansl. Mfg. **35-45**

CCC&STLRY-(Cleveland Cincinnati Chicago & St. Louis) cast down panel of brass heart shaped switch lock. "SWI"on one side of panel "TCH" on the other. Tall shackle. Mfg. A&W in hex.. **100-125**

CCC&STLRY- -(Cleveland Cincinnati Chicago & St. Louis) stamped on shackle of brass heart shaped switch lock. "C" on reverse. Mfg. A&W in hex.. **40-50**

C&SRY- (Colorado & Southern) fancy cast on body of brass heart shaped switch lock. Mfg. Fraim or Union Lock & Hdw. .... ◆

C&SRY- (Colorado & Southern) stamped on shackle of brass heart shaped switch lock. Mfg. Union Brass or Prier Brass **175-200**

C&SERR-(Colorado & Southeastern) stamped on shackle of brass heart shaped switch lock. Mfg. Adlake **200-250**

C&WRY CO- (Colorado & Wyoming) stamped on shackle of brass heart shaped switch lock. Reverse "S". Mfg. Handlan Buck.. **90-100**

CDRR-(Concord RR) stamped on panel of brass heart shaped lock. Pat: August 1853 Mfg. SC Thomson. **65-75**

CRRR-(Connecticut River RR) stamped down panel of brass heart shaped lock. Mfg. T.Slaight. Pat'd, Dec. 12, 1865 ..... **125-150**

CC&CSRY- (Cripple Creek & Colorado Springs) stamped on shackle of brass heart shaped switch lock. Mfg. Fraim. Dated 1916 .... **250-300**

CMRY- (Colorado Midland) cast down panel of brass heart shaped switch lock. MFg. Dayton or Post. .... ◆

CMRY- (Colorado Midland) stamped on shackle of brass heart shaped switch lock. Mfg. Bohannan **350-400**

DL&W- (Delaware Lackawanna & Western) stamped down panel on large brass heart shaped switch lock. Has hole through body of the lock by the shackle to hold lead seal Mfg. Romer & Co. **90-100**

DL&WRR-(Delaware Lackawanna & Western) cast down panel of brass heart shaped switch lock with steel shackle. Mfg. Fraim. **40-50**

DL&W- (Delaware Lackawanna & Western) stamped on iron shackle of brass heart shaped lock. Mfg. Fraim. Lock has double key hole **35-45**

D&RG- (Denver & Rio Grande) cast down panel of brass heart shaped switch lock. No manufacturer. **400-450**

D&RGRR- (Denver & Rio Grande)cast down panel of brass heart shaped switch lock. Mfg. Dayton .... ◆

D&RGRR- (Denver & Rio Grande) fancy cast on body of brass heart shaped switch lock. Mfg. Slaymaker .... ◆

D&RGRR-(Denver & Rio Grande) stamped on shackle of brass heart shaped switch lock. Mfg. A&W hex **100-125**

D&RGRR- (Denver & Rio Grande) "WS" stamped on shackle of brass heart shaped switch lock. Mfg. Fraim **150-175**

D&RGRY- (Denver & Rio Grande) stamped down panel of brass heart shaped switch lock. Mfg. Post & Co. **500-550**

D&RGW- (Denver & Rio Grande Western) "WS" stamped on shackle of brass heart shaped switch lock. Mfg. Fraim..................... **100-125**

DSP&PRR- (Denver South Park & Pacific) stamped on shackle of brass heart shaped switch lock with "S" on reverse. Mfg. MM Buck .. ◆

DSP&PRR- (Denver South Park & Pacific) stamped on shackle of brass heart shaped switch lock with "C" on reverse. Mfg. MM Buck............................ ◆

ERIE RR- cast down panel of brass heart shaped switch lock. Mfg. Fraim. **100-125**

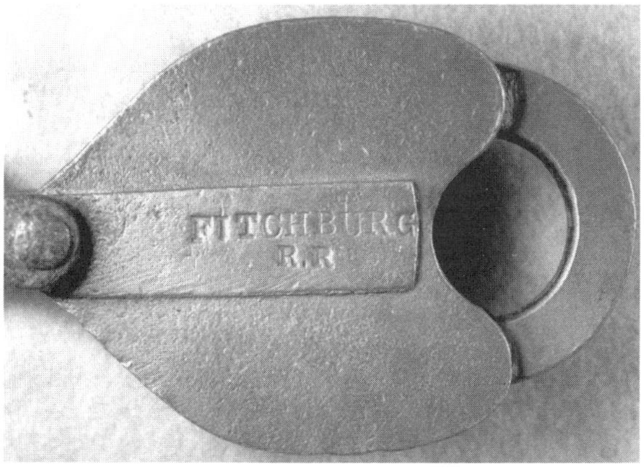

FITCHBURG – stamped down panel of brass heart shaped switch lock. Mfg. Romer & Co. **100-125**

FTS&WRR- (Ft Smith & Western) stamped on shackle of brass heart shaped switch lock. Mfg. OM Edwards **90-100**

FWSYCO- (Ft Worth Stock Yard Co.) stamped on key cover on brass heart shaped switch lock. Mfg. Bohannan **20-30**

F&CCRRCO- (Florence & Cripple Creek) stamped on shackle of brass heart shaped switch lock. Mfg. Fraim **500-550**

FL&CCRRCO- (Florence & Cripple Creek) cast down panel of brass heart shaped switch lock with pebbled finish. .... ◆

FRISCO-S- (St. Louis & San Francisco) stamped on shackle of brass heart shaped switch lock. "S" on reverse. Mfg. Prier Brass **50-60**

FRISCO-S- (St. Louis & San Francisco) stamped on shackle of brass heart shaped switch lock. "CAR" on reverse. Mfg. Prier Brass **65-75**

GR&IRY- (Grand Rapids & Indiana) stamped on shackle of brass heart shaped switch lock. Mfg. Fraim. Lock dated 1910 .... **75-85**

GNRY- (Great Northern) fancy cast on body of brass heart shaped switch lock. Mfg. Slaymaker **500-550**

GBWRR- (Green Bay & Western) stamped on shackle of brass heart shaped switch lock. "S" on reverse. Mfg. Bohannan **90-100**

GM&O- ND- (Gulf Mobile & Ohio) stamped on shackle of brass heart shaped switch lock. Mfg. FS Hdw **15-20**

H&TCRR- (Houston & Texas Central) stamped on shackle of brass heart shaped switch Mfg. Fraim **50-60**

ICGRR- (Illinois Central Gulf) stamped on shackle of brass heart shaped switch lock. Mfg. Hansl. Mfg. **20-25**

IHB- (Indiana Harbor Belt) stamped on shackle of brass heart shaped switch lock. **45-55**

II&I- (Indiana, Illinois & Iowa)-stamped on shackle of brass heart shaped switch lock. Reverse "S". Mfg. Union Brass **125-150**

JSERR- (Jacksonville Southeastern) stamped on shackle of brass heart shaped switch lock. "S" on reverse **150-175**

KCFS&GRR- (Kansas City Ft Scott & Gulf) cast down panel of brass heart shaped switch lock.. **400-450**

KCFS&MRR- (Kansas City Fort Scott & Memphis) cast down panel of brass heart shaped switch lock....................................... **400-450**

KCSRR-(Kansas City Southern) cast down panel of brass heart shaped switch lock with iron shackle... **350-400**

LIRR-(Long Island) stamped on shackle of iron heart shaped lock. Mfg. Climax **50-60**

L&NRR- (Louisville & Nashville) cast down panel on brass heart shaped switch lock. "To Get Key Out Close the Lock" cast on key cover.............................. **60-70**

MTRYCO-(Midland Terminal) cast down panel of brass heart shaped switch style lock with extended slotted panel & key cover for locking car seal....................... ◆

M&STPRY- (Milwaukee & St. Paul) stamped down panel on brass heart shaped switch lock. "C" on reverse. Mfg. Loeffelholz or Prier Brass. **175-200**

MK&T over RY- (Missouri Kansas & Texas) cast down panel of brass heart shaped switch lock. Mfg. Dayton **150-175**

MISSOURI PACIFIC LINES MAINTENANCE WAY-cast on face of brass heart shaped lock with iron shackle........................ **125-150**

MOPRR- or MOPAC RR (Missouri Pacific) stamped on shackle of iron heart shaped lock. Reverse shackle stamped "Switch". Mfg. Bohannan **45-50**

MO-PAC-(Missouri Pacific) stamped on shackle of iron heart shaped switch lock. "M-W" stamped on reverse of shackle. Mfg. Fraim **60-70**

MRR CO- (Mononghela) cast down panel of brass heart shaped lock. Pebbled finish. Mfg. Miller **100-125**

MCRR- (Michigan Central) stamped on shackle of brass heart shaped switch lock. Mfg. Miller **55-65**

NC&STLRY-(Nashville Chattanooga & St. Louis) cast down panel of brass heart shaped switch lock. Mfg. Fraim **200-250**

NC&STLRY--(Nashville Chattanooga & St. Louis) stamped on shackle of brass heart shaped switch lock. **40-50**

NY&NERR S- (New York&New England) stamped down panel of brass heart shaped switch lock. Mfg.Slaight. Lock pat'd Dec. 12 1866 .... **60-70**

NYC&HRRR- (New York Central & Hudson River) stamped on shackle of brass heart shaped switch lock. "S" on reverse. Mfg. Bohannan **50-60**

NYNH&HRR- (New York, New Haven & Hartford) cast on face of iron heart shaped switch lock. Brass key cover has star & is cast "CAR LOCK". **100-125**

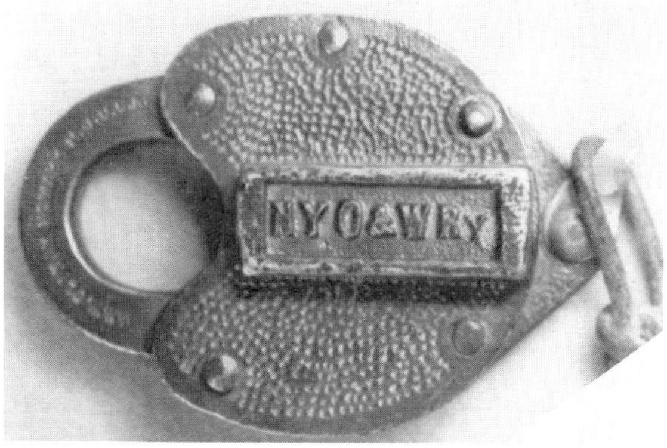

NYO&WRY-(New York Ontario & Western) cast on key cover on brass heart shaped switch lock. Mfg. JH Climax....................... **250-300**

NPR- (Northern Pacific) cast down panel of brass heart shaped switch lock **100-125**

NPRR-(Northern Pacific) cast down panel of brass heart shaped switch lock. "S" on shackle **100-125**

NPRR- (Northern Pacific) stamped on shackle of brass heart shaped switch lock. "S" on reverse. Mfg. Bohannan......................... **90-100**

NORTHERN PACIFIC- cast down panel of brass heart shaped lock. Also cast "SWI" on one side of panel and "TCH" on the other. Mfg. A&W or Adlake **100-125**

N&WRR CO- (Norfolk & Western) fancy cast on face of brass heart shaped switch lock. **350-400**

N&WRYCO-(Norfolk & Western) fancy cast on face of brass heart shaped switch lock. Mfg. Slaymaker or FS Hdw. **75-100**

NWPRR- (Northwestern Pacific) **"Switch CS8"** cast on face of brass heart shaped switch lock. Mfg. A&W **700-800**

OCRR-(Old Colony) large letters incised down panel of brass heart shaped switch lock. Mfg. Bohannan **250-300**

OR&NCO- (Oregon Railroad & Navigation) cast down panel of brass heart shaped switch lock. Key cover cast "Close the Lock to Get Key Out". Mfg. A&W **750-850**

OR&NCO- (Oregon Railroad & Navigation) CS-43 SPECIAL cast on face of brass heart shaped switch lock. Mfg. A&W **750-850**

OSLRR-(Oregon Short Line) SWITCH CS2- cast on face of brass heart shaped switch lock. Mfg. A&W **325-375**

OREGON SHORT LINE- cast down panel from top to bottom. Mfg. A&W in hex. "Close the Lock To Get Key Out" cast on key cover **800-900**

OREGON SHORT LINE- cast down panel from bottom to top. Mfg. A&W in hex. "Close the Lock To Get Key Out" cast on key cover **250-300**

OWR&NCO-CS3- (Oregon Washington Railroad & Navigation) cast down panel of brass heart shaped switch lock. Mfg. A&W in hex. **450-500**

PRRCO-(Pennsylvania) fancy cast on face of brass heart shaped switch lock. Mfg. Fraim. **175-200**

PRR-S- (Pennsylvania) stamped down panel on early brass heart shaped lock. Mfg. J.L. Howard **65-75**

PENNA CO-(Pennsylvania) cast down panel of brass heart shaped lock. **150-175**

P&LERR- (Pittsburgh & Lake Erie) cast down panel on brass heart shaped switch lock **70-80**

P&SRY- (Portland & Seattle) cast down panel on brass heart shaped switch lock .... ◆

RW&ORR- (Rome Watertown & Ogdensburg) stamped down panel of brass heart shaped switch lock. Mfg. Roemer & Co. **60-70**

RGWRY-(Rio Grande Western) cast down panel of brass heart shaped switch lock. Mfg. Adams & Westlake .... ◆

R&BRR S-(Rutland & Burlington) stamped down panel on brass heart shaped switch lock. MFg. T. Slaight **50-60**

RRR- (Rutland RR) stamped on shackle of brass heart shaped lock. Mfg. Bohannan ... **125-150**

SNRRCO- (Sacramento Northern) cast down panel on brass heart shaped switch lock. **600-650**

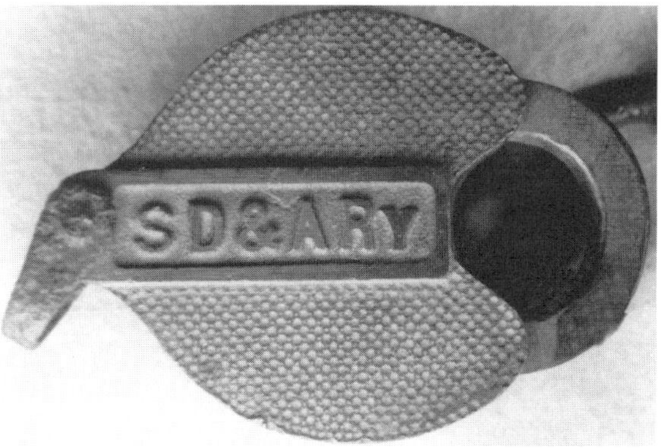

SD&ARY-(San Diego & Arizona) cast down panel of brass heart shaped switch lock with pebbled finish. Mfg. Miller .. ◆

SANTA FE- stamped on shackle of brass heart shaped switch lock. "S" on reverse. Mfg. A&W in hex **70-80**

SANTA FE- stamped on shackle of brass heart shaped switch lock. "TH" on reverse. Mfg. A&W in hex **100-125**

SANTA FE ROUTE- stamped on shackle of brass heart shaped switch lock. Mfg. A&W in hex 100-125

SANTA FE ROUTE –stamped on shackle of brass heart shaped switch lock. "TH" stamped on reverse. Mfg. A&W in hex 150-175

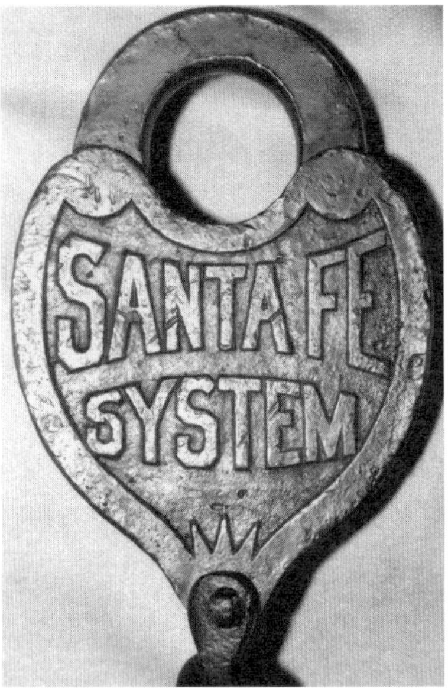

SANTA FE SYSTEM- fancy cast on face of brass heart shaped switch lock. You will find the shackle on these locks sometimes stamped with "MTRY, CMRY & SC" as well as others. Mfg. SB Co. .... ◆

SCSYCO-(Sioux City Stock Yard) stamped on shackle of brass heart shaped switch lock. "SWITCH" cast on the face of lock. Key cover cast "ADLAKE" 10-15

SOO LINE- stamped on shackle of brass heart shaped switch lock. MFg. Hansel, ... 25-35

SR- (Southern) with arrow incised down panel on brass heart shaped switch lock. "ESS" stamped on the shackle 100-125

STJ&DCRR- (St. Joseph & Denver City) stamped on shackle of brass heart shaped switch lock. "S" on reverse. Mfg. Union Brass 250-300

STJ&GIRY- (St. Joseph & Grand Island) stamped on shackle of brass heart shaped switch lock. "S" on reverse. Mfg. Prier Brass 100-125

STL&SF- (St.Louis & San Francisco)stamped on shackle in large seriff letters on brass switch lock. Reverse shackle stamped "CAR" in large letters 90-100

STL-SWRYCO-(St Louis Southwestern)-cast in square box on body of brass heart shaped switch lock. 250-300

STLIM&SRR- (St. Louis Iron Mountain & Southern) stamped on shackle of brass heart shaped switch lock. "S" on reverse. Mfg. Bohannan 125-150

STLRM&PRR- (St. Louis Rocky Mountain & Pacific) stamped on shackle of brass heart shaped switch lock. Mfg. Handlan Buck. Stamped with either "C or S" on reverse 100-125

STPUSYCO- (St. Paul Union Stock Yards) stamped on shackle of brass heart shaped switch lock. Mfg. A&W 50-60

SP&SRY- (Spokane Portland & Seattle) stamped on shackle of brass heart shaped switch lock. Mfg. FS Hdw 50-60

SO PAC CO- (Southern Pacific) cast down panel & key cover on brass heart shaped lock. Shackle stamped "Switch:". 175-200

SO PACIFIC CO-(Southern Pacific) cast down panel on brass heart shaped switch lock. "CS 4 SWITCH" also cast on face. Mfg. A&W **40-50**

SO PACIFIC CO- (Southern Pacific) cast down panel on brass heart shaped switch lock.. "CS-5 SWITCH" also cast on face. Mfg. A&W **750-850**

TEX & PAC-(Texas & Pacific) cast down panel of brass heart shaped switch lock. "Mfg. Miller & Co. .... ◆

TA&W- (Toledo Angola & Western) stamped on shackle of brass heart shaped switch lock. Mfg. Bohannan **40-50**

T&OCRR- (Toledo & Ohio Central) incised down panel of brass heart shaped switch lock. "TRACK" stamped on iron shackle. Mfg. Bohannan **100-125**

UPRR- (Union Pacific) stamped on shackle of brass heart shaped switch lock. Mfg. Bohannan **50-60**

UPRR (Union Pacific) SWITCH- cast on face of brass heart shaped switch lock. 1951 stamped on shackle **80-90**

UNION PACIFIC CS-1 SWITCH – cast on face of brass heart shaped switch lock. Mfg. A&W or Adlake **50-60**

UNION PACIFIC TOOL RACK- cast on face of brass heart shaped switch lock. MFg. Adlake or A&W **450-500**

UNION PACIFIC- cast down panel of brass heart shaped switch lock. "Water" stamped on shackle. Mfg. A&W in hex **200-250**

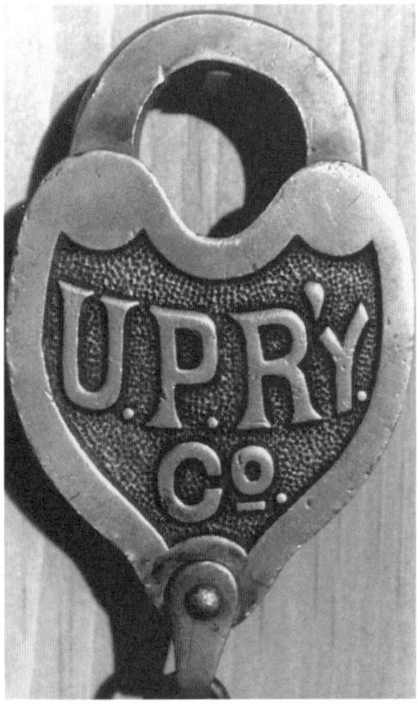

UPR'YCo-(Union Pacific Railway) -fancy cast on body of brass heart shaped switch lock. Mfg. Fraim. Pebbled finish .... ◆

UPDandGR'Y-(Union Pacific Denver & Gulf) -fancy cast on body of brass heart shaped switch lock. Mfg. Union Hardware .... ◆

V&T RR-(Virginia & Truckee) stamped on shackle of brass heart shaped switch lock. Mfg. Bohannan. **450-500**

WSTL&PRR-(Wabash St. Louis & Pacific) stamped on shackle of brass heart shaped switch lock. Mfg. Bohannan **100-125**

WES. PAC. RY-(Western Pacific) _cast on both sides down panel of brass heart shaped switch lock. Mfg. A&W **700-800**

CHAPTER 24

LOCKS SPECIAL PURPOSE

This category includes brass, steel & iron locks and covers a wide variety of styles. These can be found square, round, banjo shaped, Keen Kutter style and many others. These are the locks that were used to lock the outer buildings in the yards, including the train cars, tool boxes, oil tanks, water tanks & signals. These are usually smaller in size than their brass heart shaped cousins and can be quite ornate in their design and appearance. Remember as with all other collectibles the locks must be in good condition with no visible damage. Highly polished locks are not as desirable as those found in their natural state. And again it is not necessary to have a key for these to be collectible. It helps and is considered a great bonus but the value is squarely on the lock.

REMEMBER: PRICES SHOWN ARE SUGGESTED VALUES ONLY. VALUES VARY FROM REGION TO REGION. THIS IS MEANT ONLY AS A GUIDE. (◆) **Denotes value over $1000.00**

ACL SIGNAL-(Atlantic Coast Line) stamped on body of brass square style Corbin lock 10-15

ACLRR- -(Atlantic Coast Line) stamped on body of brass square style Corbin lock, "XLCR" incised on side 20-30

AT&SFRY- (Atchison Topeka & Santa Fe) stamped on shackle "General Purpose" cast on brass key cover of lock 35-45

AT&SFRY-(Atchison Topeka & Santa Fe) stamped on shackle , "SIGNAL" cast on brass key cover of lock 50-60

AT&SFRY- (Atchison Topeka & Santa Fe) stamped on shackle of small steel utility lock. Mfg. Fraim. 15-20

AT&SFRY- (Atchison Topeka & Santa Fe) cast on body of round six lever lock. Mfg. Miller .... ◆

B&ORR-(Baltimore & Ohio) STORES DEPT stamped on body of small square brass lock. 20-30

B&O SIGNAL- -(Baltimore & Ohio) stamped on body of small brass square utility lock. Mfg. Yale & Towne. Different divisions stamped on back side of lock. 10-15

B&ARR-(Boston & Albany) stamped on shackle of small steel special purpose lock. Mfg. Corbin. Pat. 1915 10-15

B&MRR-(Boston & Maine) stamped on shackle of small steel Corbin lock with brass rivets 20-30

BR&P-(Buffalo Rochester & Pittsburgh) "Property of BR&P Co." cast on body of small steel special purpose lock. 90-100

BR&PRY--(Buffalo Rochester & Pittsburgh) intertwined letters cast on body of square brass Yale lock. "Engineering Dept" stamped below letters 25-35

C&O SIGNAL DEPT-(Chesapeake & Ohio) incised on side of brass Yale lock 25-35

C&NW (Chicago & Northwestern) "General Purpose" stamped on key cover.steel lock Mfg. Eagle. 10-15

CB&QRR-(Chicago Burlington & Quincy) stamped on shackle of small brass special purpose heart shaped lock 20-30

CB&QRR-(Chicago Burlington & Quincy) cast on dust cover of small steel utility lock 15-20

CCC&STLRY-(Cleveland, Cincinnati, Chicago & St. Louis) SIGNAL DEPT.in circle on body of square brass Yale lock **15-20**

CM&STP SIGNAL-(Chicago Milwaukee & St Paul) cast down panel of brass lock with steel shackle. Mfg. Slaymaker **25-35**

C&SRR (Colorado & Southern) -Cast on face of Keen Kutter brass lock. Found with red orange enameled paint in the background ...... ◆

DL&WRR-(Delaware Lackawanna & Western) cast down panel of small brass heart shaped lock. Mfg. Slaymaker. Key cover reads, "Remove Key When Locking" **20-30**

The D&HCO-(Delaware & Hudson) fancy cast on body of round brass 6 lever lock...... **300-350**

D&RG- (Denver & Rio Grande) cast on body of round brass six lever lock. **300-350**

D&RG-(Denver & Rio Grande) cast down panel of small brass heart shaped lock. Mfg. Slaymaker **250-300**

D&RG (Denver & Rio Grande) SECTION HOUSE-cast on body of small brass heart shaped lock. **300-350**

D&RGRR-(Denver & Rio Grande) cast on both sides of brass Keen Kutter style lock. **350-400**

D&RGRYCO -(Denver & Rio Grande Railway) TRAIN BOX-cast on body of round brass six lever lock. Mfg. Miller .... ◆

D&RGRWYCO-(Denver & Rio Grande Railway) CAR LOCK-cast on body of round brass six lever lock. Mfg. Miller ◆

D&RGRY -(Denver & Rio Grande Railway) ICE HOUSE LOCK-cast on body of round brass six lever lock. Mfg. Miller ◆

D&RGRYCO -(Denver & Rio Grande Railway) WATER SERVICE- cast on body of round brass six lever lock. MFg. Miller ◆

D&RGW-(Denver & Rio Grande Western) stamped on both sides of shopped made large iron lock, referred to as a "Reefer" lock 60-70

ERIE RAILROAD COMPANY-cast on face of round brass six lever lock. 250-300

ERIE-stamped on body of steel Corbin special purpose lock 10-15

FRISCO-(St. Louis & San Francisco) stamped on key cover "Signal" stamped on shackle of brass lock. Mfg. Yale & Towne 20-25

FRISCO--(St. Louis & San Francisco) logo cast on one side of key cover, Signal cast on the other side on brass Keen Kutter style lock. 300-350

GTR (Grand Trunk Railway) **SIGNAL**-cast on brass key cover. Iron lock manufactured by Fraim. Patented 1908 has brass shackle as well. 65-75

GTW-(Grand Trunk Western) stamped on shackle of brass heart shaped lock. "Adlake-17 Signal Lock" cast on reverse. 45-55

GNRY (Great Northern) SIGNAL-cast down panel of small brass heart shaped lock. Remove Key When Locking cast on the key cover. Mfg. Slaymaker........ 65-75

GM&O-(Gulf Mobile & Ohio) stamped on shackle of small brass Slaymaker special purpose lock 10-15

ILLINOIS CENTRAL SIGNAL-cast down panel of small brass lock. "Remove Key When Locking" cast on key cover. .. 15-20

ICRR SIGNAL-(Illinois Central) stamped down panel on small brass heart shaped special purpose lock 10-15

KCSRY-(Kansas City Southern) stamped on shackle of steel banjo style lock. Mfg. Yale 20-30

LACKAWANNA RAILROAD-incised on face of brass Yale Signal style lock .. 35-45

LS&MSRY-(Lake Shore & Michigan Southern) incised on body of square brass XLCR signal lock.............................. 25-35

LS&MS--(Lake Shore & Michigan Southern)stamped on key cover of small steel Yale lock 15-20

LEHIGH VALLEY- stamped on shackle of Corbin style special purpose lock. Pat'd 1905. 50-60

L&NRR-(Louisville & Nashville) stamped in large letters on body of Corbin style lock. **15-20**

L&NRR CO--(Louisville & Nashville) cast on face of round brass six lever lock. **80-90**

MCRR-(Maine or Michigan Central) stamped on shackle of steel Banjo style lock. Mfg. Yale **20-30**

MCRRCO--(Maine or Michigan Central)stamped on shackle of steel Corbin style special purpose lock **25-35**

M&STLRR-(Minneapolis & St. Louis) stamped on shackle of small brass heart shaped lock. "Road Dept." stamped on reverse of shackle. **100-125**

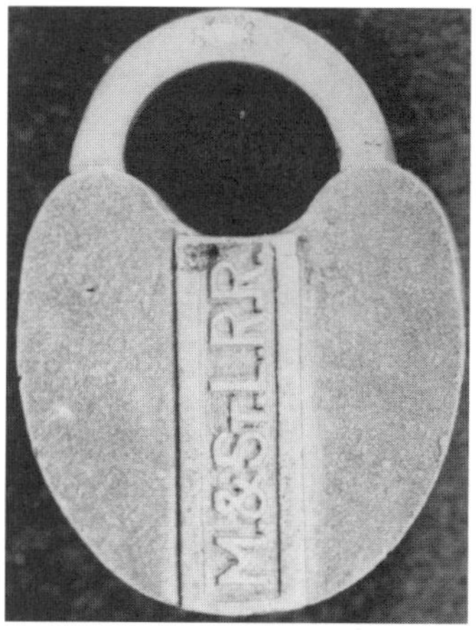

M&STLRR--(Minneapolis & St. Louis)cast down panel of small brass special purpose lock. "Road Department" stamped on shackle. **300-350**

MK&T-(Missouri Kansas & Texas) cast in center of square brass Signal Dept. lock. Mfg. Yale & Towne **30-40**

MISSOURI PACIFIC RAILWAY-cast on face of brass Keen Kutter style lock. Reverse reads, "Don't Use Oil But Plenty Of Graphite" stamped on reverse. Iron shackle. **300-350**

MISSOURI PACIFIC-cast on front of small brass general purpose lock **100-125**

FRONT

BACK

MISSOURI PACIFIC-cast on body, reverse cast "Section Tool House A-1 or A-2". "Remove Key When Locking" cast on key cover. Iron shackle. Mfg. Slaymaker **150-200**

NEW JERSEY CENTRAL- circle logo on body of square brass Corbin Signal lock. **25-35**

NYCRR-(New York Central) stamped on shackle of small steel special purpose lock. Pat'd 1915. .... **15-20**

NYCRR--(New York Central) stamped on body of brass XLCR lock **10-15**

NYC&HRRRCO-(New York Central & Hudson River) stamped on shackle of steel Corbin style lock. **10-15**

NEW YORK NEW HAVEN & HARTFORD -logo on side of Signal Dept. Yale & Towne lock **125-150**

NICKEL PLATE RR-circle logo on side of square brass Yale & Town Signal Dept. lock 25-35

N.K.P.-(New York Chicago & St. Louis) stamped on side of square brass Signal lock 10-15

N&WRY-(Norfolk & Western) cast on body of small FS Hardware special purpose lock 25-35

NPR-(Northern Pacific) stamped on shackle of small steel utility lock. Mfg. Corbin. 15-20

OR&NCO (Oregon Railroad & Navigation) CS23 ROADWAY & BRIDGE DEPARTMENT-cast on body of brass heart shaped lock. Mfg. A&W 375-425

OR&NCO (Oregon Railroad & Navigation) CS63 SIGNAL LOCK-stamped on body of small steel lock. "Use No Oil" stamped on reverse. 90-100

OSLRR (Oregon Short Line) CS 22 ROADWAY & BRIDGE DEPARTMENT.-cast on body of small brass heart shaped lock. Mfg. A&W 400-450

OWR&NCO (Oregon Washington Railroad & Navigation) CS 23 ROADWAY & BRIDGE DEPARTMENT-cast on body of small brass heart shaped lock. Mfg. A&W 500-550

OWRR&N (Oregon Washington Railroad & Navigation) CS73 SIGNAL DEPT.-stamped on body of small steel lock with brass rivets. 125-150

O-WR&NCO (Oregon Washington Railroad & Navigation)SIGNAL "Use No Oil" CS 63 stamped on body of brass signal lock... 90-100

PRR--(Pennsylvania RR)Keystone logo cast on side of large iron Scandinavian lock....... 75-85

PRR CO-(Pennsylvania RR) cast on key cover on small steel utility lock 15-20

PRR CO-(Pennsylvania RR)intertwined letters cast on brass key cover of steel lock. Mfg. Fraim. Dated 1920 35-45

PRR-(Pennsylvania RR)Keystone logo stamped on key cover of small steel special purpose lock. 5-10

PRR--(Pennsylvania RR)M.P.D. or S.D. stamped in large block letters on side of square brass lock with steel shackle. 25-35

PRR -(Pennsylvania RR)SIGNAL DEPT-stamped on body of square brass XLCR lock 15-20

PENNA RR CO-stamped on shackle of Corbin style special purpose lock with 1905 Pat'd date. 10-15

PENNA LINES SIGNAL- stamped on front of square brass Yale signal lock. 15-20

P&LERR- (Pittsburgh & Lake Erie) Circle logo incised on body of square brass Signal lock. Mfg. Yale 25-35

PULLMAN CO- seriff letters stamped in half moon shape on body of small brass square lock 50-60

RGWRY-(Rio Grande Western) WATER SERVICE cast on body of round six lever lock. Mfg. Miller .... ◆

ROCK ISLAND LINES SIGNAL-stamped on body of square brass lock. Mfg. Corbin 20-30

ROCK ISLAND LINES COMMU. DEPT-stamped on body of square brass lock. Mfg. Corbin 20-30

RCO SIGNAL SERVICE- (Reading Company) cast on drop of brass lock. Mfg. Fraim. 15-20

SANTA FE-cast on body of round brass six lever lock with tall shackle 350-400

SANTA FE- cast on both sides of brass Keen Kutter style lock. "General" stamped on bottom right corner. 200-250

SANTA FE- cast on front, Keen Kutter cast on back, again stamped General. 275-325

SANTA FE- cast on front, Keen Kutter cast on back across key cover., Signal stamped on the bottom right edge. **400-450**

SEABOARD AIR LINE-stamped on shackle of steel special purpose lock. Mfg. Yale **20-30**

SCLRR-(Seaboard Coast Line) stamped on body of small brass utility lock. Mfg. Bohannan **10-15**

SO RY SIGNAL-(Southern Ry) cast down panel on small brass heart shaped lock. Mfg. A&W **90-100**

SOU RY-(Southern Ry) Stamped on front of square brass Yale lock **20-30**

SORY-(Southern Ry) stamped on shackle of steel banjo style lock. Mfg. Yale **20-30**

SOUTHERN PACIFIC-sunset logo cast on front of Keen Kutter lock. Mfg. EC Simmons **350-400**

SOUTHERN PACIFIC- sunset logo cast on face of brass heart shaped lock. Large version with no manufacture shown **80-90**

SOUTHERN PACIFIC-sunset logo cast on face of brass heart shaped lock. Smaller version **65-75**

SO PACIFIC CO CS 44 SPECIAL-Cast on body of brass heart shaped lock. Mfg. A&W **100-125**

SOU PAC LINES CS 25 ROADWAY & BRIDGE DEPARTMENT-cast on face of brass heart shaped lock. Mfg. A&W. **200-250**

STL&SFRY- (St. Louis & San Francisco) stamped on shackle of small brass utility lock. **10-15**

STL&SFRY-(St. Louis & San Francisco) stamped on shackle of steel banjo style lock.Mfg. Yale **20-30**

UNION PACIFIC-Overland Shield logo cast on body of small brass special purpose lock. ... **400-450**

UNION PACIFIC-Overland Shield logo cast on body of large brass special purpose lock..... **500-600**

UNION PACIFIC OIL BOX- cast on body of round brass six lever lock. Mfg. A&W or Bohannan .... ◆

UNION PACIFIC ROAD WAY & BRIDGE DEPARTMENT CS 21-cast on body of brass heart shaped lock. Mfg. A&W **40-50**

UNION PACIFIC SYSTEM SIGNAL DEPARTMENT- stamped on body of small brass utility lock. UP stamped on shackle. Mfg. Eagle **50-60**

UPRR CS-61 SIGNAL USE NO OIL- stamped on body of small square brass lock **10-15**

WABASH FLAG LOGO- cast on body of square brass Signal Dept. lock. Mfg. Yale **35-45**

WABASH-cast on face of small brass lock. Mfg. Fraim **40-50**

WABASH RAILWAY STORES DEPT.-stamped on body of brass Corbin lock **50-55**

CHAPTER 25

LOCKS STEEL SWITCH

Finally this chapter deals with the steel switch locks which started making their appearance in 1912 and are still being manufactured in present day. Many of the initials found on these locks today represent railroads that have long since met their demise. These replaced the brass heart shaped style switch lock due to their affordability and durability. Some are found with raised letters on the key covers but most have the initials either stamped on the shackle or body. Someone just beginning to collect locks might consider these now as the values are still very affordable and given the appreciation of the other railroad collectibles it won't take long for the steel lock to be just as desirable and sought after. Locks must not be rusted, pitted, bent or otherwise altered from their original state to command the suggested prices listed here. The most common manufacturers of these locks were Adlake, Keline, Mitchell, Fraim, FS Hardware & Slaymaker. The photos below show the style of these steel switch locks.

Back of lock showing Mfg. mark of ADLAKE

Front of lock showing the initials of C&S for Colorado & Southern

AC&Y- (Akron Canton & Youngstown) stamped on body of steel Adlake lock.... **15-20**

ARR- (Alaska RR) stamped on body of steel Adlake lock **20-25**

A&BB-(Akron & Barberton Belt) stamped on body of steel Adlake switch lock **30-35**

AT&SFRY- (Atchison Topeka & Santa Fe) stamped on body of steel Adlake switch lock **5-10**

AT&SFD- (Atchison Topeka & Santa Fe) stamped on body of steel Adlake switch lock **5-10**

B&ORR-(Baltimore & Ohio) stamped on body of steel Adlake switch lock **5-10**

B&ORT- (Baltimore & Ohio) stampedon shackle of steel Slaymaker switch lock ... **10-15**

B&O LSTA- (Baltimore & Ohio)stampedon body of steel Adlake switch lock **10-15**

BELT- stamped on body of steel Adlake switch lock **5-10**

B&LE- (Bessemer & Lake Erie) stamped on body of steel Keline switch lock **15-20**

B&ARR-(Boston & Albany) stamped on body of steel Adlake switch lock **10-15**

B&M- (Boston & Maine) stamped on body of steel Adlake switch lock with brass shackle **10-15**

BN INC- (Burlington Northern) stamped on body of steel Adlake switch lock **5-10**

BR- (Burlington Route) stamped on body of steel Adlake switch lock **10-15**

CNR- (Canadian National) cast on key cover. Mfg. Mitchell **10-15**

CPR- (Canadian Pacific) cast on key cover. Mfg. Mitchell **15-20**

CCRY- (Carbon County) stamped on body of steel Adlake switch lock **40-50**

CVRY- (Central Vermont) stamped on body of steel Adlake switch lock **10-15**

C&EI- (Chicago & Eastern Illinois) stamped on body of steel Adlake switch lock **10-15**

C&NWRY- (Chicago & Northwestern) stamped on body of steel Adlake switch lock **5-10**

C&WI- (Chicago & Western Indiana) stamped on body of steel Adlake switch lock 10-15

C&SRY- (Colorado & Southern) stamped on body of steel Adlake switch lock **40-50**

C&WRY-(Colorado & Wyoming) stamped on body of steel Adlake switch lock **35-45**

CGW- (Chicago Great Western) stamped on body of steel Adlake switch lock **15-20**

CMSTP&P-(Chicago Milwaukee St Paul & Pacific) stamped on body of steel Adlake switch lock **5-10**

CSTPM&O- (Chicago St. Paul Minneapolis & Omaho) stamped on body of steel Adlake switch lock **15-20**

CSS&SB-(Chicago South Shore & South Bend) stamped on body of steel Adlake switch lock **10-15**

CRI&P- (Chicago Rock Island & Pacific) stamped on body of steel Adlake switch lock **10-15**

D&HCO- (Delaware & Hudson) stamped on shackle of steel switch lock. Mfg. Slaymaker 10-15

DL&W- (Delaware Lackawanna & Western) stamped on body of steel Adlake switch lock .. 5-10

D&RGRR- (Denver & Rio Grande) stamped on shackle of steel Adlake switch lock ... 35-45

D&RGW- (Denver & Rio Grande Western) stamped on body of steel Adlake switch lock 20-25

D&SLRY- (Denver & Salt Lake) stamped on body of steel Adlake switch lock 65-75

EJ&ERY- (Elgin Joliet & Eastern) stamped on body of steel Adlake switch lock 10-15

ERIE- stamped on shackle of steel switch lock. Mfg. Slaymaker 10-15

FECRY-(Florida East Coast) stamped on body of steel Adlake switch lock 10-15

FW&D- (Ft Worth & Denver) stamped on body of steel Adlake switch lock 30-35

FRISCO- (St. Louis & San Francisco) cast on brass key cover of steel Adlake switch lock 100-125

GTW- (Grand Trunk Western) stamped on body of steel Adlake switch lock 5-10

GNRY- (Great Northern) stamped on shackle of steel switch lock. Mfg. Slaymaker 10-15

GWRY- (Great Western) stamped on body of steel Adlake switch lock 30-35

GM&N-(Gulf Mobile & Northern stamped on body of steel Adlake switch lock 25-30

GM&O- -(Gulf Mobile & Ohio) stamped on body of steel Adlake switch lock 5-10

ICRR- (Illinois Central) stamped on body of steel Adlake switch lock 5-10

ICGRR-(Illinois Central Gulf) stamped on body of steel Adlake switch lock 5-10

IHBRR- (Indiana Harbor Belt) stamped on body of steel Adlake switch lock 10-15

ITRR- (Illinois Terminal) stamped on body of steel Adlake switch lock 20-25

KCSRR- (Kansas City Southern) stamped on body of steel Adlake switch lock 10-15

LVRR- (Lehigh Valley) stamped on body of steel Adlake switch lock 10-15

LIRR- (Long Island) stamped on shackle of steel switch lock. Mfg. FS Hardware 15-20

L&A-(Louisiana & Arkansas) stamped on body of steel Adlake switch lock 15-20

L&N- (Louisville & Nashville) stamped on body of steel Adlake switch lock 5-10

L&NRR- (Louisville & Nashville) stamped on shackle of steel switch lock. Mfg. Slaymaker 10-15

MSERR- (Manitoba Southeastern) stamped on body of steel Adlake switch lock 15-20

MCCRR-(Mason County Central) stamped on shackle of steel switch lock. Mfg. Slaymaker 40-50

M&STLRY- (Minneapolis & St. Louis) stampedon shackle of steel switch lock. Mfg. Slaymaker **15-20**

MN&SRWY- (Minneapolis Northfield & Southern) stamped on body of steel Adlake switch lock **20-25**

MK&T- (Missouri Kansas & Texas) stamped on body of steel Adlake switch lock **10-15**

MK&TRR- (Missouri Kansas & Texas) stamped on body of steel Adlake switch lock **10-15**

MOPAC-(Missouri Pacific) stamped on body of steel Adlake switch lock **5-10**

MOPAC LINES-(Missouri Pacific) stamped on body of steel Adlake switch lock 10-15

MOPAC SWITCH-(Missouri Pacific) stamped on body of steel Adlake switch lock 10-15

NYCS- (New York Central System) stamped on body of steel Adlake switch lock **5-10**

NYNH&H- (New York New Haven & Hartford) stamped on body of steel Adlake switch lock **10-15**

NYS&W- (New York Susquehanna & Western) stamped on body of steel Adlake switch lock **25-30**

NAR-(Northern Alberta) stamped on body of steel Mitchell switch lock **5-10**

N&W- (Norfolk & Western) stamped on body of steel Adlake switch lock **5-10**

NP SWITCH- (Northern Pacific) stamped on body of steel Adlake switch lock **10-15**

NORTHERN PACIFIC SWITCH - stamped on body of steel Adlake switch lock **15-20**

OMAHA RY- stamped on body of steel Adlake switch lock **20-25**

ONRY-(Okmulgee Northern) stamped on shackle of steel Adlake switch lock **20-30**

PERY-(Pacific Electric) stamped on shackle of steel Fraim switch lock **10-15**

PRR CO-(Pennsylvania RR) stamped on shackle of steel FS Hardware switch lock. Lock also has brass cast PRRCO key cover..... **85-95**

PRR-(Pennsylvania RR) stamped on shackle of steel Slaymaker switch lock **5-10**

PRR—(Pennsylvania RR) cast on key cover on steel Slaymaker switch lock **20-25**

PCRR- (Pennsylvania Central) stamped on body of steel Adlake switch lock **5-10**

P&PU- (Peoria & Pekin Union) stamped on body of steel Adlake switch lock **5-10**

P&LE- (Pittsburgh & Lake Erie) stamped on body of steel Adlake switch lock **10-15**

P&WV-(Pittsburgh & West Virginia) stamped on body of steel Adlake switch lock with brass shackle **30-40**

RDGCOS-(Reading Co) stamped on body of steel Adlake switch lock **5-10**

RCO-(Reading Co.) stamped on shackle of steel Slaymaker switch lock 5-10

SALRR-(Seaboard Air Line) stamped on body of steel Slaymaker switch lock with brass shackle 25-30

SCLRR-(Seaboard Coast Line) stamped on body of steel Adlake switch lock 10-15

SCSYCO-(Souix City Stock Yards) stamped on body of brass Adlake switch lock 5-10

SOO LINE- stamped on body of steel Adlake switch lock.. 10-15

SOO-SW-stamped on brass shackle of steel Slaymaker switch lock 15-20

SPCO- (Southern Pacific) stamped on body of steel Adlake switch lock 5-10

SPTCO CS4S- (Southern Pacific Transportation Co) stamped on body of steel Adlake switch lock .. 5-10

TH&B-(Toronto Hamilton & Buffalo) stamped on body of steel Adlake switch lock.................... 10-15

TRRA- (Terminal Railroad Association) stamped on body of steel Adlake switch lock.................... 5-10

UPRR NO.1- (Union Pacific) stamped on body of steel Adlake switch lock 10-15

UPRR NO.1-(Union Pacific) stamped on body of brass Adlake switch lock 20-25

UPRR R&B DEPT-s(Union Pacific Roadway & Bridge) tamped on body of brass Adlake switch lock... 15-20

WPRR- (Western Pacific) stamped on body of steel Adlake switch lock 10-15

WVRR- (Western Vermont) stamped on body of steel Adlake switch lock...................... 20-25

Y&S- (Youngstown & Southern) stamped on body of steel Adlake switch lock 30-35

REMEMBER: PRICES SHOWN ARE SUGGESTED VALUES ONLY. VALUES VARY FROM REGION TO REGION. THIS IS MEANT ONLY AS A GUIDE. **(◆) Denotes value over $1000.00**

CHAPTER 26

PASSES

Passes were issued by the railroads to employees, government officials, clergy, shippers, important clients and many others to offer free passage when riding the trains. Passes most often were made of card board but can be found in buckskin, silver, gold & brass. It is not uncommon to find a pass which is quite ornate with great lithography and vignettes found on the early issues. Collecting passes can be very rewarding. Enthusiasts tend to collect not only for the railroad but for who the pass might be issued to or who may have signed it. It is amazing to consider that so many of these card board passes can be found still today in like new condition. Passes must be in mint condition to command the prices listed here. If they are stained, folded, torn, cut or otherwise altered from their original state they are worth much less than the prices suggested here.

REMEMBER: PRICES SHOWN ARE SUGGESTED VALUES ONLY. VALUES VARY FROM REGION TO REGION. THIS IS MEANT ONLY AS A GUIDE. (◆) **Denotes value over $1000.00**

ALABAMA GREAT SOUTHERN-black on light blue dated 1906 .... **5-10**

ANN ARBOR RR CO.- black on blue dated 1914 .... **15-20**

ARGENTINE CENTRAL RR CO.- black on light blue dated 1911 .... **550-600**

ARGENTINE & GRAYS PEAK-black on white dated 1919 .... **375-425**

ATCHISON TOPEKA & SANTA FE RR- black on beige dated 1896 .... **20-30**

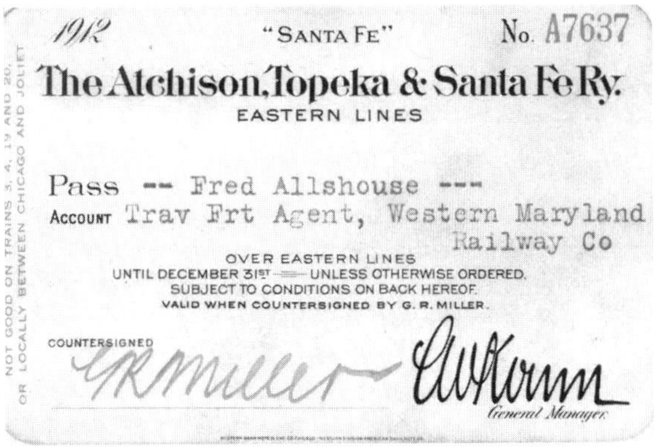

ATCHISON TOPEKA & SANTA FE RR- black on purple dated 1912 .... **5-10**

ATLANTA & WEST POINT- black on white dated 1914 .... **20-30**

BURLINGTON CEDAR RAPIDS & NORTHERN- black on blue dated 1884 .... **25-35**

BURLINGTON & MISSOURI RIVER- black on pink dated 1898 .... **40-50**

BUTTE ANACONDA & PACIFIC RR- black on cream dated 1933 .... **25-35**

CALIFORNIA WESTERN RR & NAV. CO.-black on white with red logo dated 1933 .... **35-45**

CEDAR RAPIDS & IOWA CITY RY- black on blue dated 1912 .... **10-15**

CENTRAL IOWA RY CO- black on green dated 1886 .... **20-30**

CENTRAL VERMONT RY- black on white dated 1879 .... **35-45**

CHARLESTON & WEST CAROLINA- black on cream dated 1923 .... **20-30**

CHESAPEAKE & OHIO RY- black on yellow dated 1911 .... **10-15**

CHICAGO & OHIO RIVER RY- black on blue dated 1892 .... **15-20**

CHICAGO & NORTHWESTERN RY- black on blue dated 1905 .... **10-15**

CHICAGO BURLINGTON & QUINCY RR- yellow on black employee pass dated 1890 .... **20-25**

CHICAGO BURLINGTON & QUINCY RR- black on cream dated 1908 .... **15-20**

CHICAGO BURLINGTON & QUINCY RR-black on white dated 1940 .... **1-3**

CHICAGO GREAT WESTERN RR CO- Black on green with red highlights dated 1931 .... **5-10**

CHICAGO MILWAUKEE & ST PAUL RY- black on grey dated 1904 .... **15-20**

CHICAGO ST PAUL MINNEAPOLIS & OMAHA RY- blue on blue dated 1906 **10-15**

CHICAGO PEKIN & SOUTHWESTERN- black on beige dated 1880 .... **30-40**

CINNCINATI, LAFAYETTE & CHICAGO- black on green dated 1877 .... **40-50**

CINNCINATI & MUSKINGUM VALLEY RR- orange on yellow dated 1899 .... **20-30**

CINNCINATI, HAMILTON & DAYTON RR- black on white dated 1906............. **10-15**

CLEVELAND & LAKE ERIE- black on blue dated 1864 .... **50-60**

CLEVELAND & PITTSBURG RY- green on tan dated 1869 .... **55-65**

CLEVELAND AKRON & COLUMBUS RY- black on white dated 1909 .... **10-15**

CLINCHFIELD RR- black on green dated 1926 .... **15-20**

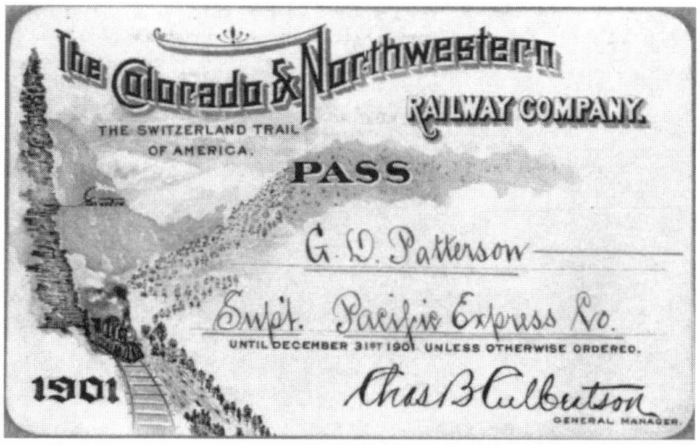

COLORADO & NORTHWESTERN RY- black on blue dated 1901 .... **500-550**

COLORADO & NORTHWESTERN RY- black on blue dated 1905 .... **450-500**

COLORADO & SOUTHERN RY- black on white with logo dated 1899 .... **550-600**

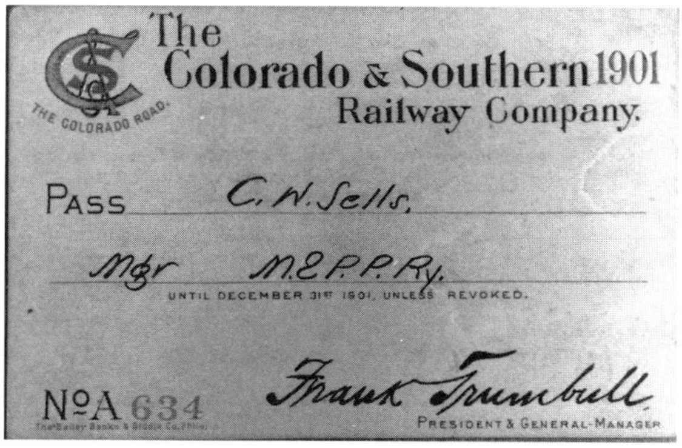

COLORADO & SOUTHERN RY-black on white with logo dated 1901 .... **350-400**

COLORADO & SOUTHERN RY- 1912 black on white **20-30**

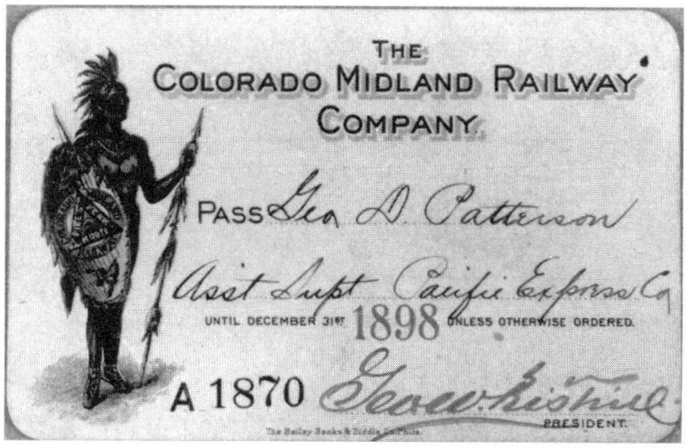

COLORADO MIDLAND RY- black on pink with embossed standing Indian dated 1898 ...... **550-600**

COLORADO MIDLAND RY- black on blue dated 1900 .... **400-450**

COLORADO MIDLAND RY-black on blue dated 1910 .... **125-150**

COLORADO MIDLAND RY- black pink dated 1915 .... **100-125**

COLORADO SPRINGS & CRIPPLE CREEK RY- black on white dated 1911 .... **250-300**

CRYSTAL RIVER RAILROAD-black on white dated 1912 .... **400-450**

CRYSTAL RIVER RAILROAD-black on white dated 1916 .... **400-450**

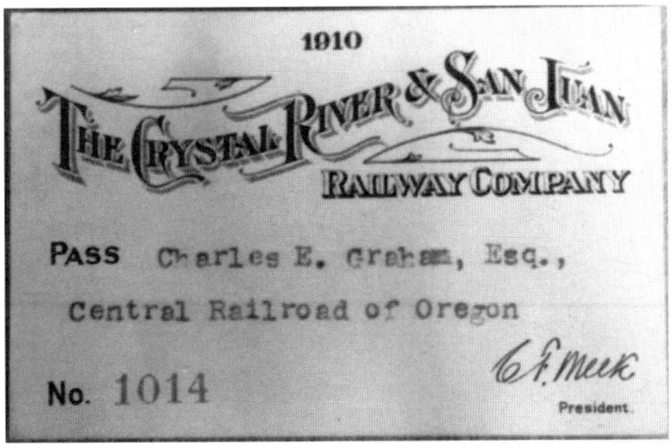

Cover view

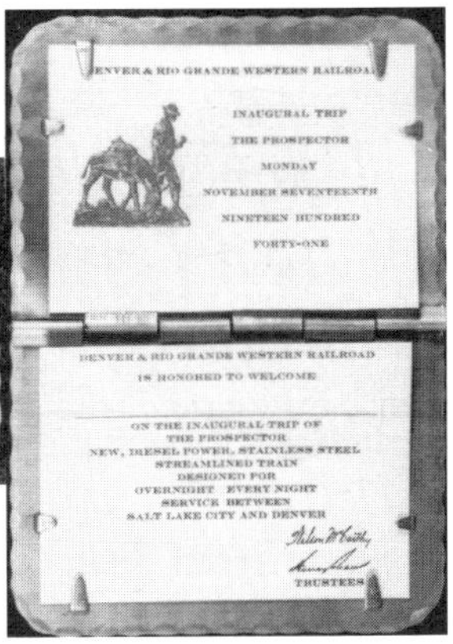

CRYSTAL RIVER & SAN JUAN RWY CO- black on white dated 1910 .... **450-500**

CRYSTAL RIVER & SAN JUAN RWY CO.- black on cream dated 1912 .... **450-500**

DELAWARE & HUDSON RY- black on yellow dated 1903 .... **10-15**

DENVER & RIO GRANDE RR- brown on beige dated 1906 .... **80-90**

DENVER & RIO GRANDE RR- black on pink dated 1907 .... **65-75**

DENVER & RIO GRANDE/ RIO GRANDE SOUTHERN –joint pass black on light green dated 1912 .... **40-50**

DENVER & RIO GRANDE WESTERN RR- black on white dated 1927 .... **15-20**

DENVER & RIO GRANDE WESTERN RR- black on white dated 1928 .... **15-20**

DENVER & RIO GRANDE WESTERN- 1941 inaugural trip pass. Two cards housed in stainless steel embossed case **400-450**

DENVER & SALT LAKE RR- black on white dated 1929 .... **50-60**

DENVER SOUTH PARK & PACIFIC RR- black on white dated 1878 .... ◆

DES MOINES & KANSAS CITY RR- black on green dated 1896 .... **55-65**

DES MOINES, IOWA FALLS & NORTHERN RR- black on yellow dated 1905 .. **25-35**

DES MOINES VALLEY RR- black on white with fancy design dated 1869 .... **35-45**

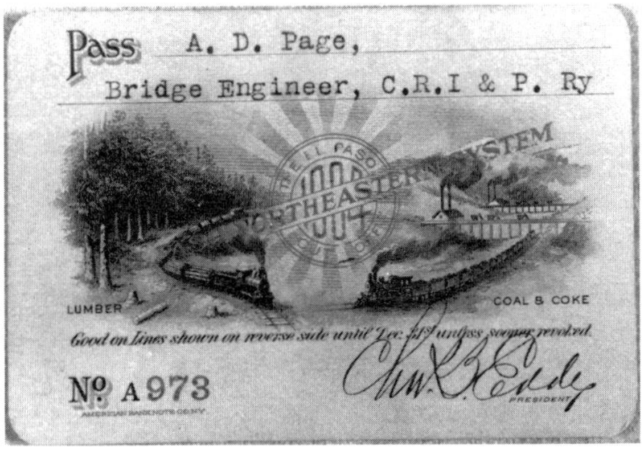

EL PASO & NORTHEASTERN RR- black on pink with colorful sunburst highlights. Dated 1904 .... **100-125**

EL PASO & SOUTHWESTERN RR- green on white with red highlights dated 1918 .... **10-15**

EL PASO & SOUTHWESTERN RR- dated 1908 .... **20-30**

ERIE- black on white dated 1913 .... **10-15**

EVANSVILLE & CRAWFORDSVILLE RR- red on white dated 1860 .... **50-60**

EVANSVILLE & CRAWFORDSVILLE RR- black on orange dated 1865 .... **45-55**

EVANSVILLE & TERRE HAUTE RR- black on green dated 1901 .... **20-30**

EVANSVILLE PADUCAH & CAIRO RR- black on beige dated 1879 .... **30-40**

FITCHBURG RR- blue on white dated 1881 .... **35-45**

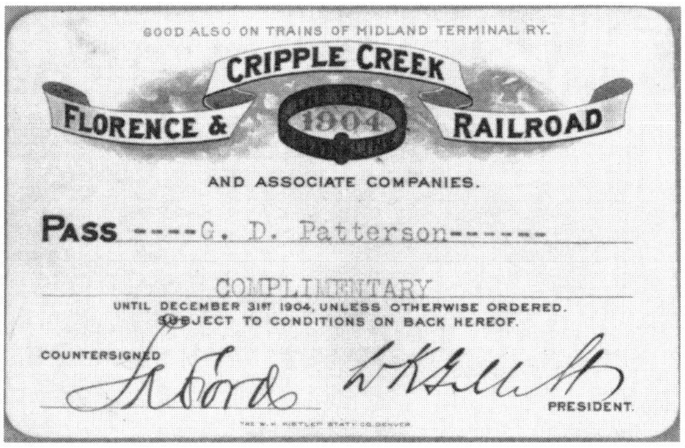

FLORENCE & CRIPPLE CREEK RR- black on white dated 1904 .... **500-550**

FLORENCE & CRIPPLE CREEK RR- black on yellow dated 1914 .... **100-125**

FLORIDA EAST COAST RR- black on yellow dated 1915 .... **15-20**

FT SMITH & WESTERN RR- black on green dated 1912 .... **25-35**

FT WORTH & DENVER CITY- green on light green dated 1900 .... **40-50**

FT WORTH & DENVER CITY- black on pink dated 1903 .... **30-40**

FRISCO SYSTEM- black on gray dated 1901 .... **10-15**

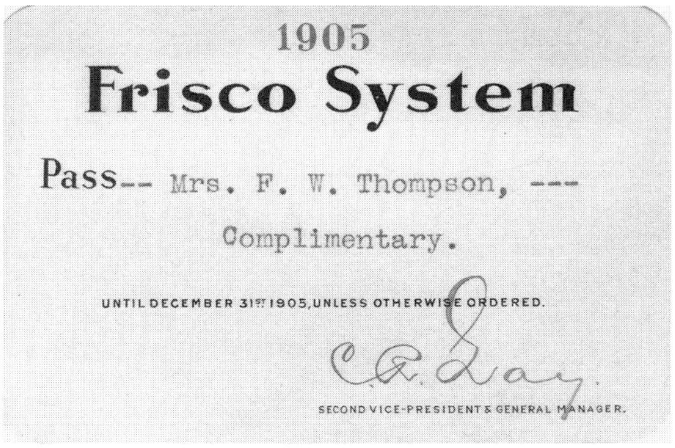

FRISCO SYSTEM – black on yellow dated 1902 .... **10-15**

GREEN BAY & WESTERN RR- black on brown dated 1926 .... **10-15**

GRAND RAPIDS & INDIANA RR- black on white dated 1912 .... **10-15**

GREAT NORTHERN RY- black on white dated 1916 .... **10-15**

GULF COLORADO & SANTA FE RY- black on white dated 1895 .... **45-55**

GULF COLORADO & SANTA FE RY-black on blue dated 1909 .... **15-20**

HANNIBAL & ST.JOSEPH RY- purple on white dated 1876 .... **65-75**

HANNIBAL & ST. JOSEPH RY- brown on beige dated 1902 15-20

HOCKING VALLEY RY CO.- black on white dated 1910 20-30

HOUSTON & TEXAS CENTRAL RR- black on beige dated 1900 20-30

ILLINOIS CENTRAL RR-black on beige dated 1899 15-20

ILLINOIS CENTRAL RR-black on white dated 1904 10-15

INTERNATIONAL & GREAT NORTHERN RY-black on brown dated 1914 10-15

IOWA CENTRAL RY- brown on pink dated 1894 50-60

IOWA CENTRAL RY- black on blue dated 1910 25-35

IRON MOUNTAIN CHESTER & EASTERN RY- dated 1875 45-55

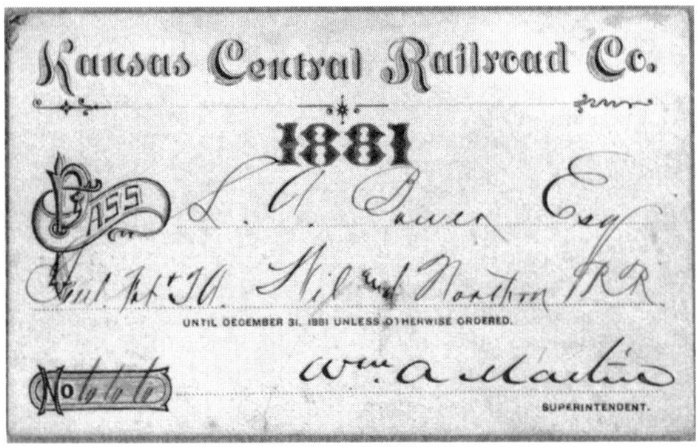

KANSAS CENTRAL RR CO-black on pink dated 1881 200-250

KANSAS CITY & OMAHA RY-Black on blue dated 1897 30-40

KANSAS CITY FT SCOTT & MEMPHIS- brown on beige dated 1897 30-40

KANSAS CITY MEXICO & ORIENT RY- black on blue dated 1910 25-35

KANSAS CITY NORTHWESTERN RY-blue on blue dated 1897 65-75

KANSAS CITY OSCEOLA & SOUTHERN RY-black on pink 1895 35-45

KANSAS CITY PITTSBURGH & GULF RY- black on blue dated 1895 20-30

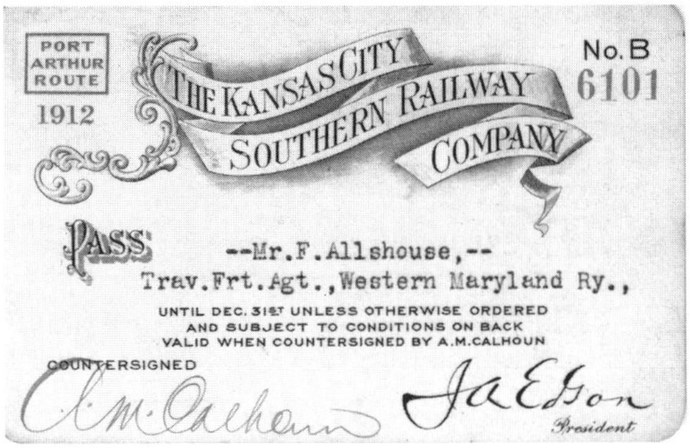

KANSAS CITY SOUTHERN RY-black on beige dated 1912 15-25

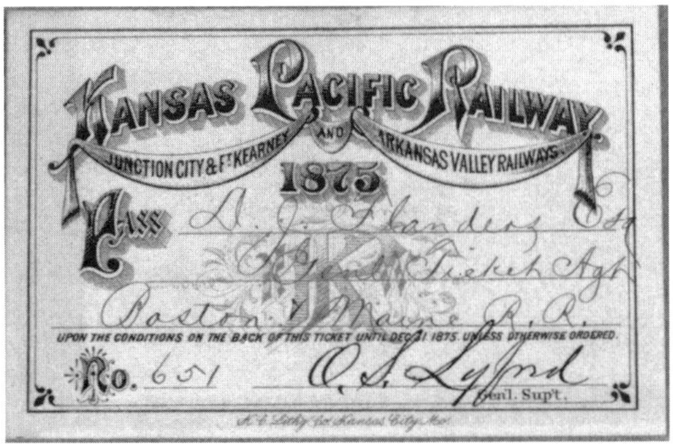

KANSAS PACIFIC RY-black on white dated 1875 450-500

LAKE CHARLES & NORTHERN RY-black on beige dated 1927 15-20

LAKE ERIE & WESTERN RY- black on white dated 1892 35-40

LAKE ERIE & WESTERN RY- black on green dated 1906 15-20

LAKE SHORE LINE- black & blue on white ornate dated 1865 75-85

LAKE SHORE & MICHIGAN SOUTHERN RY- black on yellow dated 1909 .... **10-15**

LAKE SHORE & TUSCARAWAS VALLEY RY- blue on white dated 1875 .... **50-60**

LOS ANGELES & REDONDO RAILWAY CO-black on beige with great vignette dated 1902 .... **90-100**

LOUISVILLE & NASHVILLE RR-black on white dated 1916 .... **5-10**

MARIETTA & CINNCINATI RR- black on white dated 1865 .... **50-60**

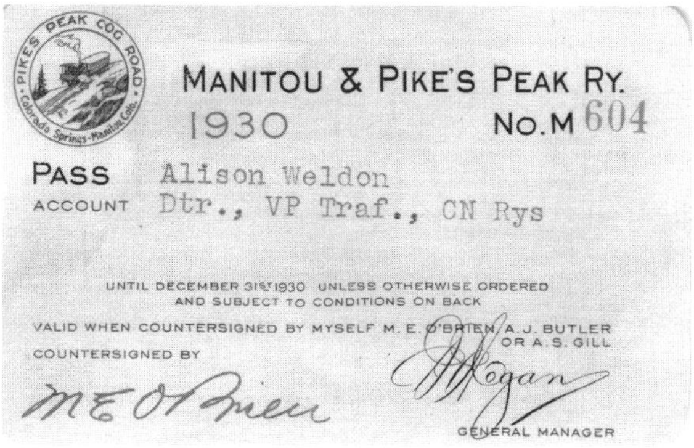

MANITOU & PIKES PEAK RR- black on beige dated 1930 .... **10-15**

MIDLAND CONTINENTAL RR- blue on white dated 1928 .... **5-10**

MIDLAND TERMINAL RR-red on light green dated 1899 .... **300-350**

MIDLAND TERMINAL & CRIPPLE CREEK & COLORADO SPRINGS- joint pass black on white dated 1919 .... **75-85**

MIDLAND VALLEY RR- black on blue dated 1908 .... **10-15**

MISSISSIPPI & OHIO RR- black on blue dated 1896 .... **20-30**

MISSISSIPPI & TENNESEE RR- green on light green dated 1877 .... **60-70**

MISSOURI KANSAS & TEXAS RR- black on orange dated 1900 .... **10-15**

MISSOURI KANSAS & TEXAS RR- black on orange dated 1927 .... **5-10**

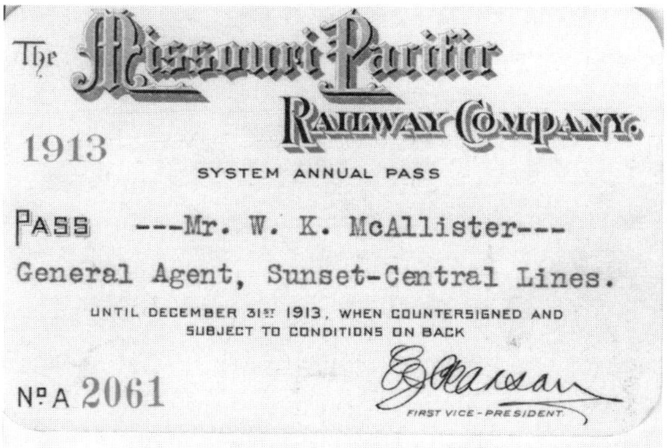

MISSOURI PACIFIC RY CO-black on white dated 1913 .... **15-25**

NASHVILLE CHATTANOOGA & ST LOUIS RY- blue on beige dated 1909 .... **15-25**

NEW HAVEN & NORTH HAMPTON RY- black on white dated 1875 .... **35-45**

NEW YORK & NEW ENGLAND RR- blue on white dated 1892 .... **30-40**

NEW YORK CHICAGO & ST LOUIS- black on blue dated 1907 .... **10-15**

NORTHWESTERN PACIFIC RR- black on beige dated 1909 .... **20-30**

OHIO VALLEY RR- black on green dated 1897 .... **30-40**

OLD COLONY RR- black on white dated 1885 30-40

OREGON SHORT LINE- black on white dated 1913 10-15

OREGON WASHINGTON RAILROAD & NAVIGATION CO. ..... black on white dated 1913 10-15

PACIFIC & IDAHO NORTHERN RR- black on white dated 1926 20-30

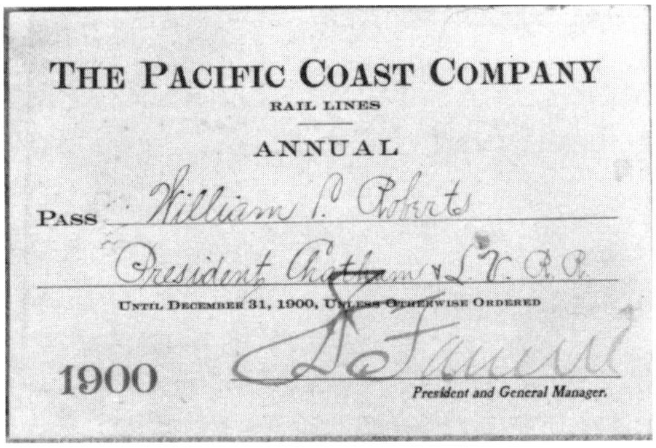

PACIFIC COAST COMPANY- Black on white dated 1900 65-75

PASSUMPSIC RR- black on white ornate dated 1883 40-50

PECOS VALLEY RR- black on green dated 1897 30-40

PHILADELPHIA & READING RY-blue on white dated 1899 10-15

PITTSBURGH & LAKE ERIE RR- black on grey dated 1911 10-15

PITTSBURGH & SHAMUT RR- black on white dated 1938 5-10

PORTLAND & OGDENSBURG RR black on beige dated 1878 40-50

QUINCY RAILROAD-black on white dated 1926 25-35

RIO GRANDE SOUTHERN – black on blue dated 1892 .... ◆

RIO GRANDE SOUTHERN –black on white dated1893 .... ◆

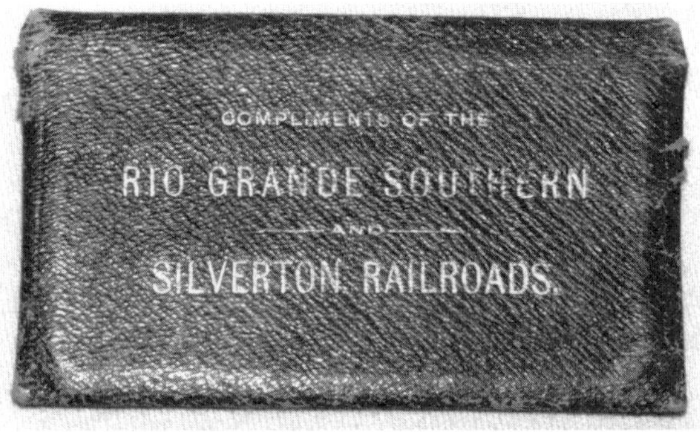

RIO GRANDE SOUTHERN & SILVERTON RR- silver ornate filigree pass issued & numbered. Made by Spitz Co. of Santa Fe Complete with leather carrying case shown above and descriptive card. .... ◆

RIO GRANDE WESTERN- black on white dated 1893 450-500

RIO GRANDE WESTERN-black on pink dated 1900 350-400

RUTLAND RAILROAD- black on pink dated 1909 45-55

ST LOUIS & IRON MOUNTAIN SOUTHERN RR- black on white dated 1876 100-125

ST LOUIS & SAN FRANCISCO RR- black on blue dated 1886 30-40

SALT LAKE ROUTE- black on white dated 1913 20-30

SAN DIEGO & ARIZONA RR- black on yellow dated 1923 20-30

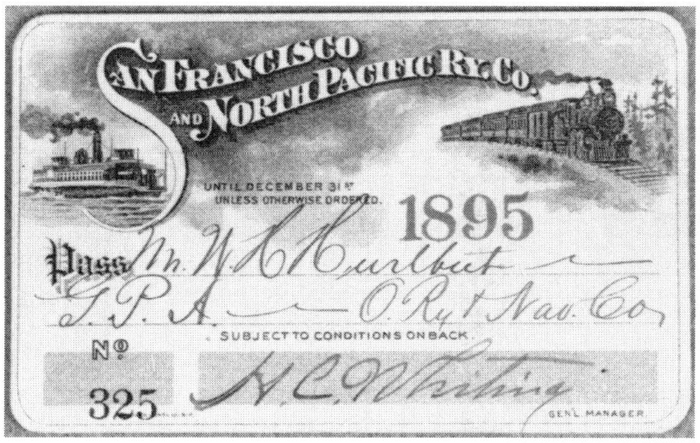

SAN FRANCISCO & NORTH PACIFIC RY- black on white with ornate vignettes. Dated 1895 200-250

SANDUSKY MANSFIELD & NEWARK RR- blue on white with red highlights and dated 1859 60-70

SAN PEDRO LOS ANGELES & SALT LAKE RR- black on green dated 1914 10-15

SAN ANTONIO & ARANSAS PASS RR- black on blue dated 1904 20-30

SAND SPRINGS RY CO-black on white dated 1940. Logo on top 10-15

SANTA FE PRESCOTT & PHOENIX RY CO-black on blue dated 1895 200-250

SILVERTON RR- black on blue dated 1893 .... ◆

SILVERTON RR CO.-black on pink dated 1897 .... ◆

SILVERTON RR- 1889 silver pass with embossed design. Issued & numbered. Mfg. Diamond Palace Co. Denver. .... ◆

SILVERTON RR-1890 silver watch fob pass. Beautiful high relief mountain scene with blue enamel inlay. Reverse side has recipients name and pass number .... ◆

SILVERTON & SILVERTON NORTHERN RR- dual pass dated 1901. Black on yellow 750-800

SILVERTON NORTHERN RR CO-black on cream dated 1909 500-550

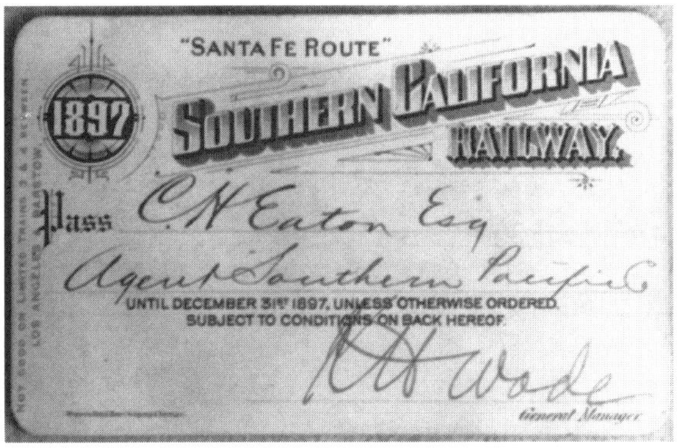

SOUTHERN CALIFORNIA RY-black on yellow dated 1897 .... **100-125**

SOUTHERN PACIFIC RR- black on pink dated 1900 .... **15-20**

TRRA OF ST LOUIS- black on blue dated 1900 .... **5-10**

TEXAS MIDLAND RR- green on white dated 1915 .... **15-20**

TEXAS & PACIFIC RR- black on beige dated 1907 .... **10-15**

TONOPAH & GOLDFIELD RR- black on green dated 1928 .... **80-90**

TPA- "Traveling Passenger Association" silver pass dated 1890. Ornate high relief mountain scene with the following railroads listed, "Denver & Rio Grande, Colorado Midland, Union Pacific issued for a convention in held in Denver .... ◆

TRINITY & BRAZOS VALLEY RR- black on brown dated 1916 .... **10-15**

UINTAH RAILWAY- black on white dated 1914 .... **125-150**

UINTAH RAILWAY- black on pink dated 1928 .... **75-85**

UNION PACIFIC RY- blue on white dated 1886 .... **80-90**

UNION PACIFIC RY- black on white dated 1907 .... **10-15**

UNION PACIFIC DENVER & GULF RY- black on white dated 1898 .... **450-500**

UTAH CENTRAL RY- black on blue dated 1877 .... **125-150**

UPPER COOS & HEREFORD RR- black on pink dated 1890 .... **25-35**

WABASH RR- black on pink dated 1913 .... **10-15**

WABASH RR-black on orange dated 1927 ... **5-10**

WEST JERSEY RR-black on green dated 1873 .... **45-55**

WESTERN PACIFIC RR- black on green dated 1913 .... **20-30**

WICHITA VALLEY RR- black on white dated 1909 .... **30-40**

WISCASSET, WATERVILLE & FARMINGTON RY- black on blue dated 1911 .... **40-50**

YREKA RR- black on blue dated 1931 .... **15-20**

CHAPTER 27

PHOTOS POSTERS & PRINTS

This chapter covers the many different advertising posters, depot photographs as well as stereoviews and cabinet cards that relate to the railroads. The advertising posters are often times very ornate and full of wonderful offers to entice the traveling public. The photographs that adorned the many depots and business offices were beautiful shots of scenes along the lines offered by a variety of early and sought after photographers. The many different stereoviews and cabinet cards that were offered by the railroads as souvenirs and traveling giveaways are also another great collectible sure to please. To find a depot photograph still housed in its orginal frame and proudly matted with the railroad logo and subject title as well is a true treasure. Many of these beautiful photographs were taken at the turn of the century without the help of todays modern photographic equipment and yet the photographer still managed to capture a beautiful landscape surrounding a train coming through a valley while keeping all the details in focus. Even todays photograhers wrestle with those effects. The stories of great photographers like William Henry Jackson who was commissioned by the Denver & Rio Grande to capture its beauty are endless. The camera used to take his "Mammoth Prints" which measured approximately 21" x18" was the actual size of the glass plate negative. He would travel for miles with pack mules carrying all of his equipment and develop his glass plates on sight as he had suffered too many losses from mules falling to continue to travel back to his offices to complete his work. These wonderful pieces of history can be a very rewarding and enjoyable part of the railroadiana hobby. Condition is imperative. Photos must not be faded, torn, stained or otherwise altered from their original condition to command the suggested prices shown here.

REMEMBER: PRICES SHOWN ARE SUGGESTED VALUES ONLY. VALUES VARY FROM REGION TO REGION. THIS IS MEANT ONLY AS A GUIDE. (◆) **Denotes value over $1000.00**

ATCHISON TOPEKA & SANTA FE-Advertising poster showing a "Special Excursion to the Arkansas Valley". Poster is trying to lure the settlers to the Great Fertile Wheat Fields in Kansas. 350-400

AT&SF-SANTA FE-Advertising broadsides used in depots, offices, hotels and other businesses to help attract the traveling public to the Southwest. These same prints were reduced and used on wall calendars, pocket calendars and sometimes timetables, menu covers and a host of other advertising venues. The large posters listed here measure approximately 18" x 24". They are colorful and quite collectible with some versions harder to find than others. The Santa Fe blue and white logo can be found on each version.

Arizona 200-250

Chico Drawing in the Sand 250-300

Chief Way 200-250

California Palm Trees 150-200

Grand Canyon Arizona 250-300

Hopi Land 200-250

Land of the Pueblos New Mexico 200-250

Meeting of the Chiefs 200-250

Navajo Land Arizona & New Mexico 250-300

Red Cliffs Continental Divide New Mexico 225-275

San Francisco Golden Gate 225-275

Southwest Dude Ranches 200-250

Sunspots in the Southwest 175-225

Ten Indian Children 250-300

Texas Famous Brands of the Lone Star State 200-250

Texas San Jacinto Monument 200-250

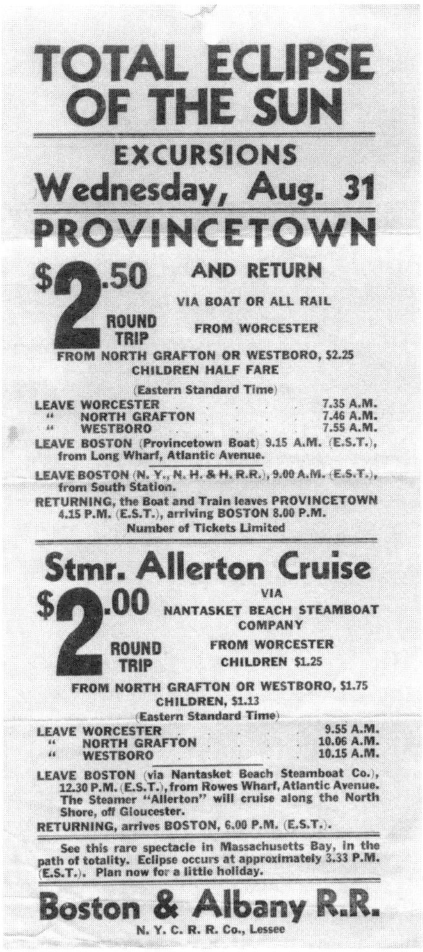

BOSTON & MAINE- Excursion poster measures 5" x 11". Black on orange advertising the "Total Eclipse of the Sun" Circa 1930's 25-30

BURLINGTON ROUTE-Depot print measures 32" x 24" framed. Colorized photo by Detroit Photographic showing 6 car passenger train behind B&MRRR engine 346 along the front range in the Colorado Rockies. Mat has gold BR logo and reads, "Chicago Special Burlington Route Denver to Omaha & Chicago, Denver to St. Joseph & St. Louis .... ♦

BURLINGTON ROUTE-depot print with 2 trains. Mat reads, "Along Burlingtons Scenic Mississippi River Route" with BR logo's in each corner 65-75

CABINET CARDS-black & white or color photos mounted on hard stock mat showing various railroad scenes. Usual size is 5" x 7" although that can vary. Cards showing trains in the scenes are usually worth more than just a scenic view. Known photographers can also command more money such as WH Jackson, Alex Martin or Charles Savage to name a few. Some cards can be worth as little as 5.00 or be worth as much as 300.00 depending on the scene and the quality of the photograph as well as the photographer. These cards dated from the 1870's to the 1900's. Sold by the railroads to travelers as a souvenir to document their journey. On the back of the cards the railroads name can be found as the sponsor of the scene. Cards cannot be faded, folded, torn or stained.

Clear Creek Canyon colored version by WH Jackson 75-85

Animas Canyon without train 25-35

Animas Canyon showing train on ledge 65-75

Balancing Rock 10-15

Denver South Park & Pacific Boreas Pass with train 250-300

Garden of the Gods 25-35

Georgetown Loop 50-60

Leadville Colorado street scene 40-50

Marshall Pass with train 100-125

Marshall Pass without train 50-60

Mother Grundy Clear Creek Canyon ... 30-40

Royal Gorge 20-30

Ute Pass 20-30

CENTRAL VERMONT-Excursion fare broadside measures 5" x 18". Blue on white dated 1932. Shows picture of Capitol advertising trip to the Washington. 35-45

CHICAGO & ALTON-black & white framed depot print showing front of engine next to rear platform of another train side by side. Brass applied plaque reads, "Coming & Going Chicago & Alton Railway The Only Way" .... ◆

CHICAGO & NORTHWESTERN-Color photochrome depot print. Mat reads, "A Limited Train The Northwestern Line" by Detroit Photographic. Measures 37" x 26". .. 375-425

CHICAGO MILWAUKEE ST PAUL-black & white depot photo. Mat reads, "Dells of the Wisconsin on the Line of The Chicago Milwaukee & ST. Paul". Frame also engraved CM&STPRY 250-300

COLORADO MIDLAND-Advertising poster showing snarling head of Mountain Lion. Several different versions can be found. Some with head only, some with Midland logo in bottom corners, some with Indian on Horseback on bottom. Also can be found with Shield logo on bottom .... 750-◆

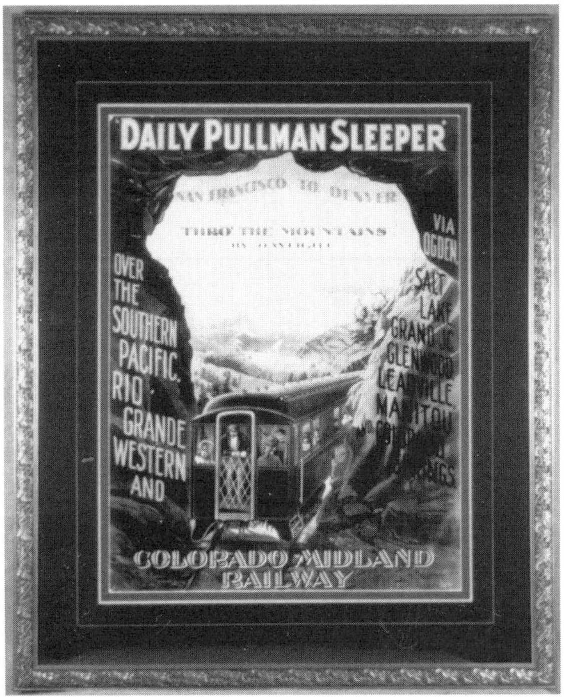

COLORADO MIDLAND-Depot print advertising the "Daily Pullman Sleeper". Measures 22" x 28 framed. Shows rear end of car coming out of tunnel on Ute Pass with destinations listed on either side. Beautiful lithography........... ◆

COLORADO & SOUTHERN-depot photo with color print of the "Gila" wildflower. Mat reads, "Found Along the Line of the Colorado & Southern". Measures 15" x 20" in gold gilt frame 200-250

COLORADO & SOUTHERN-depot photo showing Platte Canon. Chromolithograph by Detroit Photographic. Measures 26 ½" x 31" in original frame. Mat reads, "Picturesque Colorado" on the top and "Platte Canon On the "Colorado Road" Colorado & Southern" on the bottom. 800-850

DENVER & RIO GRANDE RAILROAD-Depot print showing Royal Gorge or Tunnel 2.in Glenwood Canyon. Chromolithograph by Detroit Photographic measures 33 ½" x 29" in original frame with Curecanti logo on mat. Mat reads, "Scenes Along the Line of the Denver & Rio Grande Railroad". 500-550

DENVER & RIO GRANDE RAILROAD-depot advertising poster red on white measures 6 ½" x 20" framed. Shows both the D&RG Curecanti logo and the Rio Grande Southern logo's in each corner. Advertising the Around the Circle excursion. Listing many sights and towns passed along the way. .... ◆

DENVER & SALT LAKE-color photo of Yankee Doodle Lake measures 21" x 25 ½" framed. 100-125

DENVER & SALT LAKE-colorful advertising poster titled "Top O The World TheMoffat Road. Shows lady standing on edge of rock overlooking the valley. Measures 16" X 26" **450-500**

ERIE-depot print showing large color photo of landscape and tracks. Brass plaque on frame reads, "Mile Post 188 Near Susquehanna, PA Erie Railroad". Measures 33" x 24" framed. **100-125**

INDIANAPOLIS & ST LOUIS-The Bee Line Route, colorful advertising broadside. Circa 1880's. Made of heavy cardboard. **400-450**

KANSAS PACIFIC-advertising broadside dated 1879. Blue on white measures 10" x 18". Advertising Colorado and the goldfields. Reverse shows full system map. .... ◆

MAINE CENTRAL-Advertising poster "Something New". Green on beige measures 7" x 19". Dated 1932. Advertising a $5.50 trip to the summit of Mt. Washington. **25-35**

MISSOURI PACIFIC-depot print advertising the "Sunshine Special". Dated 1946 measures 28 1/2" x 23". Brass applied plaque reads, "The Sunshine Special, Serving the Southwest & Mexico, Missouri Pacific Lines". **150-175**

NEW YORK CENTRAL- advertising poster titled "Montreal" Measures 71/2" x 17". Blue on white with things to do and special planned tours **25-35**

NORTHERN PACIFIC- Kentucky Derby advertising poster measures 10" x 13 ½" . Made of heavy card board. Shows jockey on horse with round trip fairs from Seattle & Montana to Louisville, Kentucky. NP logos in each corner **100-125**

RICHMOND & DANVILLE RAILROAD-broadside advertising the Royal Train Service to the Northeast & Northwest. **175-200**

ROCK ISLAND- depot print showing maroon & silver engine pulling passenger train with caption reading "Rock Island Rocket" in original frame. **50-60**

RUTLAND RAILROAD CO.-poster showing rate of $6.50 round trip from Burlington to New York. "Spend A Glorious Week End In the World's Greatest City". 25-35

STEREOVIEWS-are the early day version of a postcard. Purchased by the traveling public as souvenirs of their journey. From every part of the country the ones with train subject matter are very collectible. These can show railroads, towns, mining scenes, landscape shots and a host of other subjects. On the back of the cards you can often find a sticker stating the railroad name and subject matter and photographer. These can be as little as $2.00 to as high as several hundred.

Central Pacific showing Cape Horn with train by Savage 70-80

Central Pacific showing Colfax, California with train by Hart 200-250

Central Pacific showing snow shed interior by Wadkins 60-70

Chicago & Northwestern showing the railroad depot in Council Bluffs, Ia by Everett & Co 100-125

Chicago & Northwestern showing men cutting ice blocks by Elmer & Tenney 30-40

Colorado Central showing Clear Creek Canyon by Gurnseys 20-30

Denver & Rio Grande showing Royal Gorge by Keystone 5-10

Denver & Rio Grande showing Royal Gorge by WH Jackson 35-45

Lehigh Valley railroad showing two set of train tracks dated 1890 5-10

Mt Washington, New Hampshire railroad showing building of water tank 25-35

New York Central showing four tracks with train by Keystone 5-10

Northern Pacific showing grading of Eagle Butte by American Scenery 50-60

Pennsylvania Railroad view showing Onestoga Bridge 5-10

Pikes Peak Cog Railroad winter scene by Keystone 3-5

Union Pacific Denver & Gulf showing Georgetown Loop by WH Jackson 60-70

UNION PACIFIC-WWII patriotic poster "Together Well Win"-"Keep Em Rolling". Measures 22 ½" x 15 ¾". 150-175

UNION PACIFIC Las Vegas advertising poster showing colorful scene of downtown Las Vegas reached via the UP. Measures 24" x 36". 100-125

CHAPTER 28

PLAYING CARDS

The practice of collecting railroad playing cards can be very rewarding. The railroads as with everything used the playing cards to boast their logos and many times to show great scenes found along the line as you traveled. These scenes were proudly photographed and placed on the back of each card. A great way to advertise and what a fun way to play cards while enjoying the scenes shown on each one. Many of the early decks are quite collectible. Decks need to be complete and in good condition. Showing little or no use. They must not have any bends, tears or soiling to command the suggested prices shown here.

AMTRAK-Amtrack logo on white box with orange, blue or red border. Circa 1975..... **5-8**

AMTRAK-Shows color picture across farmlands. Circa 1988 .... **3-5**

AMTRAK- Glenwood Canyon color picture Circa 1987... **5-7**

AMTRAK- Winter-Summer painting circa 1990 .... **3-5**

AT&SF—(Atchison Topeka & Santa Fe) Santa Fe front facing early F-7 diesel engine on red or blue background Circa 1960 .... **10-15**

AT&SF- -(Atchison Topeka & Santa Fe) double deck housed in original box shows one freight & one passenger F unit going through the mountains. Circa 1949 .... **55-65**

AT&SF- -(Atchison Topeka & Santa Fe) Shows colorful scene of two trains in desert circa 1972 .... **10-15**

AT&SF-(Atchison Topeka & Santa Fe) **shows black & white photo of early E unit. Late 40's era** **75-85**

BN- (Burlington Northern) BN logo green on white circa 1975. .... **5-7**

BR- (Burlington Route) shows 5 engines with ghost riders c. 1963 .... **10-15**

BR- (Burlington Route) Zephyrs at Sunset on cover. Silver Zephyr with rust, gray or blue background. C. 1938 .... **30-40**

BR- (Burlington Route) Shows passing Zephyrs with rust, gray or blue background. . **25-35**

CN- (Canadian National) stacked logos on red or blue with white letters. Double deck housed in original case. **20-30**

CZ-(California Zephyr) Cover shows Zephrus Greek God with blue or red border. C. 1949 .... **20-30**

C&O- (Chesapeake & Ohio) Peake the cat in sitting position. Yellow with gold border or black with gold border. Circa 1950's **25-35**

C&O—(Chesapeake & Ohio) Peake the cat, head only. Circa 1970's........................ **25-35**

C&O- - (Chesapeake & Ohio) Sleep Like A Kitten. Tan with gold border circa 1973 .... **25-35**

CM&STPRY- (Chicago Milwaukee & St Paul) Cover shows Mountains & pines with scenes along the line on reverse. C. 1910 .... **40-50**

CM&STPRY- (Chicago Milwaukee & St Paul) Cover shows Old Faithful. C. 1927 .... **40-50**

CMSTP&PRY- (Chicago Milwaukee St Paul & Pacific) Milwaukee Road Hiawatha logo on cover, "Route of the Super Dome Hiawathas and Western Cities Streamliners" Red, blue or green. C. 1957 .... **10-15**

CMSTP&PRY- (Chicago Milwaukee St Paul & Pacific) "The Olympian" orange or blue with red border. **25-35**

C&A- (Chicago & Alton) Girl with sword in oval picture. "Chicago & Alton the Only Way". Circa 1910....................................... **200-250**

C&A- (Chicago & Alton) Logo over "The Line of the Streamliners" with blue, red or Maroon background. Circa 1940's. **100-125**

C&NW- (Chicago & Northwestern) "The 400 Fleet" with yellow diesel engine. Circa 1948 .... **25-35**

C&NW-(Chicago & Northwestern) Blacksmith with two boys & dog, train in background. Circa 1952 .... **25-35**

C&NW-(Chicago & Northwestern) Bathing Beauty waving at passing train. Circa 1952 .... **20-30**

C&NW- (Chicago & Northwestern) Logo with Safety First on green background. Circa 1984 .... **10-15**

CGW-(Chicago Great Western) logo on red or black background. Circa 1960 .... **10-15**

CRI&P-(Chicago Rock Island & Pacific) Great Rock Island Route logo in mirrored immage design. Blue background circa early 1900's.................................... **200-250**

CRI&P-(Chicago Rock Island & Pacific) Rock Island logo over "Route of the Rockets" in red or black. Circa 1950 .... **20-30**

CRI&P-(Chicago Rock Island & Pacific) Small Rock Island logo in center on red background. Circa 1960's.. **5-10**

D&RGRR-(Denver & Rio Grande) Wide deck with Curecanti Logo in center. Blue & white or red & white. Photos on the reverse shows scenes along the line. Circa 1900 ...... **175-200**

D&RGWRR- (Denver & Rio Grande Western) Steam Passenger train in Royal Gorge. Circa 1935 .... **45-55**

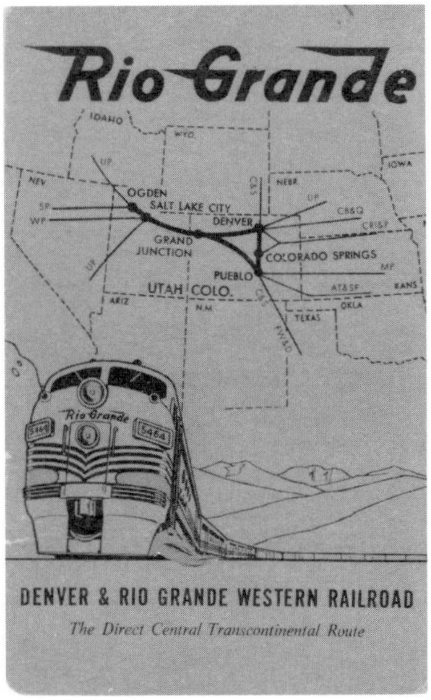

D&RGWRR- (Denver & Rio Grande Western) Shows F Diesel Unit below system map. Black on Silver or Orange. Circa 1950's......... **25-35**

D&RGWRR- (Denver & Rio Grande Western) Durango & Silverton steam train. Circa 1965 .... **10-15**

D&RGWRR-(Denver & Rio Grande Western) Mainline Through the Rockies logo in red or yellow box. Circa 1960. .... **20-30**

D&SLRR- (Denver & Salt Lake) Shows Girl on edge of cliff waving. Circa 1915 ... **175-200**

DM&IR- (Duluth Missabe & Iron Range) Logo on cover with Safety First. Red with blue border. Circa 1960 .... **5-10**

DM&IR- (Duluth Missabe & Iron Range) Shows engine 222 under "Ship Missabe". Circa 1970's **10-15**

EJ&E-(Elgin Joliet & Eastern) shows Steel Mills with green or red border. Colorful. Circa 1925 .... **25-35**

ERIE- shows Diesel train through bottom of Erie Logo. Yellow & blue circa 1955 .... **20-30**

FRED HARVEY- Indians with train in background. Circa 1915. .... **75-85**

FRED HARVEY- Hopi Indian boy sitting on ladder. Circa 1910 .... **200-250**

FRED HARVEY- Shows Indian symbol in circle. Tan & red. Circa 1910 .... **200-250**

FRISCO-(St. Louis San Francisco) White logo on red or blue cards circa 1955............. **10-15**

FRISCO—(St. Louis San Francisco) Double deck housed in velveteen case. **25-35**

FRISCO—(St. Louis San Francisco) Diesel engine below Frisco Lines logo with blue or green background Circa 1945 .... **35-45**

FRISCO- -(St. Louis San Francisco) gold Frisco logo on red or blue background housed in velveteen slipbox. **8-12**

GNRY-(Great Northern) Buckskin Pinto Woman with red border circa 1962....... **10-15**

GNRY-(Great Northern) Chief Middle Rider with blue border. Circa 1962 .... **35-45**

GNRY-(Great Northern) Double deck housing the two previous listings **75-85**

GNRY- (Great Northern) Julia Wades in the Water with blue border. Circa 1939 ...... **35-45**

GNRY- (Great Northern) Steam engine #1408, "Great Northern Railway" on cow catcher. Circa 1905 .... **250-300**

GNRY- (Great Northern) Shows two front facing goat logos on red or blue background **100-125**

ICRR- (Illinois Central) Shows Diesel Engine above "Panama Limited" with logo below. Circa 1940 .... **45-55**

ICRR-(Illinois Central) Shows Diesel Engine above "City of Miami" with logo top right corner. Circa 1940 .... **150-175**

ICRR- (Illinois Central) Shows Chicago Train Yard, with cardboard slip cover advertising the Panama Limited. Circa 1953 .... **30-40**

KCS- (Kansas City Southern) logo in center in white on red background **10-15**

KCS- (Kansas City Southern) Logo over "Route of the Southern Belle". Tan or green circa 1951. .... **25-35**

KCS- (Kansas City Southern) Logo over with train over "Southern Belle". Red or blue circa 1953 .... **25-35**

L&N- (Louisville & Nashville) 100th Anniversary with 4 trains on card. Circa 1950 .... **30-40**

L&N- S(Louisville & Nashville) hows "The General" steam engine next to Diesel engine. Circa 1962 .... **5-10**

L&N-(Louisville & Nashville) Shows "The General" steam engine next to Diesel engine with Dixie Line Logo. **10-15**

L&N-(Louisville & Nashville) Double deck housed in original velveteen box with two decks listed above. **25-35**

MAINE CENTRAL- Shows large MC logo incenter with green or yellow background. C. 1958 .... **25-35**

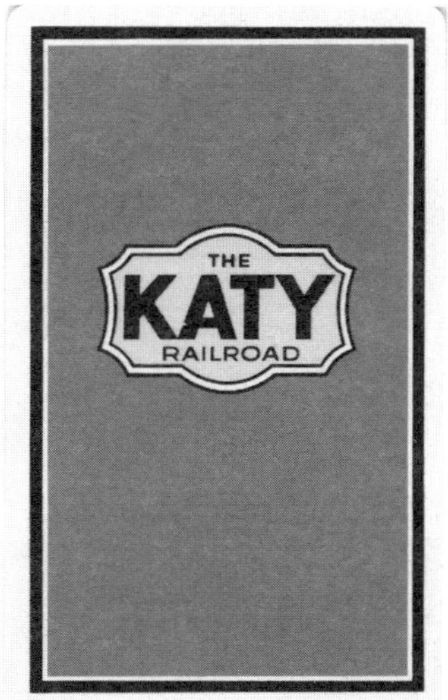

MKT-(Missouri Kansas & Texas) shows black letters on yellow logo in center with red background **10-15**

MKT-(Missouri Kansas & Texas) Has MKT logo with three vertical lines down the center. Blue logo circa 1966 .... **20-30**

MKT-(Missouri Kansas & Texas) Shows girl holding flowers and reads, "Count on Katy". Circa 1965 .... **20-30**

MP- (Missouri Pacific) Has red buzz saw logo in center on white card. **5-10**

MP- (Missouri Pacific) Modern MP logo shows eagle in circle above "MO-PAC" on red, blue orange or light blue cards. Circa 1975 .... **15-20**

MP- (Missouri Pacific) Steam engine on tracks above "Sunshine Special" with logo bottom right corner. Circa 1930 .... **125-150**

MP-(Missouri Pacific) One steam & one diesel engine side by side circa 1937 .... **125-150**

MONON-(Chicago Indianapolis & Louisville) shows red & silver engine on bridge. Circa 1948 .... **25-35**

MONON- -(Chicago Indianapolis & Louisville) yellow & black engine along hillside. Circa 1948 .... **25-35**

MONON- -(Chicago Indianapolis & Louisville) double deck with above cards in velveteen box with Monon logo in gold............... **55-65**

NICKLE PLATE-(New York Chicago & St. Louis) Nickel Plate Road logo on red blue or black background. Circa 1950................. **5-10**

NYNH&H-(New York New Haven & Hartford) double deck housed in original case with logo & 4 diesel engines as design on cards. Red or blue circa 1954 .... **30-40**

NYNH&H- (New York New Haven & Hartford) single deck with logo & 4 diesel engines on red or blue cards **10-15**

NYC- (New York Central) Shows 20th Century Limited engine running next to water. Pink border, circa 1940 .... **100-125**

NYC-"(New York Central) The Pacemaker Famous Deluxe Coach Train" over engines. Blue border. Circa 1941 .... **75-85**

NYC-(New York Central) Shows colorful scene of New York Skyline. Circa 1961 .... **10-15**

NP- (Northern Pacific) Yellowstone Park Line logo on vertical lines with red or black background. Circa 1940 .... **15-20**

NP-(Northern Pacific) Monad logo on card with diagonal lines on black or orange background. Circa 1950 .... **15-20**

PRR-(Pennsylvania RR) red & gold logo in center of card with white background **5-10**

PRR-(Pennsylvania RR) Colorful scene with engines reads, "Serving the Nation" over Pennsylvania Railroad. Circa 1944 .... **25-35**

PRR (Pennsylvania RR) -Scene on Horseshoe Curve with gold border. Circa 1950 ..... **15-20**

PC-(Penn Central) Logo in center on green or white. Circa 1968 .... **5-10**

P&LE-(Pittsburgh & Lake Erie) Intertwined logo in center of red or blue cards with gold border. Circa 1977 .... **10-15**

PULLMAN-Bridge playing cards complete with instructions. **5-10**

QA&P-(Quanah Acme & Pacific) Shows Chief quanah "Last of the Commanches". Double deck with red or blue border **75-85**

STL&SW- (St. Louis & Southwestern) Cotton Belt Route logo on cards showing small black girl eating watermelon. Circa 1903 .. **250-300**

STL&SW-(St. Louis & Southwestern) Shows SSW logo on red & white cards circa 1983 .... **5-10**

SCL-(Seaboard Coast Line) Shows red, white & blue engine 1776 celebrating the bicentennial. Circa 1976 .... **10-15**

SOO LINE-(Minneapolis St. Paul & Sault Ste. Marie) Shows red & white caboose circa 1960 .... **20-30**

SOO LINE—(Minneapolis St. Paul & Sault Ste. Marie) Shows dam spillway with logo. Circa 1955 .... **10-15**

SOO LINE- -(Minneapolis St. Paul & Sault Ste. Marie) Centennial deck 1883-1983 in red & gold. **10-15**

SP-(Southern Pacific) Shows colorful Daylight steam engine train on wide souvenir deck. Circa 1945 .... **25-35**

SP-(Southern Pacific) Shows colorful Daylight diesel engine crossing bridge on wide souvenir deck. Circa 1950 .... **25-35**

UP-(Union Pacific) Centennial double deck 1869-1969 housed in original tin box. Circa 1987 .... **15-20**

UP-(Union Pacific) Shows "The Challenger" yellow diesel engine with Overland Shield logo. Circa 1940 .... **75-85**

UP-(Union Pacific) Shows Jackson Lake & the Tetons. Circa 1960 .... **5-10**

UP-(Union Pacific) "Driving of the Golden Spike", circa 1969 .... **5-10**

UP-(Union Pacific) Modern Shield logo on red or blue deck. Circa 1980 .... **5-8**

UP-(Union Pacific) Overland Limitied "Evening on the Great Salt Lake" with scenes along the line on reverse. Circa 1915 .... **125-150**

WABASH-Shows diesel Bluebird Engine 1002 coming around bend with logo Circa 1951 .... **50-60**

WP&Y-(White Pass & Yukon) Wide souvenir deck showing logo on card in red & blue. Circa 1900 .... **100-125**

CHAPTER 29

TIMETABLES

The next time you pick up a free brochure or timetable think about the future and take good care of it. Who would have thought that something that was mass produced would have become a valuable collectible. Collecting timetables can be a great hobby. The early versions can be found with beautiful ornate covers which were often times like great works of art. The information inside brings back great memories of those stations along the way that are in many cases long gone now. Early timetables were packed full of not only the various departure times but also with great advertising and information on fine hotels, steamship companies and things to do along the travel route. Timetables must be in good to excellent condition. The folds tend to become brittle so they must be strong & not torn, soiled or otherwise altered from their original state to command the suggested prices shown here.

ALASKA RAILROAD-measures 3" x 6" with dated 1957 .... **10-15**

ALTON RAILROAD- dated 1939 with 34 pages **10-15**

ATLANTIC COAST LINE- dated May 1, 1928 with logo on cover and 72 pages .. **25-35**

BALTIMORE & OHIO RR- dated September 1902 with 54 pages **40-50**

BALTIMORE & OHIO RR- dated December 1936 with 102 pages **15-20**

BALTIMORE & OHIO RR-dated July 1946 with 32 pages **10-15**

BELFAST & MOOSEHEAD LAKE RR- dated May 1944 pocket size timetable with two panels and 4 pages **15-20**

BOSTON & ALBANY RR- dated 1904 small pocket timetable for Suburban trains with 6 panels. **15-20**

BOSTON & MAINE RR- dated September 1915 Fitchburg Division **20-25**

BOSTON & MAINE RR- dated April 1924 with 51 pages **15-20**

BOSTON & MAINE RR- dated September 1939 with 124 pages **10-15**

BURLINGTON & MISSOURI RIVER RAILROAD- dated July 1892 with 29 pages **125-150**

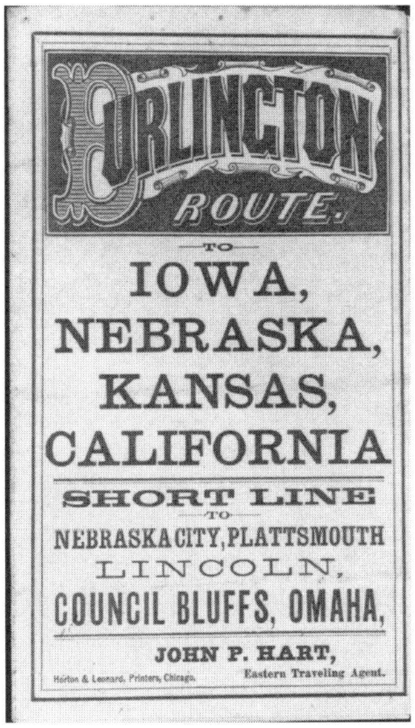

BURLINGTON ROUTE- dated November 27, 1870. Eight panels unfold to reveal system map showing B&MRRR as well **200-225**

BURLINGTON ROUTE- November 1897 46 pages with advertising & timetables **75-85**

BURLINGTON ROUTE- December 1916 with 49 pages **20-25**

BURLINGTON ROUTE-January-April 1939 "Everywhere West" on cover. With 36 pages **10-15**

BURLINGTON ROUTE- October 1962 with 25 pages **1-5**

CANADIAN PACIFIC- dated June 1918. With 49 pages **10-15**

CANADIAN PACIFIC- dated June 1926 Eastern Lines **5-10**

CHESAPEAKE & OHIO RR- dated July 20, 1947 unfolds to reveal system map........ **10-15**

CHICAGO & ALTON RR- dated 1916 with 8 panels opens to reveal system map...... **15-20**

CHICAGO & ALTON RR- Dated August September 1929 with 46 pages **15-20**

CHICAGO & ALTON RR- dated March 1931. 46 pages **10-15**

CHICAGO & NORTHWESTERN RR- dated 1906 with 26 pages of photos and timetables **20-25**

CHICAGO & NORTHWESTERN RR- dated May 1924 with photos & timetables **15-20**

CHICAGO BURLINGTON & QUINCY- dated 1870 with 8 panels & ornate cover advertising, "Kansas, Colorado, Nebraska, Utah, Montana, Idaho, Nevada, California & Oregon" destinations. **250-300**

CHICAGO INDIANAPOLIS & LOUISVILLE RR- dated 1927 "Monon Route" logo on cover. 2 panels with 14 pages........... **20-30**

CHICAGO MILWAUKEE & ST PAUL RY- dated August 1905 with 2 panels and 38 pages, "Colorful cover boasting "7000 Miles Of Thoroughly Equipped Road" **65-75**

CHICAGO MILWAUKEE ST PAUL & PACIFIC RY- dated May 1938 foled two panel with 46 pages.......................... **15-20**

CHICAGO MILWAUKEE ST PAUL & PACIFIC RY- dated May-June 1939 with 46 pages **10-15**

CHICAGO MILWAUKEE ST PAUL & PACIFIC RY- dated September 1948 with 42 pages **5-10**

COLORADO & SOUTHERN RY- dated August 1905 with large blue C&S logo on red cover **150-175**

COLORADO & SOUTHERN RY- dated November 1927 with 30 pages **25-35**

DELAWARE & HUDSON- dated 1926 with 19 pages and 2 panels. "Route of the Montreal Limited" **15-20**

DELAWARE & HUDSON- dated 1930 with 15 pages and 2 panels. **10-15**

DELAWARE LACKAWANNA & WESTERN- Dated January 1920 with 30 pages **15-20**

DENVER & RIO GRANDE RR- dated November 1887 booklet showing advertising, pictures & text. 93 pages **90-100**

JULY, 1910.
DENVER & RIO GRANDE SYSTEM
The Scenic Line of the World

DENVER & RIO GRANDE RR- dated July 1910 with 38 pages **45-55**

DENVER & RIO GRANDE RR-dated July-August 1912 with 40 pages **40-50**

DENVER & RIO GRANDE WESTERN RR- dated June 12, 1938 with 2 panels and 54 pages **10-15**

DENVER & RIO GRANDE WESTERN RR- dated February 1, 1953 with 2 panels and 16 pages **5-10**

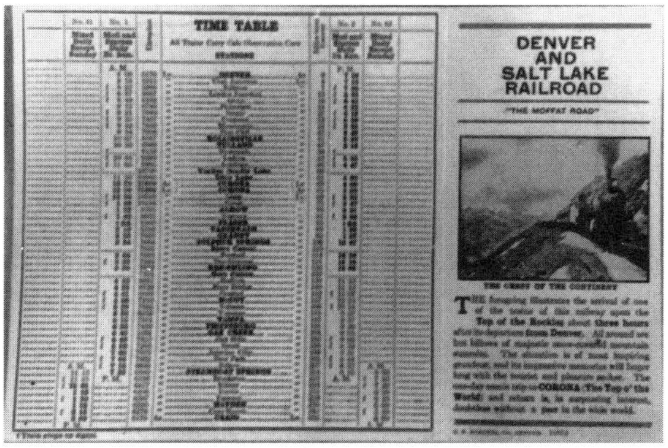

DENVER & SALT LAKE RY- dated 1928 "The Moffat Road" small pocket timetable with 4 panels **50-60**

DENVER & SALT LAKE RY- dated 1936 "The Moffat Road" small pocket timetable with 4 panels **35-45**

DENVER BOULDER & WESTERN RY- dated 1909 timetable and brochure with color photos of wildflowers and text. **125-150**

ERIE RR- dated August 1893 with 40 pages and photos **45-55**

ERIE RR- dated July 1910 "Orange Branch & Caldwell Branch" with 4 panels. **35-45**

FORT DODGE DES MOINES & SOUTHERN- dated 1948 with 15 pages & colorful red & yellow cover **10-15**

GRAND TRUNK RY- dated July 1904 with 59 pages and two panels **30-40**

GRAND TRUCK RY- dated 1920 with 81 pages & 3 panels with photos & text..... **10-15**

GREAT NORTHERN- dated 1894 with 10 panels opens to reveal system map....... **90-100**

GREAT NORTHERN- dated June 1918 with 4 panels and 62 pages **35-45**

GREAT NORTHERN- dated Spring 1967 with 28 pages... **1-5**

GULF MOBILE & OHIO- dated Winter Spring 1957 with 2 panels **5-10**

HOCKING VALLEY- dated December 1906 with 2 panels and 23 pages brochure and timetable... **70-80**

ILLINOIS CENTRAL RR- dated January 1894 with 48 pages and ornate cover **50-60**

ILLINOIS CENTRAL RR- dated January 1923 with 2 panels and 70 pages **10-15**

ILLINOIS CENTRAL RR- dated 1944 with 2 panels & 62 pages **5-10**

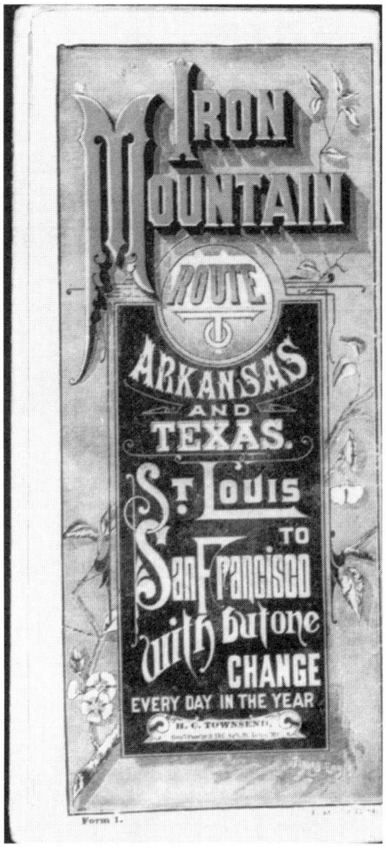

IRON MOUNTAIN ROUTE- dated 1884 timetable & brochure with 8 panels. Opens to reveal system map. Ornate cover **150-175**

LEHIGH VALLEY RR- dated July 25, 1916 with 2 panels and 19 pages **20-30**

LEHIGH VALLEY RR- dated May 8 1927 "Route of the Black Diamond" 2 panels with 19 pages **15-20**

LOUISVILLE & NASHVILLE- dated August 1901 with fancy cover & 36 pages **50-60**

LOUISVILLE & NASHVILLE- dated December 1950 with 24 pages **5-10**

MAINE CENTRAL- dated June 25, 1934 with 15 pages **10-15**

MAINE CENTRAL-dated March 1950 with 15 pages and two panels **5-10**

MINNEAPOLIS ST PAUL & SAULT STE.MARIE RY CO-"SOO LINE" dated June 1932. Two folded panels with 44 pages **20-30**

MISSOURI KANSAS & TEXAS- dated July-August 1907 with 4 panels and 27 pages **35-45**

MT. WASHINGTON RY- dated 1915 with 8 pages of pictures & history as well as timetable **15-20**

MISSOURI PACIFIC- dated June 1929 with 4 panels and 84 pages **15-20**

MISSOURI PACIFIC- dated September 1936 with 4 panels and 52 pages **10-15**

NASHVILLE CHATTANOOGA & ST LOUIS- dated December 1950 with 20 pages **10-15**

NEW YORK CENTRAL LINES- "Big Four" dated February 1910 with 15 pages **25-35**

NEW YORK CENTRAL- Dated October 1919 "Buffalo & West Divisions". 10 panels **20-30**

NEW YORK CENTRAL- Dated June 1933 with 62 pages **10-15**

NEW YORK CENTRAL-dated March 1965 with 16 pages **1-5**

NEW YORK CENTRAL & HUDSON RIVER RR- dated 1914 timetable and brochure with pictures and text **40-50**

NEW YORK CENTRAL & HUDSON RIVER RR-dated 1925 timetable and brochure with pictures & text **20-30**

NEW YORK CHICAGO & ST LOUIS- (Nickle Plate) dated 1895 timetable and brochure with 8 panels that open to reveal system map **50-60**

NICKEL PLATE – dated February 1909 public timetable with 30 pages of pictures & text as well **50-60**

NICKEL PLATE-dated January 1965 public timetable with 16 pages **1-5**

NORTHERN PACIFIC- dated 1897 with 9 panels opens to reveal system map **90-100**

NORTHERN PACIFIC-Spring 1883 with 10 panels opens to reveal system map..... **250-300**

NORTHERN PACIFIC-dated 1892 with approximately 27 pages with full color map inside. Yellow highlights shows Old Faithful on cover **125-150**

NORTHERN PACIFIC- dated December-January 1920 with 80 pages **20-25**

NORTHWESTERN PACIFIC-dated September 1956 with 4 pages **5-10**

OHIO & MISSISSIPPI RY- dated August 1885. Panels open to reveal system map **100-125**

OREGON SHORT LINE- dated May 1911. 12 pages **50-60**

PENNSYLVANIA RR dated May 28, 1919 with 8 folded panels revealing system map **20-30**

PENNSYLVANIA RR- dated June 1938 with 84 pages of text photos &timetables...... **15-20**

PIKES PEAK BY RAIL- dated 1908 public timetable & brochure **10-15**

QUEEN & CRESCENT ROUTE- dated 1914 with 3 panels of pictures & text............ **25-35**

READING RR- dated September 1925 with 20 pages **15-20**

ROCK ISLAND RR- dated August 1899 with 54 pages **90-100**

ROCK ISLAND RR- dated June 1911 with 35 pages **40-50**

ROCK ISLAND RR- dated November 1936 with 35 pages **15-20**

ROCK ISLAND RR- dated May 1957, black & white logo on cover **5-10**

RUTLAND & BURLINGTON- dated 1851 small double sided pocket timetable **70-80**

RUTLAND RR- dated September 1932 with 19 pages. Cover shows Hudson River, Green Mountain & Lake Champlain **20-25**

RUTLAND RR-dated 1945 with 19 pages. Two folded panels **15-20**

SANTA FE-dated April 1, 1902. Blue on white with 70 pages & two folded panels. Photos, text and system map **65-75**

SANTA FE- dated March 20, 1913 with 96 pages & two panels. **50-60**

SANTA FE- dated April 15, 1920 with two panels & 96 pages. **20-25**

SANTA FE ROUTE- dated March 10, 1901 with two panels & 62 pages **125-150**

SEABOARD AIRLINE- dated May 1898 with 32 pages & ornate cover **100-125**

SEABOARD AIRLINE- dated November 22, 1938 with 70 pages **10-15**

SOUTHERN RY- dated June 1942 with 4 panels & 35 pages **15-20**

SOUTHERN PACIFIC-dated 1894 with 20 pages and colorful yellow & black cover. Opens to reveal map of Railroad & Steamship lines **200-250**

SOUTHERN PACIFIC- dated January 1912 with 2 panels and 35 pages **30-35**

SOUTHERN PACIFIC- dated October 1933 with 2 panels & 28 pages **15-20**

SOUTHERN PACIFIC- dated 1940 with 2 panels & 23 pages **10-15**

TEXAS & PACIFIC RY- dated 1894 with 8 panels open to reveal system map **125-150**

TEXAS & PACIFIC RY- dated 1908 with 9 panels opens to reveal system map **50-60**

UNION PACIFIC & CENTRAL PACIFIC- dated 1881 "The Great American Overland Route" with 10 panels that open to reveal system map **350-400**

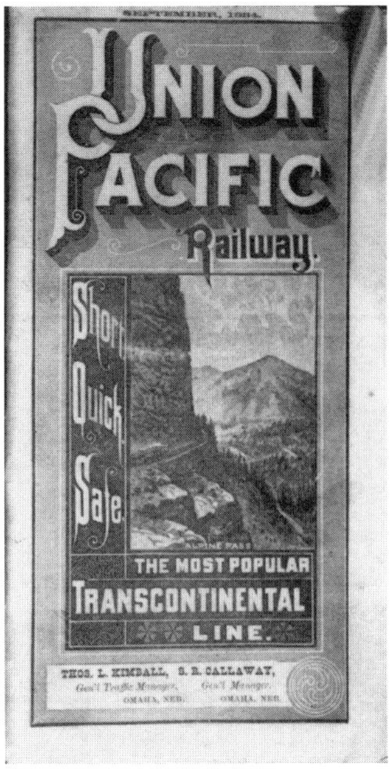

UNION PACIFIC- dated 1884 cover shows "Alpine Pass". 8 panel design **300-350**

UNION PACIFIC-dated September 1887 with 8 panels, opens to reveal system map.... **250-300**

UNION PACIFIC- dated 1897 4th edition "The Pathfinder" brochure & timetable with 80 pages **100-125**

UNION PACIFIC-dated May 1899 with 60 pages of timetables, text & pictures with ornate blue cover **125-150**

UNION PACIFIC dated June 12, 1938 with 63 pages **10-15**

UNION PACIFIC dated February 1944 for the "Diamond Anniversary", timetable ... **5-10**

WABASH- dated May 1903 with 18 panels that open to reveal colorful system map **40-50**

WABASH- dated 1912 with 52 pages of pictures & text as well as timetable **20-30**

WEST PENNSYLVANIA RR- dated 1951 with 2 panels **10-15**

UTAH & IDAHO CENTRAL RR- dated 1939 with 4 panels **30-35**

EMPLOYEE TIMETABLES

The employee timetables were issued strictly to the employees and gave them the information needed to get the traveling passengers to and from their selected destinations. These differ from the public timetables as they are full of the technical information only of interest to the folks operating the trains. The earlier timetables were referred to as saddle blanket style. These tend to be the most collectible. Below are photos of the different styles. Remember as with their public cousins these must also be in good to excellent condition with no tears or stains to command the prices suggested here. It is often times much harder to find these in good condition as the employees tended to use them much more than the traveling public.

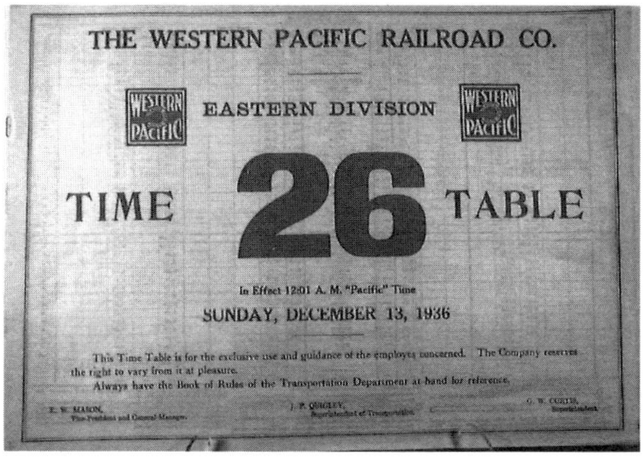

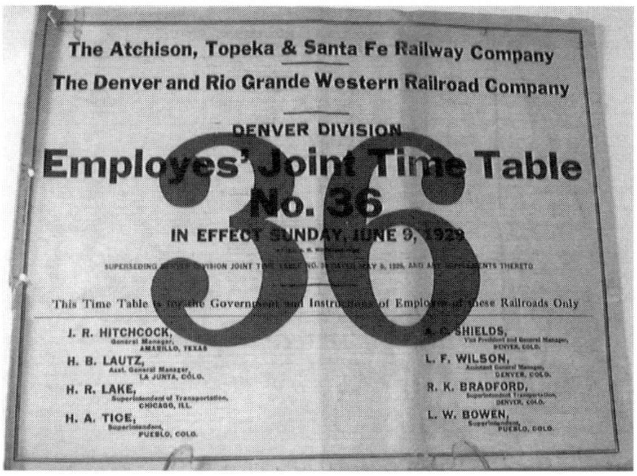

EMPLOYEE TIMETABLES - SADDLE BLANKET STYLE MEASURES 15"X12"

MODERN ISSUE EMPLOYEE TIMETABLE

ALABAMA GREAT SOUTHERN- dated May 31, 1908 #44 .... **45-55**

ATCHISON TOPEKA & SANTA FE RR- dated April 29, 1883. "Las Vegas Division" #41. Saddle blanket style **85-95**

ATCHISON TOPEKA & SANTA FE RR- dated December 17, 1893 "Colorado Midland Division" timetable #58. Saddle blanket style **150-175**

ATCHISON TOPEKA & SANTA FE RR- dated June 8, 1969 #12 with 15 pages, "Albuquerque Division" **5-10**

ATCHISON TOPEKA & SANTA FE/ DENVER & RIO GRANDE WESTERN- joint timetable #84 dated November 11, 1945 with 12 pages **10-15**

BOSTON & MAINE- dated September 29, 1929 timetable #5 .... **15-20**

BOSTON & MAINE- dated September 25, 1938 timetable #26 with 12 pages......... **10-15**

BURLINGTON & MISSOURI RIVER RR IN NEBRASKA- dated August 25, 1888. Timetable #97 .... **100-125**

BURLINGTON NORTHERN- dated in the 70's & 80's all divisions **5-10**

CARSON & COLORADO dated January 1, 1882 timetable #7. Saddle blanket style **175-200**

CEDAR RAPIDS & IOWA CITY RY- timetable #29 dated October 12, 1937 .... **10-15**

CENTRAL VERMONT- dated December 20, 1875 measures 8 ½" x 11" with 4 pages **100-125**

CENTRAL VERMONT- timetable #44 dated June 27, 1915 for the Southern Division. Saddle blanket style.. **20-30**

CHICAGO & ALTON RR- timetable #30 dated June 9, 1929 .... **15-20**

CHICAGO GREAT WESTERN- timetable #11A. Minnesota Division **15-20**

CHICAGO MILWAUKEE ST PAUL & PACIFIC- 1970's & 80's most divisions **5-10**

CHICAGO ROCK ISLAND & PACIFIC RY- timetable #22, Eastern Division, dated April 7 1895 .... **50-60**

CHICAGO ROCK ISLAND & PACIFIC RY- timetable #4A Colorado Division dated March 25, 1906 .... **40-50**

CHICAGO ROCK ISLAND & PACIFIC RY- timetable #27, St Louis Division dated 1918 .... **25-35**

CHICAGO ROCK ISLAND & PACIFIC RY- timetable #5, Missouri Kansas Division dated February 13, 1938 .... **15-20**

CHICAGO ROCK ISLAND & PACIFIC/ ROCK ISLAND – 1970's most division **5-10**

CHICAGO ST PAUL MINNEAPOLIS & OMAHA RY- timetable #158 dated October 21, 1934 .... **10-15**

DENVER & RIO GRANDE RR- timetable #57 dated March 25, 1900. All Divisions **100-125**

DENVER & RIO GRANDE WESTERN RR- Salida Division #118 dated June 28, 1928 .... **75-85**

DENVER & RIO GRANDE WESTERN RR- timetable #114 dated June 17, 1928 Alamosa Division, shows RGSRR. **200-225**

DENVER & RIO GRANDE WESTERN RR- timetable #117 Alamosa Division/June 1928 /no RGSRR **125-150**

DENVER & RIO GRANDE WESTERN RR- timetable #4 dated March 20, 1949 with 10 pages **15-20**

DENVER & RIO GRANDE WESTERN RR- 1970's & 1980's most divisions **5-10**

DENVER & SALT LAKE RR- dated June 14, 1934 timetable #33 saddle blanket style ... **65-75**

FITCHBURG RR- dated 1881 for the Boston, Mainroad & Watertown Branch **20-30**

FORT DODGE DES MOINES & SOUTHERN- timetable #46 dated November 21, 1954 .... **10-15**

FORT WORTH & DENVER CITY RY- timetable #33 system timetable dated May 28, 1899 .... **75-85**

GARDEN CITY, GULF & NORTHERN RY- timetable #35 dated June 11, 1911 .... **75-85**

GREAT NORTHERN- timetable #44 dated May 23, 1948 for the Cascade Division **10-15**

GREAT NORTHERN- timetable #380 for the Willmar Division dated October 30, 1966 .... **5-10**

INDIANA RR- timetable #301 dated September 27, 1931. Poster style measures 16" x 19" for the Indianapolis & Terre Haute Divisions **35-45**

LIGONIER VALLEY RR- timetable #28 dated September 1938 .... **40-50**

LONG ISLAND RR- timetable dated May 20, 1968 .... **5-10**

MAINE CENTRAL- timetable #14 dated September 29, 1929 Mountain Division **35-45**

MIDLAND TERMINAL- timetable #37 dated March 30, 1941 .... **70-80**

NASHVILLE CHATTANOOGA & ST.LOUIS RY- dated October 24, 1949 for the Paducah & Memphis Division **20-30**

NEW YORK CENTRAL RR CO.- timetable #50 dated September 24, 1939 for the "River Division" **15-20**

OGDENSBURG & LAKE CHAMPLAIN- timetable #9 dated June 25, 1899 .... **20-30**

PECOS RIVER RR- timetable #1 dated December 8, 1912 .... **60-70**

RIO GRANDE JUNCTION- timetable #92 dated October 21, 1912 saddle blanket style **175-200**

RIO GRANDE SOUTHERN – timetable #4 dated November 26, 1890. Measures 6" x 9 ½". Two pages. **700-750**

RIO GRANDE SOUTHERN- timetable #63 dated May 2, 1915 .... **225-250**

RIO GRANDE SOUTHERN- timetable 5 dated February 18, 1948 .... **50-60**

SOO LINE- timetable #2 dated April 27, 1986 system timetable **3-5**

SOUTHERN PACIFIC- timetable #176 dated June 17, 1940 for the LA Division **10-15**

SOUTHERN PACIFIC- 1970's to 1980's most divisions **3-5**

ST LOUIS ROCKY MOUNTAIN & PACIFIC RY CO.- timetable #1 dated October 5, 1913 .... **90-100**

UNION PACIFIC- timetable #29 for the Wyoming Division dated September 21, 1958 **5-10**

UNION PACIFIC- 1970's to 1980's most divisions **3-5**

WESTERN PACIFIC- timetable #26 dated 1936 .... **20-30**

WHITE PASS & YUKON- timetable #151 dated October 26, 1951 .... **10-15**

WICHITA NORTHWESTERN RR- timetable #30 dated January 1939 .... **35-45**

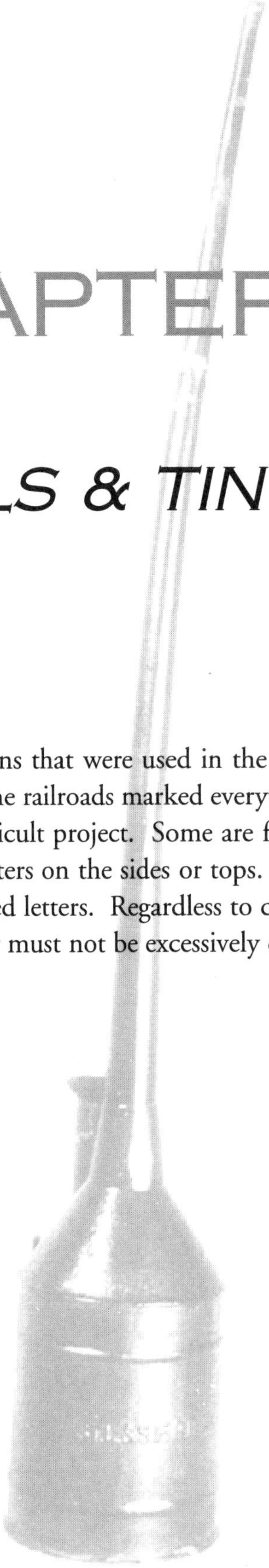

CHAPTER 30

TOOLS & TINWARE

Collecting the various tools and cans that were used in the yards and on the trains can be very fulfilling yet inexpensive hobby. The railroads marked everything as we have discussed so finding marked cans and tools is not a difficult project. Some are found stamped on the bottom of the item and also found with raised letters on the sides or tops. Tools are stamped with initials and again many can be found with raised letters. Regardless to command the suggested prices shown here they must be marked and they must not be excessively dented or rusted.

AT&SFRR-(Atchison Topeka & Santa Fe) embossed on side of cone shaped torch **60-70**

AT&SFRY-(Atchison Topeka & Santa Fe) stamped on bottom of cone shaped torch **20-30**

AT&SFRY—(Atchison Topeka & Santa Fe) marked on side of 14 ½" tall oiler. Mfg. J.Urbana **50-60**

AT&SF—(Atchison Topeka & Santa Fe) stamped on 17" long chisel **5-10**

AT&SF—(Atchison Topeka & Santa Fe) bottom stamped on talo pot **10-15**

AT&SFRY- -(Atchison Topeka & Santa Fe) stamped on the side of a one gallon kerosene can **10-15**

B&ORR- (Baltimore & Ohio) stamped on signal oil can. Small ½ gallon size. **30-40**

B&MRR- (Boston & Maine) side marked on ½ gallon size kerosene can. **10-15**

B&MRR- (Boston & Maine) cast on side of long handled torch. **20-30**

CNR-(Canadian National) cast on side of long handled torch **20-30**

C OF G A RR- (Central of Georgia) stamped on blade of hatchet. Wood handle. **15-20**

C&NWRYCO-(Chicago & Northwestern) stamped on side of 18 ½" "S" shaped double headed wrench **10-15**

CB&Q- (Chicago Burlington & Quincy) stamped on 12" monkey wrench **10-15**

CB&Q- (Chicago Burlington & Quincy) cast on side of 18" brass tank car wrench **40-50**

CB&QRR- (Chicago Burlington & Quincy) stamped on base of wood handle attached to shovel. **20-30**

CB&QRR CO-(Chicago Burlington & Quincy) on applied plate attached to top of 2 gallon kersene can **20-30**

CB&QRR CO-(Chicago Burlington & Quincy) stamped on small tin funnel ... **20-30**

CGWRR-(Chicago Great Western) stamped on shovel. Mfg. Bulldog **30-40**

CM&PSRY- (Chicago Milwaukee & Puget Sound) stamped on side of chisel. No manufacturer **10-15**

CM&PSRY- (Chicago Milwaukee & Puget Sound) stamped on side of 9" "S" shaped wrench **20-30**

CM&PSRY- (Chicago Milwaukee & Puget Sound) 5 gallon water can. With screw top lid. **25-35**

CMSTP&PRR- (Chicago Milwaukee St Paul & Pacific) stamped on side of one gallon water can **10-15**

CMSTP&PRR-(Chicago Milwaukee St Paul & Pacific) side marked on tin talo pot **20-30**

CMSTP&PRR- (Chicago Milwaukee St Paul & Pacific) stamped on side of iron chisel **10-15**

CRI&PRY-(Chicago Rock Island & Pacific) stamped on bottom of talo pot. Mfg. Eagle **20-30**

CRI&P- (Chicago Rock Island & Pacific) stamped on small 8" pipe wrench **15-20**

CRI&PRY-(Chicago Rock Island & Pacific) cast on bottom of long handle torch. Mfg. General Mfg. Co. **25-35**

C&SRY- (Colorado & Southern) cast on side of two gallon water can **25-35**

C&S-(Colorado & Southern) stamped on both ends of double headed "S" wrench **20-30**

C&SRY-(Colorado & Southern) cast on side of tallow pot. Mfg. Handlan St. Louis **35-45**

CMRY-(Colorado Midland) stamped on head of sledge hammer. **50-60**

D&SLRR-(Denver & Salt Lake) stamped on side of small oil can with 8" spout **50-60**

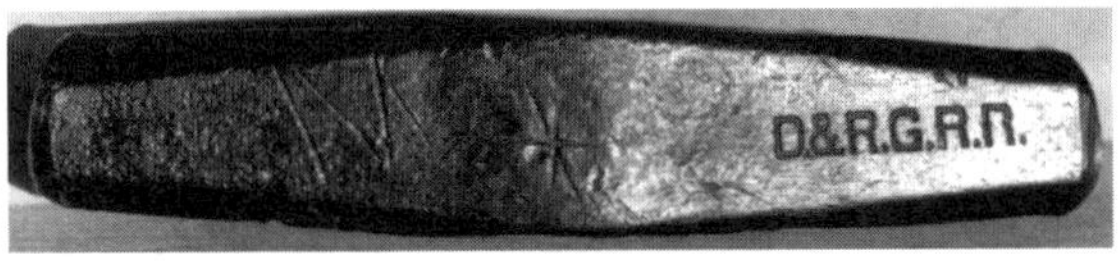

D&RG-(Denver & Rio Grande) stamped on 8" long brass chisel. **10-15**

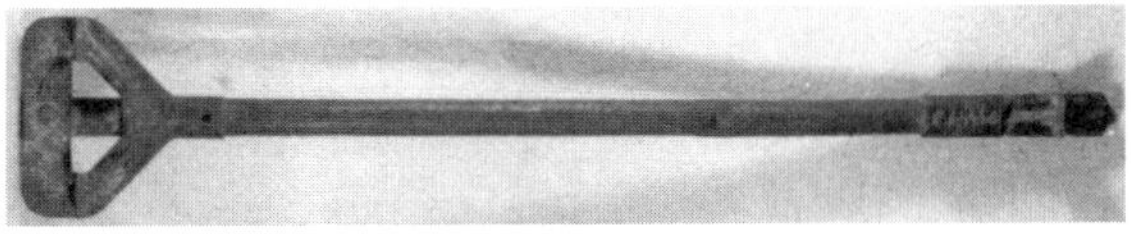

D&RG-(Denver & Rio Grande) cast on both ends of cast iron track gauge measures 36" wide for narrow gauge track. **250-300**

D&RGRR-(Denver & Rio Grande) embossed on side of 2 gallon bucket **25-35**

D&RGRR-(Denver & Rio Grande) stamped on bottom of sledge hammer **20-30**

D&RGW- (Denver & Rio Grande Western) embossed on applied plate on side of 2 gallon size water can **30-40**

EJ&ERYCO-(Elgin Joliet & Eastern) bottom marked on talo pot **20-30**

FTW&DCRR-(Ft Worth & Denver City) stamped on "S" shaped 20" double handled wrench **20-30**

GNRY-(Great Northern) stamped on hammer with wood handle. Mfg. Briarwood **15-20**

GNRY--(Great Northern) switch stand broom with ice scrapper on one end. **35-45**

GNRY—(Great Northern) cast on top of 12" tall water can 15-20

GNRY—(Great Northern) cast on bottom of kerosene can **10-15**

GNRY—(Great Northern) top marked on 12 " tall water can. **15-20**

G.N.R.- -(Great Northern) side marked on cone shaped torch **45-50**

GC&SF-(Gulf Colorado & Santa Fe) side marked on applied plate on side of cone shaped torch **60-70**

ICRR- (Illinois Central) side marked on tall oiler **40-50**

ICRR-(Illinois Central) embossed on shoulder of 2 gallon water can 20-30

KCS-(Kansas City Southern) marked on wooden track gauge with brass measuring guides & built in level 175-200

LEHIGH VALLEY- cast on cap of long handled torch 35-45

MP-(Missouri Pacific) stamped on cast iron tamping pick 10-15

MP LINES-(Missouri Pacific) cast around bottom edge of one gallon can 15-20

MOPAC – (Missouri Pacific) side marked on talo pot. Mfg. Eagle 20-30

NYCRR- (New York Central) stamped on 15" monkey wrench. Mfg. Pexico 10-15

N&WRYCO- (Norfolk & Western) cast on side of water can 15-20

NPRY- (Northern Pacific) bottom marked on tall oiler. 35-45

NPR- (Northern Pacific) stamped on double headed 12" wrench. Mfg. Williams 10-15

NP-(Northern Pacific) stamped on cast iron track chisel 5-10

NPRY-(Northern Pacific) stamped on 12" pipe wrench with wood handle 10-15

NPRY-(Northern Pacific) stamped on 1 gallon size kerosene can 10-15

NPRY- (Northern Pacific) cast on side of small handled torch. 25-35

OSL- (Oregon Short Line) stamped on metal part of shovel with wooden handle 30-40

OSL-(Oregon Short Line) stamped on 8" pipe wrench with wood handle 35-45

OSLRR-(Oregon Short Line) stamped on bottom of 2 gallon kerosene can 25-35

OWR&N-(Oregon Washington Railroad & Navigation) stamped on 8" pipe wrench 35-45

PS-(Pennsylvania System) Keystone logo cast on bottom of small handled torch 10-15

PRR-(Pennsylvania RR) Keystone logo side marked on 26" tall oiler can 45-55

P&R-(Philadelphia & Reading) stamped on 12 ½" pipe wrench. Mfg. Pexio 10-15

SANTA FE ROUTE-stamped on 15" long wrench. Mfg. WB & Co. 20-25

SANTA FE ROUTE-stamped on 8 ½" wrench. Mfg. WB&Co. 15-20

SANTA FE ROUTE-cast on side of cone shaped torch 75-85

SPCO- (Southern Pacific) stamped on 8" pipe wrench. Mfg. Bemis & Callwall co........ **10-15**

STJ&GIRY- (St. Joseph & Grand Island) cast on side of long handled torch **65-75**

SL&SF-(St. Louis & San Francisco) stamped on applied plate on one gallon kerosene can **20-30**

STL&SFRR-(St. Louis & San Francisco) embossed on side of 20" tall oiler **75-85**

STL&SF- (St Louis & San Francisco) side marked on cone shaped torch **25-35**

STL&SFRY- (St Louis & San Francisco) side marked on two gallon can. Mfg. Handlan **25-35**

T&P- (Texas & Pacific) side marked on kerosene can **20-30**

TRACK GAUGE cast iron 5 foot long with gauge on both ends. No railroad markings **40-50**

UP—(Union Pacific) stamped on side of coal bucket.. **50-60**

UP—(Union Pacific) stamped on bottom of 1 gallon kerosene can............................... **15-20**

UPRY—(Union Pacific) side marked on tall oiler **75-85**

UPRR—(Union Pacific) stamped on 22" wrench. Mfg. Williams **10-15**

UPRR—(Union Pacific) stamped on handle of switch stand broom with ice scrapper **20-30**

UP SYSTEM- stamped on metal part of shovel with wood handle **10-15**

UNION PACIFIC- cast on side of 2 gallon water can **10-15**

UNION PACIFIC- cast on cap on tallow pot **20-30**

UNION PACIFIC-raised letters on applied plate on side of long handled torch **35-45**

WPRR- (Western Pacific) cast on bottom of 10" small oil can. Mfg. Eagle **50-60**

WPRR- (Western Pacific) side marked on applied tag on side of cone shaped torch ... **30-40**

CHAPTER 31

TRAIN COLLECTIBLES

This section covers a wide variety of items. From bells and whistles to step stools and door plaques you'll find something for everyone in this chapter. We have tried to list the more commonly sought after items in this section, but certainly some things are undoubtly overlooked given the amount of different accessories the railroads used. A step stool certainly brings back the memories of the fully uniformed conductor stepping off the train and offering the stool to boost the oncoming passenger into the coach. The sight of a whistle evokes the sound of a train coming into town signaling as it would get closer to the depot. The ornate lighting fixtures bring us back to the elegance offered aboard a fully appointed coach many years ago. Whatever the item we can all probably look back and remember those great days gone by and see why so many have become obsessed with collecting and preserving these great pieces of history. As with all items discussed in this book, condition is paramount to realizing the suggested prices shown here.

REMEMBER: PRICES SHOWN ARE SUGGESTED VALUES ONLY. VALUES VARY FROM REGION TO REGION. THIS IS MEANT ONLY AS A GUIDE. (◆) **Denotes value over $1000.00**

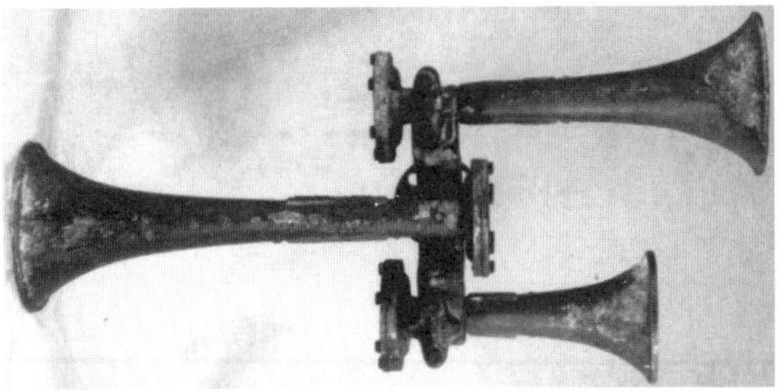

AIRHORN- *diesel horn* 3 chime. Mfg. Nathan Air Horn. #1, #2,&#4 .... **200-250**

AIRHORN- *diesel horn* 3 chime. Mfg. Leslie Super Typhon, #25, #31 & #44. .... **200-250**

AIRHORN- *air horns* from diesel engine. 3 horn set distributed by IEC-Holden, Canada. **275-325**

AIRHORN- *diesel airhorn* solid bronze. Single chime manufacturer by Leslie Typhon Model A-200 .... **275-325**

AT&SFRY- (Atchison Topeka & Santa Fe) *step stool* cast on side of iron. Mfg. Morton. 4 rubber feet with underside rag holder. Grated top to prevent slippage. **300-350**

AT&SFRY (Atchison Topeka & Santa Fe) *steam engine whistle* cast on top of five chime cast iron stairstepped. These were shop made by the Santa Fe Railroad. Measures approximately 24" tall & weighs about 40lbs. .... ◆

AT&SFRY CHEMICAL DEPT- (Atchison Topeka & Santa Fe) *bottle* cast on side of approximately quart size glass. Used for taking water samples from the steam engines **100-125**

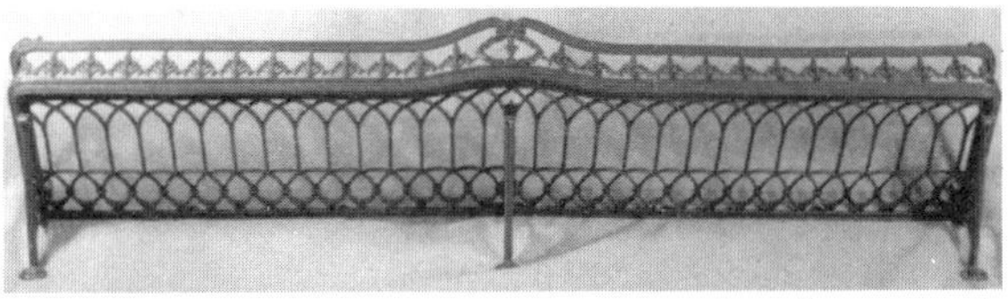

BAGGAGE OR LUGGAGE RACK- brass rack measures 27 ½" x 6". Rounded corners with mounting brackets on each end **200-250**

B&O- (Baltimore & Ohio) *front engine plate* Capitol logo skeleton type steam engine cast iron. Has three mounting holes. Original yellow paint **175-200**

B&O- (Baltimore & Ohio) *Concessionaires basket.* Metal basket with blue & white B&O Capitol logo on side. Mfg. Kennett. **175-200**

BELL- cast brass steam engine bell. Measures 12" diameter across the bottom. Complete with cast iron yoke and cradle. Mfg. Howard cast in the base. **750-850**

BELL- AT&SFRYCO-(Atchison Topeka & Santa Fe) presentation logo plate dated 1959, attached to side of 16" diameter brass locomotive bell. Complete with yoke & cradle. The Santa Fe donated these bells to different charities. .... ◆

BELL- RIO GRANDE steam locomotive bell. Has "Rio Grande" speed lettering logo engraved across front of bell. Measures 16" diameter complete with yoke & cradle. .... ◆

BELL-Diesel engine bell. Brass bell measures 12" diameter. These are distinguished by the lack of a hanger & cradle. They weigh about 60lbs and usually have to have some sort of homemade bracket to hang them. Diesel bells have a hole in the top for an air actuator 200-250

B&MRR-(Boston & Maine) *conductors ticket box* made of metal & marked with raised letters on top. Measures 13x9x9. Mfg. Peter Gray Boston. 100-125

BRAKE CLUB- *hickory wood stick* found with railroad markings used to turn the brake wheel 10-15

BN –(Burlington Northern) *hard hat.* Green BN logo on front 5-10

BN-(Burlington Northern) *first aid kit* with green BN logo on white metal box. 10-15

BURLINGTON ROUTE- *shovel* cast into handle of 22" iron shovel for caboose stove 60-70

BURLINGTON ROUTE-*cuspidor* with black enameled letters on green porcelain. 150-175

BURLINGTON ROUTE-*first aid kit* with box logo stenciled on top. Metal box complete with all supplies 40-50

BURLINGTON ROUTE- *door mat rug* with box logo interwoven in center Measures 47" x 26" with rubber threshold on one end & two grommet holes on the other for securing to floor. Brown with 1 ½" red stripe bordered by two pinstripes on either side. 500-600

CPR- (Canadian Pacific) *first aid kit* stenciled on top of metal box. Measures 5 ¾"x 2 ½". 5-10

CPR- (Canadian Pacific) *granitewear drinking cup* with black enameled letters on side of white cup. 150-175

CNR- (Canadian National) *graniteware drinking cup* with black marbilized finish. Embossed CNR in black enameled letters on side. 150-175

CANADIAN PACIFIC RY- interwoven in center of *wool blanket.* Colorful red, orange & blue design. 50-60

CABOOSE –*flare & flag kit.* Metal can with holders for flags on the side 10-15

CABOOSE- *interior wall light.* Kerosene light with spring loaded bracket to adjust tension. Comes complete with shade. Mfg. Aladdin. **100-125**

CANDLE LAMP- small brass wall lamp with bracket used in the RPO's as emergency lighting. Mfg. A&W. Spring loaded to force candle up as it burns. Glass pyrex chimney **45-55**

C&NWRY–(Chicago & Northwestern) logo on side of *ceramic jug.* One gallon size. **250-300**

C&NWRY- (Chicago & Northwestern) *glass fire extinguisher* bottle. Cast C&NWRY on side. Complete with cast iron wall mount **100-125**

CB&QRR- (Chicago Burlington & Quincy) cast on top of small brass *fire extinquisher.* Measures 14" long. Manufacturer Pyrene. **65-75**

CB&Q-(Chicago Burlington & Quincy) stainless steel *door plate* reads, "SILVER THREADS". Measures 20" long by 2 ¼" wide with black enameled letters. **125-150**

CMSTP&P-(Chicago Milwaukee St. Paul & Pacific) interwoven in center of *wool blanket.* Beige on brown and dated 1947. .... **125-150**

CLOCK- *locomotive nickel or brass clock.* Measures 6 ½" diameter. Mfg. Seth Thomas. One day wind up clock for the inside of the locomotive. **250-300**

CLOCK- *brass wall clock* from observation or business car. Measures 8" diameter. Mfg. Seth Thomas **250-300**

C&SRY- (Colorado & Southern) *canvas water bag* stenciled "Property of." Mfg. Superior Waterbag. **70-80**

COTTON BELT-(St. Louis Southwestern) *iron step stool* cast on side . Mfg. Morton. Grated top to prevent slipping. Four rubber feet and rag holder on underside **500-550**

D&H (Delaware & Hudson) *fire extinquisher.* Brass with cast D&H on top edge. Measures 14" long. Manufactured by Pyrex. **65-75**

D&H-(Delaware & Hudson) *step stool.* Cast in fancy script letters "THE D&H CO" on side of iron step stool. Mfg. Morton. Grated top to prevent slipping. Four rubber feet and rag holder on inside **250-300**

D&RG- (Denver & Rio Grande) *single chime whistle* cast on top edge. Measures 18" tall by 5" diameter. .... ◆

D&RGW-(Denver & Rio Grande Western) *cast iron step stool* in raised letters on side of. Mfg. Morton. Grated top to prevent slipping. Four rubber feet and rag holder on underside **500-550**

D&RGW-(Denver & Rio Grande Western) *canvas water bag* with stenciled letters on the side. Comes with cork stopper. Mfg. Chief Co. **50-60**

D&RGW—(Denver & Rio Grande Western) *stainless steel sign* from passenger car doorway. "Rio Grande" speed letters measures 28 ¾" x 5". Black enameled background. **150-175**

D&RGW- *Drumhead.* "Denver & Rio Grande Western San Juan" around edge with colorful mountain scene in center. All housed in lighted metal can measuring 28" diameter .... ◆

D&RGW- (Denver & Rio Grande Western) *wall mount bracket* with raised letters on side of cast iron. Also includes tin fuel font cast on side "D&RGW" or "D&RGRR" with glass chimney. **175-200**

D&RGW—(Denver & Rio Grande Western) raised letters on door, top or base of cast *iron caboose stove.* Stands approximately 36" tall. Stove usually comes apart in sections. **450-500**

DINING CAR CHIMES-4 chimes manufactured by Deagan, Inc. Chicago. Complete with wooden mallet **175-200**

FRISCO –*Drumhead.* "The Meteor" logo in black, white & red design housed in lighted can measuring 28" diameter .... ◆

GAUGE-brass ring on 8" diameter 400lb gauge. Manufactured by Ashcroft. Cast iron backing & black letters on white face 35-45

GAUGE- brass gauge measures 6" diameter. Face reads, "Car Heating & Lighting Co., The Pintsch System". 20 lb. Patented 1906. 50-60

GAUGE-"Climax Locomotive Co. Seattle, Wash" on face of Locomotive Double Spring 300 pound guage. Mfg. Marshall Town Mfg.Co. Marshalltown, IA. 7 ¼" diameter with brass ring around face and cast iron body. 350-400

GREAT NORTHERN- *first aid kit* with logo stenciled on top of. Blue & white enameling. Complete 25-35

GNRY- (Great Northern) *shop rag* stenciled with Goat logo "Safety All Day Every Day" 5-7

GNRY-(Great Northern) *hard hat* with Goat logo on front 10-15

GNRY—(Great Northern) *box car tie* cast on metal strip used to lock the boxcars 1-2

GNRY- -(Great Northern) *collapsible aluminum cup* cast "Great Northern Ry Co. News Service" with 5cent denomination 35-45

GNRY—(Great Northern) same only 10c denomination 40-50

GNRY—(Great Northern) same only 15c denomination 45-55

HEADLIGHT- steam engine locomotive *headlight* with winged glass number boards. Mfg. Pyle National with 16" lens. Overall width of light is 35" from end to end. 550-600

ICRR-(Illinois Central) *hard hat* with IC logo on front 10-15

ILL CENTRAL- stamped on side of square *ticket punch.* Nickel finish with no manufacturer shown 20-25

INTERIOR LIGHT- brass kerosene wall lamp with ornate mounting bracket. Mfg. Handlan Buck St. Louis. Brass fuel container fits into brass strap with wall mount 175-200

INTERIOR LIGHT- brass kerosene wall lamp with smoke dome attached to wall mount and kerosene fount. Pyrex chimney. Mfg. A&W. **350-375**

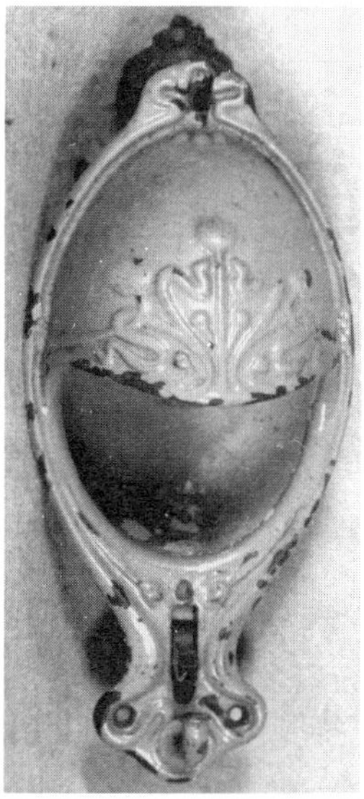

LIGHT FIXTURE- cast iron recessed electric berth light. Green enamel finish. Ornate design. **35-45**

LIGHT FIXTURE- ornate brass ceiling mount chandelier. Brass tree holds two ornate fuel containers with burner, chimneys shades& glass fuel drip cups. Manufactured by Adams & Westlake and pat'd 1890's. These hung from the ceiling of early coaches & Pullman cars. These fixtures will vary with some being quite plain & others very ornate. .... ◆

MILWAUKEE ROAD- *First Aid Kit* metal box measures 5"x8". Top reads, "The Milwaukee Road First Aid Kit State of Washington". **20-30**

MK&T- (Missouri Kansas & Texas) *iron caboose stove* with raised letters on door . Measures approximately 38" tall. **350-400**

NEW JERSEY CENTRAL/READING- *wooden cigar box.* stenciled on top of Box reads, "Special selected for Reading-NJC Dining Cars". **125-150**

NYC-(New York Central) *electric table lamp.* Applied plate in fancy diamond shape wreath on side of shade on brass table lamp. Measures 20" tall & 12" wide at the bottom. ... **450-500**

NYC—(New York Central) *brass fire extinquisher* cast on top edge Manufacturer is Badger. **50-60**

NYC LINES—(New York Central) *metal first aid kit* embossed on top painted green, complete **15-20**

NEW YORK CENTRAL- *wooden hanger* with black enameled letters reads, "Sleeping Car Dept.". **10-15**

NEW YORK NEW HAVEN & HARTFORD- *kerosene gauge lamp*, made of brass with fancy cast logo on attached mounting bracket. Fluted top with twist out off fuel font. Measures 6 ½" tall with 3" diameter. 275-300

N&W- (Norfolk & Western) *cast iron cuspidor* with large raised letters on top shoulder of 75-85

NORTHERN PACIFIC- *smoking stand* with Monad logo applied to base. Nickel finish. Has shelf for drinks and cigarette rests in center with hinged ash trap. 375-425

NP- (Northern Pacific) *caboose or work car* light with raised letters on side Made of cast iron. Bracket holds tin font 50-60

NORTHERN PACIFIC RAILWAY CO- *feather duster* with red wood handle..... 90-100

NPRY-(Northern Pacific) *brass fire extinquisher* cast on top edge Measures 14" long and mfg. by Pyrene. 75-85

NP-(Northern Pacific) *iron step stool* with Monad logo cast on side . Mfg. Morton. Grated top with rag holder on the underside and 4 rubber feet. 350-400

NP-(Northern Pacific) *whistle* with raised letters on top edge of 5 chime stairstepped cast iron whistle. .... ◆

OSLRR-(Oregon Short Line) *feather duster* with red wood handle. 90-100

PASSENGER SIGN-enameled sign with blue background and white letters reads, "Passengers Are Prohibited From Standing on Platform While Train Is In Motion" 125-150

PASSENGER SIGN-brass sign reads "Passengers Are Not Allowed To Stand On the Platform". Measures 3" x 10 ¼" **90-100**

PRR-(Pennsylvania) *wool blanket* with Keystone logo interwoven in center of charcoal colored blanket .Measures 74"x 62" **200-250**

PULLMAN CO.- *ceramic jug* marked on side of ½ gallon size. Housed in original wicker basket **100-125**

PULLMAN CO.- *ceramic jug* marked on side of one gallon jug. Tan with brown top **50-60**

PULLMAN CO- *nickel plated cuspidor* bottom marked with twist off top. Also found marked "PPCCo." **50-60**

PULLMAN CO- *aluminum step stool* embossed on side of with grated top. Rubber feet and rag compartment on the underside. **175-200**

PULLMAN CO- *wooden hanger* stenciled on side Also reads, "Travel & Sleep in Safety & Comfort" **5-10**

PULLMAN CO- *brass smoking stand* with applied plate attached to base Shelf for drinks and hinged ash trap. **350-400**

PULLMAN CO- *wool blanket* with interwoven logo in center of salmon colored.blanket. Mfg. Pendelton. **90-100**

ROCK ISLAND LINES- *iron step stool* cast on both ends with grated top and four rubber feet. Mfg. Morton. **350-400**

ROCK ISLAND –*Diesel engine nose plate.* Stainless steel in logo design with red tuscan background and silver letters and border **450-500**

ROCK ISLAND OR ROCK ISLAND LINES- *ceramic jug* marked on side. One gallon size tan bottom and brown top with either blue or black lettering. **200-250**

ROCK ISLAND – *caboose stove shovel* cast iron with raised "RI LINES" in handle **60-70**

ROCK ISLAND- *desk lamp or wall mount lamp*. Fuel font has brass applied plate in football shape, reads, "ROCK ISLAND LINES" **175-200**

ROCK ISLAND- *white hard hat* with modern RI logo in blue on front **10-15**

ROCK ISLAND- *linen head rest* interwoven with "Route of the Rockets" **20-25**

ROCK ISLAND- *white shop rag* interwoven with blue logo Reads, "Don't get hurt look, think & be alert" **1-5**

ROCK ISLAND-*Magazine cover* with "Rocky Mountain Rocket" in silver on red leatherette cover **50-60**

ROCK ISLAND LINES- *brass fire extinguisher* marked on side. Measures 24" tall by 8" diameter. **75-85**

RUTLAND RR- cast on aluminum *box car seal* **1-3**

STL&SFRY-(St. Louis & San Francisco) *ceramic jug* marked on side of two gallon.size jug. Black letters on tan with brown top. **300-350**

STL-SF RWY CO- (St. Louis & San Francisco) *flashlight* stamped on side. Mfg. Ray-O-Vac **3-5**

STJ&GIRYCO-(St. Joseph & Grand Island) *cast iron step stool* with raised letters on side and with wooden top. Probably shop made...................................... **400-450**

SAN ANTONIO & ARANSAS PASS RWY CO- *Money Bag*-stenciled on side of canvas money bag Reads, "$250 in Silver" on side. **60-70**

SANTA FE- *Steam gauge* with Santa Fe in black enameled letters on face of 100 lb gauge. Mfg. Ashcroft. **30-35**

SANTA FE- *Shop rag* logo interwoven in center of white rag."Work Safely Wipe Out Any AxyDent on the Santa Fe" **3-4**

SANTA FE- *Cloths hanger* black letters stenciled on wooden cloths hanger...................... **10-15**

SANTA FE- *Striker plate* incused logo on center of brass match striker plate. **175-200**

SANTA FE-*Drumhead.* "El Capitan" logo in yellow, red & black. 28" diameter .... ◆

SANTA FE-*Drumhead,* "Super Chief", logo in blue red & black 28" diameter .... ◆

SANTA FE- *smoking stand* with logo applied to base. Nickel finish with shelf for drinks and hinged ash trap in center **350-400**

SANTA FE ROUTE-*soap bar* with letters molded in the top. Measures 3" x 2" **15-20**

SEABOARD COAST LINE-*linen headrest* mustard colored with light blue embroidered letters **10-15**

SINK- *wall sink* from sleeping car compartment made of aluminum. Mfg. A&W pat'd Jan.19, 1915. White porcelain tips on knobs designate hot, cold & drain. **175-200**

SP LINES- (Southern Pacific) *cuspidor* with blue stenciled letters on top edge of white porcelain spittoon **65-75**

SP CO-(Southern Pacific) *step stool* cast on side. Metal grated top with 4 rubber feet. Mfg. Morton Step **250-300**

TICKET PUNCH- nickel plated punch with different designs. Sometimes railroad marked **10-15**

TEXAS & PACIFIC- *step stool.* Marked on both ends "T&P". Grated top with four rubber feet and rag holder on the underside. **250-300**

UPRR- (Union Pacific) *Brake club.* Birch wood brake handle stenciled on side UPRR Link. **15-20**

UPRR CO- (Union Pacific) *Fire extinguisher.* Cast on top edge of brass fire extinguisher. Mfg. General Fire **60-65**

UPRR-(Union Pacific) *Graniteware cup.* Blue with white letters. "UPRR" letters on porcelain finish. **250-275**

UNION PACIFIC- Blanket. Grey wool blanket with interwoven Overland Shield logo in center. Mfg. Pendelton **200-250**

UNION PACIFIC- *Blanket* grey wool with interwoven modern Shield Logo in center **100-125**

UNION PACIFIC- *cigar box.* Modern shield logo on cedar box. Missing cigars. **25-35**

UNION PACIFIC-*toilet paper holder.* Letters cast on top plate that mounts to wall. Nickel plated. Also found marked just "UNION PACIFIC SYSTEM" **65-75**

UNION PACIFIC-*smoking stand* with Overland Shield logo applied to base. Chrome drink base with ashtray in center. **350-400**

UNION PACIFIC-*porcelain cuspidor.* Marked on top rim in either black on green enamel or black on white enamel. **100-125**

UNION PACIFIC-***step stool.*** Cast letters on side. Manufacturered by Morton with four rubber feet and underside rag holders **300-350**

WHISTLE-*brass single chime* measures 14" tall with 2 ½" diameter. Mfg. Crane. **175-200**

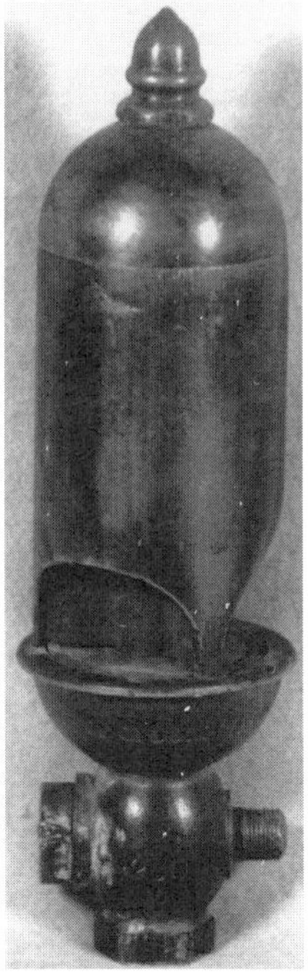

WHISTLE-*brass three chime* measures 20" tall with 5" diameter. Mfg. Lukenheimer **550-600**

WHISTLE-brass five chime stairstepped steam engine era whistle with casting numbers around the base. Mfg. unknown. .... ◆

CHAPTER 32

TRAVEL BROCHURES & BOOKLETS

Collecting travel brochures and booklets is just another rewarding facet of the railroadiana hobby. Many of the early brochures are full of incredible illustrations, photographs and wonderful advertising to lure and entice the traveling public along the route of their trip. There are many different versions of these available from the folded panel styles that unfold to reveal system maps to the string tied large format styles that boasted the beautiful views that could be seen along the route. The advertising is varied from hotels and soothing spa's to undertakers and bankers. The great history and photos shown in these wonderful pieces is what makes collecting them so rewarding. Remember condition is paramount. They must not be stained or torn to command the prices suggested here.

REMEMBER: PRICES SHOWN ARE SUGGESTED VALUES ONLY. VALUES VARY FROM REGION TO REGION. THIS IS MEANT ONLY AS A GUIDE. (◆) **Denotes value over $1000.00**

ALASKA RAILROAD- 1926 "Come to Alaska" travel brochure & timetable. 39 pages with photos **15-20**

ATCHISON TOPEKA & SANTA FE- dated 1881 map & tourist information in brochure format. Map shows all points in "Colorado, New Mexico, Arizona & Old Mexico" 10 folded panels reveal map and information, beautiful ornate cover **250-300**

BALTIMORE & OHIO- "The Story of the Railroad That Grew Up With Us" soft bound booklet dated 1951 with history of the B&O **10-15**

BOSTON & MAINE RR-booklet "Picturesque New England" shows black &white photos with approximately 100 pages of information along the line. Circa 1920's **15-20**

BOSTON & MAINE RR "Seashores of New England" shows black & white photos with approximately 100 pages of information. Measures 6" x 9" Circa 1920's **15-20**

BOSTON & MAINE RR- "New England Lakes" shows black & white photos with approximately 100 pages of information Measures 6" x9" circa 1920's............................... **15-20**

BURLINGTON ROUTE- "Dude Ranches" in Wyoming, Montana & Colorado dated 1950. 15 pages with photos & text.................... **5-10**

BURLINGTON ROUTE- "Colorado" has 56 pages dated 1957 with photos and text of places to visit while in Colorado **5-10**

BURLINGTON ROUTE- "Excursions the Summer" dated 1897 with two panels. Opens to reveal photos & text **15-20**

BURLINGTON ROUTE- "California Travel Booklet" with 71 pages dated 1919. Opens to reveal system map. **15-25**

BURLINGTON ROUTE- "Scenic Colorado & Utah" with 35 pages circa 1925. Photos and places to visit in Colorado & Utah **10-15**

BURLINGTON ROUTE- "Black Hill s of South Dakota" with 28 pages dated 1929. Photos and text of places to visit in South Dakota **10-15**

CANADIAN NATIONAL RR- "Scenic Canada" string tied book measures 8 ½" x 11". Black & white photos dated 1925 .... **10-15**

CANADIAN NATIONAL RR- "We Serve the West" brochure with 48 pages & system map dated in the 40's **5-10**

CANADIAN PACIFIC RR-F "Eastward Across Canada" brochures with 31 pages of pictures & text **10-15**

CENTRAL PACIFIC RAILROAD- "Nelsons Pictorial Guide Book" hard bound, dated 1874 Piece measures 6 ½" x 4" with approximately 50 pages of text & color lithographs. **350-400**

CENTRAL VERMONT RY- "Album of Central Vermont RR Scenery" hard bound with accordian style fold out pictures. Measures 3 ½" x 5" with ornate gold cover, circa 1890's **25-35**

CHESAPEAKE & OHIO RY- "The Rhine, The Alps, The Battlefield Line" dated 1913 with 3 panels measures 10 ½"x 4" **10-15**

CHICAGO & ALTON - 1889 "Summer Resorts" measures 8 x 9 ½" with 40 pages of photos and text **65-75**

CHICAGO BURLINGTON & QUINCY- "All Points in Kansas, Colorado, Nebraska, Utah, Montana, Idaho, Nevada & California shows 8 panels with system maps for UP, CB&Q & CPRR. 1870 .... **225-275**

CHICAGO MILWAUKEE & PUGET SOUND- "Across the Continent" measures 8 ¼" x 11 ¼" circa 1911 with colorful photos **45-55**

CHICAGO MILWAUKEE & ST PAUL RY- "Lake Michigan to Puget Sound" string tied travel booklet. Colorful pictures circa 1920's **25-35**

COLORADO & SOUTHERN RY-"Over the Loop" string tied 12 ½" x 13" travel booklet with pictures and descriptions of scenes along the line, circa 1900's **65-75**

COLORADO & SOUTHERN RY - "Rocky Mountain National Park, Estes Park, Colorado" dated 1923 with 32 pages. B&W photos & descriptions **15-25**

COLORADO & SOUTHERN RY - "Picturesque Colorado" dated 1914 measures 7" x 9" with 50 pages **30-40**

COLORADO & SOUTHERN RY -"One Day Mountain Excursions" with 21 pages. Black & white pictures of scenes in Colorado **40-50**

COLORADO & SOUTHERN RY -"Hotels & Resorts In Colorado" measures 3 ½" x 6" with 55 pages. Black & white photos & descriptions of places to stay & enjoy while visiting Colorado **40-50**

COLORADO & SOUTHERN RY - "Yellowstone National Park" measures 6"x9" with 52 pages with photos & text **15-25**

COLORADO & SOUTHERN RY –"Platte Canyon Resorts" dated 1920 with 8 pages in 3 panel design **35-45**

COLORADO MIDLAND RY "Panoramic Scenes Along the Line of the Colorado Midland" brochure. Folds out with 12 panels. Colorful cover circa 1917 .... **125-150**

COLORADO MIDLAND RY "Scenes of the Midland Railway" measures 8" x 5 ¾" with 24 pages circa 1913 .... **80-90**

COLORADO MIDLAND RY "Thru the Rockies" travel booklet measures 6" x 9" with 20 pages. Color photo's circa 1910 .... **60-70**

COLORADO MIDLAND RY "Thru Hellgate" travel booklet with red cover. Shows Hellgate on front & Cougar on reverse. Color pictures circa 1909 .... **80-90**

COLORADO SPRINGS & CRIPPLE CREEK DISTRICT RY- "Short Line Blue Book" dated August 1903 with 82 pages of photos, advertising & scenes along the line **50-60**

COLORADO SPRINGS & CRIPPLE CREEK DISTRICT RY- "O'er Canon & Crag to the Land of Gold" string tied travel book dated 1912 with photos & text **50-60**

CRIPPLE CREEK SHORT LINE- fold out brochure with black & white photos. 6 panel double sided design with scenes along the line **15-25**

DENVER & RIO GRANDE RAILWAY- "The Beautiful Denver & Rio Grande" ornate gold cover on string tied 7" x 9" travel booklet. Text with black & white photos of scenes along the line **150-175**

DENVER & RIO GRANDE RAILROAD- large format travel booklet. "Gems of Colorado Scenery". Circa 1900's. Great photos of scenes along the line **25-35**

DENVER & RIO GRANDE RAILROAD- "The Peaks of the Rockies" travel booklet measures 6" x 9" with photos and descriptions of mountain peaks in Colorado. Circa 1910 .... **30-40**

DENVER & RIO GRANDE RAILROAD "Rocky Mountain Views" string tied travel booklet. Circa 1900's with color & black & white photos **15-20**

DENVER & RIO GRANDE/WESTERN PACIFIC- 1915 Panama California Exposition brochure. 2 panels with text & photos of places of interest in California **20-30**

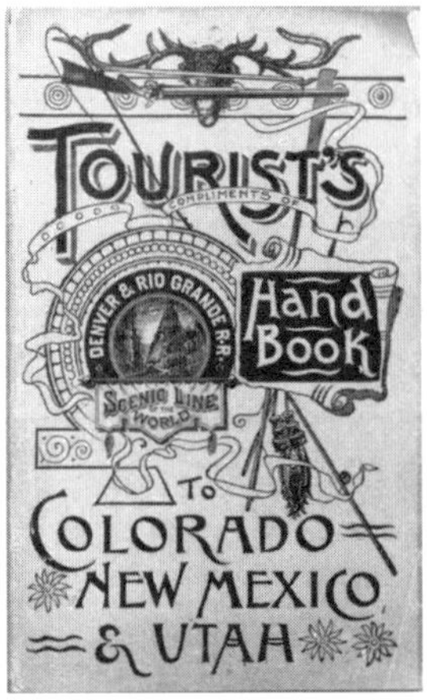

DENVER & RIO GRANDE RAILROAD- "Tourists Handbook" approximately 100 pages with pictures, descriptions & advertising dated 1887 .... **100-125**

DENVER & SALT LAKE- "Thru the Continental Divide, The Moffat Road" 10 panels with black & white photos dated 1930 .... **20-30**

DENVER & SALT LAKE "Hunting Fishing & Camping Along the Moffat Road" dated 1910 with 18 pages, measures 3 ½" x6" 30-40

DENVER & SALT LAKE-"Over the Rockies To the Top of the World" string tied travel booklet measures 8 ½" x 11 .... **30-40**

DENVER & SALT LAKE- "The Moffat Road" brochure measures 8"x 6" with 25 pages & color photos **25-35**

DENVER LEADVILLE & GUNNISON- "Boreass, Breckenridge and the Blue" travel booklet. Black & white photos with text in blue ink. Dated 1896 .... **225-275**

DENVER NORTHWEST & PACIFIC- "The Moffat Road" 1905 pictorial folder with orange border. 16 pages with Columbine flower on cover **35-45**

DENVER NORTHWEST & PACIFIC- "Wonders In Transit Over Rollins Pass, Colo" travel book measures 13" x 10" with 36 pages of photos of the early Moffat Line **65-75**

DENVER SOUTH PARK &PACIFIC RAILROAD- "Over the South Park to Leadville" in gold letters on green embossed hard bound cover measuring approximately 3" x 5". Opens to reveal 18 black & white photos attached accordian style **200-250**

FRED HARVEY- "The Great Southwest", stringtied booklet dated 1911 with color pictures of scenes along the line. Measures 8 ½" x 11" **40-50**

FRED HARVEY- "El Tovar" brochure dated 1905. 31 pages of photos & text describing the wonderful accomodations & scenery..... **60-70**

FRED HARVEY- souvenir item. 16 black & white photos of the Grand Canyon National Park. Measures 4" x 2 ¾". Housed in a silver folder for mailing **25-35**

FLORIDA EAST COAST- "Story of a Pioneer" booklet sharing the history of the line ... **15-25**

FLORENCE & CRIPPLE CREEK-folding postcard, accordian style double sided with scenes along the line dated 1908 .... **30-40**

FRISCO- "There Is Something To See Along the Frisco Line" travel booklet measures 9 ¾" x 11 ¾". Circa 1900. 32 pages of color & black & white photos & text of scences along the line. **60-70**

GREAT NORTHERN - "The Scenic Northwest" travel brochure. 52 pages of text & photos advertising scenes along the line **15-25**

GREAT NORTHERN- "Scenic Route West" brochure measures 8"x 9" with 23 pages & dated 1939 .... **15-25**

GREAT NORTHERN- "Montana Free Homestead Land" dated 1913 with 8 panels that open to reveal system map **45-55**

GREAT NORTHERN-"New Cascade Tunnel" brochure measures 5 ¼" x 8 ¾" with tunnel statistics & photos **15-20**

GREAT NORTHERN- "Views As Seen Along the Great Northern Railway" string tied travel booklet, circa 1900's & measures 8"x 10" **55-65**

KANSAS PACIFIC RAILWAY- "The Colorado Tourist" and illustrated guide with 80 pages measures 8 ½" x 11". Pictures and text circa late 1870's. **250-300**

LARAMIE, NORTH PARK & WESTERN "The Fisherman's Paradise" 8 panel brochure with photos & descriptions. Circa 1920"s **150-175**

LOUISVILLE & NASHVILLE- "Gulf Coast Nature Adventure"measures 10" x18", mostly photos **10-15**

MISSOURI PACIFIC- "COLORADO" travel booklet with photos & descriptions of scenes found along the way. 25 pages long........ **5-15**

MISSOURI PACIFIC- "COLORADO ROCKIES" travel booklet with 16 pages. Circa 1940's with photos and descriptions...... **10-15**

NASHVILLE, CHATANOOGA & ST. LOUIS The Story of the General" 24 pages circa 1900 .... **15-20**

NASHVILLE, CHATANOOGA & ST. LOUIS -"Mile by Mile" dated 1928 with pictures & descriptions **20-30**

NEW YORK CENTRAL- 1936 "Streamline Convention" brochure opens into 16 panels with 27 color prints. **5-10**

NEW YORK CENTRAL- "Arrow Train" brochure with 8 panels has drawings and interior photos of the new "Arrow Train". **5-10**

NORTHERN PACIFIC- "Yellowstone" travel booklet with 64 pages of text and photos of scenes along the line, circa 1920's.......... **15-25**

NORTHERN PACIFIC- "2000 Miles of Startling Beauty" 46 page brochure dated 1925. Travelers can read along as they travel in the train. **5-10**

NORTHERN PACIFIC-"Northern Pacific Wonderland" dated 1901 with 108 pages of black & white pictures and text describing scenes along the line. Pull out system map...... **40-50**

NORTHERN PACIFIC-"The Grand Canyon of the Yellowstone" dated 1913 opens into two panels with photos and text. **25-30**

NORTHERN PACIFIC- "The Land of Geysers, Yellowstone Park" dated 1913. Measures 8" x 9" booklet style. **25-30**

NORTHERN PACIFIC- "The Storied Northwest" measures 8" x 11" with 20 pages of black & white photos and text. **20-30**

NORTHERN PACIFIC- "Yellowstone Park Line & Dining Car Route" circa 1895 opens into nine panels and system map **50-60**

NORTHERN PACIFIC- "Scenic Route Across America" with 24 pages of black &white photos and text **15-20**

OREGON SHORT LINE RAILROAD- "Yellowstone National Park" dated 1910 opens in to 4 panels with pictures & text **50-60**

OREGON SHORT LINE RAILROAD- "Thunder Mountain" dated 1904 brochure with 32 pages and system map **100-125**

PENNSYLVANIA RAILROAD- "Photographic Views" booklet measures 9 ¾" x 7 ½" with black & white photos and text **15-20**

PENNSYLVANIA RAILROAD- "A La Photoviews Penna Railroad" by Rand McNally measures 4" x 5" Hard bound book with accordian style pull out black & white photos of scenes along the line. Circa 1900's ... **20-30**

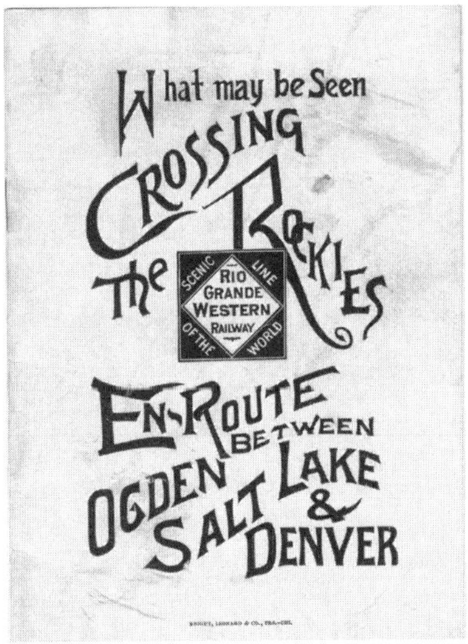

RIO GRANDE WESTERN RY- "Crossing the Rockies" 1898 travel brochure. Measures 3"x6" with 47 pages of history along the RGW line...... **90-100**

ROCK ISLAND- "Colorado Under the Turquoise Sky" dated 1911 with 48 pages of descriptions and photos of scenes along the line. **20-30**

ROCK ISLAND- "Thru Scenic Colorado & Yellowstone Park To The Pacific Coast" brochure with 23 pages of photos and text. Dated 1911 ...... **25-35**

ROCK ISLAND- "The Garden of Allahi" dated 1930 brochure with black & white photos and text **20-30**

SANTA FE- "Travel the Chief Way" brochure with 4 folded panels & color photos dated in the 60's. **5-7**

SANTA FE- "Century of Progress" brochure dated 1933 advertising the Worlds Fair Expo, measures 7 ½" x 10" with black & white photos and text **25-35**

SANTA FE- "Petrified Forest Arizona" brochure dated 1916 with black & white photos and text **25-35**

SANTA FE- "Dude Ranches Of The Southwest" dated 1935 with black & white pictures & text of vacation ideas at Dude Ranches. **25-35**

SANTA FE- "El Capitan" 1950's brochure advertising the amenities aboard the "El Capitan" **5-10**

SANTA FE- "California Limited" brochure circa 1920's advertising the amenities found aboard the "Limited" trains. **40-50**

SANTA FE- "By the Way" booklet measures 8"x 9" shows Mission Church on cover with scenes along the line. **25-35**

SANTA FE- "California Picture Book" dated 1942 booklet measures 8" x 9" with black & white & tinted photos of scenes along the way. **20-30**

SANTA FE- "Grand Canyon Outings" dated April 1913 brochures with 62 pages of black & white photos and text. **30-40**

SOUTH PARK LINE- "Colorado Views" in gold on cover of hard cover box resembling book, binding reads, "The South Park Line Vol.1"in gold. Cover opens to release accordian style photos of scenes along the line **450-500**

SOUTHERN PACIFIC- "California" measures 8 1/2" x 12" with reproduced oil painting cover. Houses approximately 60 pages of black & white photos. Circa 1920's 30-40

SOUTHERN PACIFIC- "A Picture Journey Over the Shasta Route" string tied 8 ½" x 11" booklet dated 1920's. Photos of scenes along the line 20-30

SOUTHERN PACIFIC-"Oregon Outdoors" measures 4"x9" with 62 pages dated 1916. Black & white photos of text of scenes along the line 20-30

SOUTHERN PACIFIC- "The Overland Trail" string tied book measures 12" x 9 ¼" Circa 1920's with color photos of scenes along the line 20-30

SOUTHERN PACIFIC- "Hunting & Fishing in Louisiana & Texas" 48 pages booklet with fold out system map 15-20

SOUTHERN PACIFIC -"Gulf Bend Country" with 50 pages of information on crops. Circa 1920's. 15-20

SOUTHERN PACIFIC- "Wayside Notes Shasta Route" folded two panel brochure from the 30's 25-35

UNION PACIFIC- "Summer Tours Season" dated 1937 measures 7"x 9" with 56 pages of photos and text 10-15

UNION PACIFIC- "Boulder Dam" measures 3" x 8" pocket size brochure dated 1940 5-10

UNION PACIFIC- "Rocky Mountain National Parks" 6" x9" booklet with 31 pages dated 1922 with photos and text 10-15

UNION PACIFIC- "Utah Idaho Outings" dated 1925 measures 7"x10" with pictures and text of scenes along the line 15-20

UNION PACIFIC- "Louisiana Purchase Exposition St. Louis" dated 1904 with 86 pages. Large UP logo on cover. 15-20

UNION PACIFIC – "Summer Tours Season 1935" has C&NW & UP Logos on the cover. Joint brochure advertising summer vacations via the lines. 10-15

UNION PACIFIC- "Sights & Scenes For the Tourist". Circa 1894 with 76 pages of photos of text 45-55

UNION PACIFIC- "Tomorrows Train Today". Small pocket sized brochure measures 3" x 5 1/2" advertising the new Streamlined Trains from the 30's 3-5

UNION PACIFIC- "Scenery" hardbound booklet measures 6" x9" with black & white photos, circa 1890's. 35-45

UNION PACIFIC- "The Overland Limited Crossing the Great Salt Lake" dated 1906 with color photos and text 20-30

UNION PACIFIC- "Colorado & Utah Rockies" brochure dated 1920 with photos and text 10-15

UNION PACIFIC- "California" dated 1937 brochure with gold and orange cover. Photos of text of scenes along the line 10-15

UNION PACIFIC- "Southern California" dated 1930's with 32 pages. Gold cover embossed with Overland logo 10-15

UNION PACIFIC- "Zion Brice & Grand Canyon" dated 1929 with 56 pages. Measures 7" x10" with photos and text 10-15

UNION PACIFIC- "Colorado Mountain Playgrounds" dated 1930's with 47 pages of photos and text. UP Overland logo embossed on cover .. 10-15

UNION PACIFIC SYSTEM- "Yellowstone National Park" brochure dated 1914 with pictures and text of scenes along the line 20-30

UNION PACIFIC DENVER & GULF- "Manitou" brochure dated 1896 with photos and text of scenes in Manitou 35-45

WESTERN PACIFIC- ten selected black & white postcard views housed in a folding souvenir cover 10-15

WESTERN PACIFIC- "Views Along the Line Of the Western Pacific, From San Francisco to Salt Lake City" string tied travel book measures 10" x11" with pictures and text 20-30

WHITE PASS & YUKON- "Alaska and the Yukon Territory Through Line to the Interior" brochure with 29 pages of photos and text. Dated 1909 125-150

WHITE PASS & YUKON- "A Handbook of Vacation Trips In Alaska & the Yokon" booklet measures 3"x 6" dated 1899 with 60 pages of photos and text 150-175

WHITE PASS & YUKON- 1930's travel booklet measures 7" x 10" with black & white photos and text 50-60

YOSEMITE VALLEY RR CO- "Yosemite Via Merced Canyon Route". 8 folded panels two sided with text & color photos 20-30

CHAPTER 33

MISCELLANEOUS RAILROAD

This section is devoted to those few items that really did not fall into any particular listed category. This includes Safety Banners, office equipment, loading dock equipment just miscellaneous odds and ends either used by the railroads or related to the railroads.

REMEMBER: PRICES SHOWN ARE SUGGESTED VALUES ONLY. VALUES VARY FROM REGION TO REGION. THIS IS MEANT ONLY AS A GUIDE. (◆) Denotes value over $1000.00

CANDY CONTAINERS-glass container in the shape of a lantern given to children containing candy pellets **15-20**

CEREAL TIN LOGOS-small aluminum tins showing various railroad logos. First issued in the 50's as a cereal box premium, reissued in the 70's. .... each **5-10**

CEREAL TIN LOGOS-complete set of 28 logos from the 50's **250-300**

CORPORATE SEALER- from the Silverton Railroad. Older style hand press sealer. "Seal reads, "The Silverton Railroad Co. Colorado".............................. **500-550**

DATE NAILS-cast iron nail with embossed numbers representing the year. These were placed in the railroad ties to show the year the tie was laid **1-3**

DOOR PLATE-Chicago & Northwestern "The Northwestern Line" logo cast on top of large door plate with brass door handle. Logo cast on handle as well **175-200**

FREIGHT SCALE-large floor style manufactured by Howe. Stands approximately 24" tall with brass weights............................. **100-125**

HARD HAT-White hard plastic with BN logo in green on side **5-10**

INSTRUCTOR-cast iron piece with brass fittings used to teach the basics of steam engine operation. **200-250**

NEW JERSEY CENTRAL- stainless steel plate measures 6" x 5" from North Pole Sanitary Drinking Fountain. Patented 10/31/22 .... **70-80**

PAPERWEIGHT-salemans sample showing aluminum rail joint. Mfg. Atlas Rail Joint, Chicago. **150-175**

POCKET WATCH-marked on face "Santa Fe Special". Mfg. Illinois. 21 jewels with ornate case **500-550**

POCKET WATCH- Manufactured by Hamilton. 21 Jewel with Montgomery dial **350-400**

POCKET WATCH-manufactured by Waltham. 21 Jewel with yellow gold filled case **250-300**

SAN ANTONIO & ARANSAS PASS- canvas money bag. Stenciled on the front "$250.00 in Silver" Measures 7" x 13" **70-80**

SOUTHERN PACIFIC-bottle embossed "Hospital Department" with cork stopper. Measures 4 ½" tall **20-30**

SPIKE- cast iron railroad spike .... **.50-1.00**

UNION PACIFIC-Safety Award Banner. Given to different divisions for outstanding safety practices. Heavily embroidered and colorful these were proudly displaying in division offices. Measures approximately 29" x 44" .... ◆

UNION PACIFIC-enameled motor car safety award plaque. With enameled years of recognition plates included **350-400**

CHAPTER 34

REPRODUCTION & FANTASY RAILROADIANA

Reproductions and forgeries are the one thing with any collectible that tends to be a continuous problem. It seems that everyday something new is brought to the attention of the hobby. It is only through the efforts of collectors to continually educate and document these forgeries that we will be able to stay ahead of the problems. Railroadiana collecting is no longer the dusty junk Uncle Edward stores in the garage. It is now an investment vehicle that continues to increase in value. Due in part to this change of status is the production of reproduced items, for the most part produced for the buyer who cannot afford authentic, but would in fact wish a respresentative piece. Because of this change of status it is also the means by which the greedy see a quick way to make a buck. Many unmarked reproduced items are easily detectable due to the lack of quality, but on the reverse many fool even the most seasoned collector. The only items listed here are the ones that are not permanently marked as reproductions and the items that are known forgeries or fantasy pieces. We urge you to deal with people who will stand behind what they sell. You also owe it to yourself to do your homework. We have listed in the front of the book the two railroadiana associations that we highly recommend any collector, enthusiast or dealer join. These two organizations offer a constant source of information as well as aquainting the collector with others sharing your interests as well. This can be a most rewarding hobby, full of great history and lots of wonderful people to meet and share your hobby with.

ADVERTISING MIRRORS- small pocket mirrors with advertising on reverse. Known issues include **Cotton Belt Route** showing little girl eating watermellon, **Missouri Pacific Lines** showing a black porter with passengers, **Chesapeake & Ohio,** showing the Chessie Cat, & **New York Central** in red oval with a diesel train.

BADGES-worn by the railroad police and employees are very sought after. Unfortunately they have the worst reputation for reproductions, fakes & fantasies. Listed and shown here are examples of only a small percentage of the many badges available. **Know your source and deal only with people who will stand behind what they sell.** Photos in the next column show a small round brass badge with steam engine imprint. Done in Santa Fe, Union Pacific & Wells Fargo, the little steam engine is the definite giveaway. These are fantasy badges. The railroad did not put little steam engines on their badges. Also shown is a 6 point brass star with the **Santa Fe** logo in center. These also are found with many different railroad designations. The **Union Pacific** Guard badge is very well done and a heavy badge. Unfortunately these are sold as reproductions but not permanently marked as such so they are easily misrepresented.

SANTA FE PORTER BADGE WITH ENGINE

SANTA FE POLICE

UNION PACIFIC GUARD

BUTTONS-railroad buttons have become a source of confusion. The best way to describe this is: If the Hallmark reads, "**WATERBURY CO'S**" it is a modern reproduction. The apostrohy "S" is the giveaway.

BELLS-brass reproduction dinner bells with wood handles. Logo's are engraved on side of bell. **GWRR AND PRR** are the two roads known at this time. Many more may exist.

BUILDERS PLATES-There are many companies today reproducing builders plates. In the late 60's a company offered for public sale over 60 different reproduced full size builders plates. Made from either fiber glass, aluminum or bronze these plates were advertised as exact duplicates. Plates offered includes: **AMERICAN LOCOMOTIVE COMPANY BROOKS WORKS, LIMA LOCOMOTIVE WORKS, WESTINGHOUSE & THE B&O CAPITAL LOGO PLATE.** One important factor in distinquishing an authentic plate from a reproduced one is to look for evidence of boiler scale. This is a natural build-up of rust and deposits that occurs on the back of a plate after years of being exposed to the elements and due to being mounted against the boiler.

CHINA-a large percentage of these items are really considered fantasy pieces as the patterns were never used by the railroads. The china is cheap and often times found with heavy glaze crazing which was not characteristic at all of the authentic china. Shown above are samples of fantasy patterns that are found quite often in various antique stores and flea markets. These are all white bone china with applied logos and pinstripes. Found in **Chicago Northwestern, New York Central & Southern Pacific.** One version plaguing

the hobby today is shown above. A white bone china with a blue **Denver & Rio Grande "Scenic Line of the World"** logo applied to the side with blue pinstriped borders. Pieces include a creamer, mustard pot, pedestal egg, coffee cup, bread plate and oval platter. This is a fantasy pattern. The butter pat & creamer shown below are found in **SANTA FE, UNION PACIFIC, MKT, PRR, MISSOURI PACIFIC** and probably many more by now. These are heavily crazed with applied logos.

CLOCKS-The clock shown above is **Southern Pacific.** The dial is a paper reproduction with the Sunset Logo and Tuscon, Ariz. The sticker on the back of the clock is also a reproduction aged, weathered and torn to appear authentic. There is also a **Pennsylvania Railroad** version. These are easily misrepresented. The clock it turned out had modern works.

GLASSWARE-above photo shows two different sizes of bottles. The larger is a milk bottle and the smaller is suppose to be creamer. The milk bottle is easily misrepresented as authentic. Railroads represented include: **Rock Island, Chesapeake & Ohio & Frisco.**

KEYS-Keys are without a doubt the most easily faked of all railroadiana. If you are considering collecting keys we highly recommend that you do your homework. Purchase books on the subject, join collecting organizations and solicit the help of a fellow collector who can guide you. The following keys have been mass produced. If you find a key marked identical to any listed here steer clear.

KEYS SHOWING FRONT MARKS

ACL	ADLAKE	37813
C&EI	ADLAKE	803
D&ERR	ADLAKE	
FECRY	ADLAKE	7029
GR&I	ADLAKE	2705
NYO&W	ADLAKE	1320
NCORY	FRAIM	104
SEABOARD	SLAYMAKER	39247
SNSY	FRAIM	104

KEYS SHOWING REVERSE MARKS

LANTERNS- & GLOBES Lanterns do not seem to have the trouble with reproductions, fakes or forgeries as keys and badges do. But as always know your source. There have been questionable lanterns that have appeared over the years. One of the lanterns shown here does not fall into the forgery category but rather the fantasy area. One was originally sold in a gift shop the other in a museum.

The **RGSR DURANGO** is a flat top Handlan frame with a 4 ¼" Handlan St. Louis clear globe. Usually found in mint condition this is often times mistaken for the Rio Grande Southern Railroad which was long gone when this lantern frame was produced. The other is **GC&SJ** which stands for Golden City & San Juan the name of the Colorado Railroad Museums railroad. Lantern globes on the other hand are more abundant when talking reproductions. One globe that continues to plague the hobby is a tall 5 ½" extended base version. The letters are embossed inside of a panel. The giveaway is the panel ends which angle in toward the bottom.

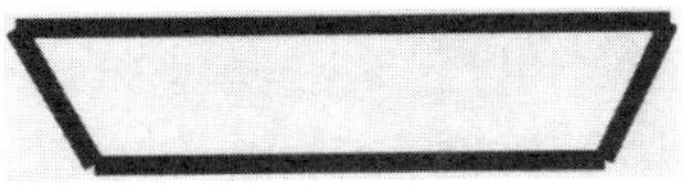

Available in clear, red, amber, blue and green. Here is the railroads represented: **AT&SFRY, CH&DRR, CNO&TPRY, D&MRY, FRISCO, ICRR, L&NRR, MONON ROUTE, SOUTHERN, T&PRR, VIRGINIAN RY AND WABASH.**

LOCKS-Brass cast railroad locks have become increasingly valuable and the knowledge that they are desirable has played a major role in their reproduction. As with the keys we urge collectors to familiarize yourselves with the correct versions of these locks. The faked locks are very well done and easily fool even the most seasoned of collectors. The fancy cast locks command the most money when they are authentic. They have reproduced a fancy cast **D&RGRR, SANTA FE, UP PRIVY which never existed AND WELLS FARGO. The manufacturer is Climax and the key cut is not right.** Also showing up everywhere are a group of locks coming out of Taiwan. These are found in **SOUTHERN PACIFIC CS-44, UNION PACIFIC CS-21.** The reproduction tends to be slightly smaller and lighter in color. Also looking closely at the cast you can see it is not smooth like the authentic locks. These have fooled a lot of collectors.

REAL FAKE

PAPER ITEMS-There have been a tremendous amount of brochures and timetables that have been reproduced over the years from original copies. Most are easily recognizable and many have been printed with the year of reproduction shown. Below is a pass which tends to still pop up from time to time.

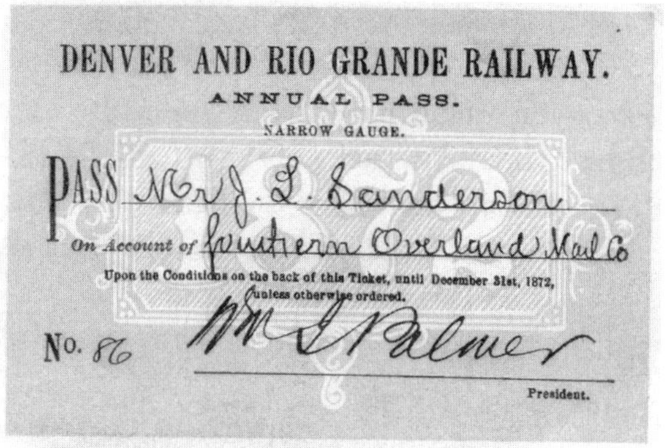

Denver & Rio Grande Railway 1872 annual passs issued to Mr. J.L. Sanderson on account of Frontier Overland Mail Co. & No. 86. Signed by W.J. Palmer, President. This pass was made as a giveaway for a bank anniversary celebration in 1972. The one and only original is owned by a museum. Also below is a list of employee & public timetables that have been reproduced by the Colorado Railroad Museum. These were all marked as reproductions but unfortunately are easily misrepresented. We graciously thank the Museum for compiling this list and allowing us to reprint it here.

EMPLOYEE TIMETABLES

ATCHISON TOPEKA & SANTA FE NEW MEXICO DIV. 56, 8/30/31

COLORADO & SOUTHERN GEORGETOWN LOOP 6/3/1904

COLORADO & SOUTHERN NORTHERN DIV.56, 6/6/1920

COLORADO & SOUTHERN SOUTH PARK DIVISION 17, 10/15/1910

COLORADO & SOUTHERN DENVER TERMINAL DIV. 9, 5/15/1924

COLORADO SPRINGS & CRIPPLE CREEK DISTRICT 1, 7/15/1919

COLORADO MIDLAND (AT&SF) #66, 1/1/1895

COLORADO MIDLAND #2 11/18/1917

COLORADO & WYOMING #17, 5/30/1909

DENVER & INTERMOUNTAIN #20, 3/1/43

DENVER & INTERMOUNTAIN #23, 3/10/46

DENVER & INTERURBAN #5, 5/27, 1923

DENVER BOULDER & WESTERN #10, 6/29/1913

DENVER NORTHWESTERN & PACIFIC #1, 6/23/04

DENVER NORTHWESTERN & PACIFIC #31, 7/1/1911

DENVER & RIO GRANDE #19, 7/23/1882

DENVER & RIO GRANDE 3RD DIVISION #99, 7/20/1919

DENVER & RIO GRANDE 3RD DIVISION #100, 3/28, 1920

DENVER & RIO GRANDE 4TH DIVISION #102, 7/20/1919

DENVER & RIO GRANDE 4TH DIVISION #104, 1/29/1922

DENVER & SALT LAKE #19, 7/6/1919

DENVER SOUTH PARK & PACIFIC (UNION PACIFIC) #4, 1/11/ 1883

PUEBLO UNION DEPOT #203, 4/13/1913

RIO GRANDE JUNCTION #106, 7/20/1919

RIO GRANDE SOUTHERN #57, 6/18/1911

RIO GRANDE SOUTHERN #65 7/20/1919

RIO GRANDE SOUTHERN #3, 7/1/1933

UNITAH #27, 12/25/1938

PUBLIC TIMETABLES

ATCHISON TOPEKA & SANTA FE, NOVEMBER 5, 1939

CHICAGO BURLINGTON & QUINCY JULY 8, 1928

CHICAGO ROCK ISLAND & PACIFIC 1891

COLORADO MIDLAND DECEMBER 1902

COLORADO MIDLAND OCTOBER 1899

COLORADO & SOUTHERN APRIL 1899

DENVER LARAMIE & NORTHWESTERN 10/22/1911

DENVER LEADVILLE & GUNNISON / UNION PACIFIC DENVER & GULF AUGUST 1897

DENVER NORTHWESTERN & PACIFIC JUNE 1905

DENVER NORTHWESTERN & PACIFIC JUNE 6, 1912

DENVER & RIO GRANDE AUGUST 1890

DENVER & RIO GRANDE/ WESTERN PACIFIC JULY 1915

DENVER & SALT LAKE JANUARY 16, 1944

DENVER SOUTH PARK & PACIFIC DECEMBER 1880

FLORENCE & CRIPPLE CREEK JUNE 1896

UNION PACIFIC (SOUTH PARK DIVISION) 1880

UNION PACIFIC (NEBRASKA/WYOMING DIVS.) NOVEMBER 1917

UNION PACIFIC JANUARY 16, 1939

WISHBONE ROUTE (DENVER & NORTHWESTERN) C. 1910

REPRODUCTIONS & FANTASY PIECES

SIGNS-Glass depot signs have hit the market with full swing. Most of the railroad hobby has been made aware of the problem, but antique stores continue to be plagued with these and usually do not want to hear that they are faked. When these signs first appeared they seemed good. The glass is old, and the purveyors of these pieces are well trained. A couple with a child first appeared with these on the west coast. We had one dealer tell us if you did not know better you would have invited them to your home. Their rehearsed story of grandpa working in a depot and finding the signs in the attic worked well at first. Unfortunately they offered these in quantities that were very unrealistic even if it was true. The signs in question are black glass reverse painted signs with gold lettering that measure anywhere from 32" to 36" long and 4" to 5" wide. Three different versions are being made available. One with **Railroad Name only**; One reads, **"TICKETS"** with railroad

name and the third version is **"WHITES ONLY"** with railroad name. Railroads include: **ATLANTIC COAST LINE, BALTIMORE & OHIO, BOSTON & MAINE, FLORIDA EAST COAST, ILLINOIS CENTRAL, NORTHERN PACIFIC, PENNSYLVANIA RY, SANTA FE, SEABOARD, SOUTHERN RY, SOUTHERN PACIFIC & UNION PACIFIC.** Others probably exist as well.

TINWARE- The originals always had the letters baked right into the enamel while the reproductions have an applied brass tag that reads, **"Property of over Southern Pacific Lines Sunset Logo over Carson & Colorado Division Railroad"**. You will also find the chamber pots made of brass or tin with applied plate that reads **"Notice to Passengers Do Not Empty this chamber pot out of train window Central Pacific Railroad"**. Also available are reproduced oil and talo pots. Reproductions are marked Urbano, O. However, originals are marked <J> Urbano, O.

CONCLUSION

Our purpose in preparing this price guide was to hopefully bring about continued interest in this wonderful collectible as well as show the incredible variety of items available. We hope you will find it to be your main resource. Prices are subjective, we are very aware of that and our purpose is more to allow the reader a wealth of information, as well as provide a guide for your purchases. We urge you to locate all means to purchase and find your items. Certainly our auction catalogs are a great resource for collectors and have been supplying the hobby for over 14 years with quality merchandise. If you are not a subscriber we urge you to join today. Your $15.00 per year subscription insures you four future catalogs plus a complete prices realized list for each. With 500-700 lots in each as well as hundreds of photos, the catalogs will become a resource for you the collector to keep up with current market values. Everything we sell comes with a full money back guarantee. If you are not pleased with your purchase your money is refunded in full. We are one of the few companies that can make that guarantee. We are so sure you will be pleased that we offer a full money back guarantee on your subscription fee as well. Should you ever not be satisfied with your dealings with our company your money is refunded in full. You can write, call, email or fax us at:

Railroad Memories

Bill & Sue Knous

1903 S. Niagara St

Denver, Colorado 80224

303-759-1290

303-757-6063 fax

email rrm@uswest.net

website: www.railroadmemories.com

Lastly, remember to do your homework. Join the organizations using the information we provided in the front of the book. Through these you will learn about the other resources available to collectors. There are many books specific to the railroad hobby. You can learn how to obtain these books to further educate you in the hobby. Try to attend railroadiana shows around the country, these are a great way to also get a feel for current prices and see first hand many of the wonderful items that are available to the enthusiast. You will also get to meet the wonderful folks who enjoy this as much as you do. We hope you have enjoyed this book and find it a welcome addition to your library. We have enjoyed doing it. Happy hunting.